Editor's Choice
Smithsonian

Editor's Choice

Smithsonian

Smithsonian Books,
Washington, DC

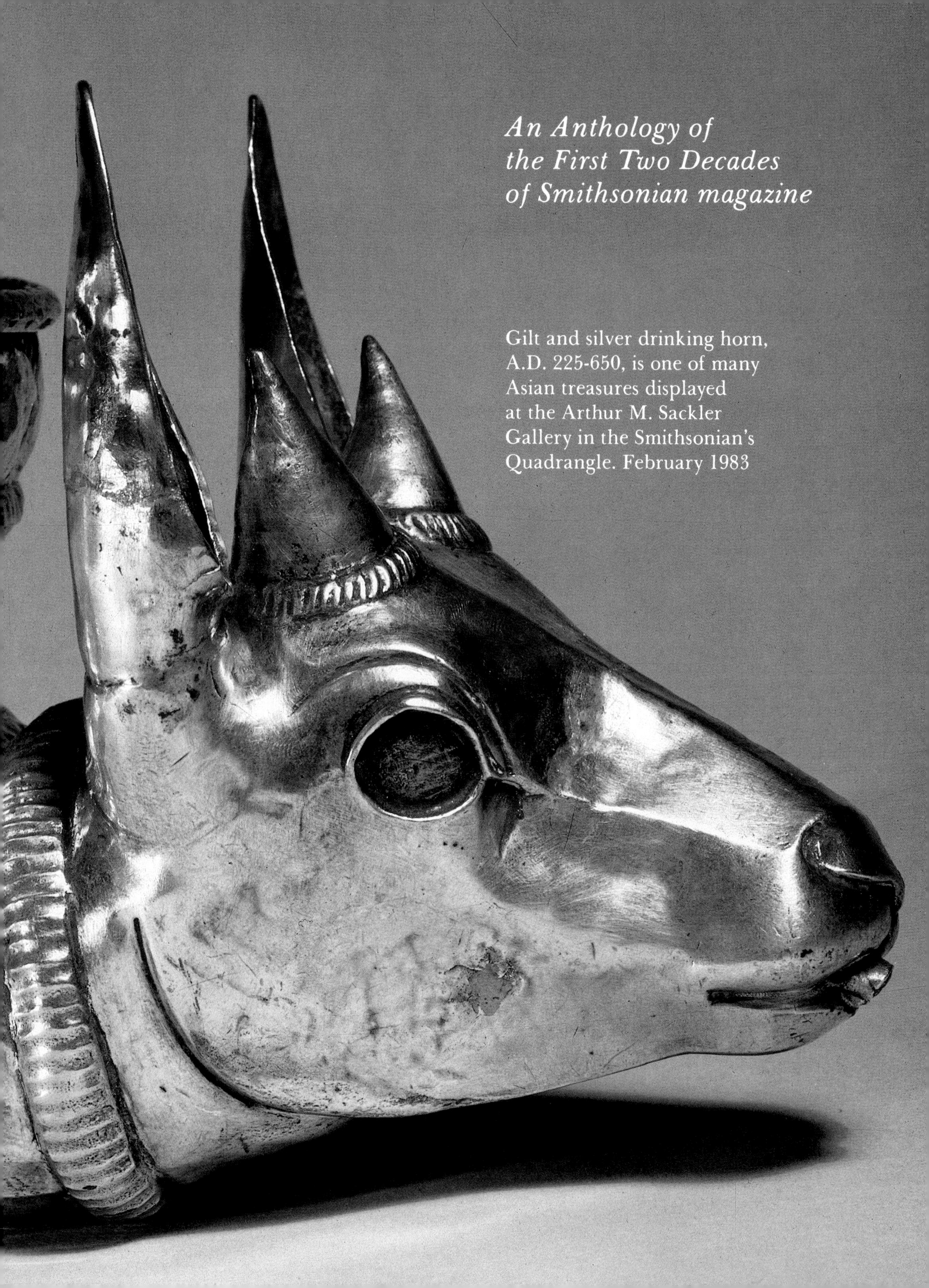

*An Anthology of
the First Two Decades
of Smithsonian magazine*

Gilt and silver drinking horn,
A.D. 225-650, is one of many
Asian treasures displayed
at the Arthur M. Sackler
Gallery in the Smithsonian's
Quadrangle. February 1983

First Edition

**Library of Congress Cataloging in
Publication Data**

Editor's choice: Smithsonian: an anthology of the
first two decades of Smithsonian magazine.

     p.   cm.

ISBN 0-89599-027-X (alk. paper)

AC5.E43 1990

081—dc20   90-9499
                                   CIP

Manufactured in the United States of America

10   9   8   7   6   5   4   3   2   1

Table of Contents

February 1972

Smithsonian

Noguchi's vibrant universal
art on national tour (p. 46);
above, an example in Detroit

April 1978

June 1972

Detail from *A Hundred Monkeys,* a 35-foot-long
handscroll by child prodigy Wang Yani. September 1989

Introduction

This year SMITHSONIAN magazine celebrates its twentieth anniversary, and it has been my privilege to have served as editor for half of that span. In trying to assist the editors of Smithsonian Books in preparing this volume of the best of SMITHSONIAN, I have had the chance to look back over 240 issues and more than 2,000 articles. In the process I've been able to renew my acquaintance with some old personal favorites—William MacLeish's eloquent essay on his father, Archibald; James Atwater's moving piece about the doomed Newfoundlanders in the battle of the Somme; Charles Elliott's sly spoof on the reading of Proust. And I was delighted to encounter once again Robert Wernick's story about the ill-starred romance of Camille Claudel and Rodin, to meet Peter Chew's handsome and intelligent mules, and to trace my way through the world of quantum physics with James Trefil leading me by the hand.

To be honest about it, looking back through all those issues I also found some mistakes, both of commission (don't worry, none of those why-on-earth-did-we-ever-do-that? stories are included here) and of omission. In April of 1986 we ran an article on meerkats, cunning little animals that live in the Kalahari Desert. For reasons that must have seemed logical at the time, I passed up a photograph of a group of these engaging critters, standing erect and peering about as if waiting for a bus, and ran instead on the magazine's cover a picture of a chair. Well, the meerkat story turned out to be one of the most popular features ever to run in SMITHSONIAN, and the picture that we never used went on to become a kind of Smithsonian Institu-

tion icon, reproduced on everything from posters to coffee mugs to T-shirts. Fortunately, the editors of this volume had more sense than the editor of the magazine, and those meerkats stand tall on the facing page.

Part of the fun of going through old magazines, of course, is looking at the pictures: Gail Mooney's photographs of Sears houses (how'd you like to buy one of those for $1,584 today?); Thomas Wiewandt's astonishing portraits of lizards; Jacob Lawrence's straining athletes; the madcap cartoons of John Huehnergarth (what does go on in that man's head?). One remarkable set of photographs simply turned up in our mail. Albert G. Richards, a teacher of dental radiography, had focussed his x-ray machine not on teeth but on blossoms, thus revealing the startling inner beauty of familiar flowers.

Although editors have a role to play in the making of a magazine (and have even been known to occasionally sneak out of the office to do a story themselves) the end product really depends on the people who do the foot-slogging, mind-frying but often intensely satisfying work—the writers, photographers and artists who are out there hanging 200 feet above the ground in tower cranes or laboring away way down in the seventh level of the library stacks. The book that you hold in your hands is the product of their brains and their talent. Enjoy it.

11

Around the Mall and beyond

While the rest of the world was fussing about the *America*'s Cup, we at the Smithsonian were fascinated by a bitterly contested match race, roiling the waters of the reflecting pool below the Capital at the eastern end of the Mall. This was the struggle for the Smithson Challenge Cup. It was held with considerable ceremony, sailed by two flamboyant skippers and followed breathlessly by the media—me. These features duplicate the larger affair.

But there were differences. The Smithson Cup vessels are about four feet overall; as opposed to 65-70 feet; their captains control them by radio instead of by growling orders to crews of muscular young men; they cost a pittance instead of several million dollars. Also, they are produced and sailed not by some of the world's most elite yacht clubs, but by staff members of the Smithsonian.

Ben Lawless, assistant director for exhibits at the Museum of History and Technology and builder-skipper of the vintage 1876 New York pilot boat *Centennial*, and Porter Kier, director of the Museum of Natural History and captain of the schooner *Emma C. Berry* of similar vintage, came to the line at a steaming summer noontime, bottoms cleaned, decks cleared, sails trimmed and radio transmitters ahum with vibrancy. After a great deal of racing around by the committee boat (a power cruiser, also radio-controlled) and of setting out handmade buoys by a barefooted young spectator and of jockeying for a windward position at the start, the "gun" went off—not the thud of a starting cannon, but the clack of two boards smacked together—and away they went.

As in any sailing race, all friendship

and association between the rival skippers vanished instantly. Instead of sitting side by side, antennae poised, as they were before the start, Captains Kier and Lawless separated and engrossed themselves in their own guidance systems. From then until the finish their only communication with each other consisted of such nautical politesse as, "Clear out of my way, you swab!"

The two vessels battled down to the buoy, rounded it, then headed back for the line. *Emma C. Berry* was trapped in a small bay in the pool where the wind went flukey on her. *Centennial* took the lead. *Berry* tried to tack out and got caught in irons. *Centennial* surged farther ahead. Kier grumbled that Lawless had *Centennial* on a string. *Berry* got a good wind shift, swept out of the bay with sails filled, caught *Centennial* and shot across the line in front.

With the usual graciousness of racing skippers, Lawless and Kier made their statements about the race.

Captain Kier of the victorious *Emma C. Berry*: "A splendid and well-deserved triumph by the better ship and the better skipper."

Captain Lawless of *Centennial*: "I don't think Kier was at the same race. Anyone who had been there would have instantly recognized who was really the better skipper. Sure, his boat was faster, but it was built from a kit, not from honest old lines, scrupulously followed with enormous skill. *Anyone*

can use a kit."

Captain Kier: "Bunk!"

They agreed on one thing. They will both be building skipjacks for the next challenge, and the Smithson Cup will remain in contention between the two of them. "The cup will remain with me forever," said Kier, demurely. "Also there's a free lunch which is supposed to go with it. And which has not yet been supplied for this year."

"I shall have no trouble winning the cup next time," said Lawless, meekly. "Nor in keeping it in perpetuity."

The second Smithson Cup race featured the same two courtly sea captains, Sir Porter Kier and Gentleman Ben Lawless.

This time the two gracious yachtsmen raced with radio-controlled model skipjacks—identical except that Sir Porter's *Geneva May* cleaned up. That makes it two in a row for this generous-hearted skipper, a paragon of sportsmanship.

I asked the two for post-race comments, and as before the replies stunned me with their old-world mannerliness. "A clear example of overwhelming superiority," Sir Porter mildly suggested, burnishing the brass buttons of his yachting jacket. "Some people can sail a model skipjack; some can't."

Fumbling with my notes, I asked Sir Porter what the name of Gentlemen Ben's yacht was. "I couldn't care less," he answered with a shrug. "Would you believe, *Beaten?*"

Porter Kier (left) and Benjamin Lawless

Gentleman Ben Lawless, known in yacht club circles as the Little Commodore, was honing the point of a sailor's marlinespike when I called upon him. "Explanation?" he roared, looking up at me with inflamed eyeballs. "The swab packed the shoreline with relatives, and they managed to jam my radio transmission. You take that kind of malfeasance and combine it with blatant cheating, and there you are! Poor little *Champion Girl* never had a chance!"

"*Champion Girl?*" I repeated, quickly making a new notation.

"*Ex-Champion Girl,*" he muttered as he slammed out of the cabin and headed for the afterdeck.

November 1977, 1978

The Fonz, star of the TV show "Happy Days," is really a talented guy named Henry Winkler. Fonzie always wore a leather jacket in his show. Now the jacket belongs to the Museum of American History.

The donation was an enormous media event with flashbulbs going off like lightning and crowds of teen-agers in the museum hallways screaming in waves of frantic emotion whenever there was a hint of Mr. Winkler's presence.

He arrived at a crowded reception room looking like the nucleus of some violent atomic action. First, all you saw was the flashing of the lights; then the screams rose to a crescendo; then there was a moving ring of cops with a harried-looking guy in the middle; then he was deposited inside the room, and one of the cops, passing me, said "Sheesh!"

Fonzie wore a sincere gray suit with a double vent, an Ivy League blue button-down shirt and a tie in Harvard crimson. His hair was longer than in the show and came across his eyes in a way that made him eerily resemble a friend of mine. He kissed every woman in sight, and a good many of the men, too.

He had a small cortege of show people with him. There was a man in a houndstooth jacket with two sets of pleats, one in front and one in back, and also very pressed khakis and shoes with hard heels that made a strong noise when he walked. There were others, too. There were some beautiful women and tall, attentive men who seemed to be in control of everything they looked at. There were lots of

Fonzie (Henry Winkler) and jacket.

Smithsonian people trying to look as though they greeted TV stars every day, and there were guards and maintenance people who were having a ball and not pretending anything else.

Fonzie spoke about the show and his jacket and a little about himself. He was easy and funny and sort of endearing.

I had to leave early, and when I went out the door of the reception room a 15-year-old girl in the crowd shrieked at me "When is he coming out?"

I smiled the way one does when one knows the answers, and I said, "Soon!"

May 1980

The National Zoo's Conservation and Research Center at Front Royal, in Virginia's Blue Ridge Mountains, is a delectable place for the exotic and endangered animals that roam its 3,000 hilly acres. It's a favorite range of native species, too. And to see what effect these Appalachian critters, from wood mice to black bears, are having on the Chinese deer, Persian wild asses and European bison, Smithsonian people sometimes catch a few, fit them with radio transmitters, turn them loose and track them by their radio signals.

Early one cold autumn morning, I joined Greg Sanders in a four-wheel drive vehicle and lurched off into the dawn to check the box traps which, Greg assured me, would contain raccoons, opossums, maybe a bobcat, maybe a fox. A small voice within me whispered "Maybe not," for I am ever a

victim of the old "You-should-have-been-here-last-week" syndrome. But Greg's confidence was catching. We bounced up to the first three or four traps, all empty, and just laughed it off. Greg splattered fresh bait inside. Rather antiquated mackerel. I filled in the coded report, designed to feed some omniscient computer and so provide lasting information about the doings of the mammal population of Posey Hollow that day. I remember "04" indicated the bait. The box traps were "207" or "208," depending on size. A simple "1" in the proper place meant that the trap was empty.

I got very good at writing "1." We spent three hours in four-wheel drive, staggering up impossible grades and reeling drunkenly down again, hanging onto the ruts grimly along sidehill stretches that seemed designed to capsize a mountain goat. We covered about seven miles in all, checking 38 traps. I noted "1" 36 times and "32" twice. Thirty-two stood for box turtle. John and Greg agreed this was the worst day they had ever seen, that it was simply impossible not to snag just one lousy raccoon, that I should have been there last week. I nodded quietly, pleased with myself for having become the box turtle king of Front Royal.

There may have been no animals, but there was a wealth of stories about them, and the project. I don't believe a word of them, mind you, but I'll pass them along.

The group got one black bear which, according to its subsequent signal, uses the Smithsonian property as part of its range. Since the Center abuts Blue Ridge National Parkway in two places, the bear has plenty of room to wander around in—all of it protected. Other bears have been seen as well. They follow trails or power-line clearings

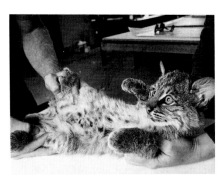

Very young bobcat, uncertain about its future, is radio tagged at Front Royal.

where blackberries grow.

Bobcats are usually too smart to get caught. One young one got into a raccoon trap. One raccoon was found spread-eagled on the floor of a trap in an attitude of total panic. Since the animals are not *that* frightened of humans, Greg took a look around the trap and found the fresh tracks of a big bobcat which obviously thought he had breakfast all lined up for that morning.

The raccoons are just as smart as all the stories about them indicate. They'll tip over a trap and shake the bait out of it or reach their little "hands" in to the bait from the outside. Opossums are stupid. As the scientists say, they play with a third of a deck.

Raccoons will fool you, though, by sometimes getting caught in dumb ways. Greg said he found two males together in adjoining traps. "They'd gone out for a couple of beers and got into trouble," said Greg, who is not a bit terrified of anthropomorphism. Another trap held a female with one of her young still outside, unwilling to leave Mom. When Greg picked it up by the scruff of its neck it screamed. "It screamed so loud I almost dropped it," said Greg. "I felt like a child molester. I thought the cops would come any minute."

Great stories. The guys at Front Royal probably sit around and make them up by the hour.

November 1981

On one of the hottest days of a steamy Washington summer I dropped in at the zoo to meet a baby elephant that had been given to the President. Despite the staggering heat and humidity, the zoo was crowded. I had to wait in my car until a slip opened in a parking lot where I could moor. I then waded through half an acre of small children to the inviting shade of the elephant house. There I found little change in temperature, and a great deal more humidity.

The baby elephant, who had been orphaned in her native Sri Lanka, stood a bit over a yard high. Obviously she relished the heat, which must have reminded her of home, and adored her keeper, who was hosing her off, playing the water all over her and rubbing her behind the ears. I realized that for this little orphan, being ward of the President of the United States is almost as good as belonging to Daddy Warbucks.

I left my little friend in good hands,

Baby elephant Jayathu, a gift from Sri Lanka, is cradled in the arms of Kathy Wallace, one of her Zoo keepers, during cooling bath in the pool.

and ventured outside again to see how other older acquaintances were handling the heat. Nancy, the African elephant, was playing in her pool, sticking her tusks through a huge tractor tire and heaving it into the air, catching it with her trunk as it came down, all the while half-submerged in the water.

All the birds had their mouths wide open, ventilating for all they were worth. I checked in with the ostriches, who, one spring, had behaved with utter abandon right before my eyes. Now they were not in the mood. I thought of that song from *Kiss Me, Kate*—"Too Darn Hot."

It was so hot, in fact, that the whole Zoo seemed smothered in a strange silence. No great roars, no calls from the gibbons, no screeches from tropical birds. And hardly a sound from the humans.

I then headed for Lion and Tiger Hill. Today there was no sound, no movement. A lion sprawled in as much shade as he could find, his maned head half over a wall. A tiger was zonked out in one of the little caves on the hillside. Then I came around the moat and suddenly confronted a beautiful white tiger—a nine-year-old female named Bharat—almost entirely submerged. The great head rested on shore; the rest of the mighty body slopped in the water with complete indifference. No playing with the empty beer keg, no slow swim-

ming, nothing but total sloth.

My God, I thought, is it dead?

Then a ubiquitous fly passed near her and one great white ear twitched. That was all, but I was relieved. I also was suddenly determined that this midsummer madness must cease. Every resident of the Zoo was handling this dreadful day more sensibly than I. Back home I knew of a pool where I could slop down, head resting on an inner tube, and put in a half-hour of sloth myself. The prospect was irresistible.

September 1984

They cleaned me up and allowed me to stand in a cold rain outside the National Air and Space Museum, one day in early spring, so that I could keep an eye on Prince Charles. He was visiting Washington and wanted to have a look at the museum because he flies and likes planes.

This was one of those occasions that has to be meticulously reported, so I filed a very careful summary of the events of the day, heavily laden with facts and figures. Here it is:

Rain in early spring has a mean temperature of 34 degrees F, or about one Celsius. Wind velocity averages 35 knots. It takes 12 minutes for spring rain to get inside the collar of a raincoat, another three minutes to work its way down to the lumbar region, and four minutes 30 seconds to soak through raincoat, jacket and shirt. Wind at 35 knots will blow an umbrella inside out in 54 seconds of the first round.

Journalists, under these atmospheric conditions, snarl a lot. But Secret Service men have learned to shiver in absolute silence. Not a tooth chatters.

Police cars, driving up fast to a museum door through a puddle of spring rain, can spray journalists effectively at a range of 43 feet. It takes four hours and 23 minutes for khaki pants to dry out after being so sprayed. Hot whiskey and lemon is nice. It doesn't cure a cold.

Dignitaries who meet Princes of Wales in a spring rain carry large, dry umbrellas. Onlookers who line fences do not cheer as loudly when they are wet as when they are dry. When they clap their hands it sounds like circus sea lions who have just finished playing *Yankee Doodle* on a set of horns.

Princes of Wales wave and smile to onlookers and shake hands with dignitaries. They eschew umbrellas. They seem sort of used to rainy weather. They are nicely dressed with white handkerchiefs in their breast pockets. They look very healthy. After Princes of Wales have entered a museum, in a cold spring rain, dignitaries crowd through after them, eight abreast, and jam each other into the door frame.

When people ask, How was the Prince of Wales, the answer is, Fine.

July 1981

Chia-Chia, the sexy British panda, arrived at our National Zoo on a cold March day and quickly agreed to a press conference. I attended, of course, expecting him to show up in an expensive dressing gown, with a silk scarf knotted at the throat. He turned out to be pleasant-mannered and healthy, but really just another panda.

He had been chosen to make romantic overtures to Ling-Ling, the National Zoo's female panda. As it turned out, he botched the job as badly as did our own male, Hsing-Hsing.

At the press conference, Chia-Chia (pronounced "Cha-Cha") paced up and down in his dressing room, tastefully decorated with shoots of bamboo, and peered out at the yard where Ling-Ling was strolling. Chia-Chia wasn't yet allowed out, being still in quarantine, but he knew she was there, by scent and sound. One of the news people suggested that he was muttering to himself,

"Where *is* the woman, anyway?" which is far too anthropomorphic to be quoted in SMITHSONIAN.

Chia-Chia's British keeper, George Callard, told me he had a good flight. "He didn't sleep, of course. He just sat there and sulked." Since that's what all air passengers do these days, no one was worried. He got to New York in a snowstorm and was trucked down to Washington. He seemed to enjoy the traffic on the New Jersey Turnpike. Mr. Callard said Chia-Chia has no track record in siring little pandas, but he seems to know how to go about it—and that's an improvement over Hsing-Hsing.

I was the only journalist, that morning, to have a chat with Hsing-Hsing while the rest of the media were absorbed with Chia-Chia, who was pacing around impatiently and munching on things that looked like dog biscuit—doubtless some sort of high-potency diet. I found Hsing-Hsing sitting in his room, legs straight out in front of him, eating carrots. He would flick one out with a claw, then snap it down with his front teeth, like Bugs Bunny. "What's up, Doc?" he asked.

"You'd be surprised," I replied.

May 1981

The marvelous Multiple Mirror Telescope, built and run jointly by the Smithsonian and the University of Arizona, rotates all right. And I was in it.

It had been a lovely day in Tucson, but I was warned of a frigid night 8,500 feet in the air, atop Mt. Hopkins. So I borrowed a parka before joining a party of young technicians in a drafty truck for the ride up the mountain to the MMT.

Conversation in the truck lurched along with the springs and shock absorbers. Someone had seen a mountain lion. There were fewer squirrels this year. Yep, that means there's a fat bobcat on the mountain. As we rose from switchback to switchback, the temperature sank. We finally reached the observatory area where two smaller telescopes, the 1.5 meter and the 61 centimeter, do their work. Observers were assigned to each of them with specific programs to follow, which had been requested by astronomers (who occasionally come themselves). Someone at, say, Harvard can simply indicate what is needed to help him in his project, and the observer does the job and sends the results to Cambridge.

We entered the building, glad of the warmth of the offices and control rooms that underlie and flank the barnlike MMT chamber. In the chamber it was cold. The instruments are very heat sensitive, and must be kept cool to retain their fine tuning. An astronomer and an operator (a woman who had come up in the truck) were carefully winching the delicate photometer out of the innards of the telescope to chill it for the night's work. Liquid nitrogen and then liquid helium were funneled into the instrument, vapor fuming.

The photometer, where the light from the six giant mirrors is gathered, is one of several specially made or adapted instruments that fit the needs of the MMT. Refinements are constantly being introduced, it seems, since the MMT is one of a kind.

From the third-floor gallery of the building you can step out onto the structure of the scope itself, maneuvering between the mirrors. From the fourth floor you can look down on the mirrors. When not in use, they are covered by a slatted metal cover that rattles out of the way like the lid of an old rolltop desk.

As we looked down, there was a grinding hum, and the whole MMT chamber slowly split apart, segments of wall and ceiling rolling back toward the corners to reveal a broad gap of open air—very cold, for by now dusk had fallen. With another brief rattle the mirror slats rolled away, revealing pools of perfectly polished glass.

To feel the disorienting effect of the building rotating, I hurried to the basement. There was a gentle sound, and I suddenly felt that the concrete floor on which I stood was turning like the deck of a carousel. But it wasn't. The building above us was, each of its four wheels following the circular steel track.

Movement of both the telescope and building comes from electronic nudges that activate small motors. Power for the telescope, in particular, is geared so it always has opposition. That keeps the actual movement smooth as silk. The computer finds the arched path of the star under investigation, then commands the telescope to swing up or down on its yoke.

We saw the result of it all in a control room. The cartoonist's standard depiction of an astronomer, old, bald, perched atop the eyepiece of a gigantic refraction telescope, is badly outdated. This one was in a warm room fed by a jumble of electrical leads. Facing him were a number of television screens. Beside him sat the operator with a pattern of control buttons at hand. One by one, she brought the mirrors into use, each producing a blob of light on the screen, then being adjusted so that the blobs came together. Thus the mirrors are focused and aligned.

It is an adage that today's astronomers are always tall, pale and bad tempered. I found this one tall and pale, but entirely affable. "Try such-and-such," he would suggest. And the operator would key in a movement of minute proportions. New spots appeared, moved together, blended.

It is a sort of game they play, I realized. A computer game with immense meaning. Not Star Wars. Just Stars.

May 1982

It looked like a World War I machine-gun nest at, say, Verdun. Soggy sandbags ringed a pool of viscous gray water, which, just beneath the surface, gelled into thin mud. A foot down, this texture became a seemingly bottomless boot-sucking clay. If you walked in it, you risked vanishing. When you wrenched your way out of it, pounds of Mother Earth remained with you, weighting every step.

At Verdun, this wretched mire might well have contained the bones of a soldier. Here, too, it contained bones. But this was not Verdun. This was a construction site a few miles outside the District of Columbia, and these were the bones of a mammoth, that early form of elephant, extinct for about 10,000 years.

On several bleak days last March the gray mudhole swarmed with Smithsonian and U.S. Geological Survey scientists, university professors, students, volunteers and interested hard-hats from the construction company. They staggered in the mud, losing boots as well as dignity. They sweated to fill with mud the burlap sacks that served to divert the stream that washed through the site. They struggled to set up a proper grid of staked lines so that a semblance of organization could be maintained in the sliding, shifting mess. They swore and they grunted and they sometimes simply laughed in total helplessness. But at the heart of the activity a couple of slime-smeared experts brushed away water and very gently,

with painstaking care, probed for bones and removed them.

The reason for the care, the explanation for the whole mammoth caper, was that along the Eastern Seaboard of the United States, mammoth bones don't show up every day—or every decade, for that matter. "If this was South Dakota," said Dennis Stanford, glaring around with mud on his beard, "no one would have been impressed."

Stanford, the Smithsonian anthropologist who cut up an elephant named Ginsberg with flint and bone knives, seeks to establish the time of Man's habitation on this continent through the evidence of the tools he used—including the knives and spearpoints with which he killed and butchered his meat. Some of the meat was certainly mammoth. So Dennis was one of the first scientists to be alerted to the Maryland find.

A geology student at the University of Maryland University College made the discovery. Dana M. D'Aria needed to make up a field trip for his class. Like many fellow students, he knew about the construction site, where bulldozers had canalized underground streamlets into a straight drainage channel. Along the banks of this cut, the clay sandwiched a dark streak, an Upper Cretaceous stratum where shells and sharks' teeth could easily be found. D'Aria headed for it on a Sunday afternoon to get some specimens.

There were other students and amateur diggers in the area. Dana moved away from them, braving the wet mud of the channel bottom. He spotted a curved stick jutting from a murky pool. He pulled it out. It was regularly curved, rather heavy, smooth. Not wood. It was a bone. A rib, in fact.

Dana said he thought it might belong to a cow. He continued working along the stream bed. Then "cow" just didn't seem right to him. He went back to the puddle where he'd found the bone and sloshed around a little more.

This time he felt, and pulled out, another hefty piece of bone, thick, rounded. And he knew it had to be part of a tusk. And the animal had to be a mammoth.

D'Aria squelched his way to a telephone, tried to call the Smithsonian, failed because we all goof off on Sundays, finally called his professor. It speaks well of Dana's scholarship that Peter Kranz, after understandable ex-

pressions of disbelief and upon viewing some of the bones that evening, agreed with his identification. Dr. Kranz notified people at the Museum of Natural History. Dennis Stanford agreed to take charge of the hastily mobilized "expedition." Gary Haynes, a Smithsonian research associate, came to back up Dennis and do the actual excavating of the bones. Other volunteers enlisted for the duration. The contractors readily agreed to the excavation and offered help. The owners of the projected industrial park, McCormick Properties, Inc., added their full cooperation.

So on a miserable morning the mammoth mob mobilized. Dennis made it clear that secrecy would be maintained lest the dig be overrun in a "mammoth rush." He also drafted every soul who was not actually taking pictures. Those sandbags had to be filled.

For an hour I tried to fake the mumbo jumbo of photography—sighting, adjusting apertures, mumbling about depth of field, shaping rectangles with my hands. Then I was found out and slapped into a work gang. I levered up dripping shovelfuls of muck and dumped them into bags held open by a muscular and imperturbable young lady—a creature, obviously, of today. No Vassar girl would have done that work in *my* day.

For all of us, every step was a sickening plunge followed by a gut-wrenching

Dennis Stanford holds rib from mired mammoth. Finder D'Aria (left) looks on.

hoist of what felt like a 50-pound boot. My pitiful physical resources were soon spent and I let my teammate do the work of two.

While we militia churned the mud, Drs. Stanford and Haynes and others of the high command went after the bones. Two construction workers, stopping by during a coffee break, were amused at the delicacy with which the bones were removed. "Hell, man," said one to the other, "I could get them bones outa there in ten seconds flat with a 'dozer. Just one run. We'd scoop up ever one of them bones." A volunteer archaeologist winced.

Quite possibly a bulldozer had already scooped up some of the bones. For though this mammoth was unusually complete, fragments of only one leg bone were found. Perhaps the other legs had been scraped away when the drainage canal was dug. Or—and this thought never fails to intrigue Stanford—was early Man somehow responsible?

An estimated 200 bones and bone fragments were removed. I saw long pieces of rib and darkened vertebrae lurking under the surface of the pool like rocks. There were also pieces of tusk, the entire lower jaw, half the pelvis, one shoulder blade and lots of skull fragments. The scientists agreed that the mammoth was about three-quarters grown—a "teen-ager," perhaps ten feet tall.

August 1982

Dr. Richard S. Fiske, director of the Museum of Natural History, decided recently that he had to get to the top of the inner dome of his building—the lofty, round ceiling of that echoing rotunda where the African elephant greets visitors. Why? Because it's *there,* of course.

Fiske is a volcanologist and so climbs mountains as readily as others dodge traffic. To climb the dome he put together a team: Jerome A. Conlon, Fiske's administrative assistant; Kim Nielsen, photographer; myself, expedition historian, preferably nonclimbing. We set off to establish base camp on a bright afternoon when we should have been on the Mall behaving sensibly by throwing Frisbees.

My idea of somehow avoiding the climb soon proved illusory. I was expected to show the right stuff. I told myself that here was my chance to experience another of the Smithsonian's

high points, and that, after all, any fool ought to be able to climb a dome, and so I shouldered my pack, lashed on my crampons and set out with rope and ice ax.

An elevator deposited us on the upper display level, where the Hope Diamond resides. Unlocking a door, we faced a large stairway that took us to a higher level where no visitor can go without a Sherpa guide. We circled around the rotunda on this gallery, finding it lined with shelves. We were all, perhaps, a little chilled to find them filled with drawers packed with human bones. Fiske chose one at random. "Tibiae" said the label, and when we pulled it out, there they were, brown with antiquity.

We continued our trek around the gallery. Leaving the Place of the Bones, we came at last to a tall door, patined with age. Jerry produced a key and the door swung grudgingly open.

We found ourselves in a lofty, dimly lit room lined with brick. Jerry found a light switch and bare bulbs flickered on. In the light we saw steep metal stairs mounting into the gloom. Roping up, we started our assault on this place, to be known as The Staircase.

Now we climbed in silence for a time. And at last we faced a doorway. Gasping in the thin air, we heaved ourselves through and emerged in a musty chamber, nearly dark except for patches of orange light that seeped out at intervals from a huge central mound of masonry. We eyed each other with wild surmise, suddenly realizing that we were beside the base of the great summit. From here, if the weather held, we would make our dash for the peak.

We circled the base until we reached a wooden ladder, seemingly acrumble with age. It rose in sections, each section angled to remain tangential to the curve of the mound.

"Men," said Fiske, "we have reached The Ladder. Well done. Conlon and Nielsen will now move up on one rope. I shall haul up . . . ah. . . ."

"Park," I suggested.

"Exactly. Park. Mind your footing, now, all of you. And watch the time. We must return to Camp Number Three before dark."

And so we made our play for the top, first hauling ourselves upward with hands as well as feet, finally standing erect and simply trudging up The Ladder, one foot at a time. Up . . . up . . . breath coming in agonized gasps . . .

The view from the inner dome

muscles screaming.

And then suddenly there was no place higher to go. We had done it. We had conquered The Inner Dome!

Well, anyway, we got up to the eye of the dome, a spooky place, predominantly lit by the similar eye of the outer dome, perhaps 15 feet above it. An eye is fashioned by keying the masonry of a dome against a ring. Reinforced glass fills the panes, and here a plastic cloth had been spread over the glass, presumably so that if the Washington weather produced a mighty precipitation, no vagrant leak would end up soaking the elephant, about 100 feet below.

I knew that I must take a look down. I don't know about the others, but I'm very uneasy about heights when I'm still connected to the ground, and I found the view from on high absolutely devastating. The world's largest mounted specimen of an African bush elephant looked like a flea. Almost more disturbing than the height was the sense of fragility.

Looking down at the tiny dots that were people surrounding the elephant, I was almost shocked to find that no one down there seemed to be looking up at the rotunda's distant top with the sudden understanding that it was about to crash down on the floor. No one realized the danger that seemed so imminent to me. I suppose life is full of such situations—someone with an overall view, shuddering at possible catastrophe while hordes of the ignorant trudge about below. But I had never before had that view. I had always been one of the people who stare at today's elephant, not at tomorrow's possibilities.

We scrambled down from the dome a little thoughtfully. It held just fine. Oh well, I suppose that an ant can walk on an eggshell.

March 1982

Edwards Park

Phenomena, comment and notes

Traditionally, the study of astronomy leads to humility: we discover that we live on a planet that orbits an unimportant star, just one of a hundred billion in this galaxy, which in turn is only one among billions. We are not the center of the universe. And yet, in a curious way, we *are* at the very center.

After a long day on a flat, solid and stationary world, I often like to stand outside on a spring evening, watch the stars come out and remember where we are. All day the sun beats back our gaze; it is so bright we do not look up, but only around at each other and down at the ground. Five miles is considered good visibility. Then the sun sets, and when that first star appears, we are seeing hundreds of trillions of miles.

One by one points of light wink on. I have been watching it happen since childhood, yet something in my mind still starts when I see a star that just a moment ago was not there. The sky is still light; the first five or six come slowly, almost teasingly; then stars turn on faster and faster, gathering like timid animals that have decided they are safe. Darkness falls, and hundreds of lights dot the celestial sphere. Once again I am standing on a planet, hurtling through space, a part of the Galaxy.

The clearer the sky, the more stars shine in the soft blackness. Even in a suburb, hundreds speckle the night. Binoculars show thousands. The sky looks crowded with stars.

An astronomer can look at one of those points of light and know how big the star is, how old it is, what it is made of, how fast it is rotating and what its future is likely to be. He or she can also tell how far away it really is. Long before astrophysics became a glamour

field, astronomers had found how far away the stars are. They are so far away from us, and from each other, that our minds cannot understand. The stars are not crowded. They are terribly alone.

In our part of the Galaxy, the typical distance between stars is about five light years, the 30 trillion miles or so that light would travel in five years. As pointed out in *The Cambridge Encyclopedia of Astronomy*, these distances are typically 30 million times the diameter of the stars themselves. If you were to take the diameter of the average person as one foot and spaced people as widely as the stars are, then there would be 5,680 miles between one person and the next. All our relatives would be distant.

My average speed going to work is about 30 miles per hour. Driving day and night, with no stops at all, it would take something like 114 million years to get to the next star. At the speed of a jetliner, I would still need more than six million years. Even if I could maintain the 25,000 miles an hour at which the Apollo astronauts began their lunar voyages, I would need 137,000 years. And this is just to get to the next star. To calculate the time to a star 100 light years away (still close—the Galaxy is 100,000 light years across), just multiply the above driving times by 20.

On a warm evening I look up at the stars and try to sense just how far away they really are. Betelgeuse glows red at the shoulder of Orion, a star so large that we can almost make out its disk from 620 light years away. I can see it so brightly, so clearly, and I can't get there. Ever. It is just too far away.

And this is just the neighborhood. Stars come in groups called galaxies, and the galaxies themselves come in groups, clusters and superclusters. Distances between clusters are measured in tens of millions and even billions of light years. And there's precious little in between.

Take our local group. There's us, the Magellanic Clouds (our little satellite galaxies that decorate the southern sky), the Andromeda Galaxy just two million light years away and perhaps 24 others. Our little group seems to be falling toward, and may already be a part of, the Virgo supercluster of galaxies, whose center lies 60 million light years away.

What I'm saying is that living on a very solid Earth with a bright sun in the day, a moon a trifling three days away

and a night sky full of stars gives us a false impression of the universe. If we look at all those stars long enough, and think about just how far apart they really are, we come to realize that the universe is essentially empty.

Thinking about all that space can be dizzying, but the feeling goes away with daylight and the return of human dimensions. No matter how much empty space is out there, things are pretty solid here on terra firma. Except . . .

Except, of course, that everything is made out of atoms and atoms are mostly empty space themselves. Our bodies, our homes, the planet itself are composed of nothing more than little clumps of spinning protons and neutrons wrapped in clouds of even smaller electrons, held together by invisible forces we cannot sense outside the lab.

Atoms are infinitesimal to begin with (100 billion billion to a drop of water), but even if we could see them there is almost nothing to see. In his book *From Atoms to Quarks*, James Trefil points out that in an atom with about the heft of an oxygen atom (say ten to 20 protons and neutrons in the nucleus and five to ten electrons in orbit), the nucleus occupies only about one quadrillionth of the atom's volume and the much smaller electrons even less.

Trefil translates that "quadrillionth" this way: if you enlarge the nucleus until it is the size of a bowling ball, then this atom would be 20 miles across with the electrons, now pea-sized, scattered around the sphere. All the rest is empty space. Toward the end of a remarkable film called *Powers of Ten* at the National Air and Space Museum, the viewer flies into an atom, and covers 90 percent of the distance from the outlying electrons to the nucleus before the latter becomes visible. There's nothing like being there to feel the emptiness. That's what we and everything else are made of. It used to bother me to think I was mostly water (somehow the image of a jellyfish would pulse through my mind). Then I was happy to learn that my hormones alone were worth a good $6 million. Now I'm faced with being 999 trillion quadrillionths empty space. Most unsettling.

On fourth thought, though, this is the perfect spot to be in. In fact, it's the only spot to be in. We are just the right size, balanced on a knife-edge between the emptiness of atoms and the emptiness between the stars. A few orders of magnitude up or down the scale, and life would be very empty indeed.

May 1982

Walking can do for our cities what our architects seem unable to do: make them people-oriented. It is a benefit that no individual walker expects, that no city planner envisions. People walk for themselves, and if in so doing they happen to alleviate global problems, so much the better. Entrepreneurs will see new opportunities, however, and in turning a buck will bring a little fun to mean streets.

As a nation we worry about global warming; we fear the ozone on the ground that injures our trees and our lungs, and the thinning ozone miles over our head that no longer protects so well against ultraviolet radiation. We worry about the nitrogen and sulfur oxides that fall again as acid precipitation and the carbon monoxide that crowds the oxygen out of our red blood cells. We're doing it to ourselves, every time we put the key in the ignition and turn it.

As individuals we also worry about our health and the urgent advice of the authorities to do grim penance for the french fries of long ago. We nod our head and tell friends we really should get out and jog, join that health club, buy a $600 machine for the bedroom. But we are rushed this morning, tired tonight. Next week for sure: we're going to get right on it. And sometimes we do, and then drop out.

Let's leave weakness of character out of this. People drop out because that kind of exercise is boring, makes you ache and, if you don't happen to be a gazelle anymore, somehow rubs your nose in your own deterioration. It has no purpose beyond the motion itself. On one of my very few excursions on horseback (Cocoa, wherever you are, thanks for keeping us right side up!), I liked it when the wrangler stopped snickering long enough to explain that while Eastern riders do it for show, out there in the West people ride horses to get somewhere.

Now what I'm driving at here (pardon the verb) is a way to exercise that does not require adding a whole new, unpleasant chapter to each day. Something that can be done without special equipment or going to a special place. Something that lessens the damage being done to the planet we love. It

Pedestrians, and merchants who cater to them, give cities a special flavor.

seems that you don't have to get your pulse up to some very high rate and keep it there for so many minutes so many times a week for exercise to do any good. Any exercise is good for you, we now learn: one of the best is just plain walking. All we really have to do in cities is what the National Park Service is forever urging us to do when we are out in the middle of nowhere: get out of the car.

The kind of walking I'm talking about has nothing to do with hardship and self-discipline. I'm talking about city walking, a delight for body and mind. Just suppose you found yourself walking five miles a day. Not all at once, mind you, but a little in the morning, a walk at lunch, a trip to the post office; later a walk part of the way home, even down to a restaurant or the movies in the evening and then home again. Find yourself noticing cloud formations or swifts spiraling down into the library chimney, bats flashing under a streetlight. Check the bookstores, the notices stapled to telephone poles. Find that faces are considerably more interesting than bumper stickers.

Paradoxically, being on your own two feet is restful. No one is climbing up your back, leaning on a horn designed to blast an opening a mile ahead while doing 130 on the Autobahn. If some-

thing catches your eye, you can stop without being rear-ended. You discover that you do not have to be training for the Iron Man Triathlon to release a few endorphins in your brain, letting the sun come out in your mind. How many times have I started out to walk somewhere, feeling tired and irritable, begun to think the whole idea was a dumb mistake, then found that despite myself the slump was even coming out of my shoulders and I was deciding not to have that troublesome writer done away with after all.

Governments dither, but there is nothing to keep us as individuals from voting with our feet. We can do something about global warming, and feel better for doing it. Each time one of us walks someplace instead of driving, that much less poison has been injected into the air we all breathe. (Actually the benefits are multiple. One less car means that the rest of the traffic will move that much more quickly and burn less fuel.) Now suppose two of us walk someplace instead of driving. What if 100 million of us did it just once a day?

As time went by, a third benefit would accrue. Paradise is not now upon us. The streets of Washington, like those of most other cities, are not yet a permanent festival, promenaded by philosopher kings. In Washington, the tide is still going out. The corner restaurant where you could sit in a booth for hours, the bakery where people lined up for the strawberry pies, the health food store that was forbidden by law to use the word "health" in its name but sold a ton of the No. 7 salad (chopped carrots, raisins and cottage cheese, with a mayonnaise-and-buttermilk dressing) are all disappearing as the old buildings come down and great glass blocks go up in their place. As urban sociologist William H. Whyte says (SMITHSONIAN, February 1989): "... prosperity [is] lowering our real standard of living." But if hordes of us take to the sidewalks, we can return these mean streets to their highest function, the bringing together of human beings.

When we reclaim them, the sight of armies of potential consumers on the march will not be lost on entrepreneurs. They will become placer miners, dipping into the stream for gold. After a couple of quick trips to Rome what I remember most fondly is not the churches, the shops or the Colosseum—but the bars. These are not establishments devoted to the consumption of alcohol but rather rest stops, places where on the way to work, or home, or your next appointment, you can stop in for a small coffee, a delicate pastry or a sandwich fresh made with whatever is in season. Places where you and a friend can go to talk. There seemed to be one in every block, and it is like having a butler who is ready at any time to produce a little something to tide you over. No one would dream of driving to one; even if you survived Roman traffic, there would be no place to park. You walk there. The day may come when we can walk to one here.

July 1989

Cities are exciting, but most Americans crave a little green as well.

Green space ranks up there with baseball and apple pie: right-thinking people everywhere recognize them as indisputably virtuous, manifestations of the "good" that by our very natures we seek. The prewar generation drove out into the country on Sundays. The postwar generation moved to the suburbs to live on plots of green space all their own. Today we crowd what green space we can find, whether we carry a pack across the backcountry or walk the dog in a neighborhood park. Cities are where the excitement is, but most Americans find they crave a little green.

When they head for the green these days, the odds are it will be crowded. On a summer weekend, parking lots will be full and late arrivals will be parked everywhere along the highway, in the bushes, perched precariously on steep banks. Picnic grills are all long appropriated, playing fields packed. Trails are busy, voices coming from every direction. Green it may be, where not trampled to dirt, but hardly tranquil.

Now, at a time when budgets on every level of government are being cut, we have the report of the President's Commission on Americans Outdoors. The Commission spent two years gathering reports and surveys, listening to the experts, holding public hearings around the country, studying case histories. Originally the Commission was boycotted by many conservation and environmental groups who feared it would not go far enough. Later it was sued by business groups, who contended it had gone too far. If everybody's mad, it must have done something right.

To me, the Commission's most exciting recommendation is its most general one: that communities across the nation establish more greenways. These are defined as "corridors of private and public recreation lands and waters, to provide people with access to open spaces close to where they live, and to link together the rural and urban spaces in the American landscape." The Commission asks us to imagine being able to walk out our front door and within minutes set off on a continuous network of corridors that could someday reach across the entire United States.

The greenways are "fingers of green" that come in many different forms: "biking and hiking trails along abandoned rail lines; boating and fishing sites on ribbons of bright water restored from neglect; vacant lots for 'just messing around' after school . . .; belts of grasslands, shrubs, and forests surrounding and threading their way through cities and countrysides like a giant circulatory system." Greenways would be corridors to connect new and existing parks, forests and refuges.

This sounds like plans I've been reading about for nature reserves in Central and South America. The idea now is not only to establish refuges where jaguars and orchids can continue to exist, but whenever possible to keep uncut corridors between them so that populations can mix and young can disperse, with the result to be greater than the sum of the two parts. (One such plan in Costa Rica was described

Rainy-day cyclist heads up a trail in Virginia that once was a railroad line.

in the July 1986 *Phenomena*.) If we can do it for animals, why not for people?

The green will appear anywhere we allow it. All the concrete and asphalt we have laid down is just a thin sheet over the potential life of the Earth itself. Sometimes I sit on a bench in the middle of the city and think of the streets, sidewalks and parking lots as so much black plastic mulch laid down over a garden bed; the buildings are the big rocks there to hold it all down. But just as with real plastic, living green things will find the tiniest cracks in sidewalk or street and grow toward the sun. I look for the green on my noontime wanderings; the thicket of black locust and ailanthus (tree of heaven) springing up along a concrete wall, tufts of grass that have found a home in the seams of a black marble fountain. Any place where we decide to forgo blanketing, we will have a greenway.

The Commission continually calls on Americans to light a "prairie fire" of community action. The best ideas may not even have been thought of yet. So, the Commission advises, "develop a dream. Define a vision. Look forward for twenty years, or fifty, and decide what you want the future . . . to be." A lot of people have a pretty good idea.

July 1987

Even unremarkable lives offer moments of heightened perception, a kind of Zen concentration that leaves the mundane world altogether. Skill is not required, age is no barrier; it is all a matter of seizing the moment.

Once the ball is in the air, nothing else exists. The game changes instantly from boredom to some higher state of consciousness, some supernatural concentration on a simple sphere moving through the air. Thought ends. No worries now, no dreams. There is only the ball against the sky, rising like a rifle shot, then arcing back to Earth. A moment ago one was a study in idleness, hand on hip, kicking at the grass. Now one is running flat out, oblivious to the rest of the world and protesting leg muscles, intent only on being there when the ball comes down.

The same thing happens at bat. Once the pitcher lets go of the ball, nothing else exists. Time slows almost to a stop. The ball looms larger and larger, spinning as it drops, while one feverishly considers whether to swing, when to swing. The decision is made in milliseconds. The back leg drives, body rotates, arms swing, wrists snap. If all goes well, there is a satisfying *thwock* and the ball departs.

Baseball is a far cry from science and natural history, the usual subjects of this column, but one could argue that a lot of science is involved. The angle at which a fielder should throw a ball to get it to a base the quickest is a question of ballistics. Equations will tell you the speed of a baseball as it leaves the bat. The recent suggestion that an outfielder calculates where a fly ball will land not by vision but by changes in his inner ears as his head tilts is applied physiology. One could even make the tongue-in-cheek argument that long hours in right field provide an opportunity to sample the local bird life. (At one field in Key West, ospreys nest in the lights.) But any such arguments would be egregious rationalizations. This magazine, like its parent institution, is interested in all of life. We certainly want to report advances in human understanding of the world, whether that world be in the interior of atomic nuclei or in the mystery of how a tiny bird can navigate for thousands of miles. But if, on summer evenings all over America, groups of people come together to try to hit a ball with a stick, that's worth reporting, too. In fact, it's hard to resist.

Not only softball but baseball itself can be played at any age, I have discovered. It is not as pretty, but it is the same game—right down to the mannerisms—that the professionals play. And the level of play often rises to the occasion. When a shot to the outfield goes between and beyond the fielders, a classic race begins, a contest between the batter who is now running the bases and the fielder who runs to the ball, and makes a desperation heave. Once again the ball is in the air, and it is not always clear which will arrive first at home plate.

During the summer I played both games, on teams composed entirely of anybody and everybody who showed up. The baseball games were at a field in Maryland appropriately called Rocky Hill. Ingenious adaptations made it possible to play with as few as four people on a side (half the normal field is declared foul territory; the team at bat provides the pitcher; when five runs have scored, that half of the inning is over). It is a friendly game, and the

Players become a study in concentration as a ball arcs through the summer air.

quality of the pitching varies exactly with the abilities of the batter. College players see nothing but curve balls. Middle-aged men flail at fat pitches grooved over the middle of the plate. Youngsters see the ball lobbed in a gentle arc.

Pitching aside, everyone is free to do his or her best. Batters swing for the fence and fielders play the ball as though a World Series were at stake. The game *is* a series of chances to excel, moments when everything turns on one individual's efforts.

Part of the fun at Rocky Hill is watching whichever of my sons has turned up to play that day. Seeing one dig a hot grounder out of the dirt with nonchalance, or another wheel at the crack of the bat and run down a sinking line drive with a sliding catch is a priceless dividend for all those hours in the backyard with little people just learning to throw and catch and hit. Their initial fear of the ball is long forgotten and they have progressed far beyond me. Once I pitched to them, first as gently as possible, then with a more level throw and finally as hard as I could throw. But I cannot throw hard enough to interest them now; my "fast ball" looks like a change-up to them.

When they first played organized ball, a hit to them was a heart stopper. Would they misjudge the fly? Would it

bounce out of their glove? When one came to the plate, my only hope was that he would make contact and not strike out. Now they worry about me. One night playing third base, I found myself camped out under a major-league pop-up, a ball hit so high there seemed to be time to put sugar and cream into a cup of coffee, stir and drink it down before the ball would descend to Earth again. I staggered around in a desperate little dance, stuck out my glove and managed to catch it. The shortstop called over, for my ears alone, "Good catch, Dad"; the old backyard relationship had reversed.

The softball was played behind a school in Virginia in the foothills of the Blue Ridge Mountains. It is the kind of community in which, when a dog wanders onto the field and stops play, everybody knows the dog's name. Age is no object: one night the second baseman on my team was eight years old; the shortstop was at least six times that age. Young girls hit the ball to the infield; 20-year-old males routinely hit the ball beyond where the field suddenly slopes downhill.

Either kind of batter hears the same encouragement from teammates, especially when runners are on base. "There's ducks on the pond!" "Let's bring 'em around!" "A hit's a run!" Batters try to hit behind the runner (so it is more difficult for the defenders to put out the runner most likely to score) just as they have been doing since before any of us were born. The fielders concentrate on that lead runner, too, with exactly the same strategy—if not the same execution—as their counterparts in the bigs.

One 95-degree Saturday I took my sons the ballplayers to watch the Baltimore Orioles try for a fourth straight win over the Chicago White Sox. I wanted to see again how the very best do the same things we try to do. And they are astonishing. The batters are so quick, the outfielders so fast. Even the routine plays amaze me. Someone hits a sharp ground ball, one that skips across the grass so hard I suspect I would leap out of the way. (I don't even think about standing in against a major-league pitcher.) The infielder whirls and lunges to his right, bends down to make a backhand stop with a suppleness forever beyond me, then makes the long throw back across the infield hard enough to catch the runner by half a step. The umpire hardly bothers to raise his thumb, the first baseman flips the ball back to the pitcher and everybody gets ready for the next batter as though nothing has happened. I'm awed. And I appreciate again the genius of the mind that decided first base should be 90 feet from home plate and not 88 or 92. The balance between batter and defense is just about perfect.

In the upper deck under the July sun, my vision blurs a little. These extraordinary players begin to look like the people I play with. Between pitches, infielders straighten up, standing idly, hands on hips. Outfielders kick at the grass as they look around the stadium, up at the sky. They are relaxing, like a heart between beats, and look bored to death.

When the pitcher winds up for his next offering, that apparent boredom is gone. Infielders crouch, ready to spring. Outfielders lean forward, ready to sprint. The concentration is so intense that the field itself seems stretched, taut, ready to spring. The next pitch is a ball, and everybody relaxes again, just standing around. Take away the manicured field, the uniforms, and they could be the gang at Rocky Hill.

We are all doing the same thing. We stand at the plate with a bat in our hands and try to see the ball so well we can drive it over everybody's head. Infielders in shorts and sneakers crouch as the pitcher delivers, and if we don't cover as much ground as our big-league counterparts, it's not for lack of trying. When the ball is in the air, we are all equal in the sense that for a moment there is nothing else in the world. We swing at it, or we try to catch it. And if sometimes we drop the ball, our glasses fall off and everybody is safe all around—and the 12-year-old girl who has scampered happily into third says "thank you" because she thinks the ball was dropped on purpose—we know that soon the ball will be in the air again and we will have another shot at it. What more can you ask for?

September 1984

The oldest dream of all may be dimming, the victim of market-place realities. But as long as people can look up it will not die.

Some dreams die harder than others. Abandoning the path to the Presidency was surprisingly easy. But other dreams remain fixed in my cosmology, always scheduled for the middle future, even as

the weeks and months flash by like lights in a subway tunnel. It has always been perfectly clear that "someday" I would travel in Australia, live a year on a salt marsh, learn to sketch. Most of all I have believed, since at least the age of five, that someday I would learn to fly.

Like millions before me, I have recurring dreams of flying. Most often I am driving a car east on the Merritt Parkway in Connecticut on a day of bright sun and blue sky. An overpass approaches. I pull back on the steering wheel and soar up and over it. Years of thinking about it have convinced me I know how to do it. Back around 1948 the Piper Aircraft Corporation sent me a kit. You put together a cardboard box with one end open. Inside was a tiny Piper Cub, operated by strings. When you pulled back on the stick in front of the box, the plane's nose went up. When you pushed the stick to the left, the plane banked to the left. I must have had at least ten hours of simulator time before the box fell apart. That was the beginning of flight training; ever since, I've simply been waiting for the right time to resume.

Now our sister publication, *Air & Space/Smithsonian*, seems bent on taking that dream from me. The message is that the era of the weekend flyer is ending; soon it will be too late to tootle out to the local airfield and learn how to drive into the sky. In issue after issue, the magazine tells of manufacturers, including my beloved Piper, getting out of the small-plane business; of the numbers of pilots falling precipitously; of young people turning their backs on aviation.

What's going on? What has happened to the dream of Icarus, of Leonardo, of every earthbound wage slave who would "slip the surly bonds of Earth and dance the skies on laughter-silvered wings"? Will we divide ourselves into professional pilots on one side and all the rest of us on the other, flatlanders confined to two dimensions?

The articles suggest reasons for the decline. The rapidly rising cost of liability insurance makes it even more expensive to build or fly planes. Layers and layers of regulations take the fun out of it. And manufacturers have concentrated their creative energies so much on larger, twin-engine business aircraft that the little planes have been left unimproved for decades.

Yet the dream goes on. Some of us

flatlanders cannot rid ourselves of a sense of wonder that people can fly. When I was three or four, my father would take me to Newark Airport to watch the silver airliners take off and land. Now, almost half a century later, I go to a park just upriver from the main runway at Washington's National Airport to watch the jets glide in over my head or take off right at me, their exhaust splitting the air.

My father took me to other fields, too, where little cloth-covered planes bounced over the grass and into the air. My most vivid memory is of standing next to a red plane, its engine running, the pilot telling me to get in. I refused, because I knew that the second I put one leg in that fragile cockpit the plane would go racing away, tearing off my leg. Finally I succumbed, and for the first time saw trees from above.

By the age of 12 fear was fading, but not the fascination. My friends and I learned to hang around the local flying club, looking eager and well-behaved, hoping to cadge rides. Some pilots would take us for safe, sensible rides; a quick climb to a prudent altitude and then a stately circling of the countryside. Others were the daredevils we wanted to be, flying so low along the beach that swimmers would dive underwater.

Nowadays my flying is pretty much confined to commercial airlines, the very antithesis of flying for fun. Yet nothing they can do can dilute the magic of the moment when you are no longer rolling along the ground but have lifted into the air, concrete and hangars and trees falling away under you. Nothing can take away the magic of leaving an airport that lies in cold, wet grayness under a heavy overcast, flying for long minutes through the clouds, and then bursting into bright sunshine and the blinding white of the cloud tops, like coming out of a dark room into a snowscape.

One of the secrets of happiness, some philosophers say, is to know when you are happy. It can be an effort to keep reminding yourself. Commercial flying is like that. If you told me when I was 12 that someday I would be seven miles above the Earth, flying along at 600 miles per hour, I would have laughed at the joke. Now I'm lucky enough to do that three or four times a year, and sometimes I forget I'm happy.

The adventure is flawed even before

you board. Check-in lines, x-ray searches, overcrowded departure lounges take some of the edge off. You board through a chute that makes it impossible to see the aircraft, and squeeze into a seat that shrinks every year. Most of your fellow passengers are oblivious to flight, busying themselves with piles of paperwork, thick novels or the fine art of magazine flipping. Flight attendants constantly push carts up and down the narrow aisles, selling drinks and serving snacks. Pilots, apparently responding to passenger demand, make fewer and fewer announcements about how high you are and how fast you are going or what the rivers and cities are you see sliding by the wing. Alone you stare out the window, wondering what invisible forces produced those cloud formations, what geologic power sculpted the shapes you see on the ground.

It could be different. Once I flew on an Air Force transport, a plane that had been modified to observe nuclear tests. It had quartz windows along the top, and a cargo hatch with windows around the curve of the plane from shoulder to knee, so we could kneel or sit on the floor and look down at the landscape flowing underneath. Each seat had headphones; with a twist of the dial we could listen to the pilots as they talked to each other or to the ground. (It concentrates the mind to hear them discuss who will do what if engines fail on take-off.) Best of all, we were welcome to wander up to the flight deck and sit with pilots and navigator. There is no view like it in the world: looking out and ahead gives a true sense of motion over the ground, of sliding along between cloud layers, of driving to the horizon. At times the plane feels as solid, as steady in its path through the sky as a locomotive.

That Air Force 707, a glass-bottomed boat of the air, is the stuff of fantasy—a modern version of Captain Nemo's submarine. But for the moment at least, small planes—in which everybody sits on the flight deck—are still around. It is still possible to sit in the front seat and fly it yourself. The possibility of flying is like that of seeing a blue whale: it is exciting to know that you can, even if you never do. After World War II, the popular wisdom was that everyone would fly. That never came to pass, but it is still true that everybody can. One of my sons has done it; I'll never forget that gray day when a suddenly small

and fragile-looking white plane sped down a dark runway and swooped up into the air, with a man who had once been my little boy at the controls.

Someday, when I no longer owe my soul to college bursars, I'll put together the money for a proper cap, aviator sunglasses and flight lessons. I'll sit in front, pull back gently on the wheel, and move from Earth to sky. In the meantime, I'll cadge rides where I can, whether with a Nature Conservancy pilot along the Platte River (*Phenom-* *ena,* June 1986) or a balloon pilot in Virginia. I'll loiter in the park at National Airport, watching the angle the jets make with the runway as they land in a crosswind. I'll go into the drugstores in neighborhoods where nobody knows me to buy, furtively, the latest copy of *Flying* magazine. And I'll hope that our colleagues at *Air & Space* don't bring out an issue announcing that it is too late.

December 1986

John P. Wiley jr.

Cruising low over the countryside once was something one could learn to do.

By John P. Wiley jr.

Polar bears mingle with people on Manitoba's Cape Churchill

Loafing along the shore while they wait for Hudson Bay to freeze, the lords of the Arctic are tolerant of human intrusion

As the warmth and the light fade each autumn in North America, those creatures that are able move south. Whales and butterflies, striped bass and half our species of birds stream down the coasts and through the interior. Others escape winter in caves and dens, turning down their thermostats until they achieve that state we call hibernation.

One animal, however, rises up out of a months-long lethargy and begins to move north, into the cold and the dark, out onto the ice that now covers more and more of the rich waters of the sub-Arctic. For this animal winter is the good time, the season to feast on seals, to put on weight and eventually to breed.

At Cape Churchill in northeastern Manitoba, where the shore of Hudson Bay makes an abrupt 90-degree turn to the west, polar bears congregate in the autumn, waiting for the ice that is their home. By November, pack ice has formed beyond the fast ice, and the bears are moving. To be at the very tip of the Cape in November is to be in the middle of a slow but steadily flowing river of bears, methodically picking their way across the jumbled ice in a straight-line push for their hunting grounds.

The flow is nearly imperceptible to a first-time observer. Driving out to the point in our strange vehicles, we pass bears sleeping in the kelp beds and gravel banks along the shore. Eight-hundred-pound males raise their heads to consider us, pull themselves to

their feet and move away unhurriedly. Cubs move in close to their mothers as they circle around us. A few bears come close to investigate, rising on their back legs to get a better fix on this strange sight emanating strange smells. But sooner or later the bears turn north again, moving out across the fast ice anchored to the tidal flats to the jumbled pack ice beyond. And then we begin to notice that far out on the ice to the east of us, on Hudson Bay proper, and to the west, over the shallow waters of La Perouse Bay, there are flashes of golden yellow appearing and disappearing in the white, a solitary male here, a mother with cubs of the year there, steadily working their way from shore, going home to the cold and the dark.

The polar bears of Hudson Bay are a distinct population thriving at the southern end of their range. Polar bears live on seals, and to hunt them they must have ice to get to where the seals are. Yet in Hudson Bay the ice melts by July and the bears have to come ashore, there to spend four months eating very little, digging into sand dunes and dirt so they can stay cool in the summer "heat," relaxing into a physiological

Tourists crowd windows as bears inspect buggy.
Vehicle is built high so bears cannot break windows.

A 600-pound male, neither threatening nor afraid, contemplates some outlandish visitors to his domain.

Photographs by Dan Guravich

In some years Cape Churchill is overrun with bears, while in others only a handful are to be seen in a day.

A young bear stands straight up to get better view. Stance is a posture of curiosity, not aggression.

state like that of black bears in winter dens. They are the polar bear population most accessible to humans, and they are not only the best studied but the most easily experienced by amateur naturalists, photographers and just plain tourists.

Forty miles to the west, where the Churchill River empties into Hudson Bay, humans have lived since the people of the pre-Dorset culture settled there some 2,000 years ago. The Hudson's Bay Company has been there for more than 250 years. Today, with a railroad and scheduled airline service (but no highway), Churchill is a jumping-off point for the far north and has the first hospital for the sick or injured being brought down from northern Hudson Bay. The community of 1,200, which has had its ups and downs as a military base and a rocket range and study center for the northern lights, now happily bills itself as the Polar Bear Capital of the World.

In February 1978, when SMITHSONIAN first reported on the town and its bears, no tourists were coming to see them. Now the town's 120 hotel beds are filled dur-

Mississippi photographer Dan Guravich has been studying polar bears for the past decade. John Wiley serves on the magazine's Board of Editors.

This scene is from 1983. Two years later the second week of a camp-out had to be canceled for lack of bears.

Pregnant females stay ashore, digging the maternity dens where they will give birth in December and January to helpless cubs that weigh only one to two pounds. Never eating, the mothers nurse the young until March or April, then bring them out of the dens and lead them in remarkably straight lines northeast to the ice, where they can feed for the first time in months. Biologists count them as they emerge, by tracks in the snow when the bears themselves are not to be seen. No one knows how the mothers navigate across as much as 65 miles of land to reach the sea. In July, when the ice melts, the mothers and cubs come ashore again with all the other bears, where the biologists are waiting for them. Older males spend much of their time on the beaches, while younger bears and mothers with cubs move inland. By October or early November the ice is forming again and the bears are moving back to the shore—and just as soon as they can—out onto the ice.

The edge of the ice is our destination, too. There are bears around Churchill itself, of course, but it is hardly their natural habitat—the streets are dotted with steel cages not for bears but for garbage, to keep the bears from getting into it, and next to the airport is a polar bear jail with 20 cages for animals that come too close to town. Driving east from Churchill in a tundra buggy, bulling through drifts and slipping on ice, we leave the world of humans and enter that of the bears.

The cold is numbing. The wind is blowing hard across the tundra. We get out to shovel when the buggy buries in a drift, and immediately our faces hurt. Take off a glove to adjust a camera, and the hand quickly becomes stiff and awkward. Back in the buggy we hold our hands over the small propane stove; it takes minutes for the pain to subside. There is a ten-year-old bear-observation tower at Cape Churchill, and beneath it caches of diesel fuel, but otherwise this

ing bear season (more hotels are under construction), while more than 3,000 camera-toting travelers pump upward of a million dollars into the local economy. Stores promote polar bear tee shirts and jackets and souvenirs such as a cloth patch with the image of a polar bear and the legend: "Churchill Household Pest Management." (Bears are not the only attraction. Birders have discovered Churchill as an accessible place to see such birds as snow geese on their northern nesting grounds, as well as beluga whales, and the tour operators that take you to bears in the fall also take you to birds in the summer.) The town has thus turned a liability into a bankable asset.

In a chain of wildlife refuges running south from Churchill there may be as many as 2,500 of the white bears, and here zoologists can do the hands-on biology necessary to understand them. The scientists census the bears from helicopters, catch them in traps or shoot them with tranquilizers from the air, so they can be weighed and aged (by later counting the rings on an extracted tooth). Ears are pierced for plastic tags, and lips are tattooed with numbers. Some are fitted with radio collars and followed out onto the ice by light plane to see where and how far they go in the search for seals.

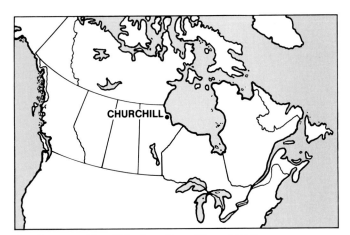

On the west side of Hudson Bay, Churchill lies at north end of historic polar bear denning area.

Nearly at the goal, a mother leads her cub across
sand dunes at Cape Churchill on her way to the ice.

A mother, center front, chases away a much larger
male, right, who had ventured too close to her cubs.

is a desolate world of tidal flats, glacial eskers and a little beach grass waving above the snow. It is November, the temperature is −5 degrees F in the daytime, −20 at night, and a strong wind is blowing unimpeded out of the northwest.

We camp between the tower and the point, on a frozen lake where the vehicles sit level. Two are the tundra buggies, about the size of school buses but built high over drivetrains originally designed for front-end loaders and dump trucks. Len Smith, an oil distributor who began the tour operation, got the idea for them when he saw an ad for the oversize low-pressure tires that would make it possible for a buggy to cross the tundra in summer with minimal damage and to move through snowdrifts in winter. The buggies are high enough so that a bear could not come crashing through the windows.

We have also brought with us a small tracked vehicle; a school bus on huge tires and fitted out with a gas stove and dining tables; and a trailer loaded with drums of diesel fuel, gas bottles and enough frozen food to feed 20 people for a week. At the tower we pick up an eight-bunk hunting lodge that rolls along on tank treads. To make camp, the buggies, the diner and the lodge are backed up to each other in the shape of a cross. "Back porches" on the two buggies and a metal landing on the diner make it possible to go from one vehicle to another without ever climbing down to the ground and risking an encounter with a bear. At night, most people sleep in the buggies and the diner, throwing their mattresses and sleeping bags on plywood panels resting on the seats. When we return to camp after a day in the buggies, the lodge becomes the Muktuk Saloon (muktuk is fermented blubber and highly aromatic, which the lodge becomes after six people sleep here for a week with no ventilation).

Bear lovers of all persuasions

Living is tight. One not only cannot leave, at least not easily, but cannot even get out and walk around. Yet this diverse group of people gets along remarkably well. We include a photographer from Quebec, an ad agency owner from Chicago, a gourmet-market owner from New Orleans, a flight attendant from San Francisco, tour operators from the Maritime Provinces and Seattle, physicians from Wisconsin, a man whose company installs insulation in oil refineries, a man who edits an oil company magazine, a young adventurer from Maryland and a retired executive from New York. What unites us is an eagerness to see polar bears.

Around us, the tidal flats and La Perouse Bay— where 20,000 snow geese nest in the summer—are covered with ice. In many places the ice has exploded upward, looking as if it had been shelled from under-

neath. These are spots where the 12-foot tide has set the ice down on rocks. The ice runs east and west to the horizon. To the north it goes only a few hundred yards to a lead of open, dark water. The lead is "steaming"— the water is much warmer than the air and is visibly evaporating into a fog bank. Beyond the lead is the pack ice, continually freezing underneath to form a mass many feet thick. This in turn has been piled up by wind and currents into pressure ridges tens of feet high. That shore lead, between the fast ice on the bottom and the pack ice, is all-important to us. A south wind will keep it open and discourage the bears from leaving. A north wind will close it and the bears will be gone.

Loafing in the kelp, dozing in the snow

We are lucky. The lead stays open, and some of the bears wait (they could easily swim across). On a typical day at the Cape we see a dozen or so. Driving from our camp out to the tip, we see two mothers with cubs of the year a mile to the east, picking their way north through the jumbled ice. At the point, we stop with three males ahead of us, a mother with two cubs on the right. The males are still lethargic, loafing along the shore, lying in kelp beds along the beach or in daybeds, holes they have dug out of the snow. They are alert to our presence, but not alarmed. When we come too close they pull themselves to their feet and amble away, looking back over their shoulders to keep an eye on us.

At one stop an 800-pound male walks up to our buggy and sits right next to us, looking up and sniffing. As the day goes on we see four more moving along out on the ice. At least one seems curious, begins to move in our direction, but then breaks off and continues his trek to the north.

All day we watch bears. Their heads look strong and potentially fierce. The black skin shows through the short hair on their snouts, which are longer than those of other bears. Biologists say their teeth have evolved from those of their omnivorous brown bear ancestor to those of a carnivore. We see their bulk, but not their strength. This animal can kill a 500-pound bearded seal with one blow—but it looks roly-poly. The rumps are almost comically rounded by the stores of blubber under the skin. The bears are downright floppy when they move, almost as if the skeleton and musculature move separately inside the envelope of blubber, skin and fur.

The eyes, nose and tongue are black; the rest is white, sometimes with a yellow wash. In the sunlight the hollow guard hairs glisten like glass. The front legs seem very long and come together at the body with no chest between them, a filled-out stick figure. The legs

Showing more agility than its shape would indicate,
a yearling leaps easily from one ice floe to another.

are bowed and the front feet pigeon-toed. When a bear ambles, the front foot remains in place until the rear foot has come up and almost kicks it forward. The foot hangs behind as the front leg swings forward, and then the hind foot flops into place, exactly into the depression made by the front foot. Even when backing up, the front feet will drop precisely into the tracks just vacated by the hind feet.

The next day we encounter an 800-pound male with the letters XX painted on his back. Biologists had marked him earlier in the year at Owl River, about 100 miles to the south. We dub him Xavier Xenophon. At first he approaches us, but then circles around us to eat kelp on the beach. By noon he has left, moving northwest across the ice. At 4:30, however, when we are back at camp on a frozen lake and the cook has started dinner, he appears over a ridge, presumably attracted by the smells.

Xavier Xenophon is not the first animal to find the camp. The very first night ghostly shapes appear beneath the buggies, patches of white against the white of the snow, flitting from place to place, disappearing and reappearing. In the morning we see them: Arctic foxes, all white luxurious fur with black eyes and noses, running humpbacked, feet close together, noses near the ground, scurrying away to cache any morsel they have found. A bear that finds something to eat is soon surrounded by foxes that make quick feints, turning the bear in circles as it tries to ward them off, until one fox dashes in, tears off a piece and races away to hide it (p. 32).

One day at the point we find that an unusually high tide has flooded in over the fast ice. Xavier Xenophon and another bear about the same size are resting in the snow. XX gets up and walks into a deep pool of the new water, ducking his head under until only his letters show above water. After about ten minutes of this

he comes out and dries himself in the snow. First he pushes his chin, chest and front legs through the snow, with his rear high in the air. Then he spreads out his back legs and drags his hindquarters along by pulling with his front legs. Finally he rolls over on his back and scrunches around in the snow with all four legs waving in the air, looking not a little human as he does so.

The other bear has been lying on his side watching all this. But now XX walks over to him and grabs him around the neck. They roll over, pushing each other off with their back legs. They tumble, mouthing each other's necks like puppies. They stand up on their back legs and grapple with their front legs. Once one bear moves its head very quickly, as if to tell the other to ease off.

Another day a smaller bear, perhaps 400 pounds, tries to cross the new ice and keeps falling through. He stands in the shallow water, pushes his chest up against the edge of the ice and spreads his front legs as far and wide as they will go and pulls himself up. The ice keeps breaking and he keeps repeating the maneuver until he is up on the ice again, where he shakes himself dry like a dog.

This bear stays with us, striking such perfect poses that we come to call him Barrymore. He has a long scar on his nose, plastic tags in his ears. And he is tough. He has found something to eat near the buggy one day when XX approaches him. Barrymore does not look up at him but repeatedly sounds a hoarse, breathy roar. Both show their teeth, XX roars once. But they never touch, and XX leaves Barrymore his

Two males about eight years old engage in the play fighting that will prepare them for the real thing.

A young bear sitting on new ice carefully licks a paw. The bears are fastidious about keeping clean.

prize. (Later XX comes back with his wrestling friend and this time Barrymore moves off quickly. The two larger bears finish eating Barrymore's discovery with no visible conflict, a sight that would have surprised the biologists of a generation ago. Then polar bears were thought to be strictly solitary.)

For a week we move among the bears, high off the ground in a heated cocoon. They are curious about us, but unconcerned. They are not afraid, and they are not threatening. We take them very, very seriously, however. Whenever anyone is down on the ground, one of the operators is there with a rifle. Polar bears are superb stalkers, and have a way of suddenly appearing heart-stoppingly close. Just two years earlier Fred Treul of Milwaukee had been leaning out of the driver's window to photograph an ivory gull when a bear reared up from under the buggy and bit down on his arm, trying to pull him out of the buggy, peeling skin and muscle as it did so. Treul nearly bled to death on the race back to town: snow blowing in 60-mile-per-hour winds meant nearly zero visibility and the trip took 14 hours. Doctors in Churchill and Winnipeg saved his arm, however, and he was back looking at bears the next year.

The buggy I spent the week on had been abandoned during that race into town when it broke through the ice and mired in a streambed. Bears had broken all the windows on one side and trashed the interior, methodically ripping the foam out of the seats. On a calm, sunny day, watching bears that seemed as friendly as the family dog, it was instructive to imagine rampaging bears tearing up the very seats we were sitting on.

In a week at the Cape, however, no bear as much as curls a lip at us. They are as lethargic as people in a railroad waiting room late at night. Even when they move, they seem to expend as little energy as possible. We are invading their world, rousing them momentarily from their resting state.

The bears appear perfectly relaxed, completely at home in what for us bundled-up humans on the buggies is a harsh, uninhabitable environment. Never have I had such a strong feeling of being an alien, an outsider. And never have I understood so well the words of Henry Beston in *The Outermost House*: "In a world older and more complete than ours they move finished and complete, gifted with extensions of the senses we have lost or never attained, living by voices we shall never hear. They are not brethren, they are not underlings; they are other nations, caught with ourselves in the net of life and time, fellow prisoners of the splendour and travail of the earth."

With Barrymore we do intrude too much. He stays with us three days, delaying his march over the ice to the seals. We chase him once with a buggy, racing the engine and blowing the horn, to make him drop a can he has found, in the fear that he will slice his tongue, wedge it over his snout or swallow it. He tries to follow us when we break camp and head back to Churchill. When firecrackers do not deter him, we finally fire a rifle in his direction, four shots kicking up the snow and gravel around him before he turns away.

The great white bears are intruding on the world of people, too, and the interactions are fatal to both. Offshore oil rigs are moving into prime bear habitat in

Awakened in its daybed, a large male keeps an eye on intruders. Polar bears sleep as much as humans do.

A bear jumps at Arctic foxes that are harassing it, feinting for an opening to dash in and steal food.

Sitting in a depression she has scooped out of the snow, a mother grooms one of her cubs as they nurse.

the western Canadian Arctic now, and bears have killed workers on the rigs. Scientists want to find out the best ways to deter bears without destroying them. A team of biologists spent the early fall in the tower at Cape Churchill, trying different techniques on bears that came too close. Rubber bullets worked best, but Canadian law strictly limits their use to police.

An individual bear is unpredictable and therefore dangerous. But the more general question of danger depends on the bears' condition. If they have fed well and are round with blubber, they are less of a menace, though still unpredictable. Churchill probably has more experience with polar bears than any community in the world, and the numbers there are instructive. In 1983, about 93 bears were captured in Churchill. A new rule was imposed after that season that requires any bear that appears in the dump or closer to town to be intercepted. Conservation officers estimate that if the new rule had prevailed in 1983, at least 200 would have been taken into custody. In 1984, only ten bears were locked up. Then last season, 70 bears were hauled in. The presumption is that during the winter and spring of 1984 the bears hunted so successfully that they came ashore with more than enough fat reserves to see them through the summer and had little interest in investigating the smells from town.

A man is killed and the rules are changed

The rule was changed after a man was killed by a bear in Churchill in 1983. Apparently he and a bear were both foraging in the kitchen of a burned-out hotel after midnight. Since then the town has drawn a line east of the town, just beyond the garbage dump. Any bear found at the dump, about six miles east of the town, or between the dump and town is picked up and taken to jail. (Mothers and cubs are kept together in large enclosures.) Any bear found between the dump and the rocket-launching range, another eight miles to the east, is captured, weighed and measured, tagged, tattooed and released.

We stopped at the jail one Saturday. A helicopter with a cargo net slung underneath had been ferrying bears to the Seal River, about 40 miles north. The jail is a triple Quonset hut with cages designed to hold 20 bears at a time. Conservation officers had trapped or tranquilized 70 bears during the 1985 season, which meant that 50 had been flown north to be released. I walked up to a culvert trap behind a pickup truck and found myself face-to-face with a 500-pound male. The

As the sunset fades and the moon brightens, a bear crosses the frozen tidal flats at Cape Churchill.

Cubs of the year, now about seven or eight months old, cuddle up with their mother in a quiet moment.

Manitoba conservation officers were trying to decide whether to drive down to the beach and release the bear on the ice. They finally decided not to, and backed the trap into the jail. Ian Thorliefsen, a Manitoba wildlife technician, told us that a mother and two cubs we had seen from town out on the ice had walked right by his van earlier in the day. They were coming from the direction of the dump.

Bears and dumps are a perennial problem in wildlife management. One of the bears in the Churchill dump last November was Linda, a regular. She was first caught there as a yearling in 1966. She is not only habituated herself, but always brings her cubs. Most of the bears found at the dump are subadults that have not yet learned to hunt well.

On occasion Churchill has been disastrous for bears. One conservation officer, quickly named Speedy by the townspeople, shot 22 before he was transferred to a less exciting post. Homeowners have shot them in the process of breaking and entering. Others have been shot while supposedly threatening human life, sometimes under questionable circumstances.

Most of the time, however, the town is remarkably relaxed about being infiltrated by half-ton carnivores. Len Smith, the man who built the tundra buggies out of scrap, tells of a day shooting geese at a pond outside of town. He shot one, he says, and his dog swam out and retrieved it. He shot another one a little farther away, and a bear emerged from the bushes, swam out and retrieved it. Smith says he just kept hunting, his dog and the bear sharing the kill equally.

North of Churchill, across the line in the Northwest Territories, polar bears are hunted regularly. Each Inuit village has a quota and even though the market for polar bear hides has shrunk and the price has dropped, they kill some every year. While we were at the Cape, hunters at Eskimo Point, a village 150 miles north, killed a 1,300-pound male. Inuit hunter and trapper associations can sell the right to shoot a bear on a guided, dogsled hunt, and in theory a U.S. citizen could go up there and kill one. He or she could not bring any part of the bear back into the United States, however. Polar bears, which spend most of their time on the sea and not a little in it (they can swim at least 40 miles), are protected under the Marine Mammal Protection Act.

Humans are pushing farther and farther into the Arctic, looking for oil and other riches. The worlds of men and bears will overlap more and more. So far, the bears are not threatened as a species. Nobody knows with any certainty, but the best estimates place the world population of polar bears at 20,000. They are completely protected in the Soviet Union and there is a moratorium on hunting in the Norwegian islands of Svalbard. In Alaska, indigenous hunters shoot 60 to 120 bears a year.

Research continues, despite budget cuts that limit the use of aircraft. As the next logical step in polar bear study, biologists are turning more attention to the seals they prey on, looking for patterns in their populations and movements. As the seals go, so go the bears.

Our week ends, and we start the long drive from the Cape back to town. About halfway we see our last bears, a mother and cubs investigating an abandoned hunting cabin. We see more creatures of the Arctic, too: a white-phase gyrfalcon hunting from a cabin roof, a snowy owl perched on a pole. At one point we get out and flounder through the willows and snowdrifts, trying to take pictures of rock and willow ptarmigan scampering across the snow. For some of us they are firsts, exciting additions to life lists. Yet after a week with the bears, everything else is anticlimax.

It is March now. Most of the great white bears have been out on the ice all winter, and now the mothers with new cubs are joining them in the hunt. The breeding season is coming, when 1,000-pound-plus males will fight for real. My thoughts turn to a day in November, the sun setting crimson over the ice, the wind whistling out of the dark northwest. We humans were packing up our cameras, thinking of getting back to camp, a drink in the Muktuk Saloon, a hot supper. But out on the ice to the west of us a mother was leading two cubs north into the night. They moved slowly over the ice, the cubs now falling back, now catching up. She set the pace of a human mother bringing her toddlers home from the park. She moved farther and farther into the dusk, the bitter cold. They were going home.

By John Skow

Having all the answers is a hard row to hoe

It gets harder and harder, being the Answer Man. In the old days, when I got out of the Answer Academy, there were questions like "What is the largest city in North Dakota?" Easy: too-far-to-go. Ergo, forgo North Dakota. And, "What do you do for termites?" A snap: serve them little wooden sandwiches.

Then about 20 years ago, I guess it was, the world got more complicated. There would be posers like "My son would be six foot six, if he ever stood up, but he just lays around looking dazed. Do you think his brain is working too hard pushing that long hair up out of his skull?" Or, "I went to a restaurant and they had raw fish. What are you supposed to do?"

I could handle those. I told the guy with the numb son to buy the boy space boots. Those are the dinguses that let you hang upside down for hours, like a wombat. That way the boy's brain wouldn't have to push so hard, and it might perk up and see the world clearly, though inverted. I saw things clearly myself in those days. Some deep thinker would write in, very sarcastically, that surely I meant a bat, not a wombat, and I would zing back "Dear Batty, You hang out with your friends and I'll hang out with mine, and we'll see whose ears drop off first."

Answers just weren't a problem. The raw fish sufferer I advised to send out for pizza. Sure, by now you've heard the pizza cure for rotten service and bad food, maybe from a joke-telling cheerful Charlie on late-night television. Probably you've seen it happen in what might loosely be called real life: some citizen waits an hour for a dried-out arrangement of animal and plant fiber that will cost him $32, plus tip. He makes a phone call, and 15 minutes later the Domino's man trots into the restaurant and delivers. Extra sauce, pepperoni, and a screaming headwaiter,

what more could you ask? An answer and a half, and I had it first.

I even had an answer for the income tax. Make the IRS unprofitable, I told my fans. Overpay your tax by some small amount, such as $3.67. Then, eventually, when you get your $3.67 refund, send back another letter thanking the federal woodchucks, but saying that recalculation makes it appear that you really do owe money. Enclose a check for $6.40. It costs the government $825 in computer time and salaries to refigure your return and send a check. If millions of civic-minded citizens overpay relentlessly, the Treasury Department will go broke, retire and grow roses, like any other elderly robber baron.

It was the New Age cult ("No, not cult," says my wife, the Answer Woman, with a smile of sweet patience) . . . OK, it was the New Age shamanistic enlightenment ("You're just sticking out your tongue and going 'nyah-nyah,'" says she) . . . All right, then, it was that gaga Shirley MacLaine and her flea-brained reincarnation ("Channeling," says the voice of reason) that curdled the Answer Man business, which up to then—as I used to tell my student answer men at the community college—had been the best scam since orthodontia, requiring only minutes of thought a week and no stoop labor.

What happened was, some fuddled husband wrote in needing help. "My wife says that she used to be Cleopatra in a past life and I used to be a water buffalo," said this Old Age hubby. "But her girlfriend Clarice also used to be Cleopatra. Are they nuts or am I?"

I should have told him to have a shot and a beer, and then get into a good, meaty argument with the guy on the next stool about whether the Seattle Kingdome or that tin can the Minnesota Twins play in is the worst ballpark in the majors. But I take my Answer Man oath seriously. "Remember you are

right, then go ahead," says the diploma on my office wall.

So I went ahead. "Channeling experts confirm that in the U.S. alone 17,283 women were actually Cleopatra in former lives," I wrote. "Oddly enough, however, neither your wife nor Clarice is among them. On the other hand, it appears certain that you really were a water buffalo."

"Not funny," said the Answer Woman as we ate supper. "That poor sap isn't the only water buffalo around."

"Sure, sure," said I. "But if all of those women really were Cleopatra, her unconscious must have sounded like high noon at a vegetarian restaurant in Santa Monica. How come nobody ever emptied slop jars in former lives?"

"Channelers are way ahead of you. Having been a beautiful serving wench in a past existence is now very popular."

"Bosh and double-bosh. Channeling is the spiritual equivalent of tofu."

"You're just closed-minded."

"Yeah, well, if you don't close the windows the bugs fly in. Like that dame on the West Coast who claims to be some kind of human megaphone for a 40,000-year-old Neanderthal condo salesman named Gronk. A complete fraud, of course. The guy who is talking through her is a bankrupt harness repairman named McCaffrey, from Linwood, New Jersey, who died in 1906. He was a loser then, and being dead hasn't made him any smarter."

"If you say so," said the Answer Woman.

"No question about it. What's this we're eating?"

"Tofu casserole. It was roast beef in a past existence, and you must have been Henry VIII, because you're on your third helping."

I am working on my answer. In the meantime, if you call my number, you will get the answering machine.

Photographs by Albert G. Richards

The secret hearts of flowers stand revealed in x rays

Using darkroom magic in a delicate process, a professor of radiography has found a way to see familiar blossoms in a whole new light

Venation in the petals of this cosmos takes on some abstract qualities associated with poster art.

Twenty-five years ago Albert G. Richards, out for a noon stroll in Ann Arbor, made a modest purchase that changed his life. A store was offering daffodils at 27 cents a dozen. Richards bought some and took them back to his office at the University of Michigan School of Dentistry, where he taught radiography to dental students and hygienists. On impulse he made a radiograph (x-ray picture) of one of the flowers, and thus began the hobby that led to hundreds of beautiful images like those on these pages.

"While many people love and appreciate flowers," he says,"they may never have realized or seen the secret beauty hidden within the blossoms."

Floral radiographs reveal details of the successive layers of tissue or petals. As you look at these pictures, you are looking into and right through the flowers. These images are perforce in black and white because there is no color at x-ray wavelengths. No shadows of the flowers are present in the radiographs that are comparable to shadows made by light in photographs.

In preparing flowers for radiography, Richards uses blotting paper to soak up rain or dewdrops. A tiny vacuum cleaner with probes like hypodermic needles sucks up any dirt lodged within the flower. Occasionally there are surprises: the radiograph of a rose re-

vealed a spider and its nest deep inside the blossom.

Some plants appear shy about it all. They close up when taken into the cooler, darker room where the x-ray machine is, or they wilt during the exposure.

The most difficult part, Richards explains, is making a photographic print from the radiograph. The x-ray film has much wider latitude than does photographic paper, and he uses darkroom "magic" to go from one to the other without losing detail.

Richards says he was hired by the University of Michigan because he had made color prints in the 1930s and "knew something about photography." He has degrees in physics and chemical engineering, but not in dentistry. He was the first to use electron microscopy to view the internal microstructure of human teeth, and he invented the recessed cone x-ray head which is now standard equipment in many dental offices. He also developed an x-ray technique for obtaining fingerprints from badly burned bodies. In 1974 he was appointed to the first Distinguished Professorship in the School of Dentistry. Retired and given emeritus status by the university in 1982, Richards devotes himself to gardening, writing and his laboratory.

Seven of the floral radiographs are at the Hunt Institute for Botanical Documentation at Carnegie-Mellon University in Pittsburgh. And one is in the collection of the J. Paul Getty Museum in Malibu, California. Richards' image was one of more than 100 flower photographs from the Getty's holdings shown in an exhibit organized last year by the Detroit Institute of Arts.

The stamens of two fuchsias emerge from multiple layers of petals and sepals that form the blossom.

A hidden bouquet

These ethereal images were chosen
from 2,000 made over 25 years.
The flowers can be cut or potted,
and are simply placed between x-ray
source and film. They are not
harmed, and no chemicals are used.

Tulip (*Tulipa* "Darwin" hybrid)

Star magnolia (*Magnolia stellata*)

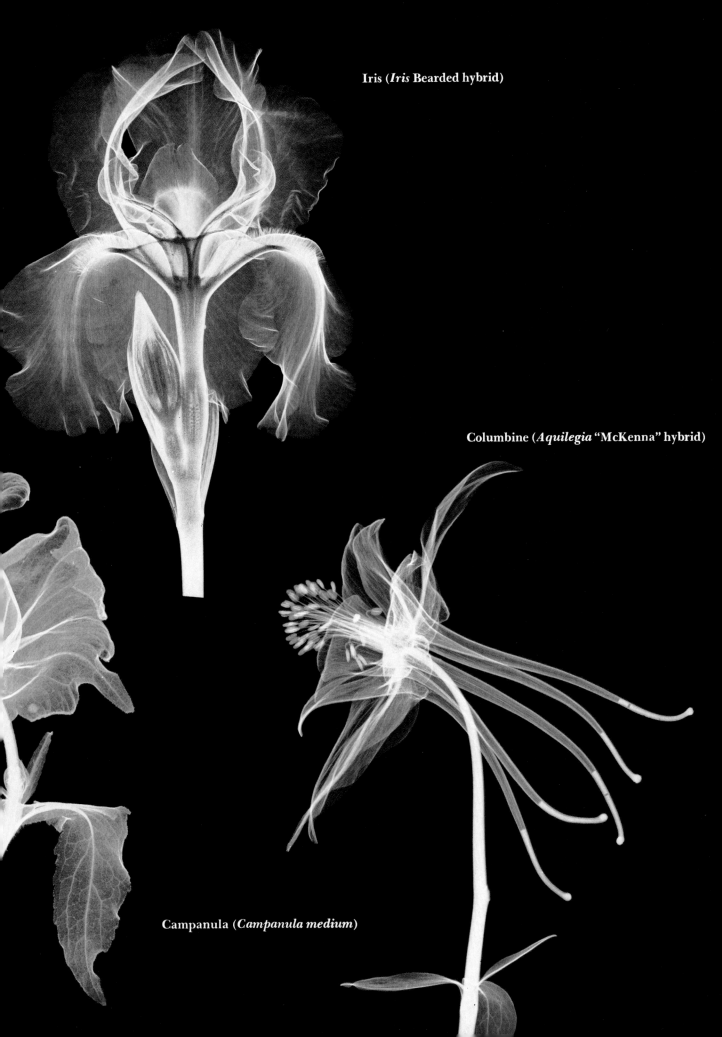

Iris (*Iris* Bearded hybrid)

Columbine (*Aquilegia* "McKenna" hybrid)

Campanula (*Campanula medium*)

Inside the flowing, cloaklike spathe of a calla lily, minuscule flowers can be seen at the base of the central spike.

Delicate petals of three cyclamen flowers
seem to wave in the breeze.

By Ruth Mehrtens Galvin

Sybaritic to some, sinful to others, but how sweet it is!

Choose up sides and thank the Maya, Cortés, Samuel Pepys, du Barry—but mostly those 20th-century chocolatiers, all vying to please

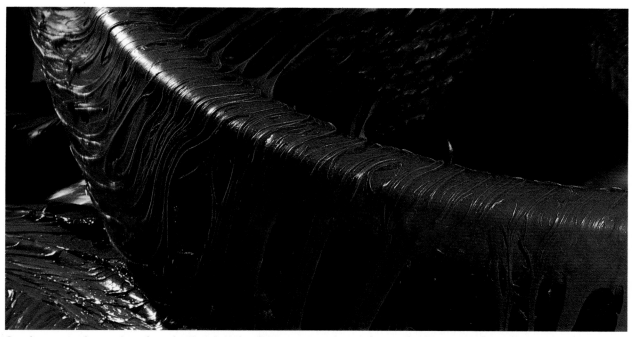

On the way to becoming chocoholics' delight, flaky, fine chocolate and cocoa butter are stirred and rolled over and over during conching at Ghirardelli's. Warm, silky-smooth, it is then ready for processing.

She was magnificent: ten feet tall, 2,200 pounds and all chocolate. Germania, proud symbol of the Stollwerck company, ensconced in a 38-foot Renaissance temple (chocolate, of course), was only one exhibit at the Chicago World's Columbian Exposition of 1893. Van Houten had so much to show off it put up a whole "chocolate house," the stucco reproduction of a 16th-century Dutch town hall. In 1894 the chocolate house was moved to Massachusetts where, painted pink, it is presently the happy home of a psychoanalyst.

Yes, sir (and madam), if you think now is the heyday of chocolate, you might take a look at the ephemera of chocolate lovers at the turn of the century. That was when Henry Maillard ("Importers of Fancy Boxes and Easter Eggs") was giving free chocolate-cooking classes at 114 West 25th Street in New York; when Hawley & Hoops ("Makers of Shaped Chocolates") were putting out "A No.1." bears and rabbits, lobsters and pigs, cigars and pipes—even chocolate violins; when you could send away to Huyler's and receive a set of picture-cards with a poem for every day in the week ("For breakfast on the day of rest/ We always get what we like best: Huyler's Cocoa" and "Monday is my washing day/ A

A dizzying array of Victorian *Theobroma cacao* ephemera shows insouciant youths, sweet little girls.

Photographs by Liane Enkelis

cup of Huyler's makes work play/Pure! Delicious! Healthful!")

All chocolate in those days was said to be pure (and certainly healthful) but Bell's Chocolates, "dipped with a fork," were both "clean *and* pure." A brochure exhibited a photograph of tastefully attired ladies wielding their forks, as well as a picture of several rather gooey-looking young women doing something else: "In the usual method of dipping," said the ad, "the HAND is continually IMMERSED in the CHOCOLATE & the creams are DIPPED with the FINGERS." Well!

I found all this, and much more, in the Wilbraham, Massachusetts, headquarters of a young man named William Frost Mobley, a chocolate fancier who maintains a business in antiquarian ephemera, dealing in the bits and pieces of everyday life that recall people's pleasures for posterity. He avers that his comely, dark-haired wife, Emily, also makes the best chocolate cake in the world, from a recipe in the box of a French product called Poulain. The afternoon I was in Wilbraham, Emily gave me a cup of Poulain cocoa. "It'll knock your sox off," she said. It did.

Small batches and the best ingredients

The Mobleys' was only one of my stops on a six-month trek that began out of utter astonishment at the continuing craze for chocolate. I had grown up in the simple era when life progressed predictably from Baker's cocoa on frosty evenings to Hershey's Kisses and Nonpareils on holidays, frozen Mars bars to take one through teenage summers and, true love at last, a Whitman's Sampler. I "knew" chocolate was vaguely naughty because it "spoiled" my meals, my teeth and my skin. I dreamed of the day my mother would let me have her collection of tiny, hand-painted cocoa cups, favors from birthday parties in her girlhood Brooklyn. As I grew older, I moved snobbishly from milk chocolate to dark, from commercial to "hand-made." Given Godiva by one of those nouveau New Yorkers who follow every fad, I thought the affectation was vaguely silly until I realized that I, too, was seeking out hand-made chocolates in capitals around the world. After I found some of the best only a stone's throw from my own Boston apartment, I learned my first lesson about what makes good chocolate: small batches, carefully made, without preservatives, from the very best ingredients. High price and a famous name guarantee nothing.

When suddenly I felt surrounded by self-styled chocoholics, chocolate portraits, chocolate perfume and chocolate cruises on the *QE2*, it seemed time to call a halt and ask what the fuss is all about. To get some answers, I drove out to my favorite local chocolate supplier, a pristine little red-and-white converted

Larger-than-life reliefs of emperors, other German bigwigs enhanced Germania's solid chocolate pedestal.

factory known as Harbor Sweets, down by the Salem, Massachusetts, waterfront. There, women of all ages, education and background—the mayor's wife and the fire chief's, college graduates and the retarded, members of the Eastern Yacht Club, Finns, Dominicans and Vietnamese—work four-hour shifts under the motto, "Love is a quality controller." Stirring caramel in a shining copper cauldron or leaping at the sound of a bell to put pecans on the caramel drops when they have reached just the right temperature; keeping an eye on the vats of chocolate "liquor" to get them to a careful 89 degrees; painting white sails on the "Sweet Sloops" (chocolate-coated buttercrunch) as they emerge along the assembly line; wrapping or packing Marblehead Mints, Sweet Shells, Sand Dollars and Barque Sarah into a Valentine heart, they make up a small ($1.5 million in sales) company, a cross between your neighborhood candy man and the big fellas.

In an informal taste test of gourmet candies by experts on one David Susskind TV show, Harbor Sweets won, hands down. To consumers, it is not only fine but one of the most expensive chocolates made in America (30 Sweet Sloops for $15). To other manufacturers, proprietor Benneville Strohecker is best known as a great marketer. Grandson of the man who made the first chocolate bunny in the United States—in Reading, Pennsylvania—he had been an executive with Schrafft's before he left to start his own company. He now turns out special chocolates for Gump's of San Francisco, the Boston Symphony Orchestra, Chicago's Field Museum, the Carnegie Museum in Pittsburgh, even the Smithsonian (from copies of old molds in the Institutions's collection). What other people see as expensive, Ben Strohecker insists is really an *in*expensive gift because "Chocolate makes everybody smile—even bankers."

Armed with Strohecker's "chocolate" library, I discovered that chocolate has been making Americans smile for 4,000 years. A Mayan treasure grown and used by the Aztecs for centuries before the Spanish discovered it in Mexico, chocolate was believed to have been brought down from the Garden of Life by the great god Quetzalcoatl as consolation to Man for having to live on Earth. In the afterlife, it was expected to be served perpetually.

On his fourth trip to America, Columbus found some cocoa beans in a canoe off Yucatán and picked them up as a curiosity. Hernán Cortés, discovering that cocoa beans were used in Mexico as currency, had the tree cultivated in earnest. Exacted as tribute by Montezuma, the beans were literally money in the

A journalist specializing in behavior and a veteran chocolate eater, Mrs. Galvin wrote about lucid dreaming in the August 1983 issue of SMITHSONIAN.

Bill and Emily Mobley go for broke with her "knock-your-sox-off" cocoa and special chocolate cupcakes.

bank. Ten could buy a rabbit; 100 a slave. Cortés sent home the recipe for a curious drink the Mexicans consumed, called *chocolatl*. Montezuma swilled it down, golden goblet after golden goblet. Mixed with water, maize and spices, the ground cocoa beans were considered an aphrodisiac, served with ceremony at weddings and said to be permitted only to the aristocracy. Chocolate had social cachet. In Chiapas, following the establishment of Catholicism, grand ladies had their maids bring them the drink in church until the bishop, annoyed, forbade the practice. One of his parishoners, so the tale goes, "somewhat too familiar with one of the Bishop's pages," got him to serve the prelate a nice cup of *chocolatl*. It killed him. The lady in question told explorer Thomas Gage that practically nobody missed the bishop.

Cocoa reached Europe before either tea or coffee, gradually moving from Spain and Portugal to Italy, Austria, France and then over to the British Isles, where a high import tax kept it special. By 1664, diarist Samuel Pepys admitted to drinking it. After a 17th-century cardinal ruled that liquids do not break a fast, cocoa became a Lenten fad. As an "inflamer of passions" it was also said to tempt monks to break their

Droplets of liquid chocolate drizzling from machine onto a steel belt form Ghirardelli's sinuous chips.

At Harbor Sweets, operator guides fluid Sweet Shells into reproduction of antique shell and animal molds.

vows, and its use by Madame du Barry and Casanova did little to dim that reputation.

In 1753 the Swedish botanist Linnaeus gave the cocoa plant its scientific name, *Theobroma cacao*—the food of the gods. (The tree is cacao, the bean is cocoa and the food is chocolate. It bears no relation to either coconuts or coca, the source of cocaine.)

Most cacao is grown between 100 and 1,000 feet above sea level and within ten degrees of the equator. In the late 19th century, the Portuguese took *Theobroma cacao* to some islands off Africa, and it soon became an established crop in the Gold Coast, Cameroon and Nigeria, where the temperature and humidity are ideal for it. Russell Cook, an authority on the subject, cautioned, in his definitive *Chocolate Production and Use*: "Regardless of species or variety, *Theobroma cacao* is a virtual prima donna in its requirements for healthy growth." A young cacao tree cannot grow in full tropical sun. It is cultivated with such trees as banana and rubber, which provide shade and alternate sources of income should the cacao crop be wiped out by fungi, pests or climatic problems.

It had become clear to me that there is more to a chocolate bar than meets the eye. One afternoon I turned on the public radio program "All Things Considered" and heard about a botany course on chocolate being given by Prof. John West at the University of California, Berkeley. I wrote to him. He wrote to

me. We talked on the telephone. Soon, there I was on his doorstep.

Botanist West, 46, made his reputation as a specialist in marine algae, but his hobby is making desserts. Through that he got interested in chocolate and, naturally, its botany and biochemistry. For the past four years he has been pursuing everything he can find out about chocolate, and he now offers a course labeled Botany 117, better known as "Chocolate." "It's a hell of a lot of work," says West. He admitted only 55 of the first 800 students who flocked to sign up (15 dropped the course when they realized he was serious).

John West looks at chocolate as a scientist. Among the myths he views with a fishy eye is the one devised a couple of years ago by several psychoanalysts, that lovelorn women binge on chocolate because it is a source of phenylethylamine, "the chemical released in the brain when people become infatuated or fall in love." There is more phenylethylamine in sauerkraut, West points out, with some disgust.

An Idaho farm boy deeply concerned about the difficulties of growing cacao—and how little the farmers themselves get from a crop that makes so many other folks rich—John West pointed out to me that while many other plants in the tropical forest have developed good defenses against disease, the cacao has not, nor have its cultivators succeeded in breeding pest-resistant strains. Fungi cause the most trouble, the

Belt moves on through refrigerated tunnel to solidify them. Process can handle up to 4,000 pounds an hour.

Toothsome blend of dark and white chocolate with buttercrunch gets dusting of nuts at Harbor Sweets.

major one worldwide being black pod disease, a relative of the fungus that created the Irish potato famine. Then, there is an insect aficionado for virtually every part of the cacao tree. The worst, capsids, use a stylet like a hypodermic syringe to suck fluid from the plants.

"I'm very keen on biocontrol," West remarked. Marine algae, he explained, must develop many natural toxins to keep from being gobbled up by every animal in the sea. There, compounds are called phytoalexins (flowering plants use them to discourage grazing and attack by fungi and bacteria) and could be extracted and put to use as substitutes for commercial pesticides and fungicides. The major cacao-producing nations have not only endless problems growing the plant, but also have oceans of seaweed right off their shores. Why not, asks West, use seaweed to solve some of the disease and pest problems of cacao?

Almost all chocolate today comes from the seeds of one or another type of the Forastero variety, a hardier breed than the Criollo, from which the legendary *chocolatl* was made. Once planted, a bean will start to grow in less than two weeks, and in another two or three will show primary leaves that look like tiny wings. Depending on shade and humidity, the tree can grow as high as 40 feet; most are only 20 to 25. Evergreen, with large, elliptical, shiny leaves, it will not bear fruit for three or four years. By age 50 it is over the hill.

A pastel beauty like a tiny jack-in-the-box, the flower can be white or rosy, pink or yellow, bright red, or any combination. It grows directly on dense "cushions" on the bark of the tree by the tens of thousands—as many as 6,000 per tree per year. Few of these marvelous flowers are ever pollinated (it was not known until 1940 that the deed is done not by birds and bees but by a tiny insect, a midge). The average tree bears annually no more than 30 pods about half the size of a football, containing between 20 and 40 seeds each—our future chocolate. Good fertilizer is essential, says John West. Harvesting, twice a year, requires skill lest the machete nick the cushion, destroying tissue needed to grow new flowers.

When the pods are cracked open, almond-shaped beans are freed from their acidic membrane, piled high and covered with banana leaves or palm fronds. Taken from the placenta and separated, the beans are still covered with pulp, something important to fermentation, the next essential process. Without fermentation, chocolate will never taste right. Philip Keeney, at the Food Science Department of Pennsylvania State University, told me it creates chocolate's "flavor precursors" by breaking down the sugar to glucose and fructose, and turning some of the protein into free amino acids and smaller peptides.

The science of fermentation pursued to perfection can create delicious varieties of cocoa beans that com-

Chocolate—sybaritic or sinful?

George Steinmetz

Tiny cacao blossom at right is hand-pollinated from detached blossom (left) in hybridization experiment.

Loren McIntyre

Great care must be exercised in harvesting mature cacao pod to avoid damage to the flower cushion.

mand premium prices. The skillful farmer will gather neither overripe pods, whose beans will not have enough flavor, nor underripe ones that tend to have a "hammy" taste. A cocoa-bean connoisseur learns to beware of gray or purple beans (signs of too little—or no—fermentation) or overfermented ones whose deep brown color is a sign of rot. Once fermented, the beans must be dried before being packed for shipment. A great agricultural gamble, cacao is also a potentially great source of income for any country that can grow a lot. In this century the chief producers have been the Ivory Coast, Brazil and Ghana, plus Nigeria and Cameroon. Thanks to its large population and prosperity, the United States is the number one purchaser, buying 11 percent (460 million pounds) of the world's cocoa beans. Per capita, though, the Swiss, Austrians, Belgians and half a dozen other countries all consume more chocolate than do we.

Cocoa beans were once a wild speculation as those who could bought up supplies, holding them to create false shortages and high prices, then dumping them on the market with a subsequent price "bust." Such a collapse just after World War I caused the creation of the New York Cocoa Exchange (now merged with the much older Coffee and Sugar Exchange), the commodities market on which cocoa futures contracts are traded in units of ten metric tons (22,000 pounds) for delivery up to 12 months in the future.

When I visited the Exchange at the World Trade Center in New York, I learned that it doesn't take a college degree to trade in cocoa-bean futures, just experience, and that the strenuous commodities market is a young persons' game. Around the cocoa pit—an octagonal fence—cocoa-bean contracts are traded by "open outcry": everyone just yells, with a few hand signals thrown in. The cocoa market is what Bennett Corn, president of the Exchange, cheerfully calls "organized chaos." Behind the pit the youngest apprentices, some looking scarcely out of high school, man rows of telephones to take orders and transmit them to the pit where by 9 A.M. traders are two and three deep. Employees of the Exchange sit on a platform, ready to record the agreements made. At 9:30, with the ringing of a bell, mayhem breaks loose. Those with contracts to sell shout their offers of delivery date, numbers of contracts and price, hoping some buyers will accept. Suddenly all shouting stops. Deals have been made. The going price appears in the middle of the pit on a television screen topped by a digital clock and is recorded on the huge wall board high above. Just as suddenly, the trading begins again. "September!" shouts a young man in a red sweater, to nobody in particular. They are back at it again.

More than 600,000 contracts were traded in New York alone last year. Speculators hope the contracts they buy and sell at one price will be worth far more by delivery time. Manufacturers join the fray not so much to speculate as to hedge, buying and selling at different times in an effort to secure prices.

Special blends, utmost secrecy

The actual beans destined for chocolate are chosen carefully from shipments delivered, for the most part, to the Port of Philadelphia. Each manufacturer has his own special blends, whose secrets he guards with his life. The Aztecs ground cacao beans in small bowls hollowed out of lava and mixed the granules with spices to produce a bitter brew; the Spanish added sugar. In the centuries since, other countries have made their own contributions. C. J. van Houten of Holland, concerned about fat, pressed the cocoa butter out of chocolate and added alkali to the remaining powder to produce a different color and taste known since, not surprisingly, as "Dutch." The cocoa butter van Houten did not want began to be added to a fluid called chocolate liquor to make chocolate. It was the Swiss who added milk, creating the most popular type.

The first North American chocolate was manufactured in 1765 in the corner of a factory at Dorchester Lower Mills on the outskirts of Boston by John Hannon, an Irish immigrant. When Hannon disappeared, his backer took over and named the company for his own grandson, Walter Baker. America's most famous chocolate man was a Pennsylvania Dutchman named Milton Hershey, who went broke repeatedly before making his first million. Today, Hershey Foods

John West describes branching pattern and leaf shape of young cacao tree to his students at Berkeley.

is the foremost researcher in the chemistry of the cocoa bean, using its findings to start an experimental cacao tree farm in Belize. The Mars family, now in its third generation in the candy business, makes the most popular candy bar in this country, Snickers. M&M's rank second. Third is Reese's peanut butter cup, made by Hershey.

As chocolate has become big business, so too has the machinery, much of it made in Germany and Italy. To get a glimpse of it, I headed for San Leandro, California, home of the Ghirardelli Chocolate Company. One of the smaller manufacturers but perhaps as diversified as any, Ghirardelli has a typical history of immigrant enterprise, true grit and hard times.

Once Domingo Ghirardelli was the largest chocolate manufacturer in the western United States. He came into the world in Rapallo, Italy, in 1818, nearly 50 years before Milton Hershey was born in Pennsylvania. Apprenticed to a candy maker, he and his bride eventually reached the United States by way of Uruguay and Peru. When he sent 600 pounds of his chocolate north to San Francisco with a neighboring merchant headed for the Gold Rush, it was such a hit that Domingo swiftly followed. At first successful as a merchant and shipper, financial reverses sent him back to making chocolate, and his family owned the business for the next 110 years. In 1962 it was sold to another Italian family, the DeDomenicos, makers of Rice-a-Roni, who moved it to San Leandro. There, the director of quality control, Ned Russell, took me through the plant.

Making chocolate is not as simple as grinding a bag

Eight-year-old Alex Heaslett of Palo Alto steals
a march on his birthday by getting to lick the bowl.

of beans. The machinery in a chocolate factory towers over you, rumbling and whirring. A huge cleaner first blows the beans away from their accompanying debris —sticks and stones, coins and even bullets can fall among cocoa beans being bagged. Then they go into another machine for roasting. Next comes separation in a winnower, shells sliding out one side, beans falling from the other. Grinding follows, resulting in chocolate liquor. Fermentation, roasting and "conching" all influence the flavor of chocolate.

Chocolate is "conched"—rolled over and over against itself like pebbles in the sea—in enormous circular machines named conches for the shells they once resembled. Climbing a flight of steps to peer into this huge, slow-moving glacier, I was expecting something like molten mud, but found myself forced to conclude it resembled nothing so much as chocolate.

Ghirardelli makes its own chocolate as well as special blends for other firms, as does Nabisco, the huge candy and cookie company that custom-makes "Merckens Bordeaux" for Harbor Sweets. ("Handmade" chocolate, Ben Strohecker had informed me, is handmade only at the end.) Ghirardelli also specializes in cocoa, which comes out of a press in wheels like small brown manhole covers. The extracted cocoa butter is added to the liquor reserved for making edible chocolate. Cocoa butter determines how fluid the chocolate feels on your tongue; texture also comes from refining and conching.

Manufacturers have tried for years to make chocolate synthetically, with little success, because chocolate contains hundreds of substances and no one knows which are responsible for its distinctive flavor. Forty or 50 separate compounds are crucial to the taste, John West told his class the week that I was there. After a rapid-fire introduction to flavor chemistry, the students were provided with cotton swabs and rows of tiny paper cups containing various strengths of sucrose, acetic acid, saccharin, hydrochloric, propionic and citric acid, and set out to discover just where on their tongues they appreciated each substance and what it tasted like. "I'm not training them to be professional flavorists," West explained to me, "just to perceive the basis for what they are doing when they taste chocolate." When I got back to Berkeley from San Leandro the whole ground floor of the Life Sciences Building reeked with the odors of several dozen chocolate components with which West had anointed thin strips of balsa for a "sniffing exercise.

As I left Botany 117, the class had still to tackle the toxicity of chocolate, a subject much studied in animals but not so much in people. The major concern about chocolate is theobromine, often suspected of being a problem because its molecular structure so resembles caffeine's. What caffeine is to coffee and theophylline is to tea, theobromine is to chocolate. With his staff of more than 150, Barry Zoumas, vice president of science and technology for Hershey, has studied the chemistry of theobromine for a dozen years. Chocolate would have to be virtually your entire diet, he told me, for the theobromine in it to do you any harm.

Scientists have long since proved to their own satisfaction that chocolate does not cause acne and that almost nobody is allergic to it. Studies have even shown that the cocoa bean may have properties that protect teeth from plaque formation. "There is always the sugar, you know," my dentist reminded me with a smile (even dentists smile when you say "chocolate").

With the price of cocoa beans going up, I did one last thing when I left the Cocoa Exchange. I stopped downstairs to visit what I presumed would be a friendly banker. "Can I borrow some money to speculate on the cocoa market?" I asked. "Sixteen percent, $10,000 limit," he declared, barely glancing in my direction. Without the glimmer of a smile.

From bean to binge: a cascade of dried beans flows
around open cacao pod and into a pool of chocolates.

Article and photographs by David W. Macdonald

A meerkat volunteers for guard duty so its comrades can live in peace

These feisty inhabitants of the Kalahari help each other with everything from raising children to waging war on their neighbors

Imagine a furry brigand about 12 inches tall standing up on its hind legs and leaning heavily on its stiff tail. Its flat triangular head features a sharply tapered snout festooned with whiskers and two impressively pointed canine teeth protruding well below the upper lip. Its beady eyes glitter behind a dark bandit's mask and each of its front paws is equipped with a set of elegantly curved long claws. You may think that you've conjured up the image of a mythical beast, but in fact this creature is real. It's a gray meerkat, distant kin to Rudyard Kipling's Rikki-tikki-tavi, one of the most sociable mammals on Earth—and one of the most pugnacious as well.

Also known as sticktails or, more precisely, suricates, gray meerkats inhabit the vast expanses of wilderness in southern Africa that comprise the Kalahari Desert. The conditions of life in the Kalahari are so unremittingly harsh that these curious little creatures must band together in order to survive. The size of their groups varies from a few individuals up to 30. The degree of cooperation within those societies is so remarkable and the selflessness of the meerkats so conspicuous that their escutcheon, if they had one, would almost certainly be emblazoned with the motto, "All for one and one for all."

Meerkats help each other to do just about everything. They forage and hunt together. They guard each other from predators, baby-sit for each other and

Author "interviews" a sentry, taping its call for later analysis as part of study on meerkat social behavior.

pick up the slack when a pregnant female stops working. They help each other raise and protect youngsters, often risking their own lives in the process. They share food with one another. Last but not least, they attack their enemies together, ganging up on any would-be competitors for prey or territory like brawling bands of buccaneers.

In recent years, field studies of wolves, chimpanzees, gorillas and other social animals have revealed how extraordinarily complex their behavior can be. Until I began following meerkats a few years ago, the details of their lives had never been studied in the wild. My previous research had been on the behavior of other animals, ranging from red foxes in Britain to capybaras in Venezuela. I selected suricates for study because of the tightly knit structure of their groups. I wanted to weigh the various costs and benefits of their sociality and to consider how natural selection might have led to the evolution of their cooperative life-style.

The sands of the Kalahari form an unbroken blanket that underlies the tropical forests of Zaire, runs through Angola and Namibia and surfaces in south-

Scanning the horizon for danger, lone guard stands watch on a termite mound in the full glare of the sun.

The sociable life of the meerkat

Female named Interloper looks after another animal's young. While baby-sitter fasts, mother hunts for food.

western Botswana and northern South Africa as the dunes of the Kalahari Desert. There, squinting into a heat haze as temperatures soar to 104 degrees F, it is tempting to dismiss the purist's quibble that an average annual sprinkling of nine inches of rain reduces the Kalahari's official status from a true desert to a mere semiarid zone. The vegetation consists mainly of short grasses and scrub, including fiercely-barbed blackthorns and charred, spiny skeletons of lightning-struck camelthorn acacias. Many of the rivers in the region are ephemeral streams that dry up altogether for much of the year. The Nossob River is more ephemeral than most; water flows between its dusty banks only once every decade or so. Its dry meanders delineate the border between the Gemsbok National Park in Botswana and the Kalahari Gemsbok National Park in South Africa. The two parks, which cover an area of 22,625 square miles, are administered cooperatively by the two countries.

During my study, I stayed with my wife and infant son in a trailer located in the South African park. I found a group of meerkats living nearby, along a parched meander of the Nossob called the Kwang. This was the community in whose company I would spend almost every day for the next six months. I called them the Kwang Raiders because of their unremitting enmity to any and all outsiders, most especially toward their neighbors. Considering their penchant for thuggery, the word "group" is too bland a term for a gathering of meerkats. A gang, a rabble or a mob better captures the tenor of their society.

One day I witnessed a dramatic encounter that told me a great deal about the nature of the beasts I was studying. Hunting for rodents, a silverbacked jackal was trotting down the Nossob when it rounded a brush pile and froze in its tracks. There, 12 members strong, were the Kwang Raiders, mouths agape, backs arched, tails held ramrod stiff. Meerkats are terrified of jackals, but on this occasion the Raiders' nearest bolt-hole lay an unattainable 130 feet off. Consequently, they jostled themselves into a bunch so compact that their fluffed-up bodies seemed to merge, and then they surged toward the startled jackal. At the spearhead was Scar Shoulder, a huge muscular male—if one can use such terms about a creature that would fit snugly into the average pocket. As the Raiders moved they uttered a hissing growl that rose and fell as the mob and the jackal skirted each other.

The jackal twirled around the churning Raiders, trying in vain to break up their formation, but always the hissing mob was at his heels. The jackal was routed

David Macdonald is a research biologist in the Department of Zoology at Oxford University. His specialty is the social behavior of mammals.

Three meerkats enjoy a midday break in the shade of a tree while another (standing, in back) keeps an eye out for trouble. The easy intimacy within this group is in sharp contrast to its hostility toward outsiders.

and, as he fled, the meerkats gave chase. Then, as if on command, they turned about and sped to their holes with two big males, Scar Shoulder and Scar Chest, covering the retreat from the rear. (I gave all of the Raiders names based on their scars and other characteristics.) Once safely at the den they fell into an orgy of greeting, sniffing and grooming. Some individuals even clasped each other around their shoulders.

Why do meerkats live in groups? That incident provided at least a partial answer. Strength of numbers can help the diminutive creatures overcome predators that could easily wipe them out one by one.

Meerkats (the name is the general Afrikaans term for mongoose) are not cats at all. They are one of 66 species belonging to the family Viverridae that includes such animals as mongooses, civets, genets and linsangs, all of which fall within the broad taxonomic order of the Carnivora. Viverrids in general are rather like the earliest fossil ancestors of modern carnivores, known as the Miacoidea, and indeed their skeletal morphology and dentition have remained virtually unchanged for 40 to 50 million years. Gray meerkats are sufficiently distinct to be classified in a genus of their own. Their closest relatives are mongooses.

Of the 31 species of mongoose, only six are thought to be highly social. The more solitary species tend to be nocturnal, whereas the social species are diurnal, but the critical difference between them may lie in their feeding behavior. The group-living species are generally more insectivorous and less carnivorous than the solitary hunters. It may be that the abundance and dispersion of the insects that they prey upon enable the social animals to forage together without getting in each other's way.

Every meerkat has two imperatives. On the one hand, it is a rapacious hunter, digging feverishly for grubs and geckos in the red sands of the Kalahari dunes, head wedged deep into tunnels, behind exposed inelegantly (p.58) and unprotected aloft. On the other hand, every meerkat is obsessed with the need to scan the skies for raptorial danger; birds of prey that threaten meerkats include the martial eagle, the tawny eagle and the snake-eating eagle. The dilemma, then, is to be both predator and prey, and the species' remarkable society is the solution. One individual can only trust to luck and waver apprehensively between feeding and vigilance, but for the member of a team there is the chance to take turns and, what is more, to develop specialities and, ultimately, a division of labor.

Meerkats take turns watching for danger in a couple of different ways. First, as the group forages, individuals will pause, stand up and scan the skies for a few seconds. Generally, there is only one animal up on its hind legs at a given instant. To achieve this constancy, each member of a smaller group has to take its turn much more frequently than each member of a larger group. Therefore, the reduction of this disruptive chore would seem to be an advantage accruing to members of larger groups.

The second approach is different, and involves an individual, or rarely two, who takes on the primary responsibility for guarding the group. Such a "profes-

Lined up like prison work crew, Kwang Raiders, as the writer refers to this gang, bask in the morning sun after emerging from their den. Their fluffy fur absorbs rays. Group may spend 20 minutes warming up.

sional" guard will perch in a bush or a tree, sometimes for an hour or more, lambasted by the wind, seared by the sun and exposed to predators for miles around. Meanwhile, comforted by the uneasy peepings which signify that a guard is on duty, the remainder of the group can forage with scarcely a glance skyward. When the incumbent eventually clambers down, hot and hungry, another volunteer relieves him.

Among the Kwang Raiders, everybody except the babies took a turn at guard duty but, intriguingly, each did so to a different extent. Scar Shoulder, the most heavily built male, acted as a guard only rarely and then generally only for periods of duty of ten minutes or less. In marked contrast, the almost equally muscular Scar Chest and the scrawnier Spot Neck volunteered often for stints which lasted for an hour or more.

The devotion to duty shown by those two males was truly remarkable. Although they seemed to be inept

climbers, they sought out the highest vantage points. Flinging themselves up into the branches, they frequently slipped and sometimes fell, crashing to the ground with lung-crushing thuds, only to scramble upward again. Of the two, Scar Chest (above) was the more exquisitely daring. Whenever I saw a tiny figure swaying 12 feet above the desert sand atop a wind-buffeted tree, I knew it was he.

The Raiders tried to avoid wildcats, honey badgers and other large predators at all costs, but they went out of their way, interestingly enough, to harass lesser animals (p. 62). Perhaps they simply wanted to banish those enemies from their territory or to discourage them from trying to catch the Raiders off guard when there might be fragile babies in the mob. I saw the Raiders intimidate bat-eared foxes (p. 60) and race along the ground beneath a low-flying goshawk, hurling themselves up into the air and snatching at the

Animals were named for physical characteristics. Third meerkat from left is Scar Chest, the brawniest Raider; to his left is Spot Neck. Scar Shoulder is sixth animal from left. Pregnada is second from right.

hawk's undercarriage. Once, the whole group clustered around a bushy shrub, leaning aggressively into its tangled roots. Suddenly a Cape fox bolted from the sanctuary and the Raiders drove it off.

To make such observations I had to inveigle my way into the lives of Scar Shoulder, Spot Neck, Slim, Lanky, Lefty, Dexter and the others. My first encounters with them were far from intimate. As my jeep trundled across the sand 300 feet or more away, they warily ran for cover. I dogged their trail from dawn to dusk, day after day, until familiarity bred, if not contempt, at least tolerance. The youngsters born to the group during my stay were rarely more than 30 feet from a two-legged shadow and, as a result, they were not averse to a game of rough-and-tumble with a wriggling finger.

The ultimate acceptance came one day when I was crouched down taking a photograph. Spot Neck launched himself at my head, scrambling for a grip in my hair. He finally got a leg up on my spectacles and hopped onto my shoulder to take up his guard duty. At first I was enraptured at this confidence, but the thrill palled when, after ten minutes, my left leg began to get pins and needles; after 25 minutes, it went completely numb. Nonetheless, some perverse code of honor kept me crumpled in a stationary heap until Spot Neck chose to dismount.

Being able to keep such close company allowed me to see every detail of the Raiders' hunting behavior. For meerkats there is no distinction between locomotion and hunting. At every footstep a hole is pawed, a crevice sniffed. A few desultory scratches break the sand's crust, and then a whiff of prey is followed by an explosion of pile-driving vigor as the meerkat digs through its own weight or more of sand in a matter of just a few minutes.

Once I was watching while a female named Slim

Bottom up and tail out, a meerkat hustles for insects. Adult can dig such a hole in about three minutes.

Six of the Raiders scurry across a dusty riverbed while a seventh pauses to glance around for predators.

stretched her long arm as far as it could reach under a log. Suddenly she leaped back, bristling, and then launched a feverish onslaught at the cranny. With a deft flick, she routed a huge red scorpion from its refuge. In a trice the scorpion was up, heavily armored pincers to the fore and slender stinging tail arched up over its body. As Slim swiped at her adversary, the scorpion grasped her long paw between its pincers. Over and over Slim somersaulted, the scorpion's sting flailing at her. Then I saw it strike her forearm, stabbing in a dose of venom. Slim finally managed to throw the scorpion free. Seemingly unaffected by an amount of poison that can incapacitate a man, even kill a child, she whirled around the scorpion, biting it again and again. Finally the prey was pinioned, the battle over and the meal begun. Now, having seen many more such battles, I can only conclude that meerkats are immune to the scorpion's poison.

In the course of foraging, the Kwang Raiders covered an expansive home range embracing a meander of the riverbed of about six square miles. They harvested the prey from that area in a highly methodical manner. Each day they explored one route, thoroughly gleaning every nook and cranny. The next day they followed a different route, and the next day yet another. Often a week or more elapsed between visits to the same spot, and that interval probably allowed the food resources to recover from the previous harvest. Some parts of the home range harbored particular sorts of prey. In the riverbed, the meerkats caught large, furry orange beetles. Grubs of tenebrionid beetles were especially numerous in the red sand dunes, whereas barking geckos and large scarabaeid beetles prevailed in the tangled roots of desert bushes.

On the day that the meerkats won their title of Raiders, they were foraging for beetles in the dry riverbed. I shall never forget what happened next. All of a sudden one meerkat gave a long peep of consternation, and a series of long trills spread from one animal to the next until they were all standing up on their hind legs, peering forward and trilling. At first I could see no cause for their alarm. Then, as they ran to join ranks, I saw another mob of meerkats in the distance, similarly agitated. The Raiders jostled for position, craning their necks and jeering at the neighboring gang.

The next moments were like a dream. The Raiders began to bound, leaping higher and higher into the air, but landing on precisely the same spot each time. The other meerkats, members of the ten-member Nutu Mob, were flinging themselves like synchronized trampolinists in a similar war dance. It seemed that each team was intent upon intimidating the other with a display of their numbers and vigor. Then the Raiders edged forward, bounding as they went. Faster and faster they moved, higher and higher they bounced, with Scar Shoulder and his lieutenants in the lead, until their formation fragmented and they raced toward the Nutu meerkats. Then, as if their morale had snapped, they halted, milling around.

They regrouped on a dusty promontory. Scar Shoulder dropped to all fours and began to dig with powerful rending strokes that lifted clods of silty crust from the riverbed. As the others began to rend the ground, the "smoke signals" rose around them. Perhaps this

The dark tips of the creatures' upright tails may function like flags, helping the group to stay together.

Adult Raider (left) shares a soft part of a relatively harmless scorpion with a youngster about six weeks old.

too was part of a signal to the adversaries of the gang's strength. Again they stood, lurching forward, then scampering back, then forward again as if egging one another on. They groomed one another. They hugged one another. Then they rushed forward and in seconds the Nutu Mob broke ranks and fled. The Raiders pursued them, some overhauling fleeing individuals, and then the contest was over.

Awash with triumph, the victors clustered around the holes where the Nutu animals had been. Scar Shoulder's behavior was extraordinary and suggested that, at least in battle, he was the chieftain of the Raiders. He fell into a frenzy of scent marking, dragging his anal pouch in ungainly sweeps across logs, burrow entrances and other Raiders. He launched quixotic attacks on little shrubs, flinging himself at them and biting and wrestling with their branches. Other Raiders joined in the scent marking and for 15 minutes or more the rapturous self-congratulation continued.

Before calm returned, Scar Chest pursued a private vendetta against a lone straggler from the other group. The two rolled over and over in snarling combat before the vanquished Nutu struggled free and sped, noticeably lamed, for the dunes. Scar Chest suddenly found himself alone more than 600 feet from his group. For half an hour he cast around and when he found the Raiders he seemed oddly cautious. Suddenly they saw him and the reason for his hesitant approach became obvious: once separated from the group, it seemed that he was no longer recognized as one of them. With tails up, the other Raiders rushed at Scar Chest, who cowered to the ground, curling up with his

Scar Chest, who often stands guard for an hour at a time, tumbles forward after losing perch in dead tree.

Raiders combine forces to drive away a bat-eared fox while Pregnada (foreground) serves as a sentinel.

The much larger fox is quite capable of killing a single meerkat, but it is intimidated by a hissing gang.

tail between his legs and rolling onto his back. As they clamored around, they recognized him and the whole group joined in a social hubbub.

The Raiders' unrelenting belligerence as far as outsiders were concerned was surpassed only by their tender tolerance of each other. As the heat of the day peaked, they retreated to the shade and, if their stomachs were full, they began to play. Everybody from the oldest to the youngest joined in a riot of acrobatic sparring. The biggest males would fling themselves on their backs, squirming and wriggling as they sparred and parried with heads thrown back and jaws wide. The scarred matriarch would hop friskily among cavorting youngsters, and meerkats four deep would pile on top of each other in pursuit of an imagined quarry.

To see such unanimous frivolity in so harsh an environment was extraordinary, and all the more so because no bars of hierarchy, age or sex seemed to inhibit the participants. The idea that wolf packs and some other animal societies can readily be described in terms of a linear hierarchy has taken firm hold on the public's imagination. But in the seemingly egalitarian so-

ciety of the meerkats, the concept of linear dominance appears to be all but irrelevant. The key role of Scar Shoulder in some situations seemed to give him a central place among the Raiders. However, other individuals were responsible for other important tasks—guard duty and baby-sitting, for example—and it is hard to know how to rank them.

The group's cohesion was greatly emphasized when the matriarch of the Raiders had babies. Pregnada, as I named her, was a rather small, almost wizened, animal, but every aspect of her demeanor signified age and authority. Her left foreleg was horribly scarred and stripped of fur and she limped slightly. Her muzzle was pockmarked with pinprick scars, and naked black skin peeped through the fur.

As she became progressively more rotund, two interesting events occurred. First, she ceased to take on

Alerted by a guard's alarm call, two jittery meerkats scramble to high ground to await further developments.

drove her back to continue with her duties as a nanny. During those days, Interloper ate little or nothing, her labors seeming to be the price of acceptance, and gradually she did become a member of the group.

It wasn't long before all of the adult Raiders were sharing the drudgery of baby-sitting. That required each of them to fast for entire days—an incredible sacrifice for a small creature accustomed to eating every few minutes. Again, specialists emerged. Spot Neck's devotion to the babies was so great that he seemed to worry about them. Occasionally, when he was several hundred yards from the den, he would detach himself from the group and travel alone—an extraordinary risk—back to the den. There he would briefly cuddle the babies. Sometimes he would even take over from the other baby-sitter, who would then run off to forage with the group.

When the babies left the den for the first time, the adults were clearly apprehensive—and with good reason. Suddenly a Lanner falcon scythed through the air, making straight for a wobbling infant. In an instant the entire group flung itself in a protective blanket over all of the youngsters. From then on, the adults were frenzied in their vigilance. Whenever a youngster lagged behind, an adult carried it back to the nearest hole. As the Raiders foraged, each baby "apprenticed" itself to an adult, and the adults in turn freely donated food to their charges (p.59).

After each day of frantic activity, the Raiders would return to the den, where they hugged and snuggled together. No single member seemed to dominate any other; each licked and nuzzled its companions. Gradually, sleep-heavy chins settled on shoulders, arms embraced necks, noses probed gently into ears, and a pile of meerkats drifted off to sleep. The unity of the group was complete.

The Kwang Raiders are only one collection of meerkats and my study of them, after 12 months in the field, is still in its infancy. As I continue to record the details of their daily lives and begin to compare them with groups of different compositions and sizes, I will gain a clearer understanding of how and why meerkats live together. It already seems obvious that members of larger groups prosper in terms of vigilance, defense and rivalry with neighbors. They have the advantage of a greater pool of labor for chores ranging from guard duty to baby-sitting. Doubtless there is an upper limit to the group size which is advantageous, and perhaps that is determined by competition for food or mates. The mating of meerkats is one of the mysteries I hope to solve next. It will take years of work to complete this picture. So far, I have seen something new on almost every day that I have worked with these remarkable creatures. I cannot even imagine how many more secrets their astonishing society holds in store.

guard duty, instead devoting all of her time to foraging. Second, a strange female appeared and began dogging the Raiders' tracks. This interloper spent a great deal of time looking around nervously, having no other meerkats with which to share the burden of vigilance. As the days passed, she edged closer to the group. She was an adult, more stocky than Pregnada.

One morning Pregnada emerged from the den having clearly given birth. All 12 meerkats set off to forage, seemingly leaving the unborn unattended. Then, to my astonishment, Interloper emerged from the den. She had been left in charge and for three days she attended the babies (p.54). Whenever she emerged from the den while Pregnada was in sight, the old female

Scar Shoulder leads attack on yellow cobra, trying to prevent snake from holing up in Raiders' territory.

By Richard Wolkomir

If the interstellar hot line rings, who gets the message?

I have a plea for Drs. Carl Sagan and Paul Horowitz: Please, gentlemen, stop before it's too late!

The Planetary Society, which Dr. Sagan cofounded, has refurbished an old radio telescope at Harvard University. And physicist Paul Horowitz is using that telescope right now to scan the skies for a message from THEM.

It's not that we Earthlings are unneighborly, precisely. It's just that some of us, contemplating the cosmos, with its myriad stars and galaxies, get the willies. What if THEY actually do give Dr. Horowitz a buzz? What then?

Scientists in Carl Sagan's camp have long argued that—unless our little plain-Jane solar system is unique—billions of stars must have planets. A percentage of those planets, the theory goes, will have life. And a percentage of those life forms will have evolved into beings bright enough to invent radio telescopes, Cuisinarts, mulching lawn mowers and other such appurtenances of a highly advanced civilization.

Such civilizations, the scientists estimate, could number a million. And they believe that at least some of them are beaming this message into the void: "We're here. Are you?"

Skeptics have asked why aliens would want to ring us up. After all, we're not dialing *them*. An advanced civilization would have so much power at its disposal that this could be just a Cub Scout project, Sagan has suggested.

Extraterrestrial Cub Scouts are mildly reassuring, but the notion of alien megapowers inclines me to crawl under the bed. What if, expecting E.T., we should find that we've reached out and touched Darth Vader? Alien fleets could simply roar into overdrive, streak through space and be here in time to sizzle the planet before cocktails.

Enthusiasts argue that any truly obnoxious civilization, at some point in its technological development, would nuke itself into molecules, which casts a certain pall over our own prospects. That being the case, it is comfortingly unlikely that any extraterrestrial Golden Horde will thunder down in hyperdrive to pillage our Stop & Shops. But there are problems.

For one thing, if we do receive a message from the stars, and somehow manage to translate it, we may turn into cosmic wallflowers, self-condemned to an eternity of sheepishness. Man has always been pretty chesty about his skills and possibilities. How will our collective self-esteem stand up to a message from Beyond sneering something like, "Uncle Miltie, indeed—you yo-yos!"

Such a curt note is possible. Carl Sagan himself has pointed out that we inadvertently began signaling to extraterrestrial civilizations in the early days of radio. Our video transmissions have also been streaming toward the stars, with shows of the 1950s starting to beam in on them just about now.

What if THEY have tuned in? As Joseph Conrad once wrote, in a different context, "The horror! The horror!" Imagine the great thinkers of planets around Aldebaran or Procyon turning up their eyestalks in dismay as they contemplate Lucy goofing around with Desi. How would they interpret Road Runner cartoons? Yogi Bear? Would Howdy Doody give them the idea that our race is actually descended from maple trees? Analyzing Sid Caesar and Imogene Coca, would they conclude that the most typical human activity is to smash scenery?

But the killer would be the Huntley-Brinkley Report on the news: Ike swatting golf balls, the Cuban missile crisis, Hula Hoop contests—surely they would have the Earth cordoned off. And when the video wares from today finally reach the interstellar confederations, and better minds than ours for the first time must decide who shot J.R., they may opt to send in a crack psychiatric team to administer global therapy.

Another possibility: the great day comes and our interstellar hot line rings . . . but we can't figure out the message. It may be the secret of existence, or it may be an advertisement for Betelgeusian water beds. What with all the chatter about mediocre education, the sheer frustration might put us into a permanent funk. What if we find out just enough to know we are too dim-witted to qualify for the galactic chapter of Mensa?

We species chauvinists who always consider the universe a stage set for our little comedy, with other life forms cast as walk-ons, would we brood petulantly, refusing to think up new, improved anti-antimissile missiles and still newer kinds of dandruff shampoo?

Or suppose that we never hear a signal. Would that really mean that *we're it*? All there is of intelligence in the expanding universe? The race that invented artificial lemonade? Somehow, that prospect is especially glum.

Now consider the worst possibility: two weeks after we pick up interstellar signals, everyone loses interest and goes back to watching *The Dukes of Hazzard*. Could we manage to survive knowing *that* about ourselves?

Gentlemen, please! Hang up the phone before it's too late!

A physicist spends part of his time with the rest of us in the familiar world where things make sense.

But he also lives in a very different place, where nothing behaves the way that it is supposed to.

By James Trefil

Quantum physics' world: now you see it, now you don't

If you have to cope with atomic particles that can read your mind even when they don't exist, it can be hard to explain what you do all day

Some people have it easy. When their kids ask them what they do at work, they can give a simple, direct answer: "I put out fires" or "I fix sick people" or "I do arbitrage." As a theoretical physicist, I never had this luxury. Society has come to expect many things from physicists. It used to be that we only had to discover the basic laws that govern the world and supply the technical breakthroughs that would fuel the next Silicon Valley. With these expectations we were fairly comfortable: they involve the sorts of things we think we know how to do. What bothers us—and what makes it hard for us to tell our kids what we're up to—is that in this century we have become, albeit unwillingly, gurus on philosophical questions such as "What is the nature of Reality?"

We now deal with a whole new class of problems. We ask how the Universe began and what is the ultimate nature of matter. The answers we are coming up with just do not lend themselves to simple explanations.

In the good old days we could explain Sir Isaac Newton's clockwork Universe by making analogies with things familiar to everyone. And if the math got a little complicated, that was all right: it gave a certain panache to the whole enterprise. But those days are gone forever. How is a physicist supposed to find a simple way of explaining that some of his colleagues think our familiar world is actually embedded in an 11-dimensional Universe? Or that space itself is curved and expanding? The math is still there; the theories are as coherent as they ever were. What's miss-ing is the link between those theories and things that "make sense"—things the average person can picture. This leads to a situation where it's easy for anyone to ask questions that can't be answered without recourse to mathematics, such as my all-time least favorite: "Well, if the Universe is really expanding, what is it expanding *into*?"

There's no place where this problem is worse than in the theory that underlies things like digital watches and personal computers. This theory, called quantum mechanics, describes the behavior of atoms and their constituents. It tells us that the world of the physicist is not at all like the world we are used to. When physicists get out of their cars in the morning, have a cup of coffee and sit down in front of computer terminals, they leave a familiar, cozy environment and enter a place where things act in strange, virtually inexplicable ways.

Let me give you an example of what I mean. When you run into a wall, you expect to bounce off. If you were an electron, however, our theories say there is some chance that you would simply appear on the other side of the wall without leaving a hole behind you. In fact, if electrons didn't behave this way, your transistor radio wouldn't work. How do you explain something like *that* to your kids? And what does it tell you about whether the electron is "real" or not?

Don't get me wrong. I don't think that people—even physicists—go around with these sorts of questions on their minds all the time. But as one friend put it to me, "It's not so much that I want to know the answers myself, it's just that I want to know that they're in good hands." It is this obligation to provide the good hands that in this century has been thrust on me and my colleagues.

Confused chitchat at cocktail parties

Physicists get involved in trying to explain these kinds of things because two of our 20th-century theories—relativity and quantum mechanics—have dealt major blows to accepted ideas about what is real in the world. The shock of relativity pretty well played itself out in the 1920s, mainly in cocktail party chitchat that confused relativity (a well-defined theory in physics) with philosophical and moral relativism, with which it has nothing in common except the name. It now looks as if quantum mechanics is about to suffer through its own period of popular misunderstanding, making physicists even more uncomfortable with their role as philosophical arbiters.

Physics has gone from studying familiar things in our everyday lives like tides and baseballs to strange things like atoms and the particles from which they are made: things we do not (indeed, cannot) ever

Illustrations by John Huehnergarth

know directly. Inside the atom we find everything in little bundles called quanta. On the subatomic level, both matter and energy always come in quanta—discrete quantities. An electron can be at one energy level or another as it orbits a nucleus, for example, but never anything in between. Or, that characteristic of the electron known as spin will always be in certain quantities and never anything else. (The singular form of the word, quantum, is combined with mechanics, an old term for the study of motion, to give us quantum mechanics.) The first great difference between the familiar world and the quantum world—the world of the atom—is that we do not "see" things in the same way in the two worlds. This difference leads to results that defy our understanding, such as the electron going through the wall without leaving a hole behind it. The electron, in effect, disappears from one side of the wall and reappears on the other. Nothing in our everyday life prepares us for this.

You probably never thought about it, but when you look at something (this magazine, for example), you're detecting light that has come from some source, bounced off the object and then come to your eye. The reason we normally don't think about seeing in this way is that in our everyday world we can safely assume that bouncing light off a magazine doesn't change the magazine in any way that matters. The light from a lamp does not push the magazine away.

When we get to the quantum world, however, this comfortable assumption no longer works. If you want to see that bundle of matter we call an electron, you have to bounce another bundle off it. In the process, the electron is bound to be changed.

Limited by the Uncertainty Principle

A simple analogy can help with this point. Suppose you wanted to find out if there was a car in a long tunnel, and suppose that the only way you could do this was to send another car into the tunnel and listen for a crash. It's obvious that you could detect the original car in this way, but it's also obvious that after your detection experiment that car wouldn't be the same as it was before. In the quantum world this is the *only* sort of experiment you can do. Therefore the first great rule of quantum mechanics is: *You cannot observe something without changing it in the process.* This is the basis of what is called the Uncertainty Principle: When you choose to observe one thing (e.g., the location of the car in the tunnel) you must forever be uncertain about something else (e.g., how fast the car was moving before the collision).

We usually associate the act of making a measurement with the presence of a conscious experimenter who wants the measurement made. Thus you some-

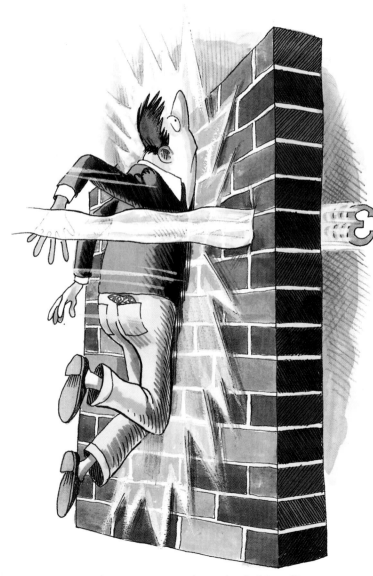

An electron can pass through a brick wall—an ability that's unfortunately denied to the rest of us.

When he sits down at his computer in the morning, a physicist leaves the rest of us behind. When he comes back, he cannot explain where he has been, or what it is that he has been doing.

times run across the comment that quantum mechanics implies that nothing could exist without the presence of consciousness. From the example of the car in the tunnel, though, it's obvious that this is the modern-day analogue to the old confusion of relativity and relativism. It's the nature of the measurement, not the one who designs the experiment, that introduces the problem.

The inability to observe things in the subatomic world without at the same time disturbing them has some surprising consequences when you start to think about the way that particles move from one point to another. Let's use another automotive analogy. Suppose I asked you to tell me where a particular car will be tomorrow. Ordinarily, you would look to see where the car is, look again to see which way it is going and look again to see how fast. After a moment with your calculator, you would come back with a definite answer. If the car is like an electron, however, you can't look at it more than once—the first look changes everything. You cannot know with precision both where it is and how fast it is going; the best you can do is to play off the uncertainties. You might, for example, be able to say that the car is somewhere in the Chicago area and heading in a generally eastward direction at roughly 40 to 60 miles per hour. You can't be more precise than that without more measurements, and more measurements would only change

James Trefil, Clarence Robinson Professor of Physics at George Mason University, is co-author of The Dictionary of Cultural History.

the car's location or velocity and therefore increase your uncertainty.

If you want to talk about where the car will be tomorrow, then, you have to speak in probabilities—it might be in Cleveland, it might be in Detroit, it might even be in New York. The chances are, though, that it would not be in Miami or London. You could make your prediction, in other words, by giving me the odds of the car being in Detroit, Cleveland or New York after 24 hours. This collection of probabilities is what physicists call a wave function, and it's exactly the way we describe the motion of things like electrons.

Up to this point, you've probably been following along pretty easily, perhaps thinking that you might as well humor this guy as he makes all these obvious statements. Well, hold on, because things are about to become curious. The reason you aren't bothered by having to describe the car in terms of probabilities is that deep in your heart, you *know* that the car is really somewhere all the time, and if you could just peek, you could see it merrily tooling along any time you wanted to. Of course, if you did you'd change it and mess up the experiment, but you have the easy feeling that somehow the car is really there, even if you don't see it. You might even imagine the whole country as an underground parking lot in which you can see the car only at the exits. You may not be able to see the car between exits, but you know it's always somewhere in the garage.

The problem is that physicists don't envision electrons this way. Their view is that until you look at a particle, you have to treat it only as a set of proba-

Using one car to find out if there is another in a tunnel is messy; similar problems arise inside atoms.

known as the Einstein-Podolsky-Rosen (EPR) paradox. This paradox was intended to show the inherent ridiculousness of treating the particle as a set of probabilities between measurements, and hence to imply that the whole probabilistic view of the world was wrong. The argument goes like this: There are some common reactions that result in two particles (like electrons) being emitted back-to-back from the same atom; electrons spin around their axes, and general laws of physics tell us that in this sort of reaction the electrons have to spin in opposite directions—if one is spinning clockwise, the other must be counterclockwise and vice versa.

Einstein applies some common sense

Einstein argued as follows. You tell me that the electrons don't really have a spin, just as they don't have a position, unless they're being measured, but I could let those two electrons travel until they were light-years apart, and then measure only one of them. For example, if you measured the right-hand electron and found it spinning clockwise, you'd know instantly that the left-hand electron was spinning counterclockwise—*without ever measuring it*. The left-hand electron, therefore, must have had that spin all along and you must be wrong about it not being anywhere or having any spin between measurements.

Well, that sounds pretty convincing, but quantum mechanics worked so well and explained so much that most physicists tacitly ignored Einstein and kept on using it. The practical payoffs—from microelectronics to lasers—have been tremendous. But the old problem of reality still rankled. Then in 1964, the Scottish physicist John Bell discovered something that has come to be known as Bell's Theorem. What he found was that in the kind of back-to-back reactions that Einstein talked about, there were certain quantities that were predicted to be different if the electrons were described as being "really there" than they would be if the electrons were described in terms of wave function. What these quantities are is not important (they have to do with the way the axes of rotation of the electrons point in space with respect to the direction in which the particles move). What is important is that with Bell's Theorem we have, for the first time, an experimental way of resolving the problem of what that electron is doing between measurements, the problem of whether it's really there or not. All we have to do is measure some of the quantities Bell talked about and see if they match up with quantum mechanics or with the common sense approach Einstein advocated.

In the 1960s, no one thought the experiments suggested by Bell's Theorem could ever be done; they had

bilities. In terms of our analogy, they say that the car isn't really at any particular place unless it's being measured. In between, it's just a set of probabilities that describe what would happen if a measurement occurred—a wave function.

The idea that there had to be some sort of underlying reality beneath the wave functions and probabilities that physicists use was probably what led Albert Einstein to his famous comment that "God does not play dice" with the Universe. This is a well-known statement, and I only wish that the reply of Niels Bohr, Nobel laureate and longtime friend and colleague of Einstein's, was as well known. "Albert," he is supposed to have said one day, "stop telling God what to do."

Einstein, being Einstein, put his objection into concrete form in 1935 when, along with Boris Podolsky and Nathan Rosen, he published what has come to be something of the status of that old sophomore problem of whether a million monkeys at typewriters could ever create *Hamlet*. It was interesting in an intellectual sort of way, but totally outside the realm of practical possibility.

Well, it never pays to underestimate experimental physicists. By the mid-1980s, a large number of EPR-type experiments had been done, and in all cases the results were unequivocal. The standard theory, the one that says that the electron has to be described by a wave function between measurements, is right. The predictions of the theories that say that the electron really has a well-defined spin before it is measured are wrong. Period. The results mean as well that the electron really is not any place between measurements. When you are not looking, it is not there.

How can we understand this? If you try to make a mental picture of what the electrons are doing, you have to say that the left-hand electron somehow knows what experiment will eventually be done—that it

When Einstein said that God does not "play dice," Bohr cautioned him against telling God what to do.

Only recently have experimentalists been able to find out if electrons spin in the ways theorists say.

changes itself depending on what happens to its right-hand partner before it can ever "know" what happened. No matter how transmitted, information—like everything else in the Universe—cannot travel faster than light. Thus in an experiment in which a pair of electrons is produced and they fly away from each other until they are light-years apart, it would take years for the results of measuring the right-hand electron to reach the left-hand electron. But the latter knows instantly.

This result is the crux of the problem in understanding quantum mechanics, and it certainly makes it tough for physicists to explain what they do to their kids. How do you talk about things in simple everyday terms when the particles you're trying to describe insist on acting as if they could read your mind? There is just no way of picturing electrons in any way that makes sense or squares with our intuition.

Having made this point, though, I have to remind you that all of the conceptual problems with figuring out what the electrons are up to have to do with what happens *between* measurements. We can never actually answer this question because the Uncertainty Principle tells us that if we try, we will change everything. Quantum mechanics succeeds beautifully in describing the result of any experiment that you can actually do.

The new wave of quantum mechanical experi-

Whether a bit of subatomic matter should be treated as a wave or a particle depends on how you look at it.

ments has produced other results that are even harder to deal with than the EPR outcome. For example, one of the old problems in quantum mechanics has to do with something called the "wave-particle duality." In essence, the problem arises because in some experiments an electron acts like a miniature baseball (a particle), but in others it seems to have the property of a wave. In classical physics, waves and particles were all there was, and everything was either one or the other. The ability of quantum particles to assume the character of either, depending on the experiment being done, constituted another of those seemingly inexplicable paradoxes of the quantum world.

Of course, you could argue that electrons were neither particle nor wave, but something different that exhibited the properties of both. Like the standard probabilistic view, however, this is a profoundly unsatisfying solution. It doesn't give a *picture* of what the particle is.

A few years ago several groups in Europe carried out experiments designed to "trick" the quantum particles into revealing their true identity. A particle would be directed toward an apparatus and then, while it was still in flight, the experiment would be changed so that either the wave or particle aspects of the moving particle would be tested. The point is that the particle, in flight, couldn't know what the experiment was to be.

For all the cleverness involved in this setup, the results were exactly as predicted by quantum mechanics: when the particle experiment was done, a particle was seen, and when a wave experiment was chosen, a wave was seen. If you insist on thinking of an electron as something analogous to a baseball or a ripple on water, this result is hard to comprehend. What *is* the electron, anyway, and how can it transform itself while it is in flight?

There are some things we will never know

The sense of frustration you are feeling right now arises because try as we may, we cannot find an intuitively pleasing way to describe what the electron is doing during those periods when we aren't actually looking at it. Does this remind you of the old college bull sessions about the tree in the forest? It should, because the quantum theory of the ultimate nature of matter seems to raise questions that simply cannot be resolved.

Some people, confronted by the sorts of paradoxical behavior we've been describing, have been driven to truly bizarre points of view. In discussing the EPR experiment, for example, some people have argued that the two particles communicate with each other by some unknown process of a kind that could also produce telepathy and extrasensory perception in humans. Others describe a Universe in which everything is connected to everything else. As the poet Francis Thompson put it, "Thou canst not stir a flower / Without troubling of a star." All this may be going overboard, but it shows how disturbing the physics is.

Many people are surprised that supposedly toughminded physicists agonize over questions like what the electron is doing when it's not being measured. But the fact is that most physicists think in pictures and have the same intuitive notions that you do. Anything that bothers you, therefore, is likely to bother them as well.

I often wonder if the real difficulty arises because there are limits to what we can know—what we can comfortably absorb. Perhaps we have moved to the limits of what our minds can picture and our intuitions can deal with. Perhaps the problems we have with 20th-century science are tokens of things to come, and in the future everything will be as strange to us as quantum mechanics. I hope things don't turn out this way, but they certainly could.

Over the years, I have talked to colleagues about their reactions to this state of affairs in our science. Some of the answers may be enlightening.

Go Away—Anonymous.

This is far and away the most common reaction. We have a theory (quantum mechanics) that allows us to make the next big technological advance, win the next Nobel Prize. Why bother about questions that can't be answered, anyway?

What's the problem?—Asher Peres, theoretical physicist.

Peres is a man who has thought deeply about the question and has come to the conclusion that the problems are all in the mind. After all, problems arise only when we try to think about the electrons as if they were baseballs. Obviously they're not, and there's no reason to expect that they will be. If we just stick to the rules of quantum mechanics and ignore the demands of intuition, no difficulties arise. The title of one of his articles, "Unperformed Experiments Have No Results," tells it all. I have to admit that I find this line of thought very attractive.

It only bothers me when I think about it—Mike Chanowitz, theoretical physicist.

A typical response of a thoughtful man. It *is* hard to stick with pure logic and give up a lifetime's worth of intuitive knowledge about the way the world really ought to be.

The mind demands more—Bernard d'Espagnat, experimental physicist.

It's not enough to have a theory that predicts what will happen in experiments; it has to give you a coherent and intuitively appealing view of the world as well. I suspect that most of you feel this way.

Anyone who isn't bothered by Bell's Theorem has rocks in his head—David Mermin, theoretical physicist, quoting a friend.

What can I say?

Today's physicists find themselves called upon to be philosophers who can deal with the ultimate question. But in the inexplicable world of quantum mechanics, comprehensible answers are few and far between.

By Carrol B. Fleming

Maidens of the sea can be alluring, but sailor, beware

In our folklore the mermaid is celebrated for her captivating charms; still, it is prudent to admire her from a safe distance

The oceans' legendary mists have long swirled with tales of exotic beasts—sea serpents, giant squid and a variety of monsters. But the stories, whether based on fact or fantasy, tell of no creature with as much age-old charm as the mermaid. The idea of near humans—both male and female—inhabiting the sea and inland waters has captured imaginations since people first ventured seaward, and for a very long time mermaids seemed every bit as real as flying fish.

The folklore of mermaids is ancient and widespread, crossing cultures, continents and centuries; stories of mer-folk and their habits correspondingly traverse every latitude of the imagination. Mer-people have been called by diverse names—Sirens, nixies, kelpies, *Morgan*, nymphs, Tritons, silkies and Nereids, among others. The stories vary more than the names; some tell of kindhearted beauties who wanted only to introduce their lovers to the rapture of the deep, while others recount mer-monsters hell-bent on ripping the drowned limb from limb. Some mermaids had hair of glimmering gold; others sported fishy tresses of blue or green that matched, in hue, their pointed teeth.

Like all folkloric characters, each group of mer-people has specific traits and habitats, but there are some features that we have come to associate with the generic mermaid. The part-woman, part-fish charmer, with a mirror in one hand and a comb in the other, gives room for a great deal of artistic variation, but most mermaids tend to merge woman with fish near or below the waist, where the female torso starts to taper with scaly grace to a fish's tail. Then things vary—mermaids have worn the speckled tails of mackerel, the flukes of dolphins and the sinewy tails of eels; some are skirted, others snakelike.

In overall form their bodies are designed for open-water seductions and quick getaways—and are, as the story goes, as soulless as water. Traditionally, the only way for a mermaid to acquire a soul is by marrying a mortal. There are many accounts of these mixed marriages—and unrequited attempts—from Undine of

Called a fake when shown in 19th-century London, "Feejee Mermaid" was later displayed by P. T. Barnum.

Herbert Draper painted this version of the Odysseus legend about 1909, taking full advantage of its drama.

drama and ballet fame to Hans Christian Andersen's "The Little Mermaid."

Often the mermaid's voice is as beguiling as her beauty. The enticements of Siren song are said to have lured ships to the rocks and sent sailors to the kingdom of the drowned. The whole idea of literally pulling good men down is a constant theme in mermaid lore. The great 20th-century poet William Butler Yeats took a rather liberal view of this in "The Mermaid." By making this particular sea-woman more unthinking than malicious, Yeats created a modern mermaid with a human forgetfulness:

> A mermaid found a swimming lad,
> Picked him for her own,
> Pressed her body to his body,
> Laughed; and plunging down
> Forgot in cruel happiness
> That even lovers drown.

This open-minded approach to mermaid imagery is

Feathered, finned (and cruel), mermaid-Sirens descend on sleeping-sailor victims in a 14th-century drawing.

240. Monstre semblable à une **Sirenne** pris à la côte de
Il étoit long de 39 pouces gros à proportion comme une
jours et sept heures. Il poussoit de temps en temps de petit
quoy qu'on luy offrit des petits poissons, des coquillages, d
fut mort quelques excrements semblables à des crottes de c

241. Ecrevisse extraordinaire qui étoit longue de 39 p.
jusques à la queuë. Voyez la Planche XLV. N.º 187.

Amboina Mermaid appears with crayfish in old natural history, which said she cried out like a mouse.

a somewhat recent development; the Sirens of the *Odyssey* were pitiless, as is the mermaid in most of our familiar folktales.

Legends often intermix and change so quickly and with such piecemeal logic that, although ancestries are traceable, it is impossible to be sure of their exact lineage. So it is with the mermaid. The first mermaid ancestor was probably Oannes, the Babylonian fish man-god. In the earliest representations of him, the benevolent Oannes had a human form and wore a cap resembling a fish's head and a long cape of fish skin. Oannes' feminine counterpart, the moon goddess Atargatis, known also as Derceto and worshiped by Syrians, Philistines and Israelites, is the earliest female fish deity. The Greek writer Lucian, in the second century A.D., described her from a Phoenician drawing saying "in the upper half she is woman, but from the waist to the lower extremities runs in the tail of a fish." As a moon goddess, Atargatis added many facets to the fish-god profile. She was associated with the more mysterious attributes of the night and the changing phases of the moon, and went on to acquire an aura of seductiveness, vanity, beauty, cruelty and unattainable love. Today's mermaids still reflect such characteristics.

Atargatis is generally regarded as the predecessor of the Greek goddess Aphrodite, who arose from the foam in a seaborne scallop shell. Although this long-haired love goddess was often pictured with a mirror and was always associated with the sea, those were her only links with the modern mermaid.

Another group of legendary Greek characters, the Sirens, also added their traits to the mermaid prototype. Greek vases of the fifth century B.C. show the

Carrol Fleming, a free-lance writer now living in California, specializes in sea-related subjects.
She wrote about conchs in March 1982 SMITHSONIAN.

Sirens as birdlike creatures with wings and claws but with women's heads. Their deadly melodies coaxed ships and sailors to destruction.

According to mythology, only Orpheus and Odysseus heard the Sirens singing and managed to escape. The legendary poet Orpheus outplayed them on his lyre; the forewarned Odysseus had himself lashed to the mast of his boat. His crew, their ears plugged with beeswax, rowed obliviously past the Sirens, and Odysseus, although enchanted by the song, could not escape his bonds (pp. 72-73).

From here it was a practical storytelling transition to meld these bird-Sirens more closely with the ocean by having them live there. And as a result, they underwent corresponding physical changes, gradually acquiring more fishy attributes; so much so that the words Siren and mermaid are now used almost synonymously. However, the Sirens went through centuries of intermediary forms when they were both feathered and finned. Throughout the transition they always kept their reputation for song, for irresistible voices that could doom the bravest sailor.

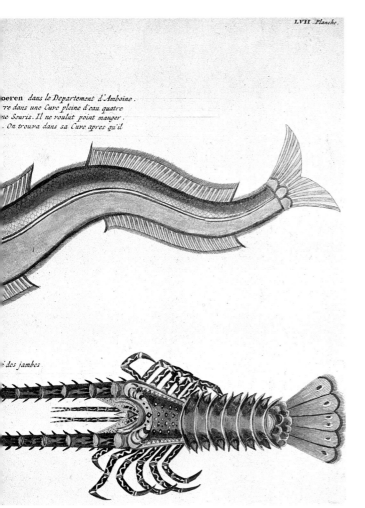

oeren dans le Departement d'Amboine .
re dans une Cuve pleine d'eau quatre
ne Souris. Il ne voulut point manger .
. On trouva dans sa Cuve apres qu'il

des jambes

A woodcut from Nuremberg Bible, 1483, shows Noah's Ark attended by mermaid, merman and mer-dog.

While the Siren was a creature of literature and myth, the mermaid was thought to be a *real* beast by natural historians and explorers. Pliny the Elder was the first naturalist to record her in detail. In his monumental work, *Natural History*, which appeared in the first century A.D., he says, "And as for the Meremaids called Nereids, it is no fabulous tale that goeth of them: for looke how painters draw them, so they are indeed: only their bodie is rough and skaled all over, even in those parts wherein they resemble woman."

The pre-Christian mermaid-Sirens were gradually incorporated as church symbols. Fish-tailed enchant-resses twined temptingly around church pillars and leered from carved pews. Among other things, mermaids came to symbolize the abduction of the Christian soul; even the story of Odysseus and the Sirens was turned into a popular moral allegory. Clement of Alexandria, in his *Exhortation to the Heathen*, managed to sum it up dramatically: "Let not a woman with a flowing train cheat you of your senses, sail past the song; it works death; exert your will, and you have overcome ruin."

In a way, the Church kept the mermaid legend active until the voyages of discovery sparked public interest in new lands and strange beasts. A flurry of mermaid sightings accompanied the early sea explorations. Mermaids are even mentioned in Christopher Columbus' journal from the voyage of 1492. He wrote of one of his seamen: "He saw three mermaids, who rose very high from the sea, but they are not so beautiful as they are painted, though to some extent they have a human appearance about the face."

There has always been a discrepancy in the descriptions of the mermaids cited by naturalists and sea captains and those representing the poetic truths of artists. Compare, for example, the lovely sea-maid of "dulcet breath" that Shakespeare wrote of in *A Midsummer Night's Dream* (p. 78) with the Amboina Mermaid that appeared in natural history volumes in the early 1700s. Although the mermaid of Amboina is given the glamour of exotic coloring, she is still described as a monster. In an original color drawing by Samuel Fallours (left) published in 1717, she has copper-colored skin highlighted with a green that matches the hula skirt of fins around her hips; her long blue tail with its central stripe ends in an elegant fluke. The naive drawing does not seem to echo the caption, which reads:

A monster resembling a Siren caught near the island of Borné . . . in the Department of Amboine. It was 59 inches long and in proportion as an eel. It lived on land for four days and seven hours in a vat full of water. From time to time it uttered little cries like those of a mouse. Although offered small fish, shells, crabs, lobsters, etc., it would not eat. After its death some excreta, like that of a cat, was found in its barrel.

This poor barreled beast uttering its mouse cries

Nineteenth-century illustration is of "real dugong" and "ideal mermaid," as it was captioned in London.

In British film *Miranda*, 1948, Glynis Johns plays comely mermaid involved with young London doctor.

seems an unlikely relative of Shakespeare's vision in *A Midsummer Night's Dream*, where Oberon

> Heard a mermaid on a dolphin's back,
> Uttering such dulcet and harmonious breath
> That the rude sea grew civil at her song
> And certain stars shot madly from their spheres,
> To hear the sea-maid's music.

These differences in story and verse gained notice as skepticism increased in the early 18th century and naturalists began to qualify their positions. When Erik Pontoppidan got around to discussing the genus of mermaids in *A Natural History of Norway*, he dismissed a lot of mermaid lore as idle talk. He complained about those who have mixed fiction with history and said that "when they give the Mermaid a melodious voice, and tell us that she is a fine singer; one need not wonder that so few people of sense will give credit to such absurdities; or that they even doubt the existence of such a creature." However, Pontoppidan follows this statement with eight folios citing the "true" natural history of the mermaid.

By the middle of the 19th century, stuffed mermaids had become spectacles in Victorian London. Showmen bought most of these so-called preserved specimens, usually trumped-up monkey-fish composites, from Japanese fishermen. Each came with an individual story of its capture, and sometimes sold for thousands of dollars.

One of the most popular (and lucrative) versions of these stuffed curiosities came to be known as the "Feejee Mermaid" (p. 73). It was first shown in a London coffee house and later brought to Broadway by P. T. Barnum in 1842. This Broadway mermaid show was so popular that it was moved to Barnum's New York American Museum, where, according to Beatrice Phillpotts in her book entitled *Mermaids*, the mermaid nearly "tripled the Museum's takings in the first month of its exhibit."

Not all Victorian mermaids were carnival freaks; there were also a number of artistic and literary fish-women. The mermaid theme of irresistible yet doomed love had great appeal for 19th-century romantics. This, along with the general interest in folk art and the classical longings of the Pre-Raphaelites, contributed to the plethora of new mermaids—some painted with a venomous beauty and others with a touching innocence. They vary from the sometimes wistful enchantresses of Herbert Draper and John William Waterhouse to the robust mer-families of Swiss artist Arnold Böcklin. Poets like Tennyson wove mer-folk into verse, while the Pre-Raphaelites Edward Burne-Jones and William Morris extended the vogue into mermaid wallpaper.

The well-known illustrators Arthur Rackham and Edmund Dulac designed small-boned sea nymphs to accompany passages from Shakespeare and Wagner. Painters like Edvard Munch (SMITHSONIAN, December

Probably most whimsical mermaid illustration of all is Norman Rockwell's magazine-cover version.

1978) and Gustav Klimt helped carry the romantic mermaid into the more psychological realm of the modern Siren. The post-Freudian era delighted in all of the innuendo of the mermaid image, and she became a symbol of political and sexual freedom, embodying a desirable lack of convention. The Surrealists found the mermaid evocatively paintable—fish-tailed femmes fatales lounged in dreamlike settings and preened on moonlit streets. Mermaids were also seen on more common ground—from ashtrays and soup bowls to movie screens. The tradition lives: next year the Disney Studios will release *Splash!*

The vitality of the mermaid legend—there is probably not a country in the world without some bit of relative folklore—indicates that there may be a substratum of fact, an animal that may appear mermaid-like from a distance. Several possibilities have been suggested: the sea cows of the order Sirenia, including the manatee and the dugong, and, of course, the many varieties of seals.

While these animals hardly have the beauty to sink a ship or even attract a sailor long at sea, they do have certain characteristics similar to those ascribed to mermaids. The nearly hairless manatee is somewhat larger than the human female, but the female manatee's breasts, which are forward near its flipperlike forelimbs, are in a position similar to the human female's. The manatee has no other limbs, and its blubbery body tapers to a horizontal flipper of a tail. The dugong is similar in shape to the manatee. It has a muzzle covered with bristly whiskers and is said to suckle its young with its upper body out of the water, cradling the baby with one flipper. These animals may very well have accounted for some of the reports of mermaid sightings in the tropical seas that manatees and dugongs prefer.

Soft-eyed seals and sailors' illusions

This leaves a large number of cold- and temperate-water illusions to be explained by one of the world's 34 seal species. To the foreflippers and tapering body, the seal adds its soft, appealing eyes; seals also cavort and pose in much the same way mermaids are said to. Sailors have often commented on the seal's similarity to a person seen far off in the water. Even now there are occasional, apparently earnest reports of mermaid sightings in remote parts of the world. But in the main, today's mermaid lives in the realm of folklore, art and cryptozoology.

Cryptozoology, according to Dr. George Zug—Chairman of the Department of Vertebrate Zoology at the Smithsonian's Museum of Natural History, who examined the photographs of the Loch Ness monster taken in 1975—is the study of mysterious animals of unexpected occurrence in time and space. When asked if mermaids would be classified as mammals or fish, Zug gives a scientific chuckle before his careful reply, "All is conjecture until we have a specimen on hand. It's possible to make anything you want out of mermaid stories. Part of the fascination is that they border on the credible.

"There are certain scientific explanations for mermaid sightings," Zug continues. "A 1975 article in *Nature* magazine described how air distortion led to the Scandinavian legends of mermen: they were really walrus. Often atmospheric conditions, fog or mist, can affect perception. Air distortion and refraction are also considered. But the stories, like those of sea serpents, continue because they *are* out of the ordinary and that is always somewhat exciting."

The stories are also of interest to folklorists like Peter Bartis at the American Folklife Center in the Library of Congress. Bartis suggests that the mermaid legend survives "not so much because it is believed, but because it was found to be an effective image. Perhaps it fills a curious psychological need for a man or woman at sea. A sort of wish fulfillment, a comforting story about drowning."

There are folktales and songs that support Bartis' sentiment; one of the most appealing versions is that in the last stanza of an English sea chantey, "Married to a Mermaid":

We lowered a boat to find him, we thought to see
    his corpse,
When up to the top, he came with a shock, and
    said in a voice so hoarse,
"My shipmates and my messmates, oh, do not
    weep for me,
For I'm married to a mermaid at the bottom of
    the deep, blue sea."

The Sirens' ancient charm continues today in the kitsch of seaside souvenirs and in the lusty mermaids traditionally tattooed on seamen's burly biceps. But the modern mermaid has also developed a broader personality. She can withstand the wry whimsy of cartoons or provide a focus for poets and painters interested in portraying the psychologies of desire.

As folklorist Bartis says, "Everyone knows what a mermaid is, how the story operates. Its long visual and oral tradition persists in figureheads, signboards, tattoos, jokes, even children's cartoons. The mermaid legend must continue to serve a function today or the stories would simply die out."

Influence of Japanese woodcuts is clear in Arthur Rackham's drawing for *A Midsummer Night's Dream*.

The subject was rich in possibilities for Pre-Raphaelite style of Isobel Gloag in *The Kiss of the Enchantress*.

The radiance of Garbo gleams against darkness in Clarence Sinclair Bull's 1930 picture: "I never had to say 'Hold it' or 'Still, please,'" he once recalled. "All I did was light that face and wait."

Gods and goddesses in graven images from old Hollywood

A touring show presents striking pictures by a handful of portrait photographers who turned flesh into glamorous fantasy

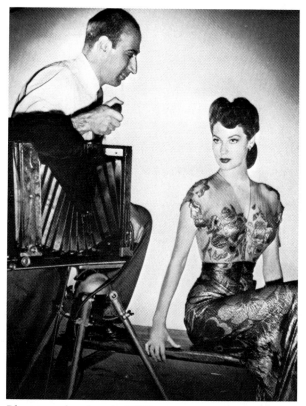

Photographer Laszlo Willinger gets ready to shoot intensely-posed Ava Gardner at an MGM still session.

"When I think of Garbo," says early film star Louise Brooks, "I do not see her moving in any particular film. I see her staring mysteriously into the camera. . . . She is a still picture—unchangeable." Brooks is referring to the face of faces (opposite), beauty and gravity and an inner joyfulness blended in proportions that defy description.

Her sentiment, though, is shared by millions of people, and the object of their photographic affection is not only Garbo. In the depths of the Depression, partly to provide escape from everyday life, Hollywood was in the business of creating something called glamour. The word came from Scotland, where for ages it was connected with creating the illusion of beauty through a kind of unwholesome magic, often practiced, as Sir Walter Scott noted, by witches and "gipsies."

In the Hollywood of the 1930s much of the magic was worked by a half-dozen gifted studio still photographers—and their retouchers. They succeeded beyond all reasonable measure. The names and faces of a handful of stars live on in the mind's eye. Gable and Lombard. Harlow and Hayworth. Cooper and Crawford, whose face often seems a sculpted mask of tragedy. Robert Taylor and John Wayne. Not to mention Dietrich the peerless, infinitely desirable, and infinitely *désabusée.*

It did not matter that Gable had Dumbo ears. That Rita Hayworth's hairline was too low. That Norma Shearer had close-set eyes and Dietrich had stubby fingers. Studios and studio photographers could fix all that. They touched out cleavage, bloodshot eyes and body hair on all male chests, and eventually permitted stars no public smoking, drinking or domestic squalor. In order to have a free hand at creating perfection in publicity photographs, some studio still men had stars use almost no make-up when they posed. What all the subjects had in common was being photogenic. Given that gift, plus a screen test, any shopgirl could aspire to be a star: immaculate, remote, perfect. And rich. By 1936 Garbo was making $250,000 a film.

Despite their impact on the careers of stars, the men who worked the magic with their lights and lenses were for years all but anonymous. Studios simply gave their portraits away—free and uncredited. In recent years, though, the Hollywood photographers have been getting serious attention in shows organized by critic and author John Kobal, whose latest effort, *The Art of the Great Hollywood Portrait Photographers, 1925-1940,* will be at the Smithsonian's National Portrait Gallery until March 21. The show includes some superb and provocative portraits by, among others, George Hurrell, Clarence Sinclair Bull, Eugene Richee, Ernest Bachrach, William Walling jr. and the only woman studio photographer, Ruth Harriet Louise.

Kobal is a master of cinema lore, with a fine eye for the way photographic effects are achieved. But he is a romantic and a man as flagrantly star-struck as any male in the Western world. He insists that the "profound beauty" of these images "will cause them to live on like Raphael's Madonnas and Botticelli's angels." It is hard to go that far. But if it is the business of art to triumph over nature, Kobal has a point.
Timothy Foote

The two faces of Dietrich, one young and vulnerable (right), the other worldly cool, were taken in 1931 and 1935 by Eugene Richee and William Walling jr. Both pictures show influence of director Josef von Sternberg, who created Dietrich's screen image as a femme fatale.

The Evolution of Hollywood's "It" girl began (above) with Clara Bow, at 18, shortly after she won a screen test in a magazine contest. But in the 1926 portrait by Eugene Richee she has traded a tousled bob and five-and-dime impishness for a vampish look and a scarf.

"There were a million women waiting to see this picture," said Hurrell about flossy portraits—like this 1933 vision of Clark Gable—that many male stars, Gable included, regarded as "sissy." In 1937 (below) Laszlo Willinger gave Gable mussy hair and an anxious expression.

Contrasting Crawfords were photographed by George Hurrell. The first, an artful 1930 blend of angst and freckles, was calculated to win her emotional roles. Retouched portrait (right) made Aldous Huxley compare her to an as-yet-unnamed product by Du Pont.

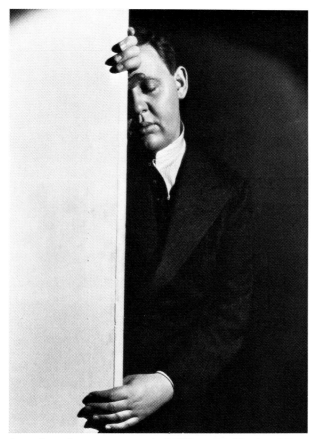

Art triumphs over nature in William Walling's oddly touching portrait of Charles Laughton. Self-conscious about his looks, the actor often played grotesques.

A Rocky-like pose, in sweat shirt against a geometric backdrop, lends Ted Allan's view of heartthrob Robert Taylor an athletic look he lacked in real life.

Classic close-up (this one by A. L. Schaefer) makes viewer feel he can reach out and touch Rita Hayworth's perfectly glazed skin and gleaming hair. Originally a plump brunette, she was redone by studio, which turned her into a strawberry blonde and heavily plucked her hairline to heighten her low forehead. After films like *Blood and Sand* and *Gilda* she became the Love Goddess personified, even to marrying a prince—Aly Khan. But the role proved treacherous. Hayworth, recalling her botched marriages: "They all married Gilda, but they woke up with me."

In this startling image of John Wayne at age 24, photographer William Fraker makes the gruff cowpoke-to-be seem sensitive yet Mephistophelian.

Going for baroque to publicize Jean Harlow, Hurrell creates an elaborate confection of clasps, curls, contrasting lights and shadows.

Carole Lombard, by Eugene Richee, looked daring in 1932 because of cigarette and lighting that emphasized her legs and shoulders.

A male desert spiny lizard distends its brightly colored throat in a threat display against an intruding male.

By Bil Gilbert

Lizards that take to the desert like ducks to water

The reptiles thrive in seemingly horrendous conditions, seizing opportune moments and fully exploiting different microhabitats

There is a great deal of talk these days about competition—about how to acquire or reacquire desirable things that, it is widely thought, we are losing to improbable foreigners. Much of it implies that the world at large is an expansion of the National Football League: that the best and natural way for individuals, populations and even species to get what they want is to take them by engaging in and winning contests with others. There is another premise: that this sort of activity is the long-range, evolutionary equivalent of jogging or eating organic. It is claimed that throughout natural history, contests have made contestants stronger and smarter, spurred them on to develop venom sacs, tusks and opposable thumbs—to say nothing of more favorable trade balances.

Much of this talk is very loose. Zoological evidence strongly suggests that for virtually all creatures, direct win-lose contests are risky and inefficient last-resort options for getting things, and are therefore best avoided. To this end many species have developed communicative, social and territorial behaviors aimed at forestalling head-to-head brawls. Confrontations sometimes still occur—no system being perfect—but are, in essence, penalties assessed when natural laws are disregarded rather than being the driving force behind those laws.

A basic and common method for dealing with the risks of contests is to get out of such situations where they are likely to occur. Most creatures locate in places and find unique ways of exploiting them so as to reduce the need to vie with others of similar appetites. Biologists call these special fields and modes of endeavor niches. The strategy to avoid rather than engage in contests seems mainly responsible for the innumerable adaptations of most animals—the diversity, possibly the tenacity, of life. Consider the Sonoran Desert lizards. The political, economic and social authorities currently urging us to bear down, suck it in and become more competitive seldom talk about, perhaps don't think much about, these animals. Nevertheless, in regard to the realities of natural competition they may offer a better model than, say, the Chicago Bears or Seattle Seahawks.

The Sonoran Desert is a tract of some 120,000 square miles extending across parts of northwestern Mexico, southern Arizona and California. In it, herpetologists think there are at least 60 species of lizards. The figure is approximate since there are differences of opinion among taxonomists about the proper classification of some of the animals. Also, in this logistically difficult area it is assumed there are probably species not yet described. As the accompanying photographs show, these creatures are an attractive lot, coming in gaudy colors and unusual shapes. Esthetics aside, however, perhaps the most interesting thing about the desert lizards is how various they are, how many niches they have found in this seemingly unpromising place.

A world of harsh, fast-changing conditions

The most dramatic, commonly noted phenomenon of deserts is that they are ungodly hot and dry. This is certainly the case with the Sonoran. Along the lower Colorado River, for example, there are places where surface temperatures approach 200 degrees F and the average annual rainfall is less than three inches, in some years nonexistent. Less obvious than these extreme conditions but at least as ecologically significant is the extraordinary diversity of climates and habitats in these areas: snow-capped peaks, swampy hollows, drifting dunes and scrub plains often exist in close proximity. At the same time environmental conditions can vary drastically from season to season, even hour to hour in the same small location. At noon, rocks on the sunny side of an outcropping can be too hot to touch, while those in the shade are coolish. At midnight the formation may be frosted and by morning submerged under the waters of a flash flood.

Deserts are wildly heterogeneous, composed of numerous, disparate, sharply delineated microenvironments. As a rule their inhabitants are confined to rather small areas and are unsuited for other nearby ones. They make do with narrow resource bases and brief, often sporadic, but frantic activity periods. Gila monsters, for example, big, venomous lizards (p. 89)

Bright orange spots on the shoulders signal that this female collared lizard is receptive toward mating.

Photographs by Thomas A. Wiewandt

Cryptic coloration of regal horned lizard allows it to blend into rocks. Some may squirt blood from eye.

that support themselves by stalking about the rocky desert scrublands, prey mostly on nestling birds and mammals—but only very occasionally. Students of the species have found that for about 98 percent of the year the surface of the desert is too hot or cold for the Gilas. Therefore they go beneath it into burrows and there, consuming at very low metabolic rates the energy stored in their stout bodies, wait for the two percent of the year when they are able to exploit the resources of their habitat. The Gila is extreme in this regard, but other lizards cope with the desert in somewhat the same fashion. For long periods they do—by the vigorous standards of birds and mammals—next to nothing, conserving their vital resources, hanging on until windows of biological opportunity open, often irregularly and briefly.

There is a theorem of classical logic to the effect that a thing cannot be and not be at one and the same time. It is applicable to the life-style of the Sonoran Desert lizards. Since they are designed, in a sense, to be patient, they cannot be impatient. In response to, say, cold, ectotherms (as cold-blooded animals are known) ration fuel rather than stoke their interior furnaces, allowing body temperature to fluctuate, up to a point, as the environmental temperature does. Survival depends upon slowing metabolic processes (reducing energy intakes and outputs) or, in a word, inactivity. Hibernating mammals make the same responses but on a seasonal basis. Lizards are more flexible, adjusting quickly to daily and even hourly changes in the temperatures of their habitat.

There are limits of patience even for lizards. While inactive they are using, though in a very miserly fashion, energy stored in their bodies. Eventually they must recharge by becoming active, taking food and increasing oxygen consumption to burn it. The conditions of heat at which they best function occur so in-

A male zebra-tailed lizard tries to look as large as it can to discourage another male on rocks below.

Black tongue of the Gila monster, one of only two venomous lizards in world, is used to track prey.

It has flattened itself vertically and extended its orange gular (throat) pouch to make itself imposing.

frequently or prevail so briefly in such small areas, however, that they cannot be entirely passive, waiting to do business until their habitat is a uniform 100 degrees or so. To be active enough to survive they must to some extent control their body temperatures. They do so by manipulating external heat sources.

Perhaps it is a basic mammalian conceit, but we tend to think of temperature in rather large, general terms: "Good morning, it is 62 degrees in Pittsburgh, 96 in Tucson. . . ." In areas much smaller than Pittsburgh, however, there are always many different temperatures because of small local differences in sunshine, wind, precipitation, topography and so on. Many of the heating-cooling mechanisms and behaviors of lizards involve exploiting the varying thermal zones that exist at a given time in their home range—which for some species may be only a few square yards.

The most obvious tactic is to cope with intolerable temperatures on the surface by leaving it—going underground, digging into leaf litter or climbing bushes and trees—to find conditions where the animal can be active or at least can survive. The differences between daytime and nighttime temperatures give further options. Even while on the surface and active, however, lizards are greatly occupied with heat management. Thus an animal will move back and forth between sunny rocks whose temperature is, say, 110 degrees to shady ones of 80 degrees. Or if the air temperature is 60 degrees, it can confine its activities to dark, heat-retentive rocks, which may be 35 degrees or so warmer. In these ways lizards, in effect, extract temperatures from various parts of their habitat and mix them. As a result, a lizard's body temperature may remain constant for several hours, during which time that precise temperature cannot be found in any single spot of the area it is using.

The blending process is abetted by a feature common to many species: the manner in which their skin colors change in response to external heat and light, becoming darker and more heat absorbent in cooler, shadier conditions and lighter and more reflective when it is hotter and brighter. Emerging from burrows to take the morning sun, some iguanids will pale so rapidly that their skins reflect three times more light at the end of a 90-minute period than they did at the beginning of it.

The lizard system for controlling body heat requires some investment of energy—for example, as it scuttles between warm and cool rocks—but it is a small investment compared to that which endotherms (warm-blooded animals) must make to operate their interior

Other topics that Bil Gilbert has written about for SMITHSONIAN *are wildflowers, coatis and groundhogs. His latest book is* On Nature, *a collection of essays.*

heating and cooling systems. Herpetologist Kenneth Nagy studied the energetics of side-blotched lizards, a species found in open areas of the Sonoran Desert, and found the amount of energy they metabolized, adjusted for weight, to be only one fifty-third of that of jackrabbits inhabiting the same area. The disparity between the energy needs of other desert lizards and birds or mammals is thought to be comparable.

The reverse side of this metabolic coin is that because they use less fuel, so to speak, lizards cannot be so energetic as mammals and birds with greater aerobic (oxygen-consuming) capacities. In short, they lack stamina. But again, in the changeable desert environment strenuous, sustained activity is often less advantageous than patience—waiting for the right moment to take quick action.

Kenneth Nagy has characterized lizards as being remarkable "low-energy machines." To carry this analogy a bit further: somewhat as automobile manufacturers have found many ways to encase the combustion engine to satisfy the demands of disparate users, so evolutionary forces, it is generally assumed, starting with the basic, low-energy lizard machine, have created a wide range of models to satisfy the disparate demands of the Sonoran Desert.

Lizards that "swim" into dunes

Open dune country, such as that found along the lower Colorado in the vicinity of Yuma, is at least in the popular imagination the classic desert environment. An animal very obviously adapted to this kind of habitat is the fringe-toed lizard (opposite). These are 5- to 7-inch-long, flattish creatures with wedge-shaped heads, velvety skins, earflaps, overlapping eyelids and traplike nasal filters that prevent the intake of sand. So equipped, they can "swim" into a dune, giving the impression, says Thomas Wiewandt, the behavioral ecologist-photographer who has spent many hours observing them, of disappearing instantly. Though they spend considerable time underground for security and because of extremely high temperatures, they are daytime hunters of small invertebrates. Their toes are fringed with flexible, outward-pointed scales. These serve them somewhat as splayed paws do a lynx in the deep snow, enabling the lizards to glide quickly and easily over soft dunes.

Though much different in shape and habits, the flat-tailed horned lizard is another resident of the open Sonoran dunes. It is not an agile animal, being a sit-and-wait feeder on insects, particularly ants. Its skin color is closely matched to that of its surroundings, a trait that in addition to being advantageous in terms of heat control serves to camouflage it from predators—large reptiles, desert birds and mammals.

Baja worm lizard, found only on the peninsula, uses head and forelimbs to work its way through loose soil.

The thorny "horns" (actually specialized scales) that armor its forequarters also have a protective function. There is a record of a western diamondback rattlesnake being killed, its throat punctured by the dagger-like scales of a regal horned lizard (p. 88) it was attempting to swallow. As an additional defensive tactic, some horned lizards squirt blood from their eyes. It is laced with substances repugnant to predators and is ejected as a sinus at the corner of the eye ruptures when the lizard is strongly provoked.

Using heat to escape predators

The desert iguana (p. 93) is often found at the base of dunes where sand is blown into windrows against creosote bushes and other scrub plants. These vegetarians are a foot or more long, including tail, and are perhaps the most heat-tolerant of all vertebrates. They are active and efficient at body temperatures of 105 to 117 degrees. In consequence, the desert iguana can be abroad, foraging in the scrub at times of day that are too hot for potential predators. In a sense, extreme brightness and heat are critical elements of the niche this species occupies.

Rocky outcroppings, slopes and cliffs are a frequently occurring desert habitat that a number of species exploit. Their home ranges are particularly rich in the number of choices provided for temperature control: mixed patches of sun and shade, crevices and ledges, rocks that vary in color and thus in their heat-absorbing and reflecting qualities.

These conditions have created some interesting lizard niches in both place and time. Geckos, for example, make up a large family of nocturnal animals whose members are most abundant in the tropics, where day- and nighttime temperatures are warm and stable. Two gecko species, however, have been able to prosper in the Sonoran Desert. Their nocturnal habits allow them to avoid water loss from the extreme daytime heat, and the rocky areas they inhabit provide heat as well as food, shelter and other vital resources. They are the most vocal lizards, communicating with, or at least identifying each other by, chirps and squeaks as they scurry nimbly about in the dark. All but the most primitive species are equipped with both sharp toenails and adhesive toepads that enable them to run along, upside down, under rock overhangs or, for that matter, on the walls and ceilings of buildings.

Like geckos, many of the rock lizards are small, quick insect hunters, but the collared lizard is a rather large (9- to 13-inch), quick hunter (p. 94) that often preys on other lizards as well as insects. It is a very sure-footed animal, able to jump over and between rocks, often running upright on its two hind legs while using its long tail for balance. So positioned, it somewhat re-

The tail of this chuckwalla is important both as a food reserve and as an indicator of its social rank.

These two whiptails are probably sister clones of one of the species recently discovered to be all female.

The well-camouflaged fringe-toed lizard, also known as a sand swimmer, is adapted to life in the dunes.

A roadrunner feeds a lizard to its chicks. Males often "tidbit"—offer a reptile to a potential mate.

sembles a miniature model of *Tyrannosaurus rex* and stands to small rock dwellers much as that giant carnivore did, it is thought, to lesser reptiles during the reign of the dinosaurs.

To continue in this vein, the common chuckwalla (p. 91) is something of a brontosaurus among lizards of the desert rocklands, being a large (up to 18 inches long), heavy-bodied vegetarian. For three years Kristin Berry studied a population of chuckwallas, marking 116, in a granite outcropping and scree area in the California desert. For about half a year these animals were inactive in underground burrows. In late winter, when surface temperatures began to rise into the 80-degree range, they started to emerge late in the morning. Usually they warmed themselves for several hours, foraged and fed in early afternoon, then basked before retiring to burrows at sundown. Midsummer activity periods were restricted to the morning. When temperatures reached 100 to 105 degrees, they went underground and stayed there.

There is considerable social interaction among chuckwallas that occupy neighboring territories. Aside from courting and mating, much of it is antagonistic and involves males. In Berry's study area, 12 dominant, tyrant males defended relatively large territories against others, mostly by threatening postures and behavior, but sometimes by chasing and fighting with them. Tyrants were usually the largest animals, but there was an interesting exception to this rule. Like that of many lizards, the tail of the chuckwalla is sometimes broken or severed, a useful attribute that no doubt has saved the life of many a lizard, leaving pursuing predators with only a bit of wriggling tail tip. But the tail is an important appendage for lizards, for balancing and often for energy storage. When a portion of it is broken off, most species grow a new one.

Regrown tails are a social disaster

Replacement tails are of a different composition, being supported by a rod of cartilage rather than vertebrae, and often of a different, duller color. Berry found that possessing a regenerated tail had a considerable negative impact on the social status of a male chuckwalla. No matter how large, an animal with a regrown tail did not become a tyrant, and those that had been tyrants ceased to be so if they had lost and then replaced their tails.

Being large animals of exotic appearance and reputation, chuckwallas and Gila monsters have been especially hunted by humans. Today this mainly involves collecting them for the pet or, more accurately, living-curio trade. At times and in places, however, desert residents have fed on them. The Seri Indians, as they traveled on the waters of the Gulf of California, often carried live chuckwallas in their canoes as a source of fresh meat. Some of these may have either escaped or been intentionally released on barren islands. However they came there, some of these islands now support endemic populations of exceptionally large chuckwallas. One of these giant species is sometimes called the piebald chuckwalla, an endangered species found on a single island off Baja.

Howard Lawler, a curator at the Arizona-Sonora Desert Museum near Tucson, has spent considerable time studying the piebalds as part of a project to breed them in captivity. According to him, much of the wild population is found along an arroyo that transects the 26-square-mile island. In midsummer, females congregate, sometimes a dozen in a hundred-square-yard

Flowers, buds and fruit of the creosote bush are a staple food for the desert iguana, a strict vegetarian.

A displaying collared lizard lifts his back feet off the hot surface of a rock so he can stay there longer.

area, in patches of loose sand and gravel where they dig nesting burrows. At the end of the tunnel a female lays 20 to 30 eggs, which hatch in a hundred days or so. After laying, the female leaves and plugs the tunnel behind her which, beyond hiding the eggs, maintains suitable conditions of heat and humidity within the nest. During the chuckwalla egg-laying period, females stand guard near the mouth of the burrow. Their objective is to ward off other, still-gravid females who, if they find an unprotected nest tunnel, will often inadvertently reopen it, dig out the eggs already there and replace them with their own. That chuckwallas gather together to lay eggs but then, paradoxically, must guard them against each other seems to be explained by the fact that good nesting soils are in scarce supply in their rocky habitat.

Though there are an estimated 4,500 piebald chuckwallas on their native island, Lawler feels the endangered species status is justified. They breed rather slowly—about a quarter of the mature females lay eggs once every four to five years— and, like all small-island populations, are vulnerable to natural catastrophes. In this case there is a continuing, potential threat of poachers, since one individual may sell for hundreds of dollars on the illegal-animal market. Several chuckwallas were stolen from open enclosures at the Desert Museum and others were killed or mangled, which forced the staff, at least temporarily, to remove the animals from public display.

Though the desert is sometimes thought of as being a uniformly barren expanse, much of it is covered with tough, water-conserving grasses, bushes and small trees. Fringes of the scrub extend into open sand and

rocky areas and species of those habitats make some use of it. Others, including the aptly named tree and brush lizards, are especially suited to exploit the vegetation. Whiptails, a New World genus of some 40 species found in deserts and grasslands from the United States to central South America, are typical residents. As the name suggests, the tails are prominent, that of the western whiptail being nearly twice the length of its body, which measures between three and four inches. They are among the speediest of lizards, and when running the tail is carried above the ground and is often lashed back and forth for balance. Like some other scrubland hunters, they dig out their prey—beetles, termites, scorpions, occasionally smaller lizards—from the soil and vegetative litter, locating them by scent.

At the moment, whiptails are the objects of an inordinate amount of scientific attention because, quite recently and surprisingly, it has been discovered that at least 13 species of them are composed only of females that, without being inseminated by males, produce fertile eggs and offspring that are clones of themselves (p. 91). That they or any other vertebrates could reproduce parthenogenetically (without fertilization) was unknown and unsuspected until 1958. In that year a Soviet zoologist, Ilya Darevsky, reported finding all-female species of lizards in Soviet Armenia. Because it was so contrary to conventional biological wisdom, the announcement was initially received with skepticism. Then, in the 1960s, herpetologists, who had never before considered looking for such things, began finding unisex species of whiptails in the western United States. Thereafter, working with captive breeding populations, Charles Cole and Carol Townsend of the American Museum of Natural History determined that generations of these animals had reproduced themselves parthenogenetically.

The existence of parthenogenetic vertebrates such as the whiptails has been accepted as incontestable only during the past decade. Understandably, behaviorists, geneticists and evolutionary zoologists currently have many more questions than answers regarding the implications of this phenomenon. In the most general terms, however, life without sex is another response to the basic preoccupation of all species: dealing effectively with their physical and social environment. In this sense it is comparable to sand swimming, squirting blood from the eyes or regenerating tails.

The evolutionary process—making, maintaining and changing niches, altering forms and behavior—can be called competitive. But figuratively it is much more like an ongoing self-help or improvement exercise than a sporting contest. Blessedly there seem to be no scoring systems that certify cloned whiptails—or any of the rest of us—as winners or losers.

By Harry Middleton

Those strange goings and comings in the sock drawer at night

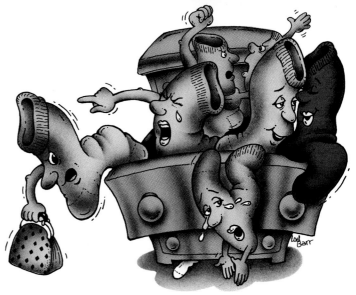

Socks and I have been close companions now for years. I might even say that we have hardly ever been more than a foot apart. But getting along with socks is no easy matter. And I place the blame squarely on the socks.

Socks are troublemakers. No sooner do you buy a pair of socks, bring them home and place them in your sock drawer than they fall into some disagreement or argument and quickly separate. Sometimes one sock is so heartbroken that it vanishes altogether. Meanwhile, the socks left behind go about their timeless ritual—slipping down into the dark bottom of the sock drawer where they multiply, each stray sock producing yet another different sock. They are like snowflakes—no two of them exactly alike. Technology has the answers to many of life's mysteries. But it has no idea why socks separate, each sock traveling its own road five minutes after you bring a pair home.

Modern design has made one improvement, I'll admit. Sulky socks used to punish you by spitefully sagging down around your ankles—unless you were unfortunate enough to wear garters, which cut off circulation in the lower leg. But frankly, I am in favor of fewer tax dollars being funneled into newer and snappier neutron bombs when they could go to sock research. The Pentagon should be interested, too. How safe can a nation be, after all, if none of its soldiers can find a pair of socks that match?

For years I blamed myself, and society, for the incredibly high divorce rate among my socks. Perhaps, I told myself, most socks are ill-matched from the start, come from broken homes, are abused and mistreated. Perhaps it was the shoddiness of my sock drawer or the peculiar aroma of my running shoes that caused the socks to split up. Whatever the problem, my socks simply refuse to stay together. You'd think that if malcontent husbands and wives can stay together, then surely a pair of socks could stick it out, settle their differences, seek counseling. Besides, what have socks really got to complain about? They get plenty of sleep. When they go out they are protected from the elements by stout shoes and pants legs.

Of course, it may be that unlike geese and teenagers, socks are born ungregarious; hating to pair off or travel in groups; rogues, irredeemable loners. This may lead them into petty disputes, rivalries. Years ago I learned never to put athletic socks in with dress socks. The outcome is always ugly. Athletic socks are bullies, always throwing their weight around. Put with gentle-tempered dress socks, athletic socks can clear out the drawer in a week's time, and leave you with perhaps a single blue and black nylon sock. The rest of the dress socks just disappear, only to be discovered later, hidden under the handkerchiefs, slumped under an ottoman, wedged in an old coat pocket or caught smuggling themselves out of the house in my gym bag.

Meanwhile, back in the sock drawer the victorious athletic socks begin bickering among themselves, splitting up, going their own way, gypsies of cotton marked with brightly colored circles of red, blue and yellow thread. The sock drawer is a rough neighborhood, a place where survival is always on the line.

When I first began to notice that my socks were vanishing and showing up with the wrong partners, I thought my son was to blame. "That's it," I told myself, "just some childish prank." I had just caught him skipping off to school dressed in one red sock and one brown. But my blame theory soon proved footless. A quick look in my son's sock drawer revealed that he was no better off than I. A fast inventory turned up one green sock, three orange ones, two that were light blue and six assorted white athletic socks. In a fit of confession my son told me that he had discovered rebellious socks under his bed, stuffed in his bookcase, hidden in his toy box, hanging from his windowsill.

What baffles me even more is that socks seem to have it in for men only. My wife never complains about a missing or vagrant sock. Her sock drawer is impeccable, everything neat and tidy, row after row of happily matched socks all rolled up in cute little bundles. Not a misfit among them.

Of course women suffer more than men do from another mysterious effect—peculiar goings-on in closets when the lights are out and the doors are closed. Every time they leave an empty coat hanger in the closet overnight, it is immediately joined by a half-dozen of its relatives. But that's another story.

The **STRATHMORE**

SIX ROOMS, BATH AND LAVATORY
No. 3306 Already Cut and Fitted
Monthly Payments as Low as $10 to $65

$1,584.00

By David M. Schwartz

When home sweet home was just a mailbox away

Hot items in Sears catalogs from 1908 to 1937, these 'Honor Bilt' houses are now the darlings of owners, preservationists

An element of perplexity mingled with the obvious sincerity in Linda Pruitt's voice. "If you come out here, we'll be delighted to talk with you, but please be aware that these are very modest Midwestern homes." The sentence was punctuated with pauses after "very" and "modest," providing an emphasis that was gently but clearly communicated over the telephone.

Carlinville is an average sort of Midwestern town, a graph-paper grid of shaded streets and well-tended buildings that crop up out of the cornfields lining Interstate 55 in west-central Illinois. In the 19th century, its greatest architectural furor was caused by wild cost overruns on the Greek Revival "Million Dollar Courthouse" of 1870 that nearly brought on a civil war among Macoupin County's enraged citizens. Now, in 1985, 152 frame dwellings in a 12-block area known as the "Standard Addition" are stirring up a lot more excitement among preservationists than their unimposing looks would suggest.

I had been undeterred by Linda Pruitt's warning. Modest the houses may be, but they also have an odd distinction: they were ordered from Sears, Roebuck and Co. A mail-order neighborhood, if you will.

To those who have known about it all along, the origin of the homes was never especially remarkable.

If you'd responded to a Sears ad something like this back in 1935, here's the house you'd have today.

Photographs by Gail Mooney

In 1918, 156 Sears homes went up in Carlinville, Illinois; today's residents voice their approval.

Houses in its Standard Addition may be "modest," as one owner says, but they are meticulously maintained.

In the early years of this century it was discovered that the entire town sat on a seven-foot seam of coal. Seeking fuel for its refineries, Standard Oil of Indiana opened the Berry Mine in 1917. Six hundred miners were employed and Carlinville was transformed virtually overnight from farm town to boom town, long on power and promise but short on adequate housing. To meet the need, Standard Oil placed a $1 million order early the next year with the company that pitched itself as "The Biggest Home Building Organization on Earth."

"These are fine houses—traditional, well-constructed, solid as the Rock of Gibraltar," explained Jayne Bowman as a small group of us ambled down North Charles Street, noting the stylistic distinctions between the various models, "but really they're nothing more than your basic Midwestern box." In the Sears catalog each had a name like The Warrenton, The Whitehall, The Gladstone and The Carlin (presumably named for Carlinville). There are at least eight models, varying in roofline, porch location, window type and other details, the diversity providing a variegated streetscape that belies the fact that all of them were ordered,

en masse, out of a catalog just bursting with options.

"It used to be that when people talked about the 'Standard Addition,'" explained Melody Tigo, "we knew that in their heads they were thinking, 'Substandard Addition.' But now we've got status. All of a sudden, we're on the right side of the tracks! Your home, wherever it is, ought to be kept up, but now a lot of us are beginning to feel, 'Hey, we really *got* something here. *Our* house is as important as the one where Abe Lincoln stopped when he visited Carlinville.' It's just a little old house. I love it, but it's just a little old house."

In 1981, *Historic Preservation* published an article on Sears houses; a year later the Associated Press put out an item. When local editors printed it and included a box asking readers to write if they knew of Sears homes in their area, the response was overwhelming. The rush to rediscover mail-order houses was on.

If the idea of Sears, Roebuck selling houses seems outrageous, it seemed logical enough in 1908. The company was formed in 1886 by Richard Sears, a railroad agent turned watch salesman, and Alvah Roebuck, his repairman. Roebuck sold out in 1895, but

Enclosing porches gave owner of house on left a larger living room, his neighbor to right a music room-den.

Sears went on to achieve vast wealth by offering Americans a "wish book" of goods that could see them from birth to death. Baby buggies to tombstones, violins to wedding gowns, bust developers to patent medicines, the Sears, Roebuck catalog had them all.

Sears stirred his public with a silver-tongued promise of quality he called "the best in the world." He also offered—and made good—a rock-ribbed money-back guarantee. Americans devoured the Sears catalog as if it were literature.

A natural progression led in 1908 to the housing business. By the turn of the century, the Sears catalog had a sizable section devoted to doors, windows, moldings and other building materials. What better way to spur sales of items for the home than to sell the home itself? The first offering of complete "Modern Homes" appeared in the general catalog for Spring 1908; later that year, the company also issued its first Modern Homes Catalog, featuring 22 models ranging from

David Schwartz's other contributions to Smithsonian *include articles on soda fountains, weather vanes and flying pests.*

$650 for a three-room cottage to $2,500 for a 9-room Queen Anne-style edifice. (In Cabin John, Maryland, a suburb of Washington, D.C., a little four-room Sears bungalow changed hands recently for $95,000, while the 1928 Hathaway, with an original kit price of $1,807, sold for $106,000.)

Copywriters left little room for doubt. "Let us save you from $500 to $1,000 or more on your next building," blared the bold print. "Don't let any contracts, don't make any arrangements, don't give an architect an order for any plans until you have carefully considered the wonderful offers we make you in this book."

Select, order—and wait for the boxcars

It was the American dream by mail order, and it couldn't have been much simpler. You picked your house, placed your order and waited for the boxcars to arrive. Sears offered nearly everything you needed —lumber, shingles, roofing, millwork, flooring, plaster, lath, doors, windows, fixtures—even sash weights and paints. (Plumbing, heating, wiring and the kitchen sink were extras.) Most vital, the shipment included a complete set of blueprints prepared by Sears' staff of architects. You provided masonry, labor and a building lot within hauling distance of a railroad siding.

Although most purchasers hired out the actual construction, many chose to build the homes themselves. Sears anticipated their every need and included with each order a 76-page instruction manual. Every board, every stud, every rafter, joist and molding had been cut, notched or mitered to fit, and numbered to match the plans. All the novice builder had to do was follow the numbers and put it all together, and the manual told him just how to do that—right down to the spacing between nails.

In the late teens and '20s, the Modern Homes program hit its stride, offering not only the materials needed to build a home but the money needed to finance it, as well. Sears, Roebuck and Co. was said to be the only institution to grant mortgages without meeting the borrowers or inspecting their property. Frequently the company advanced part of the cash needed to pay for local labor. It was an overly lenient policy that would later come back to haunt the lender, but not before more than 100,000 houses were sold.

Although Carlinville has the most extensive neighborhood ordered from Sears (Standard Oil's million-dollar check was reported to be the largest the giant mail-order company had ever received), there are other pockets of "Honor Bilt" homes around the country. Like the Standard Addition, the buildings were sometimes put up by an employer seeking housing for its workers; Hellertown, Pennsylvania, has 61 Sears homes originally occupied by Bethlehem Steel em-

Top-of-the-line Magnolia was a ten-room mansion when introduced in 1918 with a kit price of $5,140.

In Ridgewood area of Canton, Ohio, the lot, extras and construction boosted cost of this one to $18,000.

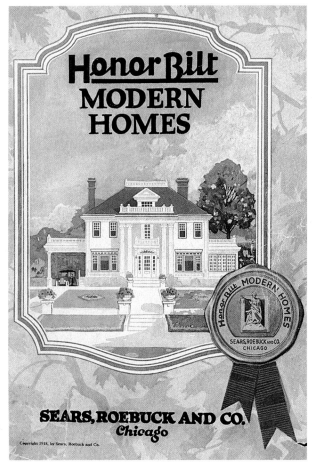

Sears proudly displayed Magnolia on cover of its 1918 catalog, first one in which houses were given names.

ployees. Often local contractors, smitten with the labor-saving benefits of Sears' ready-to-assemble homes, would promote them in their own towns. Oscar and Elmer Blume of Des Plaines, Illinois, claimed 104.

The 146-page 1918 Modern Homes catalog was the first to bestow names on its houses; on the four-color cover was the top-of-the-line Magnolia (left), a ten-room Southern-style mansion with fluted Corinthian columns, curving black-walnut banister, leaded-glass buffet, a solarium and servants' quarters. Of course, you had to pay for such luxuries; the catalog price was $5,140. In the fall of 1926, to dramatize "Our Liberal Easy Payment Plan," a chart showed what the typical customer had probably spent in rent over the past ten years, abetted by a picture of a man dropping his rent money into a garbage can.

For Carl Puffe of Meriden, Connecticut, the 1925 catalog worked exactly as Sears intended. He was browsing through, "not looking for anything in particular," when his eye was caught by The Vallonia, a neat-looking cottage with broad eaves, a prominent porch and large three-bay dormer. The price, including electric wiring, sheet plaster and a number of other options he selected: $2,803.21. Puffe had "never built even a doghouse," but with the help of an equally inexperienced brother, he decided to give it a try.

The main problem turned out to be figuring out what to do with the house *before* it was together. Although Sears shipped materials in installments, Puffe got behind schedule. Like a scene from the *Sorcerer's Apprentice*, supplies arrived faster than he could use them. "It's a good thing my mother lived next door," he says. "We shoved windows in her closets, doors under the beds, plaster, paint and everything else wherever we could."

When the Puffe brothers drove the last nail, two years after the first, Carl Puffe celebrated by betrothing May Lloyd in the living room. "She wouldn't marry me until the house was done!" the octogenarian recalls, a twinkle still dancing in his eyes.

Since the Modern Homes sales pitch stressed low cost, the company also took pains to emphasize it was not false economy. "We guarantee to furnish absolutely the most dependable grades of building material on the market." The catalog's pages were sprinkled with testimonials from overjoyed purchasers and builders. "I put up a house for Mr. James M. Ferguson," declared Henry V. Tillotson of Ossining, New York. "We have offered a reward of one dollar for every knot as large as a 10-cent piece found on this house, but no one has asked for a dollar. . . ."

"Quality? Let's have a look." Floyd Johnson kicked open a hatch that led to the crawl space beneath the front porch of his 1921 Americus, a hip-roofed Colonial in the smart-looking Chicago suburb of Glen Ellyn. Johnson knew nothing of his house's origins when he and his wife, Bev, bought it in 1967, but later, while exploring the attic, he found a set of blueprints displaying the Sears imprint.

On hands and knees, I stared up at the infrastructure of the Johnsons' porch: arrow-straight two-by-eight joists spaced 16 inches apart. If I'd relied on Henry Tillotson's offer to hand me a dollar for every knot bigger than a dime, I'd have gone broke.

Protecting the architectural integrity

Johnson showed me the blueprints, now framed and matted on the living-room wall. On each sheet a Bill of Materials enumerated every piece of wood in the house and gave its grade: floors were of clear maple, oak and pine, and framing lumber was all listed as "No. 1 Y.P." —top-grade yellow pine. I thought about the price of such lumber today—if it could be found at all.

After the grand tour, we sat among scheffleras and potted bamboos in a solar-heated addition Johnson had built on the south side of the house. The room's centerpiece was a six-foot hot tub occupied by the Johnsons' two sons. "When I found out it was a Sears house, I knew I wanted to protect the integrity of the facade," Floyd explained, "but my architectural idealism was challenged." Indeed, the sun room (p. 102), with its 20-foot expanse of glass on the south, was straight out of the '80s, but from the street, the entire

Corinthian capitals, fluted columns of yellow poplar support Magnolia's balcony, define graceful entrance.

Fine woods include black-walnut banister, birch treads and oak floor, hand-refinished by the owner.

room looked like a chip off the old house. "Don't think for a minute it was fun building this thing with a hip roof. It must have added at least a month to the job."

Five years ago Clyde and Sharon Reynolds bought a neglected 1913 Modern Home #132 in Lincoln, Illinois (p. 105). The kit price had been $2,000, at a time when the average production worker's salary was $520 a year. They set about restoring it, and the quest for authenticity has dictated every move. After sanding off textured paint, replacing a broken stained-glass window in the original pattern, refinishing floors, stenciling walls with water-based paint ("Acrylic is too bold to be authentic") and routing cracked varnish out of the dentil molding beneath the mantel with paint remover and a toothbrush, they're ready to move their operation upstairs. "We started with a five-year plan," says Sharon, "and now we've upped it to seven. I often doubt whether it's worth the work, but when people walk in with "oohs" and "ahs," I know it was."

For the Reynoldses, who have met daughters of the original owner and questioned them at length about the house's appearance during their childhood,

the building's origin makes it special. "There are millions of old homes, but only 100,000 were made by Sears," Clyde says. "That makes it a limited edition, a classic—like a classic car." And a classic it is. The Reynoldses paid $65,000 for it in 1980, along with three acres of prime farmland. But local contractor Bob Albert estimates that, using custom materials the equivalent of those sent out by Sears in 1913, you're talking about $148,000 to duplicate the house today.

In addition to the Honor Bilt line, and the no-frills Standard Bilt homes, Sears did construct some truly limited editions—one-of-a-kind designs prepared by the company architects and put up by a Construction Division that was instituted in 1929. Among these were a replica of Mount Vernon erected at the 1931 **Paris** World's Fair, a mansion for the Florsheim family in Highland Park, Illinois, and an entire cultural institution, Music Mountain, in the Connecticut Berkshires.

Designed in 1930 by founder Jacques Gordon, former concertmaster of the Chicago Symphony, in conjunction with Sears' architects, Music Mountain has as its centerpiece a concert hall engineered as the archi-

Bev and Floyd Johnson found blueprints of their 1921 Americus in attic, added the sun room with hot tub.

Reynoldses restored 1913 oak cabinet, woodwork with elbow grease; on table, "before and after" album.

Erskine Hogue's father had house shipped to Oklahoma in 1913. Oak buffet and tulip art glass were extras.

Goetz sisters' father put up Sears barn in Groveland, Illinois, in 1927. Cost including labor was $1,943.

tectural analog of a violin: stained knotty-pine walls and maple floor cushioned by air spaces; French doors positioned to function like f-holes; ceiling beams of pine that act as a violin's base bar and sound post and carry vibrations throughout the structure. According to Nicholas Gordon, son of the founder, the result is "as if you had a fifth instrument in a string quartet and that fifth instrument is the hall itself." Musicians often tell him that Music Mountain has one of the nation's three or four best chamber-music halls.

Although Music Mountain weathered the Depression, the Modern Homes program did not. The nationwide market for new housing took a nose dive, and Sears found itself spending more and more for a slow-growing slice of a fast-shrinking pie. Keeping the Modern Homes program aloft required the aptly-described "Liberal Payment Plan," and ultimately that did it in. During the dark years of the Depression, the company found itself foreclosing on thousands of delinquent mortgages. In terms of public relations, it was a disaster—Sears, "the farmer's friend," repossessing hard-earned, hard-sold homes around the country. But in terms of cold figures it was even worse: between 1909 and 1934, home sales of about $90 million had returned a profit of $4.3 million. On the other hand, mortgage losses were nearly $7 million.

The Modern Homes department was dissolved in 1937, although leftover stock was sold into the '40s. Disposing of the homes was an expedient solution to a program whose time had passed, but disposing of all the records was an act that many homeowners have come to rue. Unlike the Johnsons and the Reynoldses, most of those who own the 100,000 homes have not found blueprints or former occupants to confirm that theirs are Sears stock. At that point the trail leads to the 40th floor of the Sears Tower in Chicago.

"Some owners would like some kind of certificate suitable for framing," Lenore Swoiskin, the company archivist, told me with a bemused chuckle as we thumbed through hundreds of letters from Sears house owners and would-be owners. "Sears can't tell you that you've got a Sears house. *You've* got to tell *us.*"

It isn't easy. Since, for the most part, Sears architects copied popular styles of the day, the houses are not stylistically distinctive. Neighborhood rumors that a house came by mail don't help much either; although Sears was the largest purveyor of ready-cut kit homes, there were a few other companies in the business, including Montgomery Ward and, notably, Aladdin Readi-Cut Homes of Bay City, Michigan, which started first—in 1906, including a complete line of fixtures and home furnishings—and lasted longest, until 1983.

Still, for those who send a snapshot and a floor plan with their "We think we've got one!" letter, the archive staff scrutinizes old Modern Homes catalogs for a match, attempting as best they can to see through obscuring shrubbery, new-fashioned siding, enclosed porches and raised roofs. Their workload will be lightened next March when the National Trust for Historic Preservation in Washington publishes *Houses by Mail*, an illustrated field guide to 375 of the Sears homes.

Organized by roof type and number of stories, the book will work like a bird or wild-flower guide, drawing the reader's attention to easily observed "field marks." Each page will name and illustrate one house and floor plan, describe its distinguishing features and, to make readers weep, state its original catalog price.

Co-author Katherine Cole Stevenson believes the book will do more than verify (or refute) the hunches of genuine or would-be Sears-house owners. Conceivably, it would help the former restore lost features. Most important, she hopes it will help preservationists to identify architecturally significant neighborhoods.

Diane Maddex, editor of the National Trust's Preservation Press, says prepublication interest in *Houses by Mail* has been extraordinary. "The simple fact that Sears sold houses in the first place, and the oddity of their having come ready-cut by rail, is fascinating. Then when you see the wide variety of these house styles, and how well they all seem to have been built, it's really surprising."

Surprising, yes. Fascinating, certainly. But in several months of tracking down Sears houses and speaking with their owners past and present, I've been hard-pressed to explain all the hoopla. For the most part, as Linda Pruitt told me in Carlinville, "They're just houses!" Big or small, plain or fancy, none is unique. They're solid, but so were houses designed and built at the same time by local talent. Sometimes they conjure up an appreciation for history, but why shouldn't any older home? Certainly they're dear to their owners. But as for architectural significance, Ward Jandl, preservation specialist with the National Park Service and co-author of *Houses by Mail*, believes the distinction of being a mail-order home is offset by the fact that there are probably several hundred others just like it. "In terms of special status like inclusion in the National Register of Historic Places, the two factors probably cancel each other out."

Just the same, I've been thinking a lot lately about that Craftsman-style bungalow I lived in a few years ago in Vermont—the one with the big dormer over the scooped-in porch. I could swear it's the spitting image of the house I saw on page 82 of the 1925 Modern Homes catalog. And I seem to remember hearing that it was a kit house, although I was hardly paying attention at the time. As soon as I get my hands on *Houses by Mail*, I'm going to head up to Vermont to check it out. On the other hand, maybe I won't. If I can't find that old house in the book, it just might ruin my day.

Hogue house is listed in National Register of Historic Places. The attic "Priscilla window" is original.

Lovingly restored by Clyde and Sharon Reynolds, this house, $2,000 in 1913, would cost $148,000 today.

By William H. MacLeish

The Silver Whistler

Poet and playwright, Librarian of Congress,
Archibald MacLeish is remembered by his son

Shortly before he died last year, my father and I were sitting in the book room of Uphill Farm, the house he and my mother bought the year before my birth and which had been—except for each other—their greatest love. November blew hard across the lawn and sunken garden and on out east toward the far cone of Monadnock. Ash logs burned in the high and shallow fireplace. My father, terribly thin by then, wore a coat of Hebridean tweed that had fitted him well enough across the deep chest and small waist but now hung like a bag. He was going over some papers, and he handed one to me.

It was a poem. I could see from an attached note that it was going to be published in an anniversary issue of *The Paris Review*. The poem was short, and it was called "Whistler in the Dark":

George Barker, British poet,
writes a eulogy of Dylan Thomas:
calls him whistler in the dark
and great because the dark is getting darker.

Is it? Was the dark not always darker?
Have we not always had these silver whistlers?
Listen! . . .
             That's Chaucer like a bobolink.

I think it's not the darkness growing darker
makes for whistling well. I think
it's knowing how to whistle.
                                     Listen!
That's Dylan trilling like a lark.

At the top of the poem, he had written "Bill, from his father." There had been a few other such sudden gifts from him, so swift in the giving they outran acceptance. A dozen years ago, he sent me another sheet of paper. Over on the left, in a twitchy hand,

were the words "Archie from Father." On the right, my father had written "Bill from Dad." And typed below, the ink going, was Emerson:

"It is easy in the world to live after the world's opinion; it is easy in solitude to live after our own, but the great man is he who in the midst of the crowd keeps with perfect sweetness the independence of solitude."

I read "Whistler in the Dark" and I went to my father as he sat in his chair. I said—I was barely able to say it—"Do you know what I owe you?"

He put a hand up to my face and smiled and said in a voice that was years younger: "Only your life."

I stood, caught, above him, and then he saw me struggling with that and released me. "And I could ask of you the same unanswerable question."

When he was in the hospital, my mother and I sat beside his bed, and a connection came to me. Whistling in the dark, Dylan Thomas and what he had said to his father:

Do not go gentle into that good night,
Old age should burn and rave at close of day;
Rage, rage against the dying of the light.

And the end of it:

And you, my father, there on the sad height,
Curse, bless, me now with your fierce tears, I pray.
Do not go gentle into that good night.
Rage, rage against the dying of the light.

I cannot be sure, I cannot begin to be sure. It is hard to know if a man is raging when he is muzzled by an oxygen mask. Just as it is hard to think of Emerson and perfect sweetness when a body, big-boned and strong in its 90th year, fights to go on. But I sensed—others in the family sensed—that he had decided to

Color photographs by Cary Wolinsky

In the early 1930s, Archibald MacLeish revels
in the sun on the Massachusetts farm that was his
holdfast. Mornings were for writing, afternoons
for "cuttin' and sawin' and mowin' and suchlike."

*'She sang while my father
sat in a leaky room, trying
to teach himself Italian....'*

die, that he was following a course inward. Not raging. He did not bless me with curses. His last words to me were "You go along." I asked, "Back to Conway?" Back to the farm, back to Ada, his wife, my mother? And he whispered "Yes." I went back. I am here in this place that I owe him as often as I can be, this old town in the beginning of the Berkshire Hills of Massachusetts.

Conway was once part of Deerfield, the commons for that older and more historic village, "nine miles from ye River into ye Western woods," as the grant read. It was once on its way to growth, with waterwheels along the South River turning lathes and saws and punches. But the factories moved south and farms failed, and when my parents first came here it was the cellar holes that saddened them.

Conway was where my father's maternal grandfather, Elias Brewster Hillard, shepherded his last flock. Reverend Hillard was an outspoken man, and when he spoke out on such sins as the manufacturing of shoddy uniforms for the Union Army, he was invited to leave one parish after another. My father's mother and some of her siblings had visited their parents in the Conway parsonage. An aunt had bought a place in nearby Ashfield. When my mother and father came back after six years in Paris, he of writing, she of singing, they went

to the Ashfield house and started looking for a place to settle down.

"We wanted two things," my father told me one hot July afternoon three years ago, under the apple tree on the western terrace. "We wanted beautiful elm trees and a running brook." He was in a tearing hurry to get back to work, to writing. They found a place way over west of Conway that had been a poor farm. "It had no elm trees and it had no brook," my father said, "so we bought it."

My mother joined us under the tree. "That place was the last thing I wanted," she said. "I cried all the time about it." She smiled the smile that meant she was about to let her fancy loose on a story. "And one day, when I was busy crying, a friend told me about a house in Conway she had ridden by and it had a 'For Sale' sign out in front with the 'S' backwards. My friend said that they had put some things on the house but that they would come off easily." My parents went and peeked into the dirty and lovely rooms of a farmhouse framed probably late in the 18th century. "So," said my father, "being very cautious and careful people, we proceeded to buy this house, too."

There they were, with two houses and no money. They had spent $10,000 on two houses, about half and half: not enough for a down payment now, but all they had then. Luck smiled. A man who always wanted the poor farm, and was mad as a hornet when it was sold, took it off their hands for more than they paid for it. They sailed happily back to France while a contractor took off the "things"—columns and porches tacked on by previous owners, a Southern family so lonely for home ground that they hid the old house behind antebellum froufrou—and built a lovely gazebo over their well.

My mother and father came back late the next spring, she heavy with me, and settled into a half-finished mess. They lived among workmen tearing away plasterboard to get at

MacLeish house at Uphill Farm is in the Berkshire town of Conway.

In 1941, author and his father head for home after clearing brush.

It was used as a summer place until it could be renovated, insulated.

They fantasized as they worked, so that the chores became adventures.

magnificent mantels, scraping paint down to the soft glisten of good wood paneling beneath.

It had been my mother who was the recognized MacLeish in the early Paris days. She worked with Nadia Boulanger, the mentor of musicians, and she sang, this young American soprano, the works of Fauré and Poulenc and Stravinsky and a young compatriot just coming into the light, Aaron Copland. She sang while my father sat unrecognized in a leaky room, trying to teach himself Italian so he could read Dante in the original. For my mother, the architect in Conway proposed and built a music room, a brick wing with a huge room for her singing and servants' quarters on the second floor. "At that time," my father said, "you expected to have servants."

Work went well into the fall, when my parents discovered something. "The place was beautifully constructed," my father said. "Those beams up in the attic and the beams in the cellar were laid perfectly to their task. It was built on a ledge and always smells sweet in the spring, no matter what happens in the winter." But ah, winter! "We were so damn ignorant," my father said. "Nobody ever talked about insulation in those days, so we never bothered to find out if the house had any. It didn't. Not a bit. And when the northwest wind hit the wall of your room, it came right on through and made the hair on your head wave as you lay in your crib." There was nothing for it but to move the family to my paternal grandfather's place outside Chicago, huge and so ugly in its Victorian excess that it was beautiful. And snug.

We went back again. My mother's garden was taking shape in what had been the sunken quadrangle of an old barn foundation just east of the house. From then on, it would be the ease of our eyes, the clock of our seasons. That autumn, came ruin. My father's father had died in 1928, he of Emerson and of considerable wealth

amassed as the founder of the retail end of Carson Pirie Scott, one of Chicago's largest department stores. But in 1929 the economy came apart, and the business at hand for my father was the basic one of keeping things going.

"There were no jobs around here," my father said, under the apple tree. "I had to do something, so I began raising turkeys." He read and read, this lawyer turned poet turned farmer. He found no turkeys had been raised on the place recently, so there did not seem to be too much danger from blackhead or other turkey diseases. He raised the birds and killed them. He advertised them among his friends as Cricket Hill turkeys, fed on crickets and milk. They called the place Cricket Hill Farm—until they found that there was a Cricket Hill at the other end of town and that they were on the top of Pine Hill. "We had an old hearse of a Cadillac," my father said. "It had a sort of deck that let down between the front and back seats, and your mother and I loaded those turkeys right up to the tops of the doors and drove to New York and sold them to rich friends of ours."

"Don't say it wasn't a crazy life," my mother said.

They made several hundred dollars out of the turkey trips—until the foxes moved in. They were less fortunate with the cows; some disease got them and they all had to be killed. The dogs got the sheep. World War II got the chickens. We ran out of feed for them.

Things couldn't go on like that, and they didn't. Henry Luce was starting a new magazine, and he asked my father to work on it. Luce was even willing to give my father the time he insisted on having for his poetry, and Archibald MacLeish went off to New York to write pieces

SMITHSONIAN *has excerpted two of the author's recent books,* The Gulf Stream *and* Oil and Water.

*'But he turned out God's own
quantity of pieces, around
a hundred by his reckoning....'*

for *Fortune.* "It was the greatest single stroke of luck we ever had," my father said. It probably was. But there wasn't enough money for all of us to live in New York, so for the next decade I spent the cool seasons at my grandfather's house in Farmington, Connecticut.

This is a family of fairy grandfathers; without them, we wouldn't have made it. The Chicago one put my father through law school and supported him in Paris while he took that wonderfully long shot at becoming a poet. The Farmington one housed my governess and me (my brother and sister went away to school after a few years) through most of the Depression. My mother did what she could to divide her time between my father and us, and he came up on some weekends, but after a while I got the feeling, not uncommon in such cases, that I was adopted.

Some writers, including friends like Ernest Hemingway, did not take kindly to the appearance of my father's name on the *Fortune* masthead. Some took after him, personally and in print. But he turned out God's own quantity of pieces, around a hundred by his reckoning, in the falls, winters and springs between the years 1929 and 1937, when Harvard asked him to take on the directorship, at a pittance, of the new Nieman Fellowship program for journalists. "It

was a great advantage to me," my father said, "to be in a different category altogether from my novelist friends. They lived by their pens in the real sense of the word. The writing that we lived by was all assigned stories, and I treated them as such. But during the time I was at *Fortune* I produced more good poems than at any other time of my life. So it was pretty hard for me to assume that this was selling out."

My father had his workhouse by this time, a tiny stone saltbox on a swell of land a couple of hundred yards east of the house (p. 116). And he had his schedule: four hours there every morning, seven days a week. The work was artesian: "Einstein"; "New Found Land"; "Conquistador," which won the first of three Pulitzers; "Public Speech"; "America was Promises," many others. "This place and Paris were where I did most of my work," my father said. "That stone house is a wonderfully quiet place. Occasionally a bothersome dog down on the Shelburne Falls Road,

Kenneth MacLeish eggs his brother Bill into a belly flop off the board.

but very little even of that. Once you get going there, you keep on going—pick up from one day to the next, which I find is one of the great problems."

He was very much the morning writer, eight to noon, where writing "ought to be, in my book. I've heard people talk about the poet up in his attic at 3 o'clock in the morning. You can be damn sure nothing ever came out of that." Working as he did, he said, "you could get a rhythm not only for the work but for the day. You could work as long as you could, which is about two and a half or three hours with me, and have the afternoon for work around the place, necessary work but work that was very good for you." He switched to a hill accent: "cuttin' and sawin' and mowin' and suchlike."

He came back by himself a few times during the winters to work. He got a big fire going in the book room, the one looking out on Monadnock. A friend came up from town and cooked a set of meals and left them for him. He could listen to the drafts shrieking under the doors as the fire drew them, to his old white police dog, Finn, sighing on the hearth. It was fine, he said. Was he lonely? "No," he said. "This is the one place I never feel lonely." The slightest break in the voice. "You have the company of the house."

Uphill Farm remained a summer place until well after the Second World War, when there was enough money for insulation and renovation. And it was in the afternoons of the summers of the late '30s that I came to know my father, mostly by working with him. I was too small to help earlier, and later, in the summer of 1939, came a break that would last until the late '40s.

"Mr. Roosevelt," my father said, "decided that I wanted to be Librarian of Congress." My parents were in Washington most of the time during the war, as my father wrote speeches for the President and took on one in-

Dean and Alice Acheson were frequent visitors at Conway. In
this painting by Mrs. Acheson, the family and guests play croquet.

telligence and information job after
another, ending up as an Assistant
Secretary of State with the ticklish
assignment of helping to put together
the United Nations Educational Scientific and Cultural Organization.
There followed a severe bout of
Potomac fever. "I'd enjoyed power
for the first time in my life," my father
said. "I had had quite a taste of it,
and I had to make a bridge and get
back to being myself." It wasn't until
the early '50s, when he was well into
a long career of teaching writing at
Harvard, that he and my mother felt

they had come back to the hill. By
then, we children were away on our
own courses.

I have a few early memories, myths
perhaps, of my father, of how he
looked, in his drawers, tramping purple grapes for wine, of how he once
carried me out on the terrace to
look at a melon moon full over the
meadow. I do know that when I was
very young, in my grandfather's
house in Connecticut, my father took
me walking with him along the Farmington River. We began to play that
we were in darkest Africa. He called

me Mr. Stanley and I called him Dr.
Livingstone. The name he gave me
stuck for the rest of my life. And when
I was old enough, in those afternoons
damp with clover and timothy cooking in the heat, he and I cleared brush
and told each other that the saplings
around us were Pygmies closing in for
the kill. I hoed the big garden across
the road with him and mended
barbed-wire fences and burned tent
caterpillars out of the trees, and I
came to love the smell of his sweat.

When my parents bought the place,
the sales agreement stated that the

111

*'An artist of the spoken word
as well as the written, a man
in the line of Celtic bards....'*

transaction was "free from all encumbrances except taxes for 1927 and certain pasture rights for the 1927 season, and the right of one Bush to cut some hay." One Bush was Pa Bush to us, an old farmer of French Canadian extraction living at the foot of our hill, who fought his rheumatism and kept farming. Pa and his son Ray and his wife's blind and extraordinarily strong relative Charlie Pear hayed our fields for years. I can hear the slick shuttling of Pa's mower, the click and stumble of his horses on the sharp hillside, see him sawing on the reins, yelling "Come up in there, goddamn you!"

I started with a pitchfork, cocking windrows, then learning to fork up the cocks to the man carefully building the load on the wagon, keeping the corners firm and high. The heat leaned in and the horses lathered and twitched at the flies. We drank water laced with vinegar and ginger out of a milk can kept cool in the well inside the old gazebo. We raced thunderstorms to the barn, standing in the doorway to let the rain sluice chaff and sweat off our shoulders while the horses whickered and stomped on the thick wood floor. Once, a hurricane was coming, the big one of 1938. "Ray and Charlie Pear came up to the barn," my father said, "and the doors had been jammed open by the wind. I think the barn would have gone. But Charlie got his back where he wanted it to be and gave a couple of

shoves, and the barn doors moved."

The foundations of what I perceived my father to be were laid about then. He was one of the most lovable men I have ever met, with such warmth, with a surprising amount of natural modesty. Yet he was a secret man, as tightly chambered as a nautilus. There was the chamber of the athlete, the water-polo player, the Yale football player whom a Harvard freshman coach had called, more in admiration than in anger, "the dirtiest little sonofabitch of a center" he had ever seen. The chamber of law, the choice of his life until, walking home late on a cold Boston winter night, he chose the real one. The chamber of his art, by far the most secret. The chambers of politics, of statecraft.

Somewhere along the line he had become famous. People all over knew about him, although what they knew puzzled me. What seemed to strike them as immensely odd was that a

The author rests under the apple tree where he and his father talked.

poet could go after an opponent on the line or in a political scrimmage. That was a given to me. What I found difficult to understand was how my father could talk to me so passionately about his verities, the pillars of his soul, and yet remain hidden himself. "Live your life," he would say to us. "Don't let your life live you."

He talked about Mr. Jefferson, the Republic, freedom and the responsibilities of free men. He was an artist of the spoken word as well as the written, a man in the line of the Celtic bards, and he sang as he talked. His voice was so clear it sounded higher than it was, and he used rhythm and repetition that moved me more than any speaker ever has. But he never showed me where the words came from. In that sense, in that remove, he was more a figure of a father than a father, not so much a parent as someone on whose voyage I was a passenger. I was angered by the shadow he threw. Yet in the end, we were beloved friends.

I don't think the family was particularly close at Conway. Everyone was coming or going, everything had the impermanence of summer. Not even names seemed to stick. When he went to enlist in the Navy at the beginning of the Second World War, my brother Ken found he didn't exist. The name on his birth certificate was Archibald MacLester. I was born Peter and my name was switched early on to William when my Farmington grandfather grew sad about not having anyone to carry on his name; for a long time, I thought Bill was a nickname for Peter. My sister escaped with a mere Gallicization, from Mary to Mimi.

We were, like most children of most strong parents who depend on each other hard and on others not at all—to steal a line from my favorite essayist, Edward Hoagland—on the rim of remarkable lives. Although not always.

Early in the '30s, my father and Pa

Bush and his horses built a dam to create a pond better for swimming and diving than the small lake the Boy Scouts had built on the property. It had a diving board, with which my father, with only small success, tried to lift us to the levels of his skills with the swan dive and half gainer. I remember the look of shock and hurt on his face as I shot past him one afternoon up the length of the pond. I was wearing flippers. Without them, I lost to him in a crawl sprint until he was well into his 60s.

On hot July nights we all swam naked in that pond in the sweet, black water. On hot noons, we picnicked there on gin-and-grapefruit-and-mint cocktails and hamburgers my father cooked that were crusts on the outside and all juice in their innards. On Golden Bantam corn and salad and fresh blueberries from the garden. After, we lay on the ground, heads propped on a convenient leg or shoulder, looking up at the leaves in the light.

My brother loved to hunt and fish, and he taught me. We both had a bloodlust, and we killed far more than we needed to or should have. We even hunted each other, with bows and with padded arrows that didn't break the skin but that hurt terribly when they hit. Somewhere in midlife we both lost the lust, perhaps because we had simply killed too many woodchucks and grouse and deer, and some sharper instinct from way deep had risen to end it. I carry the shame of the excess in one memory—a kit fox, half his head shot away, whimpering himself to death at my feet. I was 17 and I stood over him and wept.

I think we killed as we did to bother my father, to rebel. "I hate killing," he said out on the terrace. "I hate seeing things killed." Even the animals that supplied those delectable hamburgers. Even Harold the Mere Steer. Even Toothsome (another beef): "He lived in a little yard by the side of the barn. He was a very

Ada MacLeish sits with her great-granddaughter, Nora Zale, age 1.

mild creature. I couldn't bear it when he was shot."

Life here was very much a life of the senses. Meals were beautifully planned and prepared. My mother always had servants, even in the worst times, and she ran a kitchen that could produce dishes that would take the blue ribbon from Cordon Bleu. We laughed most at table—at first at malaprops from the young. I was convinced that the man to be remembered at Little Big Horn was General Custard, my sister that John Steinbeck's greatest novel was *The Wrath of the Grapes*.

Because we spent so much time apart, tales of our lives together became talismanic. One story would spark another in the candlelight. Do you remember when the pen gate got opened up at the barn? When that new maid came out on the terrace where Mom was entertaining guests? She was all gussied up in black and lace, and she stood rigidly at atten-

tion and announced: "Madam, the pigs is here."

My father got his voice from his mother, a tiny woman with a pleasant face and fine mind and a strong will. She, Martha Hillard MacLeish, Granny Patty, visited us once in a while in the '30s. When she did, she read *Uncle Remus* to me in a rich alto voice that could raise to a holler: "Bred en bawn in a brier-patch, Brer Fox. Bred en bawn in a brier-patch!" My father read aloud from *The Boy's Percy*, from *The Sword in the Stone*, the wonderful tales of King Arthur's boyhood, and the "Battle of Chevy Chase." Right through our lives together, we would start each other off. "The Percy out of Northumberland," one would say. "And a vow to God made he." "That he would hunt in the mountains of Cheviot," the other would chant, "within days three." And together, "In the mauger of doughty Douglas, and all that ever with him be."

My father would read late drafts of his poems to my mother, and I listened to that magic. Later, he found stories in a collection of popular tales from the West Highlands. One, in particular, stays with me now. I memorized it: "The Brown Bear of the Green Glen." The translation from the Gaelic carried some of the word song from the original, as when the bear, hunting supper for the son of the King of Erin, "makes that wonderful, watchful turn and he catches a roebuck."

I can remember my mother singing. There is something of it left in her speaking voice now, at 91. Her voice carried music the way a spill from a spring carries water. My father told me that one day he came upon a colleague from *Fortune*, standing outside the music room by the open French doors, listening, her shoulders shaking with her crying.

My mother sang for us, too, in the evenings after supper, not so much from her repertoire as from her store of songs friends had given her: songs

Jill Krementz made a portrait of the Pulitzer Prize poet
in 1970. "In the end," says his son, "we were beloved friends."

father worked for so passionately. Later, Ken and I took up the bagpipes, and we would play them outside, because my mother hated loud noise, and just as we ended, the hills would give back the last notes of "Piobeareachd of Donald Dhu" or "Amazing Grace."

My godfather was Gerald Murphy, the painter, who, with his wife, Sara, was part of and host to the Lost Generation in the Paris of the '20s. Gerald and Sara came to the farm often before the war. So did old friends like the Achesons, the Frankfurters—we called Felix the "Little Justice"—John Dos Passos and his first wife, Katy. All were public people everywhere but on this hill. The schedule always held. My father went to his workhouse in the mornings. There was swimming and then lunch, and then a long lazy afternoon or perhaps a game of scouts in a patch of woods up by the Boy Scouts' lake, or a fierce game of croquet (p. 111) or one of its derivatives. Then cocktails on the terrace and those dinners, and then down to the music room for singing and talk.

My mother made those weekends, as she made much of the life at Conway, a time of great fun and high good taste—in the midst of which my father could always find Emerson's, his own, independence of solitude. She had given up her professional singing. "I couldn't leave the family, you know," she said under the apple tree. "That was all there was to that." I'm sure that was not all there was to that at all, but I have never heard her talk of the price she paid and I don't expect I will. She made up for some of the loss in those weekends, creating perfections of food and flowers. She kept an eye on everything. When there was a hole in the conversation, she spotted it and moved to darn it with her wit.

I will not forget gathering coral mushrooms with my father and Dos Passos in the wet September woods, and cooking them over the fire in the

taught her by James Joyce, like "The Brown and the Yellow Ale"; a song brought by my godfather, from a collection of music sung by black Union troops: "I know moonlight, I know starlight, I'm walkin' through the starlight. Lay this body down." Carl Sandburg sent her a copy of his *American Songbag* with an inscription: "Sing 'em: sing 'em by yourself, sing 'em with Archie and may your

rare singing voice stay with you long as you have wishes."

The folk songs opened the door for the rest of us. My brother and I played the recorder and the guitar. We would improvise together, each knowing what the other would do without knowing, and the rest of the family sang with us. "Sam Hall." "Dublin City." Songs of the Spanish Civil War, the Republican cause my

*'That,' said my father, 'was
just about the most satisfactory
thing I ever did in my life.'*

music room. I will not forget watching one of the most powerful men in America dancing a delicate dance of the unfolding crocus to the music of Stravinsky. And I will not forget the great bottle of champagne my godparents came with one anniversary. The next morning, Dos came down to breakfast with pouchy eyes and a poem:

Gerald brought a Jerobo-um
Very big and full of fo-um
Went to everybody's doe-um
Thank you, Gerald, glad to know-um.

"This town," my father said, "has more brooks than any other town in the Commonwealth. It's a town of old worn hills and rushing streams." About the townsfolk, he said, "We're friendly. We help each other when that's necessary. Otherwise, we leave each other alone." That was true all along. The town waited for years after my father became Librarian of Congress before asking him to serve on the library committee. "I think they probably thought I knew enough about libraries," my father said. "It's just they didn't want to intrude."

We were tolerated in the beginning. My parents were summer people: a couple from Paris in a town in the western woods. But the older they got, the longer they stayed on the hill, going south only in the bite of winter. My father worked on town prob-

lems, my mother on town flowers, and acceptance came. The 1972 report of the town was dedicated to my father on his 80th birthday.

Yet not until the late years did my father come home in his poetry. I asked him why and got only a partial answer. He referred me to Coleridge and Wordsworth and their holdings-forth on their lakes. "They aimed at naïveté," he said, "and they achieved it. And although I like their work, needless to say, I'm a little embarrassed by the naïveté." Perhaps for him writing poems about the town and his place was simply too personal, as if he were writing about his bed. He said to me, after thinking over my question a while, "I think I will write about it. I think so. If only I could make the crossover." The crossover, as I saw it, from his holdfasts to his art.

He never did make it. He died two years after the three of us talked under the apple tree. But in the other medium he loved, drama, he had already done what he said he might do in verse. In 1967, for the town's bicentennial, he wrote a play called *An Evening's Journey to Conway, Massa-*

Stones from the farm mark graves of Archibald and two of his children.

chusetts. It was given in the town park, and the set was designed to have the audience looking into the backyards of Conway residents. "That," said my father, "was just about the most satisfactory thing I ever did in my life. It turned out just the way it was supposed to turn out. It was supposed to be done by the people of the town, and to a large extent it was."

It was a magic-lantern show with music written by a composer living in the town; it was wisps of history floating at the edge of a ball field. "Neighbors," says a woman playing one of the town's settlers. "That was the great thing, neighbors." "I'll tell you what a town is," says a man playing a giant of a woodsman from the days when it took a year to clear four acres. "It's a meeting—meeting of minds. And how do you get a meeting of minds? Meeting of men." In a Civil War scene, an orator speaks to a few men and women gathered to welcome Conway's veterans. He speaks to them of a town as a place "where the living who return from the dead and the dead who are removed from the living meet each other—the common habitation of the living and the dead."

The farm today is what it was and not what it was. The great elms are gone from the front lawn, replaced by maples. The hay barn got to sagging, so my father, a worrier of worriers, asked a farmer to take it down and put it up at his own place. With it went a way of telling when the summer was ending; you knew, when the sun set south of the barn. But my mother's garden is still here, still changing its colors in the flow of days. My mother is here, her memory shortened, but not her humor. "Here are your glasses, Mom," I say. "Good," she says. "Now where are my eyes?" The cows still graze in the meadow, leaving the junipers to grow sharply sideways. Something is ending now, completing. Sitting under the apple tree, my father said, "We owe an unpayable debt to this place." So do I, as I owe him, her. But perhaps because I cannot repay, what I owe is what I will take from this place, what I will need to go along in my life.

Six years ago, my parents and my sister and I buried my brother Ken down in a cemetery of the town. My father wrote words for the minister that he could not speak himself: "Here in this pine grove, this hollow in the pines and oaks and maples, half a mile as the crow flies from the house he knew as a child, the room he loved to sleep in as a man, Kenneth has come home. Like all travelers—and he was an inveterate traveler all his life—he had more homes than one. . . . But of all his homes, this village with its meadowland and wood-land and swift streams was dearest to him." When the minister finished I climbed to a knoll with my pipes (they had been Ken's) and found I could play what my brother had asked me to play, "Amazing Grace."

Now all the men in my immediate family are in that hollow, under a big maple. Stones from the farm mark them, my father at the edge of the lot, then a space where my mother will be, then Ken, then Brewster Hitchcock MacLeish, born in 1921 and dead six months later. I never knew him. But the others I knew, travelers, as I am. They do not rest there, as I see it, for rest never interested either one very much. They are, I believe, travelers still.

My father dreamed of that voyage when he was young:

... It is colder now,
    there are many stars,
        we are drifting
North by the Great Bear,
        the leaves are falli▸
The water is stone in the scooped rocks,
        to southward▸
Red sun grey air:
    the crows are
Slow on their crooked wings,
        the jays have left us:
Long since we passed the flares of Orion.
Each man believes in his heart he will die.
Many have written last thoughts
    and last letters.
None know if our deaths are now
    or forever:
None know if this wandering earth will
    be found.

Listen! The silver whistler.

Archibald MacLeish wrote about ". . . the stone house in the rocky field where I write poems when my hand's in luck."

The lines above are from "Epistle to be Left in the Earth," *The Hu▸ Season: Selected Poems 1926-1972.* © 1972 by Archibald MacLeish. Reprinted by permission of Houghton Mifflin Company.

By William Weber Johnson

A Tale of Two Bagels *and other bits of execrable prose*

San Jose State University, originally known as Minns' Evening Normal School, claims to be the oldest public institution of higher learning in California. It has survived fire and earthquake. It was the alma mater of Edwin ("The Man with the Hoe") Markham. But until recently it had no claim to international fame. All of that has changed. In England and Indonesia, Mexico and Australia, West Germany and South Africa, the Netherlands and New Zealand, as well as the United States, people have been talking about and writing to San Jose State.

The reason: a crazy literary competition, known as the Bulwer-Lytton Fiction Contest, created by Scott Rice, a droll, bearded professor of English.

Edward George Bulwer-Lytton was a statesman and noted dandy, an accomplished rider, boxer, fencer, whist player and dabbler in spiritualism. He was also a prolific producer of plays and novels. His most famous novel, a dramatic pot-boiler, *The Last Days of Pompeii* (1834), is still read. A lesser one, *Paul Clifford* (1830), is mainly remembered for an opening sentence that begins: "It was a dark and stormy night. . . ."

Like so many of Bulwer-Lytton's phrases (*e.g.,* "the pen is mightier than the sword"), "dark and stormy night" has become a cliché particularly favored by amateur writers like Snoopy, the beagle, who shamelessly borrowed it as the first line of his unfinished novel.

To encourage students to recognize, and parody, the bad in writing—as an aid to appreciation of the good—San Jose's Professor Rice has in the past asked them to seek out and imitate the worst opening lines of novels, and in making the assignment he often used "dark and stormy night" as an example. At San Jose State,

creating and collecting bad first lines became a kind of campus game and, finally, an international competition. The response was voluminous—about 10,000 entries. Acknowledgment cards, carrying the likeness of Bulwer-Lytton, read, "We have received your execrable prose. . . ."

Some was pretty execrable. Purple prose proliferated: "The man stood in an abyss of cerebration ruminating pensively on the ebon thunderhead's impending extermination of the dark-blue suede empyrean with all its glittering, silver jewels and decided it was going to rain."

Puns were frequent. Examples: "A shameless exploiter of young female delinquents, Beauregard Fagin of Atlanta, Georgia, was a man for whom the belles stole." And, "It was raining cats and dogs and he stepped into a poodle." Also, "Colonel Winterbottom was a cold, stern man." Describing a conversation between two delicatessen owners on the eve of the French Revolution, one opener invoked Dickens with "It was the best of wursts and the worst of wursts." (The title of this "novel" was *A Tale of Two Bagels.*)

Naturally, Dickens was not the only famous novelist to have his prose rifled. One entry read, "Call me, Ishmael, any time." Another contestant, preferring poetic satire, threw grammar to the winds in mocking T. S. Eliot's *The Waste Land*: "Egg rolls is the coolest lunch."

A good many entries took aim at currently popular writing genres. Romances, Gothic or otherwise: "Even the raging wind of the wild November night could not compete with the turbulence of Everard's mind as he lay tossing in his great ancestral bed, tormented by the glittering image of Juniper, dancing. . . ." Not to mention the contest's eventual winner: "The camel died quite suddenly on the second day, and Selena fretted

sulkily and, buffing her already impeccable nails—not for the first time since the journey began—pondered snidely if this would dissolve into a vignette of minor inconveniences like all the other holidays spent with Basil."

Predictably, a majority of the parodists took potshots at science fiction: "I watched in helpless horror as the monster clawed its way up the TV tower and wondered what could be in the mutated genes of these Alaska King Crabs which caused them to snatch only Canadian aircraft from the sky."

Professor Rice reports a wide use of Wow!, suggesting that many contestants were under 30. Similes took a terrible beating: "Screaming like a banshee . . . bleeding like a side of beef in an abattoir, the Chinese sailor croaked out one word: 'Firelight' . . . and fell to the ground like an epileptic lobster. . . ."

Fractured syntax flourished: "Safeway wasn't open when Keegan pulled his Chevy into the lot, its valves chattering, gun-blue cracked-ring smoke sputtering from its tail pipe, to get some eggs."

And then there was wholehearted dullness: "The story is closely related to my own life, which has been ordinary, loveless and dull, but which I will try to make exciting in the following pages."

Professor Rice has drawn few conclusions from the sheafs of inadvertently revealing prose. One is that people capable of writing well can write terrible sentences if they put their minds to it, while others just seem to have a natural talent for bad writing. Also: there are a lot of people who want to write, but lack an audience.

The briefest and perhaps most eloquent entry in the contest came from one of Rice's faculty colleagues. It consisted of just one word: "Alas!"

By Jon Cohen

'Gone up North, Gone out West, Gone!'

A startling exhibit takes visitors on the Great Migration of a million black Americans during 1915-40 in their search for a better life

Two middle-aged black men are standing in front of a re-created 1920s Virginia train station. There are separate side-by-side entrances for "colored" and "white." One of the men walks under the "colored" sign, turns, puts his arms akimbo and says to the other, "Take my picture right here. This is *our* door." "You've got that right," replies his friend, snapping the shot.

The train station is part of a new exhibition at the Smithsonian's National Museum of American History that reveals the little-known story of the Great Migration, the exodus from the South to the North made by more than a million American blacks between 1915 and 1940. And the two visitors have reacted just as Spencer Crew, the show's curator, had intended: they have placed themselves squarely into this chapter of American history.

The exhibit, "Field to Factory: Afro-American Migration, 1915-1940," is not about American science or technology or famous figures from our history, familiar themes to Washington's museumgoers. This exhibition offers sights and sounds that are new to many who might be more accustomed to viewing First Ladies' gowns, postal-pouch locks, Wedgwood china, Joe Louis' gloves, atom smashers and Thomas A. Edison's phonograph. This is a show about people, not things: American black people. Crew's goal is for the exhibition to "speak to every person who has packed up, said good-bye and headed for strange territory in search of a better life."

The few Southern blacks who could earn money for a car often packed up the family to go North together.

This photograph, used in exhibition brochure, shows
migrants with all they own loaded on a Studebaker.

Mix of artifacts in the tenant farmhouse kitchen
reveals that families dined, played and worked there.

Obviously this exhibit, which will run throughout
March 1988 before traveling around the country, has
special appeal to Afro-Americans. "By having this at
the Smithsonian, we're saying that black American
history is important," says Crew. "By selecting an
event that occurred in the 20th century, we're also saying that recent experience—that of your grandparents
or parents—is important."

To Crew, the Great Migration embodies the great
American pioneer spirit. "But I don't think we very
often use that term to describe the black migration,"
he says. "It doesn't bring up the image of going West,
crossing the Rocky Mountains or through the Donner
Pass—this migration was lower key, though no less dramatic for the people who made the journey. We're just
beginning to understand the difficulties involved, how
people's lives were changed and its effect on American
society. It had a tremendous impact."

"Field to Factory" does not use the same language
as many museum shows. It accents people rather than
objects. It tells a story with a beginning, a middle and

an end. It creates tense, even uncomfortable tableaus.
It pounds in ideas without being didactic. And rather
than summing up a historical event, it pushes its visitors to ask questions.

Over the past four years, hundreds of people have
helped Spencer Crew bring the story of the Great Migration to life, yet there is one person with whom he
shares the title of creator: designer James Sims. Crew
is black and from Ohio; Sims is white and from California. Their backgrounds dovetail neatly. Both went
to college in the 1960s—Crew is 38, Sims 41. Both have
previously worked as professors, Crew at the University of Maryland Baltimore County (American and
Afro-American history), Sims at the University of California, San Diego (stage design). Both shifted into the
museum world during the early '80s.

Crew and Sims began working on "Field to Factory"

Writer Jon Cohen, senior editor of Washington, D.C.'s
City Paper, *spent four months following this
exhibition's progress.*

Curator Spencer Crew searched his own past to help better understand impact of the Great Migration.

Many families chose to stay in the South because of their close ties to friends, church and community.

in December 1985, along with project manager William Withuhn, who looked after the budget, solved deadline crunches and kept the peace within the 80-member team. "Never before had we done such a major exhibit on our nation's history from a black perspective," says Withuhn. Museum shows are put together like movies. Research leads to a script, which gets reviewed, rewritten and blessed. An artist—in this case, Sims—links with the writer, draws up a floor plan, makes some models. Finally, the script is worked onto a storyboard, coordinating visuals with text.

"To tell you the honest truth, when they sent me a designer I was very concerned," says Crew. "This is my heart and I wanted to make sure it was handled right. When Jim showed up with his design, it was so wonderful, I just fell over."

Essentially, Sims' design divides the baseball-diamond-size space into three sections: the rural South, a transition area (the train station) and the urban North. A typeset version of Crew's "Field to Factory" script is mounted on stands throughout the exhibit:

"The United States has been a haven for millions of immigrants fleeing war, poverty, and discrimination, or seeking freedom," it begins. "But in some places, at some times, American society has oppressed its own people. . . ." The words are set off by more than 200 period photographs and some 200 artifacts.

At the entrance is a 1935 Chevy sedan, complete with baggage roped to the roof and a 1938 Esso road map spread across the front seat. A Langston Hughes poem called "One-Way Ticket" flanks the car:

I am fed up
With Jim Crow laws,
People who are cruel
And afraid,
Who lynch and run,
Who are scared of me
And me of them.

I pick up my life
And take it away
On a one-way ticket—
Gone up North,
Gone out West,
Gone!

In 1915, more than 75 percent of America's blacks lived in the rural South; they made up nearly one-third of the South's population. Farming was the main business and cotton was the main crop. Few blacks owned homes or the land they worked; typically, they share-cropped or rented.

The first part of the exhibition creates an atmosphere of the open, rural mood of the early 20th-century South. Mannequins of a mother, father and daughter are hoeing soil. At an original tenant farmhouse with a dirt yard, a grandmother mannequin is doing her laundry. A phonograph is playing in the house. Choir voices are coming from the re-created apse of a church nearby. Not only does the church represent the place of prayer, but it was also the social center, school and news bureau.

"What we try to do," says Crew, "is play back and forth on the draw of a strong community life—the church and the family in the South—against the unknown possibilities elsewhere."

Without land, many blacks fell into debt and many sharecroppers were swindled by greedy landlords who lied about their crop profits. If a sharecropper moved to a new farm, his debt often followed him. There were incidents of landlords and local store owners stealing from Southern blacks in various credit schemes.

Jim Crow laws restricted blacks to their own restaurants, rest rooms, hotels and barbershops. Where Jim Crow laws affected publicly funded institutions such as the segregated public schools, blacks were given less money for staff and equipment. Poll taxes and literacy tests kept Southern blacks from the voting booth. And lynchings by groups like the Ku Klux Klan held back black reformers.

World War I created a labor shortage for Northern industrialists who sent recruiters to the South to hire black workers. Recruiters promised high salaries and frequently gave away train tickets to the North. Some blacks were enticed by glowing reports in Northern black newspapers and by letters of encouragement from relatives who had already uprooted. Two natural disasters, the Southern floods of 1915 and the attack of the boll weevil—a beetle that lays its eggs in the cotton seedpods called "bolls"—also encouraged farmers to put down their hoes and head North.

The decision to leave was difficult

Crew makes the point that some people, even those living in depressed conditions, choose to stay. "They don't stay because they're weak, they don't stay because they don't care, they just stay because other things are more important to them than leaving," he says. "The issue is that people have to struggle and weigh their choices. For some, it was hard to leave if the family owned property. Others may have stayed in the South to fight through the rigid segregation policies. They all had to make their own peace with their decision."

In re-created 1920s railway coach, the girl mannequin, first shown in exhibit hoeing a field, travels North.

Like this woman, thousands of Southern blacks stayed on the road for months, following the crops.

Migratory agricultural workers trudge North Carolina highway, heading North to harvest potatoes in 1940.

For the thousands who went North, it was especially difficult to leave their families and churches, and the journey was frequently perilous. Those who traveled by car or bus met discrimination on the road, in restaurants and segregated rest rooms. Traveling on overcrowded and poorly maintained trains did not lessen the anxiety of the travelers who were leaving home for the first time.

This transition is represented in "Field to Factory" by the then segregated Ashland, Virginia, train station. It provides the launching point for the trip North. The story of three migrants is told using photographs and captions. One of them is Rufus Franklin Crew, Spencer's grandfather. Another is Lillian Reuben-McNeary, an aunt of Spencer's wife. "I haven't been shy about using family connections," says Crew. (He also used his family to cast all but one of the mannequins' faces. The little girl is his daughter, the mother is his wife and the grandmother is his mother-in-law.)

Crew says his own background had nothing to do with his initial idea for the exhibition, but that while putting the show together he was prodded to learn more about his own roots. "I had a terrific summer afternoon with my aunt talking about the family," he says. "As a young child you never get to sit down and talk about family matters. It was nice to go back as an adult and listen to my aunt tell me about her own ex-

periences. I found a picture of my grandfather that I had never seen before, and another of an aunt who died before I was born. While searching the past of others, I found a sense of myself."

In addition to the train station with its "white" and "colored" entrances, through which visitors must pass, there is a re-created 1920s segregated day coach, with a mannequin of a sleeping black girl on one of the seats (p.122). It is the same girl seen earlier hoeing the field with her mother and father.

Beyond the coach, in the third and final area of the exhibit, the urban North feels cluttered and the neon lights and city noises seem abrupt. Artifacts from the Traveler's Aid Society offer a hopeful sign of welcome, but a short film about the realities of the transition from South to North tempers the initial good cheer. A testimonial from a Philadelphian is posted on a wall: "They really looked pathetic, like just off the farm."

In 1919, after the initial influx of migrants, race riots broke out in Chicago; Detroit followed in 1925. Whites instituted restrictive covenants to keep blacks out of their neighborhoods. Employers of the newly arrived blacks often paid low wages and many of the industrial jobs were low-level, unchallenging and dangerous. Frequently, women could find jobs only as maids. And when the time came for firing and layoffs, blacks were often the first to go.

In July 1936, a Eutaw, Alabama, family laboriously hoes weeds to improve the chances of a good harvest.

Metalworker in a factory in Columbus, Ohio, found better money, but jobs were often unchallenging.

While the North was not the land of milk and honey for everyone, some Afro-Americans were moving ahead. In 1928 a Chicago black man, Oscar De Priest, was elected to the U.S. House of Representatives. Many who migrated were earning more money than they ever had in the South. New communities came together through fraternities, clubs and newly formed churches. Twice as many black children were finishing high school. Black-owned businesses prospered (the exhibit features a reconstructed beauty salon). A new urban black culture was evolving with its own literature, art and music.

Spencer Crew says the Great Migration created the first black ghettos, but, he notes, they were far different from our modern perception. "Today we think of ghettos with high crime rates, drug problems and burned-out buildings. In the beginning, though, the neighborhoods were not places of despair, but offered hope and opportunity."

On the stoop of a re-created Philadelphia row house, the mannequin of the young girl is seen one last time (p.127). She sits reading a letter from her grandmother who stayed in the South. "City" music is heard through an open window in the row house, and on the bedroom floor is a jigsaw puzzle of the United States with only the East Coast pieces snapped into place. A question is posed on a nearby wall that asks, "Was it Worth It?"

Many of the 200 artifacts in "Field to Factory" were loaned directly to Spencer Crew. He tried to find objects with the strongest connection to those that were used and owned by Afro-Americans during the Great Migration. The problem with a show on the migrant poor is that their artifacts are hard to find. Who saves tattered clothes, broken tools and banged-up pots and pans? Crew drew on the help of the African American Museums Association, but "if they didn't have material pertinent to what I wanted, they put me in contact with local people who might. It was a process of letting everyone know what we were doing." He had to convince people that the Smithsonian would return their treasures and that the museum cared. "If people held on to objects, they must have had some sort of tangible or intangible importance. I had to assure them that I shared the same love for their heirlooms."

Crew tells the story about trying to get a uniform from a former domestic. "We were very close to closing negotiations and then a relative told of reading about someone local being given a lot of money for what he thought were similar artifacts." The man decided that if the Smithsonian wanted his relative's old shoes, housedress and apron, it would have to pay what he thought was the going rate—about $10,000. Says Crew, "I swallowed and told him, 'I'm sorry that you've come to that decision, but we can't accommodate that.'"

In early 1988, a smaller "Field to Factory" will begin a three-year journey around the country. Forty

A 1922 picture of brothers William and Benjamin Layton, who were members of an urban family from Richmond, Virginia, illustrates the wide economic disparity within Afro-American Southern community.

panels will feature portions of Spencer Crew's script and a selection of about 200 photographs gathered for the show. No artifacts will go on the road.

Crew hopes that the places booking the exhibit will collect and display Afro-American objects of local origin. "When you talk about migration, you talk about mobility of people, and the one thing everyone has to make a decision about is what to keep and what to throw away," he says. "What I'm trying to do, along with a number of other people who are bringing together Afro-American history, is remind the public to save their mementos and family treasures, preserve them, give them to museums, so that when your kids come along, and your grandchildren come along, there are objects they can see, offering something concrete to tell them about their own history."

One Sunday shortly after the exhibit opened, swarms of visitors fill "Field to Factory," giving it life. Though the Smithsonian's Mall museums typically attract a largely white audience, there are many black families visiting this day, some still in their church clothes—little boys in ties and sports coats, mothers in veiled hats, natty grandfathers with fancy canes and fur-collared overcoats. Many of these families went through the Great Migration.

A father of four, whose family came to Maryland from North Carolina in the '30s, prods his four-year-old to share her thoughts. "They had hard jobs," she says after much squirming. "We have it easy."

"I see things in this show that remind me of what I've seen at my grandmother's house," says a middle-aged woman. Others label the exhibit everything from "inspiring" to "depressing." A young man whose family came from Georgia says he walked through both station entrances to see what it felt like. "I just wonder how people could treat one another like animals," he says. "What kind of people were they? You're talking about churchgoing people. What was on their minds?"

A woman about 40 who moved North from Raleigh, North Carolina, in the '60s is particularly touched. "At least it shows that we did exist in American history," she says. This woman knows what segregation feels like. She remembers not being able to use her town's public library, having to see movies at a "colored" theater and sitting in the back of the bus. "I watched whites going through this exhibit saying 'This can't be so.' Now I can't be overjoyed when in 1987 people are finally recognizing we exist and what we've been through. And this is not the full story. But it's a start," she says. "It's a real positive start."

In 1940, this homeowner in Putnam County, Georgia, stayed in close touch with faraway relatives by mail.

Girl mannequin, now living in urban row house, reads letter from her grandmother who stayed in the South.

After 51 days on the bottom, bow of the resurrected
Squalus knifes out of the ocean near Portsmouth yard.

Sub was brought up by special lifting-pontoons that were inflated until she burst loose from bottom.

By Edwards Park

The death dive and brave rescue of the *Squalus*

*In May 1939 a freakish accident sank a new
U.S. fleet submarine in 240 feet of water.
Many of its men were literally saved by a bell*

Some of us still remember a half-century ago, when the film industry fell in love with the U.S. Navy. Week after week it seemed, there was Pat O'Brien playing a tough-but-tenderhearted chief petty officer. Then the newsreel would give us Navy biplanes wobbling past, and battleships digging broad bows into giant seas and shoveling green water over their foredecks while the music rose into that familiar theme and the camera lens came straight at us with "The Eyes and Ears of the World" printed across it.

Submarines were left out. By nature retiring, they quietly prowled the coast instead of parading for the cameras. They weren't photogenic. If you happened to see one, it looked like a black toothpick with a little box—the "sail," or conning tower—amidships. They weren't large or fast. The old F and H classes ran less than 200 feet; S boats a bit more. Surfaced, 15 knots was about the best they could do.

Subs seemed to rate coverage only if something happened to them. We learned a lot about the *S-4*, struck and sunk by a Coast Guard destroyer off Cape Cod in 1927 with the loss of 40 lives. Two years before that, newsboys hawked "extras" when a ship rammed the *S-51* off Block Island and sent her down with 33 men.

About 50 years ago, fleet submarines appeared, big enough (300 feet or so) to have long range, and fast enough (20 knots surface speed) to keep up with other ships. Instead of letters and numbers, they rated real names, the names of fish—*Sculpin*, a bullhead; *Tang*, a surgeonfish; *Squalus*, a small shark. Their World War

Illustrations by Arthur Shilstone

129

II triumphs were fully recorded. (The 1943 movie *Destination Tokyo*, with Cary Grant, was actually used in the Navy as a recruiting film.) But before they saw action, we didn't know much about *them* either. Unless, of course, something went wrong. . . .

May 23, 1939, dawned at Portsmouth, New Hampshire, with a chilly northeast wind. Down the Piscataqua River and out past the Isles of Shoals slipped the fleet submarine *Squalus*, slicing through the whitecaps on her way to the sea trials required before she was assigned to fleet service. For she was a spanking new vessel, proudly manned by a crew of 51, five officers and, on this trial run, three civilian observers.

"We were headed out for our 19th dive. We called it the 'Secretary of the Navy dive' because he'd stipulated that we had to get down to periscope depth—that was about 60 feet—in 60 seconds while going ahead at 16 knots. If we could dive that fast in wartime, we'd have a good chance of getting under before a patrol plane spotted us. We'd come within two seconds of it on the 18th dive. I knew we could do it this time."

The speaker is a stocky man with a spring in his step that belies his 80-odd years. He looks at you squarely with very blue eyes as he talks. And you listen to that soft, courteous voice with a vestige of New Orleans in it, because of all the people who remember the *Squalus*, none knows more about her than Rear Adm. (ret.) Oliver F. Naquin of Arlington, Virginia. He graduated from Annapolis in 1925; his classmates knew him as Nake and considered him the hottest jazz trumpet player in town. Midshipman Naquin got a nibble from the famed Paul Whiteman band, but he turned it down for a career of service and a wife and family.

Edwards Park, who is a Contributing Editor of Smithsonian, *is the longtime author of the "Around the Mall and beyond" column.*

Cutaway view shows water rushing into the sub's stern compartments from an open air valve amidships.

After submarine school at New London, Connecticut, he was assigned to Pearl Harbor and the submarine *R-14*. Life could be dangerous and demanding on "pigboats," as early subs were called. They were so tiny that human bodies were forcibly blended into the innards of the vessels. Submariners bore bruises and smells to prove it. "Diesel exhaust would be sucked belowdecks," Naquin recalls, "and we'd all reek of it. My wife wouldn't let me in the house unless I'd head straight for the shower."

Naquin became commander of the *S-46* and worked

Naquin blew ballast tanks to stop descent. "We got the bow up, but there was too much weight to surface."

at the Navy Bureau of Engineering before being assigned to Portsmouth and command of the *Squalus*. Up till now, putting her through her paces had been a pleasure: "We rigged for the 19th dive and went down somewhere around half-past eight in the morning. Here it is in the log. . . ." The Admiral produces a photocopy of a scribbled sheet and there, written in the quartermaster's hasty hand, are the words, "0840 Dived Ship."

As Naquin points out, that was quite an operation in prenuke days. Diesel engines, used on the surface,

In engine room, men reach out toward ladder as water engulfs them. In all, 26 were trapped and drowned.

had to be shut down and electric motors started up. Aboard *Squalus*, Lt. Naquin, on the bridge atop the conning tower, gave the order, "Rig for diving." Officers and men jumped to their stations in crowded compartments. Lt. (j.g.) John Nichols had charge of the forward section: its battery room and torpedo room. Ens. Joseph Patterson supervised the after compartments: the after battery room, the electric motor room, the torpedo room and two diesel engine rooms. Men stood by telephones that linked them with the control room, amidships.

There, Lt. William Doyle jr., the diving officer and Naquin's second-in-command, heard the reports that one compartment after another was rigged for diving. As a final assurance, the two junior officers reported in person to Doyle, then returned to their posts. Doyle notified the captain that the ship was rigged for dive and Naquin asked the officer beside him, Lt. (j.g.) Robert Robertson, to check the sub's position by taking a bearing. With the dive imminent, bow planes, acting as horizontal rudders, were swung out from the hull and a message was radioed to the Portsmouth

Shivering survivors began banging on hull, hoping to be heard on surface; one blow for dot, two for dash.

Navy Yard that *Squalus* was beginning to submerge.

"Stand by to dive," barked Naquin, then ducked below. Klaxons sounded through the ship. In the control room, Doyle gave the orders that would put her under, pitching bow planes downward, opening ballast tanks to let the sea into them, closing valves to keep the sea out of the watertight hull. Red lights on a panel warned of open valves. Quickly they began changing to green.

The last intakes to close included the main engine induction valve, 31 inches in diameter, which fed air to the diesels. Once they were silenced, this great opening could be closed, for electric motors don't have to breathe. A single lever controlled the hydraulic pistons which held the mushroomlike induction valve open or tugged it shut.

Aboard *Squalus* that May morning, the diesels stopped; but the momentum of 16 knots kept the vessel plowing deeper until the electric motors, fed by 252 batteries, could take over. Machinist's Mate Alfred Prien shoved the induction valve lever to the closed position. Automatically, all eyes noted the last red lights on the "Christmas tree" turning green. *Squalus* nosed into the sea at ten degrees. The skipper entered the control room. "Green board, sir," said Doyle. Naval architect Harold Preble, one of the three civilian technicians supervising the trials, checked his stop

watches. It looked as though they had the Secretary's dive in the bag.

And then a yeoman in earphones turned toward Naquin and, ashen-faced, shouted five incredible and unforgettable words: "Engine rooms are flooding, sir!"

Impossible. The Christmas tree was green. Nevertheless the Atlantic Ocean was pouring aboard through that manhole-size induction valve. Like a flash, officers and men reacted. "Blow main ballast! Blow safety tanks! Blow bow buoyancy!" Compressed air roared into tanks, driving out the water that had just been taken in for the dive. "We got the bow up, but there was too much weight to get to the surface," Naquin recalls. "We hung on for a moment, then started going down by the stern, taking an angle of about 40 degrees. People couldn't keep their footing."

Hanging to the periscope handles, Naquin ordered bulkhead doors closed. He didn't have to; his men had been trained to "dog down" those watertight doors even if friends were trapped on the wrong side. In the control room, the seaman guarding the door to the flooding after battery room had to reach down for it and haul its massive weight up against the steep pitch of the sinking boat. He had just got a good grip when frantic voices shouted, "For God's sake, keep it open!" Said the guard later, "I couldn't just let them drown." Seven men stumbled through before he dogged the door tight against the cascading sea. There were 26 others who did not get through.

"The after batteries had shorted out," says Naquin. "But while we were going down the chief electrician managed to jump down on top of the cells in the forward battery room and pull the port and starboard switches to prevent fires and explosions. From then on we had nothing but flashlights to see by."

No one felt the vessel settle into the mud, 240 feet down, but all felt the deck angle decrease. Then the cold crept through the steel hull and into the bones of 33 trapped men. It was just 0845 hours.

False position from a garbled message

Adm. Cyrus Cole, commandant of the Portsmouth yard, learned that *Squalus* hadn't reported surfacing after her 19th dive. He orchestrated a huge, coordinated search-and-rescue effort, starting with the submarine *Sculpin*, sister ship of *Squalus*. He alerted the submarine base in New London, Connecticut, and the rescue ship *Falcon*, veteran of the *S-4* and *S-51* disasters. Then he waited. And worried.

"The trouble was," says Naquin, "our diving message had gotten garbled and came across five miles off our real position." At intervals the trapped men fired smoke rockets. They'd released the marker buoy, an orange can with a brass plate bearing the message:

"Submarine Sunk Here. Telephone Inside." Now, they too waited. "I wanted the men to sleep," Naquin remembers. "That way they'd avoid building up carbon dioxide, which will kill you if it reaches a concentration of seven percent. We covered ourselves with anything we could find to keep warm, and I made them lie still and keep quiet. I wouldn't even let them go to the head. I told them to use a bucket."

Submarines carried a kit to measure the vital CO_2 buildup, and Naquin remembers that at one point during the cold, dark wait, someone asked him if it wasn't time he checked the air. "It was the last thing I wanted to do," he says. "I knew the air was foul. It was making them sleepy. If I checked it, they'd worry and breathe harder and stay awake. So I asked the Gunner's Mate to hand me the test kit. I dropped and broke it, then said, 'Oops! How stupid of me! You guys go back to sleep.'"

The log, at this point a barely legible scrawl, heightens the drama with its understatements:

—1007 Hopes of attracting Sculpin firing red rockets
—1008 Established watch in Conning tower
—1024 Fired red rocket

On Naquin's orders to conserve energy, men lay down, breathed very slowly, and attempted to go to sleep.

—1117 Spirits High men joking and planning on our escape
—1140 Fired red rocket
—1223 Chow down men joking about our chow
—1255 Heard propellers of Sculpin right overhead
—1301 Fired yellow rocket (saving our red)
—1306 Heard anchor of Sculpin drop
—1321 Made communication with Sculpin

Sculpin had seen the red rocket, then spotted the marker buoy and retrieved it. Naquin had taken care to brief Lt. Nichols about what to say on that phone: the main induction was open, the after compartments flooded. Listening, Nichols heard the welcome voice of Warren Wilkin, *Sculpin*'s commander. He passed along the message and sent for Naquin. "I got on the phone and said 'Hello, Wilkie!' and he answered 'Hello, Oliver!' and then the phone went dead."

Sculpin had been lifted on one of the blustery ocean swells and snapped the line. The line was the only link with *Squalus*. Down below, the shivering survivors broke out hammers and began banging on the hull to help *Sculpin* find them again with her listening gear. "We had four-pound sledges," Naquin recalls, "and we stripped off cork insulation inside the conning tower

Naquin, 35 at the time of the sinking, was a senior grade lieutenant, had put in ten years in submarines.

and the forward torpedo room so we could strike bare steel. One bang was a dot; two a dash."

Sculpin got a bearing on the faint taps and came close enough to anchor. Then she too settled down to wait for the rescue vessels. On the bottom, the survivors ate again—canned pineapples, canned peaches, canned tomatoes. Naquin says he could hear teeth chattering in the dark. He located the source, the youngest member of the crew, and gave him his jacket.

On the surface, in increasing darkness and worsening seas, the Navy tug *Wandank* out of Boston and the Portsmouth tug *Penacook* began dragging for *Squalus*. They had to find her for the divers on their way to the scene aboard *Falcon*. "We could hear the grapnel running around up there," says Naquin. "And then it snagged a railing on deck." Naquin and his men couldn't hear the great cheer from *Penacook* when her grapnel caught and held.

That was at 7:30 P.M. Nine long, cold hours later, *Falcon* arrived, the sound of her propellers rousing the *Squalus* men to new hope. When they faded again, and no messages came to him, Naquin ordered a last red rocket fired. He got an instant response from *Falcon's* oscillator: "Am mooring over you. Do not fire any more smoke bombs." At 10:19 A.M., 25 hours and 39 minutes after they began their dive, the crew of *Squalus* heard the clump of a diver's weighted boots on the deck above.

Naquin is amazed at the combination of good sense and good fortune that now aided the rescue. "The grapnel had caught us only a few feet from the forward hatch where the rescue bell would come down. And when the diver saw the broken end of the telephone cable lying across the hatch he had the sense to kick it out of the way. It would have broken the seal of the bell so that it couldn't have worked."

The bell was the McCann Rescue Chamber, never

before used except in training exercises. After the loss of the *S-4*, the Navy adopted the Momsen Lung, a simple breathing device invented by Lt. Comdr. Charles Momsen, to allow individuals to escape from sunken subs. Naquin had lungs aboard *Squalus* and dealt them out to the survivors, mostly as a safeguard against the chlorine gas that became a hazard when batteries got flooded by salt water. Everyone realized it would probably be fatal to try an escape with the lung at this depth and in such cold water.

The nine-ton rescue chamber, designed by Momsen and Comdr. Allan McCann, looked like an inverted pear and worked like a submarine—with compressed air, ballast tank and a closed, watertight hull. With a crew of two and air-driven power it could winch itself down to a hatch on the sub's deck. Then, sealed in position by a rubber gasket, it would blow water ballast from its lower chamber, open its hatch and the sub's hatch and take aboard about eight men. Momsen and McCann were aboard *Falcon* to lend a hand.

The diver on *Squalus'* deck rigged the bell's downhaul cable to the sub. Then the chamber was lowered into the water from *Falcon's* deck. At around half-past twelve, the weary survivors in the forward torpedo room were drenched with trapped water as the deck hatch opened. With understandable dread, they closed their lower hatch against it. Then they saw that hatch

Composite illustration shows two stages of rescue: diver reconnoitering deck, and descent of diving bell.

open, too, and heard a friendly voice: "Hello, fellows, here we are."

Naquin had selected seven men for the first ride up in the bell. Lt. Nichols would go to report on conditions below. Preble, the civilian, would go. The others were those in the worst condition. "The boy whose teeth had been chattering so badly went on that first trip," the skipper recalls. The rescuers handed down hot coffee and soda lime to absorb CO_2, and *Falcon*'s compressors blew air into the sub's hull. That made the long wait for the next trips a lot more bearable.

And then the cable jammed

Each trip took about two hours. The second and third brought up nine men. The rescue chamber started upward for the fourth time at 8:14 that evening with six enlisted men, Lt. Doyle and finally—the last to leave his ship—Oliver Naquin. Fate toyed with them. At a depth of 155 feet, the cable jammed. Clever work by McCann freed it enough to be hand-hauled to the surface but only after a four-hour wait. The cable had somehow torn and might have snapped. Naquin recalls that they all tried to keep cheerful by kidding about the great steaks they could look forward to once they got ashore. One reprobate said, "Make mine a blonde."

The Navy managed to raise and tow *Squalus* by getting chains under her and pumping air into lifting-pontoons. World War II was already two weeks old on September 15, 1939, when the mud-stained, rusting *Squalus* finally reached Portsmouth's dry dock. In the after compartments, 25 bodies were found and identified. The 26th, the second cook, must have floated out through an open hatch. A fascinated public followed both rescue and salvage in the newspapers, on the radio and in newsreels.

It takes a special breed to serve in subs—people who get on well together in ludicrously close quarters, don't panic, and make decisions with assurance. Oliver Naquin, easygoing but precise and an utterly competent engineer, was exactly the right skipper to keep 33 men very much alive. He still sorrows for the men he lost, but says "I have absolutely no sense of guilt. I know that I reacted correctly. We all did."

Yet losing a vessel can easily wreck a career. Naquin faced a court of inquiry. It ended by commending him for "outstanding leadership." He was then assigned as chief engineer of the giant battleship *California*. And he was still with her—but ashore—on the 7th of December, 1941. "If you remember Pearl Harbor," he says, "you'll recall that *California* was hit by a 1,000-pound bomb forward and two torpedoes amidships. She went down in shallow water on an even keel."

He moved on to the cruiser *New Orleans*. At Tassa-

After bell was fitted over the sub's rescue hatch, escaping crewmen climbed up into its lower chamber.

faronga in 1942, she intercepted a Japanese force on its way to relieve Guadalcanal. By then Naquin was Navigator. He remembers that his watch glimpsed the Japanese ships, close to the beach, and fired on them. The *New Orleans* caught a torpedo. Says Naquin, "We lost a third of the ship. The bow was blown off and the strands of armor plate left sticking out looked like a cat's whiskers."

As for *Squalus*, she was rebuilt and recommissioned. As the fleet submarine *Sailfish*, she at first had a career as far-flung as her former skipper's, sinking seven ships, one of them the Japanese escort carrier *Chuyo*. By a tragic irony, *Chuyo* carried 21 prisoners of war, all survivors not only of an American submarine but of the one submarine that *Squalus* men would remember all their days with special warmth and gratitude: their old sister ship, *Sculpin*, which had found them when they were 240 feet down. Many of *Sculpin*'s crew had died when she was depth-charged by the enemy on November 19, 1943. Only one of the 21 who lived to go aboard *Chuyo* escaped *Sailfish*'s victory.

Oliver Naquin's much decorated career proceeded steadily until he retired in June 1955. Last October he attended his 60th class reunion.

He says he still hears from 13 of the *Squalus'* men. "They send cards, and I'm quick to answer. There was a bond, you know. . . ." His mind goes back to a day, early in the war, when he brought the *New Orleans* into Pearl Harbor to refit after the Battle of the Coral Sea. He happened to walk past his old ship, the *California*, lying in dry dock, still undergoing repairs from the Pearl Harbor bombing. He remembered, ruefully, that his wife had kept aboard the battleship a trunk filled with small family treasures—photographs of the children, knickknacks, the things that make a house a home. It was in the trunk room, near where a torpedo hit, and had been blown to smithereens.

Now, as he tells it, "Scoop buckets were bringing debris out of the *California*, and as I walked down the dock one of these scoops dumped its load right in front of me. And there was a little silver sailing ship given me by the people on *Squalus*. Right at my feet."

He pauses and looks at you with those sky-blue eyes. "I think that's the most extraordinary thing that's ever happened to me," he says.

In pile of debris dumped on Pearl Harbor dock after sinking of battleship *California* on which he'd served, Naquin miraculously found silver sailboat given him by the *Squalus* crew three years before.

By Timothy Foote

Fifty years on, 'O Best Beloved,' Kipling is making a comeback

In the half century since his death, interest has risen about the elusive genius who created Kim, Mowgli and all of the others

It is 50 years since Rudyard Kipling died, and close to a century since—hardly more than a boy—he burst like a starshell over the sonorous gloom and decadent filigree of late Victorian literature. Esthetes like Oscar Wilde and Aubrey Beardsley had about run their course. Kipling was a new voice. He was brash and he was brilliant, and he wrote like a house afire, both in verse and prose, and readers couldn't get enough of him.

He dropped his aitches artfully and he sang rough songs about common soldiers and told tall tales about subalterns, some apparently able to run a subcontinent single-handed. In an age not noted for candor (or realism) he dealt briskly with war and casual death, cruelty and the cost of discipline, addiction to the Black Smoke (opium) and seasonal seductions in Simla, the summer capital of the British Raj in darkest India. In the world of the young Kipling, a Djinn might come out of a bottle, but a Martini was a rifle and the writer seemed to know all about its action and muzzle velocity. And if the Sahibs he chronicled were not always pukka (true), Kipling still saw in the work of empire the likeness of a noble aspiration.

He was only 23 when he turned out "The Man Who Would Be King," a matchless adventure story with a built-in moral. Soon afterward he was rich and revered, and nearly as famous as a modern rock star. In 1901 he brought out *Kim*, a long, loving and philosophical meditation upon India that masquerades as a tale of espionage and of growing up. It was a masterpiece. In 1907 he became the first Englishman to win the Nobel Prize in Literature. A citation noted "primordial imaginative power," celebration of "cour-age, self-sacrifice and loyalty" and a "feeling for the poetry of nature."

Whole generations of young readers—he addressed them as "O Best Beloved"—have joyfully learned from Kipling how the First Cat tricked the First Woman into giving it a place near the fire by making the First Baby laugh, and how with help from his insatiable curiosity the elephant's child got his trunk on the banks of the great gray-green, greasy Limpopo River. They know the Law of the Jungle as laid down for Mowgli by Baloo the Bear and Bagheera the Black Panther. Legions of parents pinned "If" to the wall, fondly hoping it would inspire their children (as late as 1937 it was the favorite poem of the graduating class of such a sophisticated place as Princeton University).

Kipling still takes up 13 pages in *Bartlett's Familiar Quotations*, and two columns in *Books in Print*. He is probably the most quoted (as well as misquoted) writer of his century. He is certainly the last to have sizable chunks of his verse learned by heart. He is also the writer who, for decades, the Higher Criticism consigned to the ash heap of history as a brute, a bully, a jingo imperialist and a committer of vulgar doggerel.

Everyone agrees, however, that this genius of perplexing reputation loved children. At the drop of a hat he would forsake adult company to play with children, listen to them and tell them stories. In all other respects he was an intensely private man, whose personal life and papers were fiercely protected. Kipling regarded curiosity about the private lives of famous people as "the Higher Cannibalism." At the end of his life he begged his readers to let him lie "quiet in that night which shall be yours anon." And for "the little, little span/ the dead are borne in mind, Seek not to question other than/ The books I leave behind."

It is easy to sympathize.

And yet, and yet. For anyone who has been happily carried away by the roll and thump of Kipling's music-hall verses, or by the austere eloquence in poems of sorrow and service, or followed the man in stories from

Prettied up illustration romanticized "Drums of the Fore and Aft," a gritty story about how two drunk drummer boys rally a collapsing British regiment.

the distant Punjab to the soft green fields of Sussex, which Kipling used as a takeoff point for time travels into English history, it is hard to feel like a cannibal for wanting to know more about the man's life. And the life, like the talent, is an astonishment.

On both sides, Kipling's people were fierce Wesleyite Methodists who believed in hard work as the key to salvation, and the Devil take the hindmost. Kipling often showed what he called his "pulpit streak." But there were other strains as well. His mother, one of the five clever Macdonald sisters, was celebrated in the family for having tossed a treasured lock of John Wesley's hair into the fire, exclaiming "Hair of the dog that bit us!" His father, John Lockwood Kipling, was devoted to learning and skilled at art and design. At age 28 he got a good appointment, to run the Sir Jamset Jeejeebhoy School of Art in Bombay, married Miss Macdonald and moved to India, where Joseph Rudyard Kipling was born December 30, 1865.

Not far away from the Bombay house stood a Tower of Silence on which Parsees exposed their dead, to be dried by the sun and borne away by kites and vultures. One of Kipling's earliest memories was of his mother's distress "when she found a child's hand in our garden and said I should not ask questions about it. I wanted to see that child's hand." Ordinarily Kipling's garden was filled with fine flowering trees and loving servants who spoke in Hindi and seem to have spoiled Ruddy; it is remembered that the unruly boy tossed lumps of clay into the classrooms at the art school. History also records that once, on a visit to England at age three, he chugged down High Street in the town of Bewdley shouting, "Out of the way, out of the way, there's an angry Ruddy coming!"

What with typhoid, cholera and heat, death did not take many holidays in India. At six, Kipling's parents packed him and his three-year-old sister, Trix, off to England for safety, to board at the house of a woman whose name they got from an ad in the newspapers.

The Bible was his punishment

Trix was made much of. But as everyone knows who has read the sad, fierce story "Baa, Baa, Black Sheep," Kipling was mistreated, unfairly punished, told he was bad and sent off to school wearing on his back a sign that said LIAR. Critics have suggested that the experience explains the cruelty that sometimes appears in his stories, and the high frequency of revenge as a theme. Kipling denied this. He did say that it made him pay attention "to the lies I soon found it necessary to tell: and this, I presume, is the foundation of literary effort." One of his punishments—until his tormentors discovered that he enjoyed it—was to be sent to his room to read the Bible. He had a prodigious

Formidable Ruddy at age six, in 1871, and (right) as a benign raconteur of 37 surrounded by shipboard friends, telling stories during trip to Capetown in 1902.

memory; the sound of the Old Testament would ring in his writings for a lifetime.

After five years of this, Kipling was sent to an army cram school in Devon for the sons of not-so-well-off officers. He was smallish, nonathletic, with dark beetling brows (Henry James would later describe him as "the little black demon of genius"). His thick, pebble glasses blocked him from any career in the army. But he was tough, funny and clever. He read his head off and made his mark as school wit and versifier. Moreover, he won a permanent role playing the part of Beetle in the genial skirmishing with housemasters and bullies that would become *Stalky & Co.*

As the time for graduation approached, his worried father wrote the headmaster about Ruddy: "I must confess that it is the moral side I dread a breakdown on. I don't think he has the stuff to resist temptation. Journalism seems to be especially invented for such desultory souls." Lockwood Kipling feared that the impressionable youth might come to grief in sinful, bohemian London. And so it was that in 1882, not yet 17, Ruddy was dispatched to Lahore, to become "50 percent of the staff" of the *Civil and Military Gazette*, a frontier daily. Lahore was in the Punjab, part of India's northwest frontier confronting Afghanistan. It was standard practice to take 30 grains of quinine in your sherry. Men and women died all about him, from typhoid and cholera. The night, Kipling

wrote, "got into my head," setting off a habit of sleeplessness that plagued him all his life. For relief he prowled the dingy world of all-night liquor shops and opium dens, looking for reportorial color.

He broke down twice from heat and fatigue and disease. But he managed to work ten to 15 hours a day under the rather hellish conditions described at the start of "The Man Who Would Be King." And as an escape from what he called "the horror of the great darkness" he wrote much of what would become his first two books, *Departmental Ditties* and *Plain Tales from the Hills.* In the latter was "The Gate of a Hundred Sorrows," a shattering monolog by an opium addict whose subtly orchestrated diminution of will and interest is more familiar to readers today than it was to shocked English audiences in 1888.

He learned to write fast, and short. He traveled as reporter, covering all the constructive work of empire which in the Punjab was largely administered by the army. He would always have an insatiable curiosity about work, how it was done, the men and even the machinery that did it. It was the people, Indian and Briton alike, who, sweating and risking their lives, actually farmed the land, dug the wells, built the dams and bridges, set up medical dispensaries, that he admired all his life. He called them the Sons of Martha (as opposed to the Sons of Mary who did not have to work) and he tended not to include politicians in this

Expressive portrait of Cat that Walked by Himself was best of pictures Kipling did for his own books.

useful group. Naturally he was interested in war, too. Though he sometimes showed an infernal, boyish glee in writing about it, there was nothing glorious in the treatment: "When you're wounded and left on Afghanistan's plains/ And the women come out to cut up what remains,/ Jest roll to your rifle and blow out your brains,/ An' go to your *Gawd* like a soldier."

He never actually saw a battle, though, the Second Afghan War having ended before his return to India. When he moved on to a job in Allahabad, he found that the newspaper there ran three- and four-thousand-word short stories, often reprints of famous writers like Bret Harte. Why waste money? he asked. I'll write them. And, on top of his full-time job, he did.

After six and a half years he sold all his stories and poems for £250 to a company that had offered them in paperback editions at railway stations in India. Putting all his money together he set out around the world. The house where he took cheap rooms when he reached London, on Villiers Street beside Charing Cross Station, now sports a royal blue medallion saying that he lived there. But in 1889, the cheeky sign he put up read: "To publishers, Classics while you wait."

In less than two years he was a celebrity, praised by everyone from Oscar Wilde to Henry James. Maga-zines and newspapers clamored for his stories and poems. No one since Dickens had had such a rapid rise, such a lightning facility with words. Perhaps partly as an attempt to exorcise the experience of falling in love with the wrong woman, a bachelor girl named Flo Garrard, he tried a novel, with Flo as the prototype for Maisie, an artist-heroine who won't agree to marry. *The Light that Failed* came with two endings, one in which boy gets girl, one in which boy loses girl—plus his sight and his life as well—but, except perhaps for love-sick youths longing for romance and adventure, modern readers are likely to find it a fizzle either way. Kipling's later poem, "The Vampire," may have gone straighter to the mark:

A fool there was and he made his prayer
    (Even as you and I!)
To a rag and a bone and a hank of hair
    (We called her the woman who did not care)
But the fool he called her his lady fair
    (Even as you and I!)

He was not much happier about some of the literary company his new fame made him keep: "I consort with long-haired things/ In velvet collar-rolls,/ Who talk about the Aims of Art,/ And 'theories' and 'goals,'/ And moo and coo with womenfolk/ About their blessed souls." In 1890, suffering from something like a nervous breakdown, Kipling quit London, setting out on a soothing voyage.

He would always say how fortunate he was that life had dealt him the cards it did, that all he had to do was play them as they lay: the two childhoods, East and West, that gave him two worlds; the journalism that taught him his trade and gave him the whole dazzling tapestry of India to work on. But beginning in 1890, fate or chance seemed to jerk him crankily about. After his sea voyage he made friends with a young American, Wolcott Balestier. He met Balestier's sister Caroline, and soon was collaborating with him on *The Naulahka*, another romantic novel featuring another girl, an American this time, who wouldn't say "Yes." Except for spots of brilliant writing about the intrigue in a petty Rajah's palace, *The Naulahka* is best forgotten. Kipling took to the seas again, but during the voyage Wolcott Balestier died suddenly. Kipling was called back. On January 18, 1891, just eight days after he reached England, he and Caroline were married. No other Kiplings were there. But Henry James gave the bride away.

They settled in Vermont where the fates pursued Kipling once more. He was looking for a home, and

A member of SMITHSONIAN'*s Board of Editors, the writer also serves on the Executive Board of the National Book Critics' Circle.*

space, outside of England—which he called "my favorite foreign country"—and he took to the New England landscape around Brattleboro where his wife's family lived. Surrounded by snow in a rented cottage in 1892, he wrote the first *Jungle Book*, his imagination dreaming backward to India and the green mysteries of the Seeonee Hills and steamy Waingunga River. Then he built a large house and wrote the *Just So Stories* and *Captains Courageous*, the latter filled with characteristically careful reporting about the work and rigging of a Gloucester fishing schooner.

Teddy Roosevelt and "reeking bounders"

Kipling liked many Americans, one of them being Theodore Roosevelt. But he was far from diplomatic. "I never got over the wonder," he wrote, after a visit to the Smithsonian, "of a people who, having extirpated the aboriginals of their continent more completely than any modern race had ever done, honestly believed that they were a godly little New England community, setting examples to brutal mankind." When he explained this to T.R., "he made the glass cases of Indian relics shake with his rebuttals."

New York he saw as "the shiftless outcome of squalid barbarism and reckless extravagance." And though many Americans in the time of Grover Cleveland agreed with his description of Washington, D.C., as a place of "reeking bounders," some did not appreciate the judgment coming from a 27-year-old English visitor, even if he *was* a genius.

Unfortunately, America outraged one of Kipling's deepest convictions, his belief in the Law. By the word he did not mean a set of statutes, or even legal justice. He meant an agreed-upon and widely held conviction of the need for self-discipline in behavior, and more or less fair dealing in public and private affairs. After his experience in India, he considered such law the only hope of holding natural disorder at bay in a world essentially inclined to chaos. The United States, he said, had "unlimited and meticulous legality, but of law abidingness, not a trace."

As if to illustrate the point, his brother-in-law Beatty Balestier, a charming deadbeat given to easy anger, got into a smoldering argument over the use of some land, and one day in a fit of rage, threatened to kill Kipling. A foolish lawsuit against Beatty, which Kipling won, gave the American papers a field day. In 1896 the Kiplings packed up and went back to England.

Three years later, when they ventured back, at least as far as New York, Beatty threatened a countersuit. He had no case, but could promise more frightful publicity. Just at that moment Kipling came down with pneumonia. Besieged by the press, which treated the story as front-page news, his wife and Frank Double-

Kipling's patriotism stirred Max Beerbohm to this cartoon showing him out with "Britannia, 'is girl."

Best of many Kipling films was 1975 *Man Who Would Be King*. Christopher Plummer (left) was Kipling.

day, his U.S. publisher and lifelong friend, stood round-the-clock watch. He finally recovered. What they could not tell him, as his own life hung in the balance, was that during his illness his daughter Josephine, seven, the "O Best Beloved" for whom he told the *Just So Stories*, had died of fever.

All his life Kipling had suffered from "deep melancholy and self-distrust," a sort of free-floating angst. His child's death was a specific wound, the first of two that he would never recover from. He lived for 37 more years. For decades to come in America, Kipling was a leader on the Doubleday sales list. But he never set foot in the United States again.

Earliest published books were these paperbacks sold for one rupee apiece in Indian railway stations.

He had long attacked his own countrymen for their sneering treatment of British soldiers and their families, and for "making mock of uniforms that guard you while you sleep": "For it's Tommy this, an' Tommy that, and 'Chuck him out, the brute!'/ But it's 'Saviour of 'is country' when the guns begin to shoot." People back home didn't understand the real England ("What should they know of England, that only England know?"). He, at least, saw England not as a remote, indifferent little island, but as a worldwide community aimed at gradual progress. Now, near the turn of the century, two poems appeared that would later draw violent criticism, but defined his view

of imperialism and foreshadowed his growing distress at Britain's increasing failure to live up to the responsibilities of empire. One was written as a warning to Teddy Roosevelt, then embarking on what Kipling correctly feared might be frivolous colonial adventures in the Philippines: "Take up the White Man's burden—/ Send forth the best ye breed—/ Go bind your sons to exile/ To serve your captives' need."

The second was "Recessional." A great hymn, whatever its sentiments, it was taken as a paean of praise to the British Empire and to Queen Victoria on her Diamond Jubilee. But it is something else, a warning written out of deep misgivings, about the brevity of power and the dangers of its arrogant misuse:

> Far-called, our navies melt away;
>   On dune and headland sinks the fire:
> Lo, all our pomp of yesterday
>   Is one with Nineveh and Tyre!
> Judge of the Nations, spare us yet,
> Lest we forget—lest we forget!
>
> If, drunk with sight of power, we loose
>   Wild tongues that have not Thee in awe,
> Such boasting as the Gentiles use,
>   Or lesser breeds without the Law—
> Lord God of Hosts, be with us yet,
> Lest we forget—lest we forget!

For more than 30 years Kipling would watch, and often protest in silly ways, as his country, in the name of peace but actually through fecklessness and failure of will, grew weak, abandoned its responsibility to the people of its empire and stumbled, unprepared, toward three wars.

The first, against the Boers, was so ineptly conducted that it cost England 22,000 unnecessary casualties. Kipling complained in polemical verses, and raised £250,000 for the relief of common soldiers. On the scene in South Africa, along with reporting, he helped see that the wounded got medical care. Afterward, when Old Boys and generals did not seem to learn from their mistakes, an angry Ruddy struck out at them, "The flannelled fools at the wicket/ The muddied oafs at the goals."

In the second war Kipling lost his son John, just 18, killed at the Battle of Loos in 1915, as a subaltern in the Irish Guards. His father had used army connections to help get the boy a commission. Mostly he spared others his grief. But one poem mercilessly said it all, for himself and all parents: "That flesh we had nursed from the first in all cleanness was given/ To corruption unveiled and assailed by the malice of Heaven/ By the heartshaking jests of Decay where it lolled on the wires/ To be blanched or gay-painted by fumes—to be cindered by fires."

The verses reproduced throughout the article were taken from *Kipling's Verse: A Definitive Edition*, Doubleday and Co. Inc.

In 1893, world-famous at 28, Kipling allowed a
rare portrait in his book-lined, Vermont study. The
mantelpiece bore an inscription carved by his father:
"The Night Cometh When No Man Can Work."

Mowgli's greatest friend and teacher in *Jungle Books* is Bagheera, the sophisticated black panther.

This splendid illustration by E. J. Detmold shows moment when the boy first learns the use of fire.

A Kipling Sampler:

Yet, if you enter the woods
Of a summer evening late,
When the night-air cools on the trout-
    ringed pools
Where the otter whistles his mate,
(They fear not men in the woods,
Because they see so few.)
You will hear the beat of a horse's feet,
And the swish of a skirt in the dew,
Steadily cantering through
The misty solitudes,
As though they perfectly knew
The old lost road through the woods. . . .
But there is no road through the woods.
(From "The Way through the Woods")

'What makes the rear-rank breathe
    so'ard?' said Files-on-Parade.
'It's bitter cold, it's bitter cold,' the
    Colour-Sergeant said.
'What makes that front-rank man fall
    down?' said Files-on-Parade.
A touch o' sun, a touch o' sun,' the
    Colour-Sergeant said.
    They are hangin' Danny Deever, they
        are marchin of 'im round,
    They 'ave 'alted Danny Deever by 'is
        coffin on the ground;
    An' 'e'll swing in 'arf a minute for a
        sneakin 'shootin 'hound—
    O they're hangin' Danny Deever in
        the mornin'!
(From "Danny Deever")

Ah! What avails the classic bent
    And what the cultured word,
Against the undoctored incident
    That actually occurred? . . .

It is not learning, grace nor gear,
    Nor easy meat and drink,
But bitter pinch of pain and fear
    That makes creation think.
(From "The Benefactors")

Oh, East is East, and West is West, and
    never the twain shall meet,
Till Earth and Sky stand presently at
    God's great Judgment Seat;
But there is neither East nor West,
    Border, nor Breed, nor Birth,
When two strong men stand face to face,
    though they come from the ends of
    the earth!
(From "The Ballad of East and West")

The female of the species is more deadly
than the male.
(From "The Female of the Species")

He went back through the Wet Wild
Woods waving his wild tail, and walking
by his wild lone. But he never told
anybody.
(From "The Cat That Walked By
    Himself")

Now this is the Law of the Jungle—as old
    and as true as the sky;
And the Wolf that shall keep it may
    prosper, but the Wolf that shall break
    it must die.

As the creeper that girdles the tree-trunk
    the Law runneth forward and back—
For the strength of the Pack is the Wolf,
    and the strength of the Wolf is the Pack.
(From The Second Jungle Book)

It takes a great deal of Christianity to
wipe out uncivilized Eastern instincts,
such as falling in love at first sight.
(From Plain Tales From the Hills)

The Camel's hump is an ugly lump
    Which well you may see at the Zoo;
But uglier yet is the Hump we get
    From having too little to do.
(From "How the Camel Got His
    Hump")

I could not dig: I dared not rob:
Therefore I lied to please the mob.
Now all my lies are proved untrue
And I must face the men I slew,
What tale shall serve me here among
Mine angry and defrauded young?
(From "A Dead Statesman")

The Devil whispered behind the leaves,
    "It's pretty but is it Art?"
(From "Conundrum Of The Workshop")

I've taken my fun where I've found it,
    An' now I must pay for my fun,
For the more you 'ave known o' the others
    The less will you settle to one;
An' the end of it's sittin' and thinkin',
    An' dreamin' Hell-fires to see;
So be warned by my lot (which I know
    you will not),
    An' learn about women from me!
(From "The Ladies")

Many religious people are deeply
suspicious. They seem—for purely
religious purposes, of course—to know
more about iniquity than the
unregenerate.
(From Plain Tales From the Hills)

Take of English earth as much
As either hand may rightly clutch.
In the taking of it breathe
Prayer for all who lie beneath.
Not the great nor well-bespoke,
But the mere uncounted folk
Of whose life and death is none
Report or lamentation.

    Lay that earth upon thy heart,
    And thy sickness shall depart!
(From Rewards and Fairies)

We're little black sheep who've gone
    astray,
    Baa—aa—aa!
Gentlemen-rankers out on the spree,
Damned from here to Eternity,
God ha' mercy on such as we,
    Baa! Yah! Bah!
(From "Gentlemen-Rankers")

More men are killed by overwork than
the importance of the world justifies.
(From "The Phantom 'Rickshaw")

I 'eard the knives be 'ind me, but I dursn't
    face my man,
    Nor I don't know where I went to,
    'cause I didn't 'alt to see,
Till I 'eard a beggar squealin' out for
    quarter as 'e ran,
    An' I thought I knew the voice an'—it
    was me!
(From "That Day")

Down to Gehenna or up to the Throne,
He travels the fastest who travels alone.
(From "The Winners")

When Earth's last picture is painted and
    the tubes are twisted and dried,
When the oldest colours have faded, and
    the youngest critic has died,
We shall rest, and, faith, we shall need it—
    lie down for an aeon or two,
Till the Master of All Good Workmen
    shall put us to work anew. . . .

And only The Master shall praise us, and
    only The Master shall blame;
And no one shall work for money, and
    no one shall work for fame,
But each for the joy of the working, and
    each, in his separate star,
Shall draw the Thing as he sees It for the
    God of Things as They are!
(From "L'Envoi" to The Seven Seas)

He would be asked to write a history of the Irish Guards and to become a commissioner of England's 750,000 war graves. With painful care he did both, and worked as he always had on behalf of veterans.

But if he had spoken for everyone's grief and patriotism during the war, after the war he was at odds with prevailing values, and an avalanche of critical scorn now fell upon him.

The fiercest attacks came from the literary left. England was exhausted from war. English liberals especially were strongly pacifist, hoping the way to untroubled rest lay through appeasement. Many of them, touched by fashionable Marxism, liked to feel that any future hope for international fairness and order lay with the communist experiment. They could see in Kipling's imperial vision only pure hypocrisy or economic exploitation. But Kipling was outraged by what was going on in the Soviet Union. Like Churchill, he also understood that another war with Germany would come unless England and France were strong, and he called for rearmament.

He had made fun of liberals all his life and once slightly referred to "brittle intellectuals who crack beneath the strain." He still spoke of heroism, duty, courage and sacrifice, words tarnished by their use to incite the young to face the horrors of trench warfare. Some attacks were genial enough, like this spoof of Kipling and his friend H. Rider Haggard, the author of *She* and *King Solomon's Mines*:

'Every Bolsh is a blackguard,'
Said Kipling to Haggard
—'And given to tippling,'
Said Haggard to Kipling
'And a blooming outsider,'
Said Rudyard to Rider.
—'Their domain is a blood-yard,'
Said Rider to Rudyard.

Some attacks were not. He found himself labeled a warmonger and a fascist. His writing was dismissed as sadistic and shallow, drenched with bourgeois sentimentality. Besides, wasn't he patronizing the working class, writing all those soldier poems in dialect?

For two decades, according to British historian Paul Johnson, critics and educationists on both sides of the Atlantic assailed him. "This attempted effacement of a great writer," Johnson notes, "is without parallel in any country this side of the Iron Curtain." Critic Edmund Wilson would put it more simply. Kipling, he wrote, "had been dropped out of modern literature."

He died in 1936. The year of Stalin's purges. The year when, unopposed by the British and French, Adolf Hitler marched into the Rhineland.

This spring seminars and ceremonies will mark the half century since Kipling's death. Partly because of that, partly because the copyright on all his work is running out, there will be a rush of new collections and studies. Fortunately for students, and readers generally, a process of critical reassessment has long been under way. It has helped turn the emphasis away from polemics to Kipling's art, to his chameleon poet's skill as a writer.

The reassessment started in the 1940s, most notably with George Orwell and poet-critic T. S. Eliot. Because he came from the political left, Orwell's comment had political impact. Kipling might sometimes be "morally insensitive and aesthetically disgusting," Orwell granted, but he was no fascist. And no capitalist exploiter, either, since he saw British imperialism

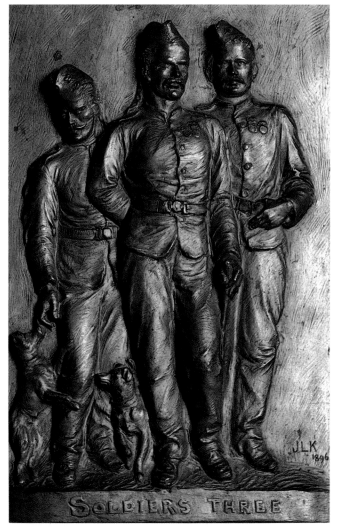

His father illustrated Kipling's three soldiers with bronze relief. From left: Ortheris, Mulvaney, Learoyd.

In 1900, as war-correspondent (lower right) Kipling covered Britain's inept and costly Boer War in South Africa. He also wrote poems and led rallies to raise money for wounded soldiers and their families.

not as a "money-making concern" but as "a sort of forcible evangelising." Orwell noted that the line "Lesser breeds without the Law" did not refer to benighted natives, but mainly to the lawlessness of the Germans. The term "white man's burden," Orwell suggested, "instantly conjures up a real problem, even if one feels that it ought to be altered to black man's burden." He pointed out the deep feeling and beauty of some of the soldier poems.

A consummate craftsman himself, Eliot praised Kipling's immense skill at verse, his concern for poetic craftsmanship. Noting his music and "remarkable" rhythmic innovations he cited the "Harp Song of the Dane Women" as an example: "What is a woman that you forsake her/ And the hearth fire and the home acre,/ To go with the old grey Widow-maker?"

More important, as one of the high priests of mod-

ern criticism, Eliot lent weight to an obvious point: Kipling's verses, written in a long and honorable tradition, were often sneered at simply because the tradition had gone out of style. Just before World War I, rhyme schemes, heavy metrics and poetic language had given way to free verse and Ezra Pound's order "to compose in the sequence of the musical phrase, not in the sequence of the metronome." The new poetry aimed at capturing the exact curve of intricate private experience, and sought the complexities that have made poetry, once widely understood and read aloud, inaccessible to the general public. Accustomed to regard obscurity in a poem as proof of its seriousness, modern critics tended to be "contemptuous of poetry which they understand without effort." Kipling's ballads were aiming at something older and more generous: a poetry of direct statement, written in order to stir a "response from all readers, and only the response which they can make in common."

The relation between serious criticism and commercial publishing, or the public acceptance of a writer, is fairly tenuous. But biographies and studies proliferate, and within the past decade there has been something of a Kipling boom.

Opinion is still divided, but on different (and more favorable) terms. Some think Kipling's real claim to a place in history owes most to the early writing on India, and soldier stories like "Black Jack" and "On Greenhow Hill." Others prefer the less well-known later stories, notably "An Habitation Enforced" and "The Wish House," mostly set in England and often intricate, abstruse, layered in meaning.

The number of visitors who journey down to Sussex to Bateman's, Kipling's spacious house, has lately jumped from about 5,000 to more than 55,000 a year. Once there they can buy books and see the dam and brook that figure in such later stories as "Under the Mill Dam" and "Friendly Brook." In 1983 in England, as a result of relaxed restrictions on the use of Kipling's letters, out came *O Beloved Kids*, a selection of his letters to his children—no doubt a shocking invasion of privacy, but funny and touching and full of marginal sketches and fond exhortation.

For the past two years actor Alec McCowen has been touring with a compelling, cranky and eloquent stage portrait of Kipling, grumping because people "half quote" him to suit "*their* prejudices," but gradually quoting himself correctly to explain his life.

What emerges is no political thinker, but a stoic man of genius and surpassing literary charm, a gentle-violent man full of affection and knowledge, who took refuge from inner and outer darkness by praising and holding to his idea of the Law, doggedly following duty and work and loyalties outside himself—even as you and I. Fortunately, he could write about, seem to inhabit, and speak for, all manner of animals, people, places and moments in history, re-creating for anyone willing to read, a vision of Victorian India and the England of his dreams.

"If you really want to know what I thought, read the books," McCowen says at the show's end, slamming his hand down on the pile of books on his desk. Pause to glare at the audience. Then he adds scornfully, "But you *won't*."

Perhaps so. But this would be an appropriate year to prove him wrong.

Desk at Bateman's, the house he lived in for 34 years, looks on Sussex countryside he grew to love.

Late in life, with Caroline. "Men and Things come round again," he would write, "eternal as the seasons."

By Henry Allen

There'll be some changes in the city when the cranes come soaring in

Over the skylines of our major urban centers loom giant 'one-legged dinosaurs' that have transformed the way we construct buildings

If only the ladder were wired a little tighter, the view from halfway up this tower crane would be beautiful. Pearl-pink clouds arch over Chicago. The moon slides behind the Amoco Building. The crane broods over the half-finished roof of a 62-story office building and about 700 feet below is the cozy emptiness of a city at dawn. The waves on Lake Michigan are tiny—they look like the patina on old silver.

Beautiful. Except for the ladder, which is fastened onto the tower crane—also known as a hammerhead crane—with scraps of old wire. It's a touch that seems startlingly casual when you consider that the wind is blowing 25 miles an hour. It catches you, shakes the ladder, makes you glance down all that breathless distance to the streets of the city, no wider from here than the back of a knife.

This is how tower-crane operators get to work every morning—one rung at a time, winter and summer, rain and shine, high and alone.

"I had a laborer panic up here one time," says **Don Dulkoski**, 44, who has climbed ahead. Dulkoski was a crane operator before he became the business agent for Local 150 of the International Union of Operating Engineers. He stands atop this Pecco SK 180 from Germany and studies a sun lifting so molten red out of the lake you can practically hear it hissing in the wind. He says: "This was back when we were wrecking the old Morrison Hotel about 20 years ago. The workman was climbing up and all of a sudden he stopped. Wouldn't let go of the ladder. Just froze. I had to call the fire department to get him off."

Dulkoski has a wary calm that could pass for pre-occupation, an attitude common to crane operators. They are the aristocrats of construction sites, making as much as $24 an hour in New York City ($19 here in Chicago). Foremen and superintendents want to please them—a happy tower-crane operator is apt to pour more cubic yards of concrete every day than a disgruntled one. They operate one of the biggest single pieces of standard construction equipment in the world. One freestanding crane used at the Seabrook, New Hampshire, nuclear plant stood 423 feet tall and could lift 182 tons at a radius of 269 feet. Another anchored to the inside of the CN Tower in Toronto was more than 1,000 feet above the street.

Loose ladder or not, this crane is yet another steeple of America's religion of progress, a harbinger of prosperity, of cities rising. The first tower crane arrived in America from Germany in 1958 (virtually all are European 27 years later). They have multiplied until they

Hook block (center) hangs still from outstretched jib of hammerhead crane 24 stories above Chicago streets.

Photographs by Kay Chernush

Lifted by hydraulic jacks, jumping seven floors at a time, a tower crane rises with edifice it is building.

surmount new buildings from Boston to San Francisco like a breed of one-legged dinosaurs: *Towersaurus rex.* Some people in Denver like to call their city "the nesting place of the one-legged crane." Among the boosters of Houston, the tower crane is widely known as "the state bird of Texas."

This particular crane at 446 Ontario Street in Chicago has a jib, or horizontal boom, that reaches out 168 feet to hold sway over more than two acres of the city. "It'll be pouring concrete for the roof today," Dulkoski says. "They park the trucks in that alley next to the building and bring it up from there."

The crane has been the "point man" for the regiment of carpenters, plumbers, ironworkers, electricians, concrete finishers, laborers and superintendents who have toiled beneath the crane operator and trusted him with their lives—one wrong twitch on a joystick could crush them with a load of reinforcing bars, a pile of plywood, three tons of concrete.

Power: with his giant drum of 18mm cable, backed by three electric motors pulling 440 volts, the operator has provided the bootstrap with which this building has lifted itself.

Every time seven or so floors are completed, the ironworkers raise the crane higher, inches at a time, hydraulic jacks hiking 75 to 140 tons while the operator sits in his cab balancing the counterweights with a load on the jib, feeling his tower sway.

Blood on the windshield in a strange Valhalla

Such power in such solitude is the province of American heroes: cowboys, eccentric millionaires, boxers, secret agents, drivers of 18-wheel trucks—people who do hard, lonely, dangerous, beautiful work. But it's a strange Valhalla up here. The crane twitches and shudders in the wind. Dulkoski is moved to start telling horror stories—the time his assistant, called an oiler, got his foot crushed in the turntable and passed out. "The first thing I knew about it was the blood running down the windshield." And the day the concrete pad collapsed beneath the 180-foot crane he was operating, and the crane lurched over till it caught at a 12-degree tilt.

Then he's talking about how you can be out of work a year at a time in this business, waiting for your name to rise to the top of the union's hiring roster. And when you do work, it can be 12 hours a day, seven days a week for months on end, with the whole world looking at you, no slack, no place to hide. "A laborer can hide—he can set a few re-bars and wander away and slough off. An operating engineer can't hide."

In fact, Dulkoski says, when you're an operator your radio will crackle all day with petitions from the tiny figures below—they need a lift on this load of plywood, how about swinging this piece of facing stone over to the northeast corner—and meanwhile everybody's waiting for another concrete form to be moved into place. The superintendent is yelling. The wind batters the jib as it swings over the site. The sun glares off the structural steel and you can't see the hand signals of the men below.

You're all by yourself with an old antifreeze jug for a bathroom and a pair of binoculars to remind you that those are real people boiling around like ants down there. You're warm in the winter, but you roast in the summer up there in that little metal cab all day; hauling concrete up from a truck you can't even see over the edge of the building—"working in the blind," they call it—but you're responsible for those lives down

Six-ton I-beam, held by a choker cable slung through tower crane's hook, is lowered onto building deck.

Jerry-built squawk box is used to relay orders between the site "super" and the crane operator high above.

Ironworker, in a precarious position, unsnags the tag line from a column just lowered into place by crane.

there. A six-inch mistake can crush a hand like a road-killed rabbit.

Or maybe the hook on the end of your cable gets away from the bucket man and accidentally snags the truck—the next thing you know the jib is lunging down, the tower is twitching as you try to lift the whole truck and the voices are screaming into the radio. . . .

It's enough to drive you crazy.

But how many Americans can say what a lot of crane operators say: that they look forward to climbing that ladder every morning, that they go home feeling good every night? "It's an art, doing this," Dulkoski says. "Some guys don't get satisfaction from their jobs. I used to leave my job every day and know I'd really done something."

Essence of simplicity: joysticks and a foot brake

The tower crane is a triumph of engineering over common sense. It is not to be confused with the whole family of conventional cranes—crawlers, cherry pickers, long booms and so on. Those are run from the ground and they are little more than analogs of a reaching arm. A tower crane is something different. The most common have one perfectly horizontal beam, called a jib, balanced on one perfectly vertical beam, called a tower. The whole thing is operated from the top with two joysticks and sometimes a foot brake. It is the essence of simplicity, solid geometry made real, with the operator sitting atop a perfect cylinder defined by his hook and cable.

The tower crane has totally altered the way we put up buildings. Before them, things had changed little since the days of the pyramids, with building materials being horsed into place by muscle power. The tower crane sets loads down precisely where they're needed.

"Before tower cranes we used hoists," says Bernard (Ben) Carbeau of Fairfax, Virginia. Now a Pecco district manager, he brought the first tower crane to America. "That was my family's business, building hoist towers. To take material up in the building you'd put it on a platform and raise it up on the construction elevator, or sometimes with a Chicago boom. Then workers would cart the concrete in a two-wheeled buggy or carry other materials to wherever they were supposed to go.

"In 1957 I went to Germany to see what they were doing in construction over there. We flew into Stuttgart. On approaching, I saw these things standing up in the city. I wondered what they were. I told the taxi driver to take me to one of those sites before we even went to my hotel. I kept wondering: How is it possible for them to reach up so far and out so far with so little at the base? But I thought that if this *was* what it *seemed* to be. . . ."

By 5:30 A.M. an operator has ridden an elevator to the topmost floor of a building under construction.

Carbeau, tweedy and reserved now at 59, was a young man out to make his mark. He knew how hard it would be to convince not only contractors but unions and building inspectors that a crane could stand, say, 265 feet tall, like the Pecco SK 560, on a tower approximately eight feet square. It's like putting something as tall as the Empire State Building on a foundation the size of a racket-ball court—one of those impossible ideas that have marked 20th-century architecture, like the cantilevered overhangs that Frank Lloyd Wright designed, personally kicking out the timber supports and standing under them to prove they were safe. The result is a machine that can lift 35 tons. The reason this load doesn't buckle the tower is the counterweight—about 25 tons of reinforced concrete to balance the load.

Carbeau says: "In Germany they told me, 'No one seems to think they need these in your country.' That was in April. I flew home and in June we had a sales conference. I did a presentation. The salesmen said,

The author is a staff writer for the Washington Post's *Style section. His novel,* Fool's Mercy, *is available in paperback from Carroll & Graf.*

Now he must climb another nine stories up a ladder to cab of the crane where he will spend the day.

Lowell Kamerer makes his 150-foot climb look easy, but it is probably the most dangerous part of his job.

Operator talks with signal man by intercom before he starts to move a load on the construction deck.

On his brief lunch break, Larry Overton suns himself on chaise longue 350 feet above the Chicago River.

'Who is this kid?' The first tower crane that actually got used was at a Sheraton Motor Inn in Binghamton, New York, a Pecco 401. It was 100 feet high with a 100-foot jib. It could only lift three-quarters of a yard of concrete—about 3,000 pounds.

"By the early '60s," Carbeau continues, "other companies were getting into it—Linden, from Sweden, and Liebherr, from Germany. It was somewhat difficult in those days to get an operator. Sometimes they didn't like the height, they didn't like the climb. Sometimes they'd turn into prima donnas and want to run the whole job from up there. We preferred younger, untrained operators we could teach ourselves."

Cranes sell now for prices between $200,000 and $1 million, but most contractors choose to rent them, with fees ranging from $5,000 to $20,000 a month with $8,000 to $9,000 the average, says Carbeau.

With a few exceptions, almost all cranes come from Europe. American crane manufacturers not only are behind in the technology and marketing, but also cannot attain European economies of scale; there, with more concrete and less lumber used in residential construction, tower cranes are used to build houses as well as skyscrapers.

During major renovation of west face of U.S. Capitol, articulating-jib cranes allow delicate maneuvering.

Cranes have grown in size, with innovations such as a self-erecting crane and a tower crane with what are known as luffing booms or articulating jibs mounted on them. Essentially, these are tower cranes with what looks like a conventional long-boom crane mounted on the top, instead of the standard horizontal jib. Cranes move on tracks and they can be rigged with a hose to pump wet concrete, rather than haul it in buckets.

Structural safety has proved to be extraordinary over the years. Tower cranes are set up so that the motors will cut out if the load is too heavy. Sometimes the operator doesn't know exactly how much weight he's picking up—it has to be judged by how much the tower bends, how much the jib arcs.

Most notable accidents have occurred during dismantling of the tower cranes or when their bases were inadequate. One mishap in New York City that killed a pedestrian in 1982 was caused by the failure of the derrick that was being used on the roof of a building to disassemble a tower crane. Another spectacular collapse in Bailey's Crossroads, Virginia, was the result of construction flaws in the building it stood on. Another in the late '60s at a Holiday Inn in Washington, D.C., was blamed on "flaws in the welding," says Morrow-Liebherr salesman Jim Harrington.

"It was 110 feet tall," he explains, "and it broke off at the base, but the operator lived—the counterweight on the back of the jib hit first, and since it was after the normal working day, there was no one on the deck for it to hit. As it happened, there was a convention of the Associated General Contractors of America going on across the street. The next day, I was there at the site and a guy with a German accent came out and said 'I thought American technology was better than that.' I told him it was a German crane."

"I thank God nobody was hurt"

Every morning when Jim Baker climbs up into his crane, he kneels down and prays. Baker, 38 and a Jehovah's Witness, says: "I thank God for my secular work. At the end of the day I kneel down and thank God nobody was hurt." Crane operators are a little like gods, themselves. Says Baker: "The hardest thing is keeping your cool. Everybody uses the tower crane. You've got carpenters, ironworkers, plumbers, electricians, finishers—they all want you at the same time."

And sometimes they don't understand that their prayers cannot be answered, though there can be lessons in that, too. Consider the day during the building of Holy Cross Hospital in Silver Spring, Maryland, when Baker found he couldn't swing his jib in third speed because it was too windy. He decided to shut down and "weathercock" the crane—let it swing free with the wind.

"But the carpenters' foreman kept after me to lift this load of plywood off a truck out in the street," Baker recalls. "I said I'd try it. As it happened, it was the foreman's son who was working on that truck. I got the jib almost all the way over there, I had the hook three or four feet away from him, but then the wind started to push it back. He reached out and grabbed it and it pulled him off the truck. The jib was gaining speed now, and he was too scared to let go of it. I could see it was going to smash him into a wall, so the only thing I could do was hoist him up eight floors and land him on the building. They never badgered me any more about working in the wind."

It takes a certain mentality to operate a tower crane. Some people don't like the height and the climb, others don't like the loneliness, others are afraid of the responsibility. And some just can't accept the fact that the crane *is* going to remain standing. "I had a student who was doing fine until he got to heavy loads," says Baker, who used to train crane operators. "He did fine with his load, but when he came down and watched the next guy work, he said to me: 'Did the jib bend that much when *I* was doing that?' I said it did and he said good-bye. When I pick up two [cubic] yards of concrete—that's over 8,000 pounds—with the trolley 120 feet out from the tower, I can look down and see the tower moving ten to 14 inches. The jib pulls down at least eight feet—I can be sure of that because when the bucket man dumps the concrete too quick, the bucket will go up so high he can't reach it." This would bother most people, but crane operators are different. Says Baker: "I try to keep a humble attitude."

Here is a vision of workingman's heaven, the ultimate sandbox, a little boy's dream you watch from 100 feet up in the Richier 1268 tower crane at the Accokeek, Maryland, training site of the Operating Engineers. Off in the distance, bulldozers scrape perfect rectangles in the earth, graders smooth them over, backhoes dig holes, front-end loaders fill them in. Trees shudder in the wind. A pond ruffles in the distant silence.

Lovely—except that just now it is proving tense, frustrating and difficult to do the simplest task with a tower crane—move, say, an empty concrete bucket in a straight line from point A across to point B. Why should it be so hard? This tower crane is stunningly simple: two joysticks controlling three speeds of trolley, three speeds of swing, three speeds of hoist. Put it all together and, like instructor Mike Holley, you too can carve invisible arcs and parabolas out of the thin air.

On the other hand, it's a little like trying to draw a straight line with a geometrician's compass—the problem of squaring the circle, which means that science and reason aren't quite enough. You have to bring in an operator willing to run on intuition, Kentucky windage, the seat of his pants.

"You've got to get in the groove"

Holley, 38, is a philosopher of the tower crane. As one of the small but growing number of blacks climbing up into cranes every morning, he has learned it all the hard way, unlike a lot of operators whose fathers had run cranes before them and brought their sons into the union and the craft to succeed them.

"You've got to get in the groove," he says. He has big, light hands that float down over yours to flick the joysticks a hair of an inch this way, that way. "You've got it going in circles now," Holley says, and he demonstrates how to "catch" the load and make it move in straight lines again.

Slow and sloppy, with much hands-on help from Holley, the bucket arrives at its target. It descends. It should be easy to judge how close it is to the ground

Operator Mike Holley, tower-crane philosopher, calls himself a "mother hen," protects everyone on job.

today—the sun is out and the bucket and its shadow draw together at ground zero. Except that a bit too much push on the joystick bangs it down with cable-bellying clumsiness, the kind of error that could kill a man standing next to a concrete truck.

"You got to move with the motion, one move, A to B, get that biorhythm going," Holley says. He is a man of great personal style, a loner given to skydiving and downhill skiing in his spare time and, like a lot of crane operators, a man who thinks about the nature of things and where he fits in. Listen to him:

"That concrete bucket's moving up and down, up and down until it's a song in your head. A song! You get working like that, it makes everybody feel good, people feel good being there, the day goes fast, you don't spend all day waiting to go home. I get on the radio, I say, 'It's show time! Let's rock and roll!' You know, you make it fun, you get into the flow and everybody's finger-poppin'. You got to work together. The man on the bucket, he can feel that motor kick in. I

to do better than that. You get old man momentum working for you...."

It's after work in Chicago at a bar called Tramps. There's a pregnant woman singing behind a piano, and a table full of men paying no attention after a while. A vodka here, a beer there and they're locked into one of those fierce, sad bull sessions about the meaning of life, which for them is inextricably mingled with the operating of tower cranes.

For one thing, *they* are tower crane operators and the rest of the world isn't. They discuss the splendid stupidity of ironworkers, the frustrating illogic of carpenters, the venality of superintendents and the vengeance of all of them when a crane operator causes someone to be hurt. After a while, though, the talk mellows out and you begin to see why they feel so superior not only to the other trades, but maybe to all the quietly desperate lives they see below them, huddling and hustling, worrying and scurrying.

It isn't just the beauty of the job, with the sun skidding across the morning lake, igniting the dome of the planetarium, the sort of sight that provokes operators to take cameras up with them. And it isn't nature's oddities, such as a raccoon that climbed 160 feet of ladder, or a nesting falcon or a bat gathered like a lump of grease against the tower one morning.

And it isn't just the high pay or the high esteem that the world gives them—"I consider myself just as important as an airplane pilot," says Lowell Kamerer, 47, bearded and green-eyed and an operating engineer for the past 28 years.

It's more.

"The best part," says Ray Jorsch, 40, a crane operator for 15 years after working as a tool and die maker, "is when you go down the road after you've finished a job, and you can look back and say: 'I did that.'"

He is sitting next to Larry Overton, who shares with Kamerer a fear that the pressure of the job will have them on operating tables for cardiac-bypass surgery any day now. Overton is 33 and "taking blood-pressure pills," he says. Kamerer, who is divorced, says he doesn't want his daughter to marry a crane operator—"I know what the pressure can do." But on balance, he doesn't have a lot of regrets.

"Every day for 28 years I've looked forward to going to work—every day," Kamerer says. "I love seeing things go up. I'm going to retire pretty soon—it gets hard climbing that ladder after a while—and when I do, I want an artist to come and paint a mural on my wall of all the projects I've worked on. Every one."

tell him, 'Don't worry about pulling it in, I'll get it within three inches,' and you do it all in one move, you don't stop and let it hang there while he pours. Just as he's hitting that lever for the last of the concrete he feels the motor kick in and he knows that bucket is already on its way....

"I'm the mother hen," Holley goes on, "that's the way I feel about it. I look out for these people, for their safety. I'm baby-sitting. It's my job to make sure everybody gets through the day without getting hurt. You have to loosen up. I usually get there half an hour or so ahead of time. You get up there, you sit there and drink your coffee, you look at the day, you look at the sunrise, look at a star that's still out. You can't go up in a crane with an attitude. You leave your personal problems behind. But that's the good part, you go up there and that's all down here, and you know you don't get a paycheck for those personal problems. You can't have problems up there. You have to watch out for addictions. A lot of guys, after work, they go to the bar, have a bunch of beers—I tell my students, don't go to that bar, take a walk in the park.

"We have the best crane operators in the country. We have operators go from this local to the manufacturers to test equipment. We're the best in the world except for Swedish women—they don't have no ego. Women don't have egos like men do. I've been to Sweden. I've been to Manila, London and Holland.

"I worked in an industrial plant when I was young— you had to go in and out of a gate. I couldn't stand it. Here, you think about it all the time, you look forward to getting to work. You're brushing your teeth and thinking about how that lid is like a concrete bucket. Then you get to the site and that first load of concrete tells you how your day is going to be. The book says that pouring 35 to 40 yards an hour is acceptable, but acceptable to me is 50 to 60 yards an hour and I try

An operator may put in 12 tense, solitary hours a day, swinging his crane "until it's a song in your head."

Photographs by Robert Noonan

Secrets of still waters

Although it may seem placid on the surface,
a freshwater pond seethes with small creatures
that compete fiercely for food and survival

Deceptively tranquil in appearance, a roadside pond
in Harford County, Maryland, teems with activity.

With a practiced and serpentine motion of his
wrist, Robert Noonan scoops a kitchen strainer
through the aquatic vegetation and lifts it up, dripping with fronds of carnivorous *Utricularia.* He empties the strainer into a Tupperware tray. Against the
white background, things begin to move among the
Utricularia plants: darting copepods; fire-red, pin-
head-size aquatic mites; a diving beetle that caroms
about like a demented Pac-Man; a delicate damselfly

In the pond, insect predators often kill vertebrate
animals. Here a one-inch water bug attacks a tadpole.

larva with feathery tracheal gills at the end of its abdomen; a squat, pugnacious-looking dragonfly nymph;
an inch-long predacious water bug—a male whose back
is encrusted with eggs his mate has cemented there,
leaving him a perambulating nursery.

Behind us, a few yards away, 18-wheelers thunder
past on a four-lane highway. At our feet lies a submerged automobile tire. Beer cans and plastic six-pack
holders are strewn among the lily pads. Noonan pokes
at his tray. He says: "You couldn't ever dream up creations like these."

Noonan has been photographing this little pond
north of Baltimore, and a couple of others nearby—one
of them backed up against the fill dirt of a Burger King

parking lot—for more than a year. He makes most of his pictures at the pond; sometimes he takes home small creatures to photograph them in an aquarium, and when their portraits have been made he returns them to the pond alive. "You have an obligation to them," he says.

The day with Noonan is an exercise in nostalgia. My pond was in northern Ohio, a half mile through the woods from the house where I grew up. To an adolescent daffily preoccupied with natural history, the pond was jungle and veldt, tundra, mountain and sea. I read stories about Paul Siple, the Eagle Scout who went to the Antarctic with Byrd, and about the young Craighead brothers who flew falcons with Indian princes, and I was painfully aware that they had set off on their adventures when they were not that much older than I was. At 13, in Euclid, Ohio, and with no such prospects, the pond was the best I could do. I marched there in hip boots, armed with a net made of a broom handle and an old cotton curtain; a peck basket full of Mason jars for live specimens; a killing bottle charged with Carbona cleaning fluid; a pair of long-nosed forceps my aunt, a nurse, had liberated from the Cleveland clinic; a collecting bag (for which read old pillow slip) in case I encountered a good snake; and a copy of Ann Haven Morgan's *Field Book of Ponds and Streams*. I slogged back to the house and my perplexed parents after dark —muddy, happy, tired and smelling of pond.

What took me there is what brings Noonan here. The richness and density of life, the accelerated pace of procreation and death, the compression of nature into a close-at-hand microcosm, the ingenious and infinite variety of adaptation. The dragonfly nymph, a sedentary, gill-breathing, aquatic lump, captures hundreds of mosquito larvae each day with thrusts of a lower lip that fires like a missile; on an afternoon in late spring it transforms into a glistening aerialist that uses huge multifaceted eyes to home in on adult mosquitoes, and scoops them up in a lethal basket formed by its legs. There are creatures here that breathe through gills on their limbs, that breathe through snorkel tubes attached to their abdomens; others, like scuba divers, carry their own air supplies beneath the surface. There are creatures with oar-shaped legs that propel them like single sculls beneath the surface; others with legs like delicate stilts on which they skate along supported only by the water's surface tension.

Consider scale. After an hour of prowling the borders of the pond and peering into Noonan's strainer at tiny insects and crustaceans, I see, hovering near an area of bottom that has been swept clean of debris, a fish—a bluegill patrolling its nest site. "Look at the big fish," I say, and realize as I say it that the bluegill is in fact only six inches long. It seems large only to my scaled-down consciousness of the moment. How awesome the bluegill must appear to the damselfly nymph. Were we on the scale of the creatures of the pond, we would be hopelessly vulnerable to their speed and strength and armor and weapons.

A small freshwater pond is sleepy-looking, in repose, but beneath the tranquil surface it is an almost unimaginably violent place, the lair of biting, rending, piercing, sucking, stinging little gangsters who spend their days and nights wreaking havoc on their neighbors. But violence fascinates, whether it be in the tragedies of Elizabethan dramatists or in the pond's voracious competition. As a boy I would sit before my aquaria transfixed by scenes of thuggery as the creatures of my day's catch went about murdering one another. My parents found my preoccupation with this mayhem disturbing, as well they might were it the only thing that drew me to the pond, but it was not.

There were also: the flash of a redwing's epaulets among young cattails; the golden burst of a prothonotary warbler among the branches of an overarching beech; the sartorial elegance of a ribbon snake; the stately curiosity of a dragonfly as it looked me over, eyeball to eyeball; the chorus of tiny frogs whose throats ballooned with springtime ardor until the throats seemed larger than the frogs themselves; the intricate patterns traced on smooth black water by fast flotillas of whirligigs; the evanescent beauty of a fairy shrimp, the clockwork of its body revealed through an abdomen transparent as glass. No trips with Byrd or falconry with princes—but I could have done worse.

Well, the little ponds along the Northeast corridor are going fast, Noonan tells me, eaten by landfill, disappearing beneath the highways and subdivisions and shopping centers. My own pond in Ohio went down that road long ago. Rivers and lakes and mountains and forests have their bands of organized, purposeful defenders, with lobbyists in Washington and professional fund-raising campaigns. But who mourns the loss of a stagnant one-acre pond with beer cans blooming among the water lilies? Noonan does, anyway.

He lifts his strainer again, pokes at it. "Long-jawed spider," he says. Pale, fragile-looking, perhaps half an inch long, it is not really aquatic but a builder of exquisite webs at the water's edge. Gently, Noonan lifts the spider on a piece of flotsam, transfers it to a plant stem above the water. The spider elongates itself, legs aligned with its body so that it becomes almost invisible, a slender mote of detritus.

Noonan observes the spider for a moment. "You could spend your entire life here," he says. "And still know nothing of what there is to know."
Don Moser

A moth, adult form of an aquatic caterpillar, rests on *Salvinia*, a plant native mostly to the tropics and subtropics. Plant may have been introduced through aquarium dumping or on the feet of waterfowl.

The voracious nymph of a dragonfly lies in ambush
as an unsuspecting mosquito larva wriggles nearer . . .

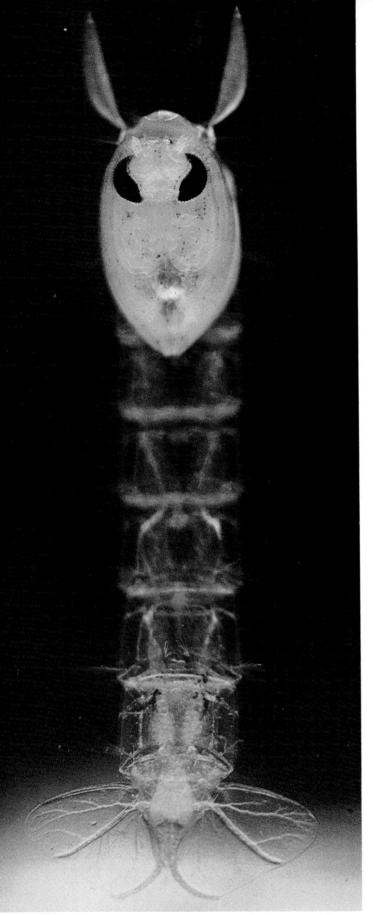

Enlarged 28 times, ghostly pupa of phantom midge
is intermediate form between the larva and the adult.

Fierce water tiger, larval stage of a diving beetle,
sucks bodily juices of its prey through curved jaws.

... and when the larva comes within range the dragonfly snares it with a quick thrust of its lip.

In a rite of spring at the pond, two crane flies, joined abdomen to abdomen, mate on cattail stem.

A hydra, a tiny freshwater polyp, feeds on an insect larva it has subdued with stinging tentacles.

Dwelling upside down in a submarine world, the backswimmer uses oarlike legs for rapid propulsion.

Though it appears the essence of fragility, larva
of a phantom midge is nevertheless a fierce predator.

An emerging adult midge struggles in the surface
film as it forsakes aquatic existence for an aerial one.

After creeping from the water and casting off its nymphal husk (right), dragonfly dries its four brand-new wings in the sunshine.

By Richard Wolkomir

By the atarnal, Yankee Jonathan!

*He was America's first national symbol;
though he could cheat the paint off a wagon,
he left an indelible mark on Uncle Sam*

Wherever the old-time peddler traveled, he could scare up customers for his New England wares.

Even before the Republic was born, the New Englander was regarded as a special type by everyone else. William Beekman, a businessman in colonial Manhattan, complained: "Seven-eighths of the people I have credited in New England have proved to be such damned, ungrateful, cheating fellows that I am now almost afraid to trust any man in Connecticut. . . ." And Stephan Collins, a Philadelphian of the same era, called Boston merchants "deceitful, canting, Presbyterian deacons."

Just after the Revolution, John Bernard, a famed English comedian, toured the States and noted that the New England peddler "is regarded by the Southern trader in the light of a visitation; he may be truly said to have Yankee-phobia, and to look upon a 'Connecticut chap' as a commercial Scythian, a Tartar of the North whose sole business in life is to make inroads upon his peace and profit. He ranks him in the list of plagues next to the yellow fever, and before locusts, taxation, and a wet spring; indeed, some go so far as to suppose that a shower of Yankees was the crowning pestilence which made Pharaoh give up the Israelites."

The Yankee was the United States' first regional stereotype. The Dutch of New Netherland might have claimed that distinction, but by 1800 they were mostly absorbed. An Englishman observed that Americans had no regional dialects, "except it be the New Englanders, who have a sort of whining cadence."

As the first uniquely American personality, the Yankee was as fascinating to the former Colonies as a first baby is to newlyweds. Like new parents, Americans couldn't resist telling and retelling stories about him, exaggerating a bit more each time.

All enduring myths have real roots. Forced to exert mind and body just to keep alive during subzero winters, early New Englanders on their stony farms had to be resourceful and energetic. And, while nature in New England was stingy with warmth and rich soil, she was generous with waterpower. Soon the old Puritan formula of a town built around a church had become in many places a town built around a factory.

Thus, while the South developed an agricultural society with a landed aristocracy resembling Europe's, New England was speaking its own lingo, producing everything from razors to clocks and carts and looking southward with interest, for there lay an inviting market. Only sketchy paths connected early America's handful of raw settlements, and so the natural way to move goods through the countryside was on foot. For men with long legs, there was money to be made.

All over New England, in Hartford, Worcester, Newport, Rutland, Hanover and a hundred other towns, enterprising young men shouldered great packs filled with combs and buttons, jewelry, needles, knives, and razors—"Yankee notions"—and started walking. They were unusual, these peddlers. Most of them were

Richard Wolkomir, who lives in Calais Stage, Vermont, wrote most recently for Smithsonian *on running shoes in September 1989.*

As a peddler, Brother Jonathan was a real buster. It was said he could sell warming pans in Jamaica, iceboxes in Quebec, a whole family of foxes to a chicken farmer and seven lean years to a pharaoh.

a kind of super Yankee. For one thing, the hike from Penobscot Bay to Savanna, Georgia, say, is no Sunday stroll, especially with a bulging pack. There probably never was a fat peddler. They were rangy and lean. They were also self-contained, used to days of lonely hiking between backwoods settlements. A stranger wherever he went, the peddler learned to trust only his own wits. And, of course, he was either going to be a sharp businessman, selling and swapping advantageously, or he was going to be hungry. Few starved.

Was the Yankee dishonest? Thomas Hamilton, an Englishman who toured the United States in 1833, leaves little doubt: "The whole race of Yankee peddlers in particular are proverbial for dishonesty. They go forth annually in the thousands to lie, cog, cheat, swindle, in short, to get possession of their neighbor's property in any manner it can be done with impunity. Their ingenuity in deception is confessedly very great. They warrant broken watches to be the best timekeep-

ers in the world; sell pinchbeck trinkets for gold; and always have a large assortment of wooden nutmegs and stagnant barometers."

However, in those days business morality was sketchy everywhere, the scandalous "purchase" of Indian lands for a few beads being one example. Thousands of bales of American cotton once lay unbought on the wharves in Liverpool because the South's planters had tried to fatten them with pebbles and sand. Probably the Yankee was no worse. But apparently he was sharper. People tried to fool him and failed. Stories arose about these crafty Yankees—so many stories, so incredible that soon the Yankee peddler was as mythological as an elf. Long-backed and thin, they said he was, "lank as a leafless elm." He always dressed in butternut brown. No door could be locked against him and, once he was in the house, silver leaped into his pocket of its own accord.

He is said to have sold warming pans in the West

Drawings by Arnold Roth

171

The strange career of Yankee Jonathan

Indies and white paper hats in Canada—but there was no market because of the cholera, and so he ground up his hats in a mortar and made them into pills. He traveled alone, didn't talk politics, drink or gamble. When he had finished bartering, he became as wooden as the dishes in his pack. Yet he was proud and prickly, capable of tart rejoinders.

"Down East," said a Southerner to a peddler, "a cow and a calf and a calico frock is said to be a girl's portion, and that's the place you come from."

"Well," said the Yankee, "and you're from that place, ain't you, where a potato patch has cracks in it so wide the grasshoppers can't jump over, and that's the portion of the eldest son? My father told me that he was drivin' by one of your great farms, observin' the wretchedness of the land, and he said, 'the fellow that owns this must be plaguey poor.' 'Not so poor as you think,' said somebody from the blackberry bushes, 'for I don't own but a third on't. My father give away one third to a man to take t'other!'"

No one could best a peddler. Rip Van Winkle's shrewish wife died when "she broke a blood vessel in a fit of passion at a New England peddler." People chuckled over how the Down East sea captain had outwitted the London dandies, and over the way a Yankee always answered a question with another question, and over the Yankee's genius for practical jokes.

British troops during the Revolution had used the word "Yankee" as a mocking epithet for New England colonials. The New Englanders, in turn, began calling themselves Yankees, and proudly. When a British officer composed the sarcastic lyrics for "Yankee Doodle," the New Englanders promptly adopted that too. During the Civil War it was banned in South Carolina.

Up until that time, though, the Yankee was an important figure to Americans in all parts of the young country, because the new United States had no cul-

tural identity, no personality. Americans had always thought of themselves as British, but after the Revolution Englishmen pilloried them as tobacco-chewing barbarians who lived in ugly towns devoid of all but the rudiments of civilization. Democracy produced nothing but rude boors, who were dishonest besides—witness the Yankee peddler!

With little history and no national identity to fall back upon, Americans were stung. "Why are we so exquisitely alive to the aspersions of England?" Washington Irving wondered. He put it mildly. As late as 1848 some British actors who had criticized American manners sparked the Astor Place Riot. Naming the three most notorious book-writing British tourists, actress Fanny Kemble warned: "I would not advise either Mrs. Trollope, Basil Hall or Captain Hamilton ever to set their feet upon this ground again, unless they are ambitious of being stoned to death."

As they had done with the mocking "Yankee Doodle," Americans now made the Yankee himself into a national symbol, like England's John Bull. The first step came in 1787, with the production of a play called

When Jonathan wasn't peddling, he was whittling.
"The Yankee boy, before he's sent to school

The Contrast, the first native comedy to be professionally produced. The author was Royall Tyler, a Boston-born, Harvard-educated lawyer who had lived in Portland, Maine, where he must have carefully observed rural New Englanders.

Tyler's plot was allegorical: An American father has engaged his daughter to a hypocritical British rake, although the girl yearns to marry a patriotic American, Colonel Manly. By the story's end the British dandy has been exposed as a plotting blackguard and Colonel Manly and the heroine are at last united. The presiding genius of all this intrigue is Manly's servingman, Jonathan, a Yankee.

In this early play the Yankee character is still undeveloped, and Jonathan is something of a rustic clown, full of queer phrases—"By the living jingo!" "What the rattle?" "Smite my timbers!" "Maple-log seize it!" and "Swamp it!" However, "the contrast" of the title was between an English personality, hypocritical and decadent, and the roughhewn American democrat, who far exceeds his counterpart in wit. Jonathan therefore frequently thunders with patriotic bombast—"True blue son of liberty!" or "True blue Bunker-Hill son of liberty!" or even "True-born Yankee American son of liberty!"

Tyler struck an enduring chord in the American character when he combined national pride with good-humored self-mockery. At one point in the play Jonathan says of "Yankee Doodle": "I can't sing but a hundred and ninety-nine verses; our Tabitha at home can sing it all." Audiences chuckled and applauded.

After *The Contrast* came the deluge. The public's appetite for plays about Yankees proved voracious, and playwrights seemed to materialize from the air. Their themes were invariable: the superiority of the rustic American to the urbane Englishman. Each play pivoted about a Yankee character, who seemed mild and dull but was really calculating and sharp. He might be a peddler, a sailor, a Vermont wool dealer or just a Green Mountain boy who swapped and whittled and upset calculations. Often the Yankee was a globe-trotter: Titles offered *The Yankee in Tripoli*, *The Yankee in China* and *Jonathan in England*. There were also *Bumps or Yankee Magnetism* and *Sam Patch, the Yankee Jumper*. Wherever in the world he was, the Yankee's stage costume usually was the same—a white bell-crowned hat, a blue coat with long tails, red and white trousers, and high bootstraps. He was on the way to becoming Uncle Sam.

Yankee roles of George H. Hill

More important to the audience than the plot was the ability of the actor who played the Yankee. Thespians like Charles Mathews, James H. Hackett, Danforth Marble and Joshua Silsbee helped form the nation's idea of Yankee character. Greatest of them all was George Handel Hill, Boston-born scion of a Rutland, Vermont, family. In Hill, Yankee myth and reality were united, for he himself was one. As esteemed in his native New England as in New York or London, Hill was often invited to "come down our way and give a show." Once a Maine farmer was irked because he thought Hill had not come and that the Yankee part was being played by one of his own neighbors. It turned out to be Hill after all.

Hill's New Englander was quiet and low-voiced, a mild man who whittled while he talked. Alone on the stage, Hill could create a gaggle of awkward young Yankees at militia training, a New England family at home, or a lecturer excessively satisfying the New England thirst for abstruse discussion. He sprinkled his monologues with vivid expressions: "strong as whitleather," "coming on full chisel," or "so thin you could pitch him clean *through* a flute."

In the late 1820s, while the Yankee theater was in full swing, a native of Maine named Seba Smith intro-

Well knows the mystery of that magic tool,
The pocket knife," wrote poet John Pierpont.

duced America to a literary creation named Colonel Jack Downing, who would keep readers laughing for 20 years. The first of the "Downing Papers" appeared in a Portland newspaper. It was in the form of a letter from young Jack Downing to the folks back home in Downingville, Maine. Jack had come to Portland to sell some ax handles and cheese, but he wasn't especially successful. However, after exhibiting his watch in a tavern, a man stepped up and offered to trade: "Says he, I'll give you my watch and five dollars. Says I, it's done! He gave me five dollars and I gave him my watch. Now, says I, give me *your* watch—and says he, with a loud laugh, I han't got none—and that kinda turned the laugh on me. Thinks I, let them laugh that lose. Soon as the laugh was well over, the feller thought he'd try the watch to his ear—Why, says he, it don't go—No, says I, not without it's carried."

Jack had ambitions, for he hoped to make "them 'ere chaps that have been asneering at me here stare at me like an owl in a thunderstorm." Before long, he was comfortably settled in Washington as President Andrew Jackson's personal adviser. Thus, as Seba Smith drew him, the Yankee became the sly oracle.

Jack Downing was the President's friend, and that relationship was humanly drawn with folksy monologue, but underneath ran an acid criticism of Jacksonian democracy. In his letters (addressed to Uncle Joshua, Aunt Nabby, or "To my old friend, the Editor of the *Portland Courier,* in the Mariners' Church Building, second story, eastern end, Fore Street, away Down East in the State of Maine") Downing dryly lampooned office seekers and land speculation. Later, of the Mexican War, Jack wrote, "Uncle Joshua always says, in nine cases out of ten it costs more to rob an orchard than it would to buy the apples."

Seba Smith's Downing Papers inspired scores of imitators. One, Sam Slick, the Yankee clock peddler, spent three decades hoodwinking customers, to the merriment of readers. James Russell Lowell's Hezekiah Biglow spoke in verse, as in this description of a New England courting:

> *He stood a spell on one foot fust,*
> *Then stood a spell on t'other,*
> *An' on which one he felt the wust*
> *He couldn't ha' told ye nuther.*

Lowell eventually used his Yankee poems to fight for abolition, combining the nasal twang, the iron-willed self-righteousness and the macabre humor of his Yankee heritage into a mixture so explosive it surprised even its author—"The success of my experiment soon began not only to astonish me, but to make me feel the responsibility of knowing that I held in my hand a weapon instead of the mere fencing-stick I had supposed."

In 1828 a newspaper called *The Yankee* was founded, and it overflowed with sketches from "about the middle of down east" and with serious definitions of Yankee traits. Actors from the Yankee theater, and scholars, too, trekked to New England to study the phenomenon in its natural habitat. Many of them, like actor James H. Hackett, composed long lists of Yankee traits and peculiarities. David Humphreys, a playwright, prepared a glossary of Yankee lingo in 1815. "Atarnal" means eternal, he noted, while "fairce" means fierce and "Varmount" means Vermont.

Writer John Neal said: The word *Yankee* is no longer a term of reproach. It is getting to be a title of distinction." To which Seba Smith added: "So far from being a talking boor, he is on the contrary singularly wise, penetrating and observant."

The United States emerged from the post-Revolutionary period as Brother Jonathan, a gawky New England country lad whose mild countenance masked a shrewd mind. But the Yankee hailed from just six small Eastern states, and a vigorous young America was straining toward the Pacific. By 1850 a new mythical figure—the Western woodsman, a ripsnorter full of braggadocio and tall tales—had eclipsed the Yankee.

He may have stepped from the spotlight, but the Yankee has never left the stage. Serious writers from Hawthorne and Melville to Robert Frost have explored the somber Puritan strain beneath Jonathan's mild mask. Even today, our picture of the New Englander is partly rooted in the stage Yankee. Foreigners still call all Americans Yankees, and an adaptation of the red, white and blue costume Yankee Jonathan sported 170 years ago is still worn by Uncle Sam.

Yankee verity: oft-proved by firm injunctions to heaven to strike him dead if. . . .

By Jim Doherty

Was he half hype or sheer hero?
Buffalo Bill takes a new bow

'The Last of the Great Scouts' is back again in a road show complete with film, posters, paintings, costumes, guns—even a stuffed bison

There's a terrific cowboy-and-Indian show playing around the country these days. The star, a husky, goateed fellow on horseback, wears a fancy buckskin jacket, shiny thigh-high boots and a white Stetson. When he's not shooting glass balls out of the air or rescuing pioneer women from Indians, he is busy attending to urgent matters backstage. He turns up in posters and playbills, in photographs and oil paintings, and even in a brief film where the public can see him announcing the show's other acts. "Ladies and gentlemen," he proclaims, doffing his hat with a courtly flourish, "permit me to introduce to you a Congress of Rough Riders of the World!"

If that sounds a tad old-fashioned, there is good reason. The stalwart showman is none other than that celebrated ex-Pony Express rider, buffalo hunter and Indian fighter without peer, Col. William Frederick Cody himself. It's Buffalo Bill!

For more than three decades around the turn of the century, "Buffalo Bill" Cody toured the country with his fabulous Wild West show, dramatizing the legendary American frontier even as the real one faded into history. Today "the last of the great scouts," as he liked to bill himself, is back in the saddle again. And, once again, he is surrounded by some of his favorite troupers from the good old days: sharpshooting Annie Oakley, cowboy star Buck Taylor, Indian chiefs Red Shirt and Iron Tail, and of course the great Sioux leader, Sitting Bull. This time around, though, the "show" is a bit more subdued than the original. It's a traveling, multimedia exhibition. Along with the films and artwork are costumes, a small arsenal of guns, and such memorabilia as a lock of his hair and a stuffed bison, all from the Buffalo Bill Historical Center in Cody, Wyoming, the town that William Cody helped found in 1895.

Last year, *Buffalo Bill and the Wild West*, as the exhibition is called, drew happy crowds and rave reviews at the Brooklyn Museum in New York before moving on to acclaim at the Carnegie Institute's Museum of Art in Pittsburgh. Next month it is to open at the Colorado Historical Society in Denver. After pulling up stakes in May, it will migrate to California for a summer at the Oakland Museum.

It is no surprise that Buffalo Bill is still packing them in. He always did. He was arguably the most famous personality of his time, an international superstar adored by the masses everywhere and feted by royalty in the capitals of Europe. (His wife, not known for her sense of humor, named Queen Victoria as cor-

Backed by braves, a buckskinned Bill salutes an evening audience in this Frederic Remington oil.

respondent in a divorce proceeding in 1905; the judge ruled the charge "preposterous.") President Theodore Roosevelt, no slouch himself at the manly arts, was one of Bill's bulliest fans. Cody was often called "the greatest showman the world has ever known."

Circuses and other barnstorming shows flourished during the 1890s, but Buffalo Bill's Western extravaganza, a forerunner of the modern rodeo and movie horse opera, was in a class by itself. Cody, however, was more than a shrewd impresario. "He was America's first media hero," says David H. Katzive, who put the current exhibition together with money from Philip Morris, Inc. and the Seven-Up Company. The irrepressible plainsman became a matinee idol on the stage. He was featured in some 3,000 dime novels and several of his ghostwritten "autobiographies" were best-sellers. In his later years he even directed a series of short films about Indian life and history, which included the Battle of Wounded Knee.

Again and again in the Wild West show, he reenacted (with some improvements) his own youthful exploits. Wherever the show played he was front-page news in the local papers—thanks to his PR man and crony, John M. Burke. He appeared in advertisements for Winchester rifles, Stetsons, Chancellor cigars and Old Crow bourbon. Says Katzive, director of the DeCordova and Dana Museum and Park in Lincoln, Massachusetts: "When it comes to self-promotion, today's showbiz celebrities just aren't in the same league."

Ironically, however, Cody's reputation has suffered in this skeptical age, partly because he was such a master of hype, partly because American attitudes toward buffalo hunters and Indian fighters have lately done an abrupt about-face. In academic circles especially, people either tend to disbelieve what they hear about the old scout's exploits, or to deplore what he was up to. Buffalo Bill the hero, it is charged, was a figment of his press agent's imagination. The intrepid

Hell-for-leather poster presents Bill pulverizing glass balls with a rifle, as he rides at full gallop.

cavalry scout was really a bloody-minded hunter and Indian hater as well as an incompetent businessman, a vain imposter, a drunk and a skirt-chaser. In Robert Altman's controversial 1976 film, *Buffalo Bill and the Indians,* the Native Americans have all the humanity and wisdom. Bill Cody, as played by Paul Newman, is a blustering hypocrite, cynically exploiting the Indians in his show. Novelist and critic Leslie Fiedler, Samuel Clemens Professor of English at the State University of New York, has suggested that Cody, like many of his contemporaries, was an instinctive champion of white supremacy whose views today might be suitable to folks clad in the sheets of the Ku Klux Klan.

Cody biographer Don Russell, and other historians of the Old West, beg to differ. Bill, they insist, is an authentic American hero. His accomplishments were real. "The man and the myth," reflects Paul Fees, curator of the Buffalo Bill Museum at the Historical Center, "were largely one and the same." Without any question, Cody was a skilled rifleman, a superb horseman, a courageous scout and an indefatigable Pony Express rider. He was also very much a man of his times, a rugged individualist fairly brimming over with grit, pluck and, yes, bluster.

In many ways, William Cody was also a complex, not to say contrary, fellow. Just over six feet tall and weighing 200 pounds, he often indulged a boyish appetite for fun and games. He would behave like a prima donna one moment and an easy-going "good ole boy" the next. His sentimental streak was as wide as his outsize belt buckle, yet he also demonstrated an entrepreneur's cold eye and driving ambition.

Chauvinsim and pure pigheadedness

Cody was even more contradictory when it came to some of the most important issues of his day. Buffalo Bill, that heralded Indian fighter, could sometimes be an eloquent champion of the Indian's cause. Time and again he insisted: "Every Indian outbreak that I have ever known has resulted from broken promises, and treaties broken by the government." Bill's rocky marriage was largely the result of his traveling habits and pure pigheadedness. For his part, at the divorce hearing, he accused his wife of serving his guests while "wearing a dirty wrapper." Yet this chauvinistic husband was, as an employer, a staunch advocate of women's rights. "If a woman can do the same work that a man can do and do it just as well," he averred, "she should have the same pay." Even more incongruously, William Cody the mighty hunter evolved into a pioneering conservationist who helped rescue from extinction the last few herds of buffalo in the West.

Historically, Cody was a transitional figure who changed with times that were changing with breath-

In action, near the end of his career, the real Bill stirs audience by stampeding buffalo with blank cartridges.

Between performances, the elegant entrepreneur relaxes in tent. Road show netted $1 million a year.

taking speed. He was born three years before the California Gold Rush; he died the year the United States entered World War I. His lifetime encompassed the Civil War, the last pioneer thrust Westward, wagon trains, cattle drives, Indian wars, the building of the great Western railroads and the burgeoning of the region's sprawling new cities. It was a time that saw the perfection of the telegraph, telephone and light bulb, of the automobile, airplane and machine gun. Not to mention Joseph Glidden's barbed wire, an 1874 invention that did as much as anything to close down the Old West for good.

By 1890, with the frontier all but gone, Bill began catering to the Eastern public's instant nostalgia for an Old West they had never known. At the same time, he did his best to get in on the ground floor of the new West, investing heavily in land and mining. "He symbolized the past to millions of people but he really wasn't much interested in it himself," says Fees. "Basically, he was a developer."

His father, a restless farmer and Kansas "free stater," died in 1857, leaving the family penniless. Will, the fourth of eight children, was just a boy, but he soon got a job as a wagon-train messenger with a Western freight company. He was only 11 when he was required to sign an employee pledge: "I agree not to use profane language, not to get drunk, not to gamble, not to treat animals cruelly and not to do anything else that is incompatible with the conduct of a gentleman." Cody never did swear much; he favored such mild expressions as "Thunderation!", "By jiminy!" and "You can bet your boots and socks!" As for the rest of that pledge, he ran with a pretty rough crowd and could

A member of Smithsonian's *Board of Editors, Jim Doherty writes frequently for these pages.*

hardly have been expected to behave much better than the company he kept.

He hung around frontier cavalry posts with bullwhackers from the wagon train and delighted in showing off his riding, roping and shooting skills. As a Pony Express rider, at age 15, he set the record for the third longest leg in company history—321 miles in less than 22 hours. He was befriended by gunfighter "Wild Bill" Hickok (the two Bills eventually did a stage number together). Cody is supposed to have killed his first Indian during a night raid on a cattle drive in Nebraska.

During the Civil War, he served 19 months with the Seventh Kansas Cavalry. Afterwards he married a pretty, citified St. Louis girl named Louisa Frederici, who, it turned out, disliked show business and hated the West as much as Bill hated staying home. He had an unhappy fling at running a hotel, served briefly as a scout with George Armstrong Custer (well before the Little Big Horn), then went to work as a hunter supplying meat for the Kansas Pacific Railroad. Riding his Indian horse Brigham (half-jokingly named for the Mormon prophet), in eight months he killed more than 4,000 buffalo with a .50-caliber Springfield rifle lethal enough to be called Lucrezia Borgia.

Derring-do with the 'Dandy Fifth'

By 1868, Cody was known throughout the West as Buffalo Bill. General Phil Sheridan took him on as chief of scouts for the Fifth Cavalry, the "Dandy Fifth." The cavalry had been sent out to protect the wagon trains of Westbound emigrants, and Cody's job was important. He served with distinction until 1872, chasing horse thieves, keeping watch on Indian bands and participating in 14 more or less hair-raising engagements. It was not all blood and thunder, though. In later years the resourceful scout liked to tell the story of a solitary ride through Indian territory, when he was outfoxed by his mount, an old Army mule that somehow got away from him when he carelessly dismounted, failing to wrap the reins around his wrist. For miles, sweat pouring down his face, Cody chased after the animal. Finally, he caught up with it. "Now, Mr. Mule, it's *my* turn," he announced, and, raising his rifle to his shoulder, shot the critter dead.

In the summer of 1869, he helped a regiment of troopers in a fight with a band of Cheyennes near Summit Springs, Colorado. As the Fifth swooped down on the Indians, killing 52 of them and rescuing a captive white woman, Cody shot and killed the famous chief Tall Bull. In due course, a reenactment of Cody's exploit in the battle became a dramatic feature in the Wild West show.

After Cody visited New York City for the first time in 1872, his life took a theatrical turn. Journalistic ac-

Soulful Buck Taylor, billed as "King of the Cowboys" in Cody's show, was the hero of many a dime novel.

Sitting Bull briefly joined his friend Cody in 1884 for $50 a week and the right to sell photos of himself.

Native Americans abroad, on *Wild West*'s 1890 tour, braved waters of the Grand Canal in a Venetian canoe.

Ohio farm girl Annie Oakley, who opened the show for 17 years, demonstrates mirror marksmanship.

"Pawnee Bill" (Major Gordon Lillie) served as Indian translator and partner during 1910 "farewell" tour.

With life at stake in 1944 film, Bill (Joel McCrea) is tied up by Chief Yellow Hand (Anthony Quinn).

A courtly Bill (Louis Calhern) bows with Howard Keel and Betty Hutton in film *Annie Get Your Gun.*

counts of his heroic deeds had preceded him and the first of the dime novels written by Ned Buntline, Prentiss Ingraham and at least 18 other scribblers were selling well. Buffalo Bill was lionized by August Belmont, the banker-diplomat, and *New York Herald* editor James Gordon Bennett jr. (SMITHSONAIN, November 1978), but what impressed him most was seeing himself portrayed on the stage. A few months later he took to the boards himself. Playing the lead in a noisy Buntline potboiler called *The Scouts of the Prairie*, he was an instant hit.

For the next decade, Cody worked part of the year as a scout and hunting guide throughout the West. Then, cashing in on his soaring reputation, he played in Western melodramas such as *The Red Right Hand; or, Buffalo Bill's First Scalp for Custer.* The proceeds helped him buy a fancy ranch in North Platte, Nebraska; it was the first of several. There, in the summer of 1882, the townsfolk asked Cody to organize a big Fourth of July celebration. Cody had long entertained the idea of producing a pageant combining dramatizations of his frontier adventures with demonstrations of cowboy skills. The local celebration gave him a chance to try out his idea with a willing cast of hundreds. Called the "Old Glory Blowout," it proved such a success in North Platte that Cody was convinced it would go over big back East. The first performance of *The Wild West* took place in Omaha in May, 1883—100 years ago.

Bill and his astute business partner, Nate Salsbury, needed a while to work the bugs out of the show. On the road, the logistics were horrendous. Three long trains were eventually required to transport 400 horses, plus steers, buffalo, 640 cowboys, Indians, Rough Riders, musicians and technicians. It was hard to keep such an army supplied with food and gunpowder. Horses kept stampeding. Train accidents and bad weather added to the difficulties. But, over the years, the show thrilled 50 million people in a thousand cities and a dozen foreign countries, and it netted as much as a million dollars a season.

Cody's theatrical sense was superb. He knew how to get a crowd on its feet and spared no expense or effort to keep it there. A report in the *Hartford* (Connecticut) *Courant* described a performance: "Thunder of hoofs, clank of spurs, rattle of pistols, glint of shattered glass balls, odor of gunpowder and cattle made it authentic. It began with a pony bareback riding race between Indians and went on to a climax with a grand realistic battle scene depicting the capture, torture and death of a scout by savages; the revenge, recapture of the dead body, and victory of the government scouts. Cowboys rode bucking broncos, roped and tied Texas steers . . . The pony express rider dashed in, changed . . . to a fresh mount and dashed off again. The startling, soul-stirring attack on the Deadwood mail coach ended in a rescue by Buffalo Bill. . . ."

Cody insisted on at least the illusion of authenticity. He never permitted his *Wild West* to be called a "show." It was billed as "the all genuine educational exhibition of the American West." In the program, Sioux Indians might be described as Arapahos or Crows, but their presence underscored the show's claim to be "the real thing." Cody's vaunted Rough

Riders of the World were actual cavalrymen from France, Germany and even Russia. The wagons used to illustrate "a prairie emigrant train crossing the plains" were genuine Conestogas. The mail coach captured by the Indians was billed as "the original old Deadwood stage" built in Concord, New Hampshire, and used for years on the run from Deadwood, South Dakota, to Cheyenne, Wyoming. For a "buffalo hunt" conducted by Cody and the Indians, firing blanks, nothing would do but to have a real herd of the shaggy creatures to pursue.

Cody lived like a king. He wore only the finest clothes. He bought another scenic mountain ranch on the south fork of the Shoshone River and a rustic hunting lodge farther north called Pahaska (for his Indian name, Longhair) Tepee. In the off-season, he caroused with cronies but took time to found his namesake, the town of Cody, where in 1902 he put up a hotel named the Irma, after his youngest daughter.

If those were the best days, they were not altogether carefree. Cody was increasingly estranged from his wife, Lulu, as he called her. She did not like his friends, his drinking, his flashy clothes, or his vagabond ways, and she made her disapproval plain. Cody fretted about her a good deal, and finally tried to get rid of her in 1905. But, after a bitter hearing, the judge refused to grant a divorce.

Bill worried about money, too, for he spent or gave away most of what he earned. Even before Salsbury died in 1902, he was overwhelmed by work and by ill health. "I can't stand so much as I used to," he wrote his sister Julia. "Now as we are getting old we must not kick at our breaking down, it can't be helped, but I don't want to break down until I get out of debt and ahead of the hounds . . . enough to take it easy."

Cody never achieved his goal. Without Salsbury's business genius, he went into a financial spin. Toward the end, he was so overextended that he was unable to borrow a mere $33,000 to keep The *Wild West* afloat. His mining interests and other investments did not pay off either. Even the Irma proved a money loser. Rather than face bankruptcy, Cody assayed several comebacks. Paunchy, wearing a wig and suffering from a variety of painful ailments, he was barely able to sit in the saddle. Somehow, though, he managed to gallop around the arena and shoot glass balls out of the air, albeit with a little trickery—his rifle shells were filled with bird shot. In January 1917, William Cody died in Denver at the home of another sister, May Cody Decker. He was one month short of his 71st birthday. The *Denver Post* attributed his death to kidney failure and nervous collapse, complicated by, of all things, a "moon eclipse." Cody wanted to be buried in Wyoming but Lulu had him interred in Colorado, atop Denver's Lookout Mountain. A gaudy funeral, arranged by a young journalist named Gene Fowler, was attended by 25,000 mourners.

Cody's legend took on new luster after he died, mainly thanks to Hollywood. He had appeared in only ten films, all silent, but over the years the character of Buffalo Bill was to be featured in 35 others. These ranged from John Ford's 1924 classic *The Iron Horse*,

Charlton Heston played a swaggering Bill in the 1953 production of *Pony Express*.

As a cruel showman in Robert Altman's version, Paul Newman reenacts killing of an Indian chief.

and the popular 1950 musical *Annie Get Your Gun*, to a 1970s Italian spoof entitled *Don't Touch the White Woman.* The roster of actors who have played Bill reads like a *Who's Who* of Western stars—among them Tim McCoy, Roy Rogers, Joel McCrea, Richard Arlen and Charlton Heston.

On the screen, Buffalo Bill usually comes off as a simple-minded, sentimental fellow. In William Wellman's *Buffalo Bill*, for example, Joel McCrea ap-

Mourning the death of a hero and the Wild West, a boy weeps in a *Boston Record* cartoon, January 15, 1917.

pears in the farewell scene riding a white horse and wearing a white hat and buckskins. Speaking to the hushed crowd, he intones, "Now the time has come to say . . . goodbye. Hand in hand, my wife and I are returning to our home in the West . . . to the sunset . . . And so my little comrades up in the gallery and you grownups who used to sit there . . . goodbye. God bless you." Then from far up in the peanut gallery chirps a youngster's shrill voice: "And God bless *you*, too, Buffalo Bill!" Cody would have loved it.

Buffalo Bill lost a fortune gambling on Wyoming's future, yet his visions of prosperity for the region he called home all came true. Today, around Cody, oil wells are pumping and ranches irrigated by water from the Buffalo Bill Reservoir are thriving. Each year, more than three million tourists visit nearby Yellowstone National Park. The town has become a prosperous community of some 7,000 residents who strive mightily to keep their founding father's legend alive. Nothing signifies that commitment more dramatically than the huge equestrian bronze of William Cody, sculpted by Gertrude Vanderbilt Whitney, outside the Buffalo Bill Historical Center which also houses three other separate collections of Western art and artifacts.

As for Cody's other principal landmark, the Irma Hotel, these days it is doing a lively business. Occasionally, Buffalo Bill's grandson, Fred Garlow, stops in for dinner or a cup of coffee. Known locally as "the best hunting guide in northern Wyoming," the chatty 72-year-old can remember slicing up apples for "Grandad" when he was feeling poorly. Another Cody resident, 82-year-old Francis Hayden, used to deliver the newspaper to Buffalo Bill whenever he stayed at the Irma. "He was such a restless man I never knew where I would find him," recalls Hayden, whose father, a surveyor, laid out the town. "Sometimes he was in his office back by the stairway. Sometimes he was out in the bar. Sometimes he was upstairs playing cards. But he always paid me a nickel and he *always* said thanks."

Annie Oakley worked for Cody for 17 years without a contract. She sized him up this way: "He was the kindest, simplest, most loyal man I ever knew."

"What more," Don Russell wonders, "could possibly be asked of a hero?" Hero or not, the old plainsman's charms are hard to resist, as anyone who sees the new show can testify. Like his traveling extravaganza, William Cody was "the real thing." You can bet your boots and socks on it.

In a theatrical, yet touching, farewell portrait,
the old scout doffs his hat and gravely bows his head.

By Louis Phillips

'Yours, not sitting on a pumpkin'

January 6, 1846

Dear Mr. Trump:

Thank you for your recent letter in which you express interest in purchasing my house for the purpose of tearing it down and building a 36-story hotel and gambling casino tentatively called THE WALDEN TRUMP CARD.

May I just point out that since we last conversed on the subject I shingled the sides of my house, which were already impervious to rain, with shingles made of the first slice of the log, whose edges I was obliged to straighten.

I hope you will keep such improvements in mind when making your bid.

Cordially,   Henry David Thoreau

January 11

Dear Mr. Thoreau:

Indeed my corporation will take into consideration anything you wish. However, what does *impervious* mean?

Yours in haste,   Donald Trump

January 14

Dear Mr. Trump:

Impervious *adj*: Not to be pervious. Or to be pervious at one's whim. Forgive me for resorting to the dictionary. It is as we both know a last resort. Last Resort—would that not be a good name for one of your pleasure palaces?

The other morning I received three dispatches (brought to me by a hound, a bay horse and a turtledove) from your lawyers. Your agents have inquired about the exact cost of my house. I give details because very few are able to tell exactly what their houses cost, and fewer still, if any, the separate cost of the various materials that compose it:

Boards	$8.03½
(mostly shanty boards)	
Refuse shingles for roof and	
sides	4.00
Laths	1.25
Two secondhand windows with	
glass	2.43
One thousand old bricks	4.00
Two casks of lime	2.40
(that was high)	
Hair	0.31
(more than I needed)	
Mantle-tree iron	0.15
Nails	3.90
Hinges and screws	0.14
Latch	0.10
Chalk	0.01
Transportation	1.40
(I carried a good part on my back)	
In all	$28.12½

Yours in leisure,   Henry Thoreau

February 3

Dear Mr. Thoreau:

Happy Groundhog's Day or thereabouts. My representatives and I wish to thank you for your candor. You are correct in pointing out that the cost for the lime was high. In future, I hope you will allow me to buy it for you wholesale.

Frankly, the mention of hair left us a bit perplexed. It strikes us as unsanitary and we believe it will cause problems with local health authorities.

While I think of it, please do not carry boards upon your back. A strong back is necessary to an essayist. I will put you in touch with the Fugazy service whose stretch limousines provide a television set and private bar. Once the neighbors see you in a stretch limousine, your work will earn a new respect.

My lawyers will contact you in a few days about a preliminary bid. In the meantime I remain, Financially secure,

Donald Trump

"We have not discussed the furnishings to my dwelling. They consist of a bed, a table, a desk, three chairs, a looking glass three inches in diameter . . . three plates, one cup, one spoon, a jug for oil and a japanned lamp."

February 12

Dear Mr. Trump:

Thank you for yours of February 3d.

Your representatives have been in touch with me. I must say that your offer of $14,789,000 is quite tempting. It does represent a substantial increase over my original investment.

I should like to point out that last year I made $23.44 by selling farm produce. I also earned by day labor $13.34. I hope you will take these figures into consideration when revising your offer. Sincerely,   Henry

February 20

Dear Henry Thoreau:

You *are* a Yankee. $17,500,000 is as high as I am prepared to go. After all, even you must admit that Walden is no Monte Carlo. Sincerely,   Donald

March 1
Dear Donald:

I am not an extravagant man, and I am certain that $17,500,000 would make it possible for me to survive two or three years as a Concord gentleman. I could also publish another edition of my book, since so-called commercial publishers want no part of it.

However, we have not discussed the furnishings to my dwelling. They consist of a bed, a table, a desk, three chairs, a looking glass three inches in diameter, a pair of tongs and andirons, a kettle, a skillet and a frying-pan, a dipper, a wash-bowl, two knives and forks, three plates, one cup, one spoon, a jug for oil and a japanned lamp.
Yours, not sitting on a pumpkin,

Henry

March 8
Dear Hank:

Is there anything else we should know?
Yours (I don't sit on pumpkins either),

Don

March 15
Dear Don:

My nearest neighbor is a mile distant, and no house is visible from any place but the hill-tops within half a mile of my own. That should be worth something.
Take your time,   Hank

March 26
Dear Hank:

We'll throw in $340,000 for the furnishings and $500,000 for the view. For God's sake, man, stop being so stubborn. We would like you out by June 15 at the latest. Yours,   D.T.

May 2
Dear DT:

Your offer is most tempting, especially since last year I turned a pecuniary profit of $8.71½.

However, a lady once offered me a mat, but as I had no room to spare within the house, nor time to spare within or without to shake it, I declined it, preferring to wipe my feet on the sod before my door. It is best to avoid the beginnings of evil.
Yours,   HDT

June 1
Dear HDT:

You have delayed the construction of my proposed casino far too long. Just

"You have delayed construction of my proposed casino far too long. Just what game are you playing? It is obvious you cannot make a decent living from your writing or farming."

what game are you playing? It is obvious to everyone you cannot make a decent living from your writing or your farming. Just what trade are you in?
Yours,   Donald Trump

June 13
Dear Donald Trump:

I have as many trades as fingers.
Yours,   Henry Thoreau

June 21
Dear Mr. Thoreau:

I believe it. Sincerely,
                        Donald Trump
P.S. By any chance are you a friend of Mayor Koch? Or Mort Zuckerman?

July 1
Dear Mr. Trump:

No, I have no acquaintance of the gentlemen you mentioned. I never knew, and never shall know, a worse man than myself. Sincerely,
                    Henry David Thoreau

January 3, 1847
Dear Mr. Thoreau:

I can imagine that winters at Walden must be no picnic. My new partners and I are prepared to offer you $21,000,000 for that shanty of yours, but we must have a response within three days of your receipt of this certified letter.
Yours,   Donald Trump

January 6
Dear Mr. Trump:

After a winter night I awoke with the impression that some question had been put to me, which I had been endeavoring in vain to answer in my sleep.

I hereby decline your offer of

$21,000,000 for my cottage and acreage. You have not taken into account that I have all of Walden Pond for a well. This is valuable as it keeps butter cool.
Yours,   Henry David Thoreau

January 12
Dear Mr. Thoreau:

Please do not lecture me about the value of things. Make the new offer $22,000,000. You have three more days.
Yours,   Donald Trump and Co.

February 3
Dear Sir:

Time is but the stream I go a-fishing in. Yours,
[This letter was unsigned.]

February 7
What does that mean?
                        Trump Corporation

February 27
Dear Mr. Corporation:

I have no idea. But I thank you for your letters. To speak critically, I never received more than one or two letters in my life that were worth the postage. Your postage bills must be enormous.
Yours,   Henry D. Thoreau

[The following letter was undated and unsigned.]
$35,000,000. Is that worth the postage?

March 13
Dear Sirs:
[Alas, Thoreau's reply, written in ink, was obliterated by rain that leaked through the ceiling of his cottage. The best we can make out is that it made some mention of a japanned lamp.]

Illustrations by Brenda Losey-Sumpter

"Fanny and Rosey were both in awe of the kitchen.
Neither had ever seen anything so terrifyingly modern.

188

By Shirley Abbott

The epic tale of one noonday meal, hot and on time

How easy it sounds, but how hard it was to do, for a bride in Manhattan in 1855 with a new husband and an imposing stove

There are times, as anyone knows, when the collapse of a soufflé can be as catastrophic as the fall of Rome. And in the mid-19th century the trials of a housewife could be anguishing indeed, even with the help and counsel of Home Cookery by Mrs. J. Chadwick and Ladies' Indispensable Companion. These two historic books, which contained almost all there was to know about domestic problems—from preparing puddings to teething ("lance the gums of the child")—have just been reissued by Oxmoor House in a single volume. The following story of Fanny Van Courtlandt's hectic noon meal, a fictional yet authentic account of how things were for a hard-pressed young wife in the 1850s, has been adapted from the Introduction.

Every story needs a heroine, and imagine the heroine of this one as a bride of one month, age 20. In June 1855 she came to live in Manhattan as the wife of Charles Algernon Van Courtlandt, the ambitious new junior partner in the dry-goods importing business run by his uncle, Henry Van Courtlandt. Caroline Frances was her name, but everyone called her Fanny except her husband, who called her Mrs. Van Courtlandt. That was, after all, her proper title, and Charles took pride in his polished manners, as well as in his pretty new wife, and Fanny loved the "Mrs." Their household servant Rosey, age 16, was just off the boat from Cork. She called her new employer Mrs. Van.

Maid and mistress had laid eyes on each other for the first time when Charles and Fanny came home on their

"The room's centerpiece was a black monster unlike anything the girls had ever seen: a cast-iron cookstove."

wedding day. Rosey had been waiting for hours in the front hall, weeping from dread. Would the new lady like her? Beat her? But Mrs. Van turned out to be quite human, and almost as inexperienced as Rosey herself. Fanny had grown up on her parents' prosperous dairy farm on the Cow Neck peninsula in western Long Island. She was not accustomed to servants but, as the eldest daughter, she knew about hard work. Her mother had sometimes hired a girl, but only by days and only when she was lying-in, which was often: Fanny was one of ten. Fanny liked the outdoor work better than the cooking and sweeping. But she was a fine embroiderer and she *could* bake bread.

Charles had offered her a better situation in life than

"On the fateful morning, Fanny sat in the front parlor, more or less like the lady she knew she must be."

she had dreamed possible. His Uncle Henry, a successful importer, was about to open a fancy new carriage-trade store on Broadway, where he planned to sell fine silks from the looms of France and cottons from England. Charles and his younger cousin Samuel were to come into the firm as junior partners. And to spare the newlyweds the ignominy of living in a boardinghouse, Uncle Henry had generously advanced the money for them to set up housekeeping—provided only that they should live near the store so that Uncle Henry could dine with them daily and that Cousin Samuel could occupy their spare bedroom. Charles had fitted out the house down to the last spoon, for he wanted a home to reflect his present and future position.

Fanny and Rosey were as one in their awe of the kitchen in the basement of the Van Courtlandt town house. Neither had ever seen anything so terrifyingly modern. Rosey had learned to cook over a peat fire, out in the open, and Fanny had learned to cook on an open hearth in the ample kitchen of her parents' house. This kitchen was much smaller than her mother's; it had a fireplace of modest dimensions for the spitting and roasting of meats, but the room's centerpiece was a black monster unlike anything the girls had ever seen: a cast-iron cookstove. Attached to the back of it was a good-sized water tank with a little spigot: hot running water for all kitchen uses, so long as the fire stayed bright and you remembered to fill the tank! The cook top was like a small table with five lids, and there were two little doors on the sides for adding the firewood.

Fanny's first thought was that with such a stove you could cook standing up, rather than bending into the fireplace or stooping to pile hot coals around the Dutch ovens on the hearth, as her mother had done. A great improvement, she thought, and Charles reminded her, with some satisfaction, that the stove used half as much firewood as an open hearth and would pay for itself (it had cost him $8) within a year or so. And what seemed more miraculous than the stove was the sink on the wall with its water pump—fresh, pure water piped right into the house. According to Charles, it came from the Croton Reservoir, many miles to the north.

The table was stacked with pots and skillets

Fanny was dubious. But at least they need not draw water from a well or buy it from a street vendor. And on a worktable next to the sink was stacked an array of gleaming new kettles, pots and skillets in cast iron, britannia and tinware, and a butcher knife, muffin rings, pudding bags, a rolling pin, an apple peeler—everything the cook could want. Fanny's heart sank. Where were the hooks and cranes, the familiar brick ovens, the toasting racks of Mama's kitchen?

On the fateful morning of which we write, Fanny sat

"Yesterday they dined on Rosey's burned beefsteak and a leaden, gray pudding. But Cousin Samuel had uncomplainingly eaten every bite. 'Why don't we go to Delmonico's tomorrow?' he proposed. Henry glared."

not in her kitchen but in the front parlor, more or less like the lady she knew she must be. Lady or no lady, dinner had to be ready for the Van Courtlandt menfolks promptly at 1 o'clock. So far Fanny had done rather poorly in the dinner department. Yesterday they had dined on Rosey's burned beefsteak and a leaden, gray pudding. Uncle Henry had eaten a quantity of bread and butter, Charles had grimly swallowed the steak and rejected the pudding. Cousin Samuel had uncomplainingly eaten every bite, smiling down the table at Fanny in a provoking manner. (He was quite dark and handsome like Charles, but being only 22, had not yet decided to cultivate a mustache.) "Why don't we all go to Delmonico's tomorrow?" he proposed. Henry glared at him.

That evening Charles had spoken solemnly to Fanny

Shirley Abbott is author of Womenfolks, Growing Up Down South, *a book about the role and responsibilities of women (and ladies) in the Old South and the New.*

about the serious nature of domestic responsibility:

"You cannot leave everything, indeed anything, to Rosey, for she is stupid and untrained. You cannot expect to spend your mornings at your needlework—your happiness can only come from the proper performance of your duties. I provide you with every comfort. Surely you can, in return, provide my uncle and Cousin Samuel and me with a palatable noonday meal, served hot and on time. Need I remind you by whose generosity we acquired this house and its furnishings?"

Fanny's cheeks had burned, and the cooling tears had rolled down them (just like the tears of the heroines in *Godey's Lady's Book* fiction), but whether she was ashamed or merely angry she couldn't have said. One objection to Charles that Fanny's mother had raised was that, although he was only five-and-twenty, he was as serious as a parson.

But today she was making a new beginning. It was only 9 o'clock, and getting hot. She rolled down her stockings and propped her feet up. Charles had specified mutton soup, fish cakes, veal chops, a pudding of some description, chocolate cream for dessert, and of course bread and butter on the side. Not a complicated dinner, he pointed out, modest in comparison with the fare Uncle Henry expected at home. Surely Fanny could produce such simple, basic dishes. Leafing anxiously through her cookbooks, Fanny ignored the ominous sounds from the kitchen below. Rosey was talking to herself and banging the stove door. Had the fire gone out again? Fanny must not think of it: she must find a pudding recipe.

At eight that morning Fanny had set the mutton soup to cook, or had attempted to, while Rosey dusted the upstairs bedrooms, carried out the slops and turned the bedclothes out to air. "Take a leg of mutton weighing five or six pounds, put it in a nicely cleaned pot, and a little more than cover it with boiling water."

Plain enough, Mrs. Chadwick. Fanny had pried the heavy joint from the icebox, noticing as she did so that the pan was running over onto the floor. On her knees, with the mutton balanced on one hand, she raised the wooden flap that hid the water pan, noting that it was not only full but slimy, which explained the sour smell. The block of ice had melted away in the night, and the meat was hardly cold at all. She sniffed the mutton suspiciously. Not too bad, if she could get it cooking fast enough. She would set Rosey to cleaning the icebox, if the dusting ever got done. Dumping the mutton into a soup kettle, Fanny turned to the great black stove. Pride of the household. It was just about warm enough to melt butter.

She covered the meat with tepid water from the tank and set the heavy pot on the range top. She could see that Rosey had cleaned out the ashes, had even brushed

"Yet 'shiftless' was hardly the word for Rosey as she walked behind Fanny in the busy market, lugging heavy baskets, or scrubbed the kitchen floor, her bony fingers clutching the scrub brush like lobster claws."

down the sides of the firebox, and had laid a nice, compact little fire, which now, inexplicably, smoldered and smoked. Had the kindling been wet? Probably. And the woodbox was empty. Fanny went to the cellar and came back with an armload of wood and the phosphorous matches. These, too, were a modern convenience and a great blessing when they did not explode in your face or shower your apron with sparks. (Faced with a cold hearth in Long Island, her mother would have had to walk to the next farm for live coals.) Fanny watched long enough to see the flames rise, then returned to Mrs. Chadwick.

"Put in a bunch of carrots, four turnips, two onions, a small cup of rice, and some salt." Having come this far, Fanny discovered that Mrs. C. had wanted the vegetables boiled before the meat was added, but perhaps Mrs. C. (and Charles) wouldn't know the difference. The vegetables had to come from the cellar. Fanny descended the stairs once more, fetched the vegetables, peeled them and soon had the soup on to boil. To boil? The stove by then was almost cool enough to touch. Flinging the side door open and bending to inspect, Fanny could see no cause. Again she restacked the wood, this time with more plentiful kindling, lit the match, blew on the flames and retreated hopefully upstairs to the parlor. Why did the smell of stewing mutton and onions not fill the house?

"Rosey, what has happened to the fire?"

Again, the sound of muttering and banging. "Rosey!" Silence. Fanny went to the top of the kitchen stairs. "Rosey, what has happened to the fire? Is the soup boiling?" "Bless you, ma'am," the cheerful cry came back, "I got her going now. She'll be red-hot in no time." Rosey's thick brogue was pleasant to hear, though Charles disliked it, wishing they had an English maid instead. But everybody hired the Irish now—almost one million of them had come to America in a single decade, driven by famine at home, by desperation, by hope. Rosey earned $4 a month and her keep, and sent $1 a month home to her younger sister in Ireland who was saving for her passage.

The ladies in the neighborhood joked about their Irish hired help, called them shiftless and dirty. And it was true that unless Fanny scolded her daily, Rosey never thought to change her dirty apron, which disgusted Charles. Yet shiftless was hardly the word for Rosey as she walked behind Fanny in the busy market, lugging the heavy baskets—or pumped water into the dishpan, or scrubbed the kitchen floor, her bony fingers clutching the scrub brush like lobster claws. Fanny knew who would be scouring the floors if Charles could not afford a maid.

The smell of cooking mutton finally crept upward to

"Half-past twelve! Hearing the cry of the milk vendor, Fanny sent Rosey rushing out into the street."

the parlor floor, and Fanny went back to her books. Instead of searching for the pudding recipe, she turned to the *Ladies' Companion*, which held a horrible fascination for her—all those lists of illnesses, diseases! She had taken for granted the doctoring her mother did at home, but now, it dawned on her, the good health of the household was in her hands. She skipped over teething ("lance the gums of the child"), "diarrhoea" (arrowroot gruel with a teaspoon of chalk) and rickets ("apply warm fomentations to the belly"). She wondered what "female obstructions" might be and whether she would ever suffer from them. She turned to consumption, and quickly prayed that no one she knew would get it. Lime water, sumac tea or a potion of hops, molasses and gin were remedies recommended. But Fanny knew nothing could cure it.

Moving on to coughs, heart palpitations and putrid sore throat, she had hope. Those she might master. But smallpox? Asiatic cholera? The first time she had read the book, Fanny had begun to cry and had to set the volume on the tea table. Here in New York, she thought, she and her family would be exempt from at least some of the disasters enumerated, for example, drowning. "There have been many extraordinary recoveries where the body has lain for hours under water," the manual sagely advised. "Let no violence of any kind, such as rolling on a barrel, be permitted." Indeed, she would not, should the time come. Well, on this sweltering morning she had no teething children, no consumptives and no drowned bodies. Fanny hitched her skirts above her knees to get some air. The parlor, with its velvet curtains, was a hotbox.

There were other sources of anxiety in housekeeping, even for the hale. Fanny knew that cleaning was no lark, but the directions for cleaning carpets, for example, sounded like a week's work. At home they had had bare floors and rag rugs but Charles had bought wool carpets and he already worried about moths. "Take up and shake at least twice a year . . . put straw under. . . . Sprinkle tobacco or ground pepper on the floor. . . . Rub on, with a new broom, pared and grated raw potatoes." How long would it take to grate enough potatoes, let alone clean the rug?

And the etiquette—would she ever learn city manners? She did not mind being told, though she already knew it, that it was better to "wear coarse clothes with a clean skin than silk stockings drawn over dirty feet." But the dinner-party manners were stifling. "When the ladies leave the table, which they do together, at the signal of the mistress of the house, the gentlemen rise and conduct them to the door of the apartment, and then return to the table." What did the ladies do next, she wondered. Sit in the next room and wait for the men to drink their port? And society had now deemed it inelegant to eat with a knife, though Papa did, and so did Uncle Henry, in spite of Charles' having replaced the old-fashioned two-tined forks with new three-tined ones. "Can't make the peas set down on 'em!" Uncle Henry had bellowed.

But this was no time to be thinking of carpets and knives. The clock was striking half past nine. What she needed now was Mrs. Chadwick. Puddings. Every dinner must have its pudding. Men loved them so, and Mrs. C. supplied a magnificent procession of them, 88 in all. Suet and plum puddings, Royal Nursery Pudding, boiled puddings and baked puddings, sweet puddings and savory. Fanny read the recipe for Charleston Pudding: six eggs and half a pound each of raisins and currants. Fanny had no raisins. In any case, the Charleston Pudding must boil four hours. She must find a two- or three-hour pudding. Here was a recipe for Marlborough Pudding, her Papa's favorite:

"Stew and strain twenty-four apples; add while hot one and a half pounds of butter, one and a half pounds of sugar; when cool add twenty-four eggs, the juice of four lemons and peel grated, two nutmegs, two or four milk biscuits. Rosewater and salt to taste."

Twenty-four eggs would deplete the week's supply, and anyhow, where could you find apples in the month of July? Besides, Mrs. Chadwick had neglected to state how long the pudding must bake, as though any right-thinking Christian would know already. Fanny turned to the page with Indian Pudding, which wouldn't do, as it "must be made the night before." Boiled Flour Pudding it would have to be—milk, eggs, flour and salt. Only an hour and a half to cook. It sounded uninteresting, but she'd make a sauce for it.

And so she descended the kitchen stairs once more, reluctant to face the wood stove, though she prayed it was red-hot as Rosey had promised. She had begun to sweat under her whalebone stays, her two petticoats and her muslin dress. Though she weighed only 100 pounds, she encased her thorax each morning in the proper corset of a matron, lacing until she gasped. Charles liked to encircle her waist with his hands, and Fanny was very vain of her figure. Now, as the heat of the kitchen hit her in the face, she had to grab hold of the stair rail. Poor Rosey had to stoke the fire, summer and winter, and split the kindling, but at least she was not obliged to wear a corset.

By the time the pudding was set to boil, securely tied in the pudding bag but with room to swell, the clock was striking 11. Rosey had not been able to manage the icebox pan alone, and had spilled the water all over the kitchen floor, and Fanny had to clean the interior of the box herself, swabbing out the drainpipe with a long stick. As they struggled, the fire almost died again. Quickly they got it going once more, and the heat in the kitchen grew so powerful that Fanny, heedless of the flies, opened all the windows.

"Yes, Mum, but what about the iceman?"

"I can't endure it," she cried in the middle of the chocolate cream (she was boiling the quart of milk just prior to adding the gelatin, and had set Rosey to grating the French chocolate, which the poor girl had never seen before). She stripped out of her dress, down to her corset cover and petticoat. "Rosey," she said, "you must warn me if you hear them coming. Mr. Van would be very angry if he caught me in this state."

"Yes, Mum," Rosey replied, "but what about the iceman? He's due in the forenoon, ain't he?"

"Not until after dinner," asserted Fanny, by now stirring her chocolate-cream mixture in a pitcher over boiling water, which would require half an hour's time. The noon chime had sounded before she poured the dessert into its individual molds, whereupon she and Rosey began putting the fish cakes together and readying the chops for frying, skimming the soup, slicing the bread and fetching the butter from the cellar. It had turned rancid in the heat.

Half-past twelve. Hearing the cry of the milk vendor, Fanny sent Rosey rushing into the street. Perhaps he would have a piece of butter she could put on the table. The table! She hadn't laid the table. She ran up the stairs to the dining room and hastily assembled the dinner plates, soup plates, knives, forks and spoons. Clutching the empty soup tureen under one arm, she descended the kitchen stairs, wondering whether she or the stair treads would wear out first.

She flew around the kitchen in a frenzy. Rosey arrived with the butter and carried it upstairs with the bread. Fanny turned the fish cakes, retrieved the pudding from its caldron (it had a suspiciously liquid look

inside its bag), noted that the chocolate cream had not set, and burned her finger on the soup-kettle lid. Tears of real anguish, quite unlike the sentimental tears in *Godey's Lady's Book*, ran down her cheeks. Then she remembered that she had forgotten to make coffee.

At that very moment, four events transpired. The clock struck one, a rapping at the back door announced the iceman, Rosey screamed and the Van Courtlandt men came down the kitchen stairs—Uncle Henry first. Snatching her discarded clothing to her bosom, Fanny took refuge behind a ladder-back chair. To the end of her days she remembered the five faces: the iceman astounded, Uncle Henry horrified, Charles chalk white, Cousin Samuel a little too amused for his own good and Rosey dabbing her eyes with her soup-stained apron. Fanny had forgotten to tell her to change.

"To the end of her days Fanny remembered the five faces: the iceman astounded, Uncle Henry horrified, Charles chalk white, Cousin Samuel a little too amused for his own good, Rosey dabbing her eyes."

195

By Peter Chew

'Mules is born in a man; you ain't gonna get it out of him'

Long bad-mouthed for cussedness, mules are in fact tough, smart, strong—and making a fast comeback today because they are fun

The old mule: wearing blinders, a team of draft mules does field work in San Marcos, Texas.

Has a secret colony of mules seized control of our destiny from somewhere in outer space?

NBC-TV's *Saturday Night Live* once posed this question. Well, television gag writers aside, the mules are having the last laugh these days. Consigned to the "killer man" for slaughter when tractors growled across the landscape in the late 1940s, the mule has come back from cast-off beast of burden to popular beast of pleasure.

More intelligent than the horse and far tougher physically, the long-eared, shave-tailed mule is sharing at last in the nation's wealth, which mules of yesteryear did so much to create by what was often brutal, life-shortening toil.

A mule is the sterile, hybrid offspring of a male donkey—or jackass—and a female horse, which was once bred selectively for work in the cotton fields of Mississippi, the sugar plantations of Louisiana, the coal mines of West Virginia and every imaginable form of heavy draft work. Today, hobbyists modify the animal's breeding to produce riding, driving and racing mules. Ways of having fun with the New Mule are limited, it appears, only by the human imagination.

"The modern mule is being asked to do everything a horse does, and he does some things better than a

The classic mule: matched pairs are judged for color, size and conformation at Missouri State Fair.

horse," notes Betsy Hutchins, editor of *The Brayer*, published by the 2,000-member American Donkey & Mule Society in Denton, Texas, which boasts 40-odd affiliates such as Montana's American Council of Spotted Asses and the Oregon Mr. Longears Club.

Trail riding and trail driving in covered wagons are popular mule activities. Mules are competing in their own rodeos, gymkhanas, hunter-hack and Western classes modeled after horse shows. They take part in multiple-hitch classes and weight-pulling contests; they race with jockeys up; they race with chariots behind. They jump fences with riders aboard; they jump riderless. Mules have become skilled at working cattle on ranches.

Mrs. Edith Harrison-Conyers of Winchester, Kentucky, rides to hounds on Kit, her five-year-old mule (p.198), a fearless jumper that finished seventh in the Mumford Farms Horse Trials in Evansville, Indiana, last May, clearing every cross-country and stadium jump, scoring well in dressage and finishing ahead of 11 of the 18 horses in the grueling three-phase event. But people also buy mules just to have them around. They want to see their long ears sticking up in the near distance and to hear the music of their braying.

At the big Reese Horse & Mule Company auction last winter in Columbia, Tennessee, when 800 mules and jacks went under the hammer, an aging mule man in bib overalls talked about the mystique of mules during a break in the bidding. "Years ago, every little farmer with half an acre of tobacco would have a one-

197

The new mule: Cathy Wieschoff takes Kit over a jump. Kit regularly competes against horses.

© Steve Wall 1983

Winfred Speed of Clayton, Georgia, rides Jezebel like a horse, but doesn't shoot from her back.

line mule to do the work, but people today have got a job in a factory or office someplace," said John C. (Tennessee) Miller, a prominent breeder of prize draft mules. "It's more or less a hobby. Mules is born in a man, and you ain't gonna get it out of him."

Miller, too, has an office that is supporting his mules. He is the multimillionaire president of Frontier Companies of Alaska, Inc., and many other firms. He commutes between his headquarters in Anchorage, where he has mules, and a farm not far from Columbia, Tennessee, where he has more mules.

Melvin Means, president of the Ruidoso Downs Mule Skinners Association of Ruidoso, New Mexico, claims that "Mule racing is the fastest-growing sport in the Southwest." Ruidoso Downs is the home of the world's richest horse race—a $2.5 million event for quarter horses—and the world's richest mule race, a 350-yard dash for a $10,000 purse. And some of these mules can pick 'em up and lay 'em down. They cover 350 yards in 20 seconds.

Jim Lackey, chairman of the Bishop, California, Mule Days Celebration, which includes mule races of more than a half-mile, says: "They come down past the stands the first time running like hell. They run on around the clubhouse turn and down the backstretch. But when they round the turn into the top of the homestretch, some of the mules just stop. They've run as far as they want to, and that's that. Mule men generally agree that mules are smarter than horses."

Bishop is the undisputed "Mule Capital of the World," a small resort community in the lush Owens Valley in the shadow of the High Sierras, 300 miles northeast of Los Angeles. There, 4,000 residents and 1,000 pack mules live in harmony with tourists and summer vacationers.

Firing skyward like a missile

Raccoon hunting on muleback, which usually takes place at night, is a tradition in places such as Arkansas, Missouri, Tennessee and Kentucky. Mules have always been the hunters' transportation of choice. Gunfire does not faze the animals once they have been trained. The little mules are nimble of foot and adept at jumping the barbed-wire fences that crisscross the country. When coming upon a fence, the rider dismounts, drapes his jacket over the top strands and lets the mule size up the obstacle. The rider goes to the far side of the fence and tugs on the reins. The mule then sinks down on his powerful haunches, tucks in his front legs —and fires himself skyward like a missile.

Mules have minds of their own, and things do not always go according to their handlers' plans in more formal jumping contests. Sometimes a mule will rub its chest up against the fence to gauge its height, start

Picking 'em up and laying 'em down, mules pound toward finish wire at Ruidoso Downs, New Mexico.

Mule racing is growing fast, and no wonder—for this 350-yard dash the purse amounted to $10,000.

to sink down in readiness to jump—then change its mind and walk under or around the obstacle in question while the crowd laughs and its handler fumes.

Endurance riding on mules is a growing sport. In 1976, some 100 riders, 175 horses and five mules (each rider was allowed to bring a spare mount if he or she wanted to) took part in a race from Frankfort, New York, to Sacramento, California, a distance of 3,200 miles. A 60-year-old Californian named Virl Norton finished first, in 98 days, with his mules Lord Fauntleroy and Lady Eloise, both of which were 16-hand animals out of thoroughbred mares. After Norton picked up the $25,000 winner's check, some of the horsemen complained about how the race had been run, so Norton offered to race them back to New York for a $10,000 ante—winner take all. There were no takers.

Conformation, or halter, classes for draft mules are a fixture at state and county fairs (p.196). A consistent winner in Kentucky is Ralph Higginbotham of Monticello, a protégé of Tennessee Miller, who ships his Belgian draft mares to Higginbotham's farm each spring to be bred to jacks.

Generally speaking, the conformation of a mule presents the body of a horse on the legs of a donkey. A mule's back is flatter than that of a horse, and its withers almost imperceptible. Head, ears and tail are those of a donkey, or ass. And a mule's foot is smaller

Peter Chew is working on a book about the bluegrass horse country. He wrote about draft horses in SMITHSONIAN, *February 1980.*

than that of a horse, although a draft mule is expected to have a big foot. A mule should have clean, straight legs, an alert eye and erect carriage.

"A good mule is like Lulubelle," said Higginbotham recently at his farm, leading her out of the barn for display (p. 204)."Everything comes out just right."

Lulubelle is a two-year-old, foaled by one of Higginbotham's 16 Belgian draft mares; she is by Henry, an irascible 11-year-old jack, one of three on the farm. A sorrel with flaxen, roached mane and flaxen tail, Lulubelle already stands nearly 16 hands and weighs more than 1,300 pounds. Today, the most fashionable draft mules are "blond" sorrels, a soft, tannish color. Lulubelle is a reddish sorrel and this bothers Higginbotham. "Ain't but one thing I would change about Lulubelle: if she had the blond color, she'd be perfect."

When the oil crisis hit a few years ago, draft horses began to come back, and their prices rose accordingly (SMITHSONIAN, February 1980). To a lesser extent, this has happened with draft mules, although good ones remain in precious short supply. Higginbotham has a pair of rare young, steel-gray mules for which he has turned down $7,500. And a few years ago at a sale in Waverly, Iowa, a pair or "span" of draft mules was knocked down for $15,000. However, the prime draft-mule market these days rises and falls with the prices that Amish farmers—the largest group of mule buyers —receive for their tobacco, and prices have been off the past two years. (Similarly, the Missouri mule market ebbed and flowed with cotton prices in the Gulf States before and after the turn of the century.)

In the South the indispensable mule helped plow cotton fields, then hauled the bales to market.

A 1905 poster advertises the popular cleanser, although by then mules were no longer hauling it.

So at the Reese sale in Tennessee last winter, draft mule pairs went for an average of $2,500, down considerably from recent years.

Even more so than Tennessee Miller and Ralph Higginbotham, Melvin Kolb of Lancaster, Pennsylvania, looks the part of a mule man. A big man who loves to eat, he dozes through mule auctions, a long whip cradled in his hands, seemingly out of the action. But when the auction is over, he has somehow managed to make the top bid for many if not most of the best mules.

Like his late father before him, Kolb sells mules to the Amish, scouting sales and farms in half a dozen states. The Amish generally do not breed and raise their own mules because their land—which ranges in value from $3,500 to $6,000 an acre—is too valuable to devote to the animals. Normally, Kolb buys at least 100 mules at the Columbia sale; this year he bought only 70, with 21 of them from Tennessee Miller in a $45,000 private deal outside the sales ring.

When pricing a mule, you must consider that your mule will never be able to reproduce himself or herself. A male or "horse" mule is born sterile, although he has genitals and must be gelded, for he has the instincts and drive of a stallion. Similarly, a mare or "Molly" mule comes in heat, but if bred to a stallion or jack either will not conceive or will abort.

Hinnies, which are the offspring of stallions and female donkeys called "jennets" or "jennies," also do not bear offspring. These creatures are fairly rare and are smaller than mules. Overly simplified, mules and hinnies cannot reproduce themselves because they lack the proper number of chromosomes, those bodies within sex cells that must match up, perfectly, two by

Mules were also indispensable in Italy in World War II. This is a British Eighth Army pack train.

Harry S. Truman, son of a Missouri mule and horse dealer, communes with team of his "favorite" animals.

two, before new life can be created. An ass or donkey has 62 chromosomes or 31 pairs; a horse has 64, or 32 pairs; while a mule or hinny is the odd-animal-out with 63 chromosomes.

There are two other equine species: *Equus zebra* and *Equus hemionus* or onager, a nearly extinct wild ass known for its ferocity. *Hemionus* is the Greek word for a "half-ass." Donkeys have been successfully bred to zebras, with the offspring known as zebronkeys.

The quirky character of the mule has been shaped in the course of 3,000 years on Earth as a faithful servant of Man, who has alternated between abusing and ridiculing the animal, and treating it royally, as Nero supposedly did when he fitted out his mules with silver shoes and other grand accoutrements.

It is hardly surprising that the mule instinctively eyes Man with suspicion. A mule *can* be stubborn, and a mule *can* kick your brains out, but these propensities have been exaggerated beyond reason, say mule men. A mule will kick when provoked or frightened, but so will a horse. Horses can be stubborn, too.

When I was a boy, we had a sweet old mule named Alice on our small farm in the Shenandoah Valley of Virginia, but you could ride her just so far across the fields and through the apple orchards before she would stop in her tracks. Through trial and error, however, I discovered that if I dismounted and led her quickly around and around in a tight circle, then remounted and headed her back, she would trot along happily enough—until she decided to stop again.

During a mule race at the Berryville Horse Show one summer, a neighbor's mule that I was riding stopped dead still in front of the grandstand—a mortifying experience. I hopped off, led the animal around

in a circle, jumped on and, sure enough, the mule galloped on. But the rest of the field had passed me by.

A mule's temperament depends in great measure upon the temperament of its dam, and on how it was treated when it was young. Today's draft mules inherit the placid dispositions of the Belgian draft mares that give them birth, and breeders of sport mules are careful to choose mares with gentle dispositions.

We speak of "horse sense" when we should, more properly, speak of "mule sense," for common sense is the mule's greatest asset. If, for example, you turn a hungry mule loose near an open corncrib, it will eat until it is satisfied and then stop. Neither will it founder from overdrinking. Under the same circumstances, a horse is likely to go on eating until it becomes ill. If you overload a pack mule, it will buck the load off or refuse to move. A mule knows what it can carry and what it can't carry. If a mule becomes tangled, say, in barbed wire, it will wait patiently for someone to come along and extricate it. A horse in the same fix is likely to tear its hide apart in a panicky effort to get free. A mule can stand the heat better than a horse, is stronger pound for pound than a horse, and is heir to far fewer ailments than a horse. A mule is what farmers call "an easy keeper," an animal that is cheap to maintain.

Mules are notorious for learning how to open gates, barn doors and the like. A Wyoming rancher recalls a team of mules that worked together to open gates: one mule would lift the sliding wooden bar with its nose, while the other mule nudged the gate open.

The surefootedness of the mule is legendary. Since the turn of the century, mules have been carrying tourists (many, if not most, of whom have never ridden any kind of animal before) down the steep, narrow trails and switchbacks into the Grand Canyon, a distance of ten miles. Interestingly, there has never been a single human fatality, although some pack mules and some mules that were being trained have plummeted to their own deaths.

There is a threadbare saying that the mule is "without pride of ancestry or hope of posterity." Not so. The mule and the donkey have been celebrated in song and story and in art form, from Homer's *Iliad* to Balaam's talking ass; from the ballads of black share-croppers in the American South to the rhythmic clip-clop of mule hooves in Ferde Grofé's *Grand Canyon Suite*; from ancient Greek pottery to the 20th-century paintings of Thomas Hart Benton.

The mule as a prime energy factor

Greek and Biblical writings indicate that mules first walked the Earth in Asia Minor some 30 centuries ago; it is not known whether they arrived by human design or natural brief encounter. One theory holds that mules were first bred in Cappadocia, which is now central Turkey. For more than a hundred years—throughout the 19th century and well into the 20th—the mule's presence was pervasive in the United States, specially so in the Southern and border states, in the cotton fields and on the sugar plantations.

"From one-mule farms in the hill country to Delta plantations with hundreds of teams, the mule for over a century was the prime energy factor in Mississippi's agriculture," notes Patti Carr Black, director of the Mississippi State Historical Museum, in the book *Mules and Mississippi.*

George Washington, no less, had foreseen all this and realized what a boon mulepower would prove to be for our agrarian economy. He had said in the early 1780s that the American farmer needed "an excellent race of mules," and he set about establishing one. There had been donkeys and mules in this country since the days of the Spanish explorers, but they were of indifferent quality and little more than curiosities. In Washington's day, Spain possessed the finest jack stock in the world: huge, powerful animals from Andalusia and Catalonia. Farmer Washington was determined to get his hands on some of these beasts even though the Spanish guarded them jealously and forbade their exportation.

"Nevertheless, by 1784, the name Washington meant something even in the courts of Europe and soon word of his quest reached the King of Spain through somewhat irregular diplomatic channels," notes John Rhodehamel, archivist of Mount Vernon, in *Fairfax Chronicles.* "Hoping to win the goodwill of the foremost citizen of the strange republican na-

James Clark rides a two-row corn planter behind a pair of handsome white mules in central Kentucky.

tion across the Atlantic, Charles III . . . caused two fine Spanish jacks [and two jennets] to be dispatched at once to George Washington, farmer."

In 1785, a leggy 16-hand Andalusian jack, which Washington named Royal Gift, arrived at Mount Vernon—and proved an immediate disappointment at stud. He was a "shy breeder," and could be coerced into mating with only two or three of the more than 30 mares that Washington had assembled for his court. The Spanish jack, wrote Washington, "was perhaps too full of Royalty to have anything to do with a plebeian race." By the next year, however, Royal Gift had redeemed himself. Farmers from up and down the East Coast sent mares to Mount Vernon, and Washington eventually sent Royal Gift on a triumphant 1,000-mile breeding tour through the Southern states.

Soon after, Washington acquired two jennets and a smaller jack from Malta, which were sent to him by the Marquis de Lafayette. The second jack, christened Knight of Malta, proved to be better suited for the breeding of saddle mules, while Royal Gift was able to sire mules for draft work. When Washington died in

The Clarks also use tractors on their farm, but
"mules don't pack the ground like a tractor."

1799, nearly 60 mules were grazing at Mount Vernon
and America did indeed have the beginnings of "an
excellent race of mules," the world's best, in fact.

In 1890, the mule population of Missouri stood at
245,273, the highest in the nation, according to U.S.
Census figures. Texas, which had developed its own
cotton fields, took the lead in 1900 with 474,737,
reaching an all-time high in 1930 of 1,040,106. Texas
absorbed its own mules, whereas Missouri shipped its
mules in vast numbers throughout the United States
and the world at large.

Missourians produced and marketed mules the way
Detroit would produce cars and trucks when the combustion engine became a reality.

Luke McClure Emerson, born in Pike County in
1860, was Missouri's most celebrated importer and
dealer. He was known to carry as much as $80,000 cash
in his pocket, buy wholesale lots of mules sight un-
seen and boast that all he needed to see of a jack, in
order to judge him, were his head and ears. Emerson
was a showman with a talent for publicity. In January
1894, nearly 100 of his Spanish jacks reportedly

escaped into the city of Liverpool, England, while being loaded from one steamer to another in the harbor.
The jacks were rounded up by police but when they
reached New York they escaped again, mysteriously,
one of them falling into a well ten miles outside the
city. In April 1911, when Missouri's Champ Clark was
elected Speaker of the U.S. House of Representatives,
Emerson drove him down Pennsylvania Avenue in
Washington behind a pair of mules named Belle of
Pike and Belle of Callaway.

A firm by the name of Guyton and Harrington in
Lathrop, Missouri, which won an exclusive contract
to provide horses and mules to the British Army during the First World War, operated on a scale that tests
credibility. On a 15,000-acre tract, with access to four
railroads, as many as 50,000 horses and mules were
assembled at one time. The company supplied an estimated 350,000 horses and mules to the British Army.

The American Army in World War I procured nearly 160,000 mules, many thousands of which were lost
to bullets and shellfire in France. Tens of thousands of
mules served American and British forces as pack ani-

The comeback of the mule

mals in Italy during the Second World War (p. 201).

Donald Willems of Portland, Michigan, was the American Fifth Army's pack troop and remount officer in Italy, with hundreds of men and 40,000 mules under his command—American mules and mules captured in the Po River Valley and elsewhere. Now 65 years old, Willems remembers his mules vividly and with affection. "Once they were settled in, they didn't panic," he recalls. "We would go in at night and take materiel up to the units in the line—ammunition, 75-millimeter gun barrels, food, medical supplies, demolition wire— up where trucks and Jeeps and even bulldozers couldn't go, up in the mountains in snow and mud." But when the Germans zeroed in on the pack train with heavy mortars, the men could hit the ground or take cover, while the mules could only stand still. Thousands of Willems' mules were wounded and killed in the Italian campaign.

Apart from war service, the most dramatic episode in the history of the amazing American mule concerns the 20-mule teams that hauled huge freight wagons loaded with borax 165 miles across California's Death Valley in the 1880s. In each train were a 1,200-gallon water-tank wagon and two freight wagons 16 feet in length with rear wheels seven feet in diameter; each freight wagon weighed four tons and was capable of carrying 36 tons of cargo.

"The life of a teamster on the desert is not only one of hardship, it is in places extremely dangerous," wrote John R. Spears, a New York *Sun* reporter from Death Valley in 1891. "There are grades, like the one on the road from Granite Spring to Mojave, where the plunge is steep, the roadbed as hard as a turnpike. The load must go down, so when the brink is reached, the driver throws his weight on the brake of the front wagon, the swamper [assistant] handles the brake on the rear, and away they go, creaking, groaning and sliding, until the bottom is reached.

"If the brake holds, all is well, but now and then a brake-block gives way, then a race with death begins. With yells and curses, the long team is started in a gallop, an effort is made to swing them around up the mountainside, a curve is reached, an animal falls, or a wheel strikes a rock or rut, and, with thunderous crash, over go the great wagons."

It is about 150 miles from Death Valley to the Owens Valley and Bishop, California, where the modern mule lives a quite different life. But we shouldn't begrudge today's mules their good times: they have paid their dues.

Ralph Higginbotham of Kentucky wishes Lulubelle were more blond, but otherwise she's "perfect."

Lucky Jonathan Chipman of Perry, Missouri, has a three-month-old mule colt, Susie, for a pet.

By Robert Wernick

Jacob Lawrence: art as seen through a people's history

Brought up in Harlem's tough and teeming streets, he encountered the fine arts in a settlement house and went on to greatness

Lawrence today: professor emeritus of art at the University of Washington, he still paints and teaches.

And he said unto me, Son of man, can these bones live?

Jacob Lawrence can still hear the words of the Prophet Ezekiel thundering through the cavernous spaces of New York's Abyssinian Baptist Church from the mouth of Adam Clayton Powell sr., the great preacher of Harlem.

Harlem in the 1930s might well have struck a sensitive boy as a valley of bones. The Depression had fallen savagely on a not very wealthy economic community to begin with. Perhaps, Lawrence says, it didn't have the devastating emotional impact it had on white communities, for American blacks were used to hard times and didn't have so far to fall. Still, it was grim enough: a world of unemployment, soup kitchens, evictions, overcrowding. Jacob Lawrence was what might pass as a statistically average kid in that world. His parents had long been separated and his mother was on welfare a good part of the time. He was a high school dropout. There were only a few odd jobs available—now delivering papers, now in a laundry, now delivering bootleg liquor in brown paper bags.

A bleak enough picture, but for an imaginative, healthy, very quiet but very determined boy, it was enormously exciting. Those overcrowded streets in the West 130s and 140s were full of vivid, racy life. People

The realities of Harlem life are fused creatively into a work of art in Lawrence's *Tombstones*, 1942.

were living somehow. Jake Lawrence's keen young eyes could see them bustling, stumbling, struggling everywhere, in the churches and the pool halls, the funeral parlors, the barbershops, the whorehouses.

At the age of 12 he was sent by his mother to a program at Utopia House, a settlement house where he could get hot lunches and some training in arts and crafts in the afternoon. There was a young teacher there named Charles Alston who set him to work making bright color patterns with cheap poster paints on wrapping paper; later he made papier-mâché masks, grotesque Halloween faces. He also decorated the insides of cardboard boxes to make them look like street scenes. From that time on, he knew he was going to become an artist.

There was little family encouragement. His mother had no notion of the arts and could only dream that he would grow up to get a safe job in the civil service. But the community around him provided a richly nourishing atmosphere. The great days of what had been

Frederick Douglass series depicts the writer-orator in 1836, planning escape along with other slaves.

Harriet Tubman series commemorates life of the early fighter for emancipation, here as plantation worker.

called the Harlem Renaissance in the 1920s were over, but there were still distinguished figures around—novelists, poets, preachers, propagandists, who stimulated the dormant energies and desires of black America. And they were always on the lookout for signs of talent in the young. Lawrence's gifts were discovered and encouraged by people like Augusta Savage, a whirlwind of a sculptor who had come back from Paris to bring the message of art to the streets of Harlem; and his first mentor, Charles Alston, who turned his studio at 306 West 141st Street into a neighborhood workshop. The 306 studio was famous in those days. It was a gathering place and debating club for all the luminaries of the Harlem cultural world: older ones like Claude McKay, Countee Cullen and Langston Hughes; younger ones like Richard Wright and Ralph Ellison, who went there to talk and argue among themselves and with pilgrims from downtown like the young William Saroyan. Alston let Lawrence rent a corner of his studio for a small sum, and he would go

A fugitive, Douglass attends lecture by Abolitionist
William Lloyd Garrison and is greatly inspired by him.

In the saga, Douglass arrives in Rochester, New York,
where he edits *North Star*, the first black newspaper.

there to work and to listen to all that was discussed.

Often he would walk the 60-odd blocks downtown
to the Metropolitan Museum of Art and study the Old
Masters. How did those Dutchmen achieve technical
feats like painting glistening drops of water on the
skins of fruit? Or how did they produce the different
effects of a white egg on a white tablecloth?

He painted as much as he could. The earliest Lawrences to survive date from 1936, when he was 19.
They contain the ideas he had worked out for himself
since the age of 12, and they also contain in embryo, or
fully developed, the elements that through a long career have made him one of America's most distinguished painters. These early works can be seen in the
big retrospective, containing some 150 paintings and
now touring the country, which will be on view at the

*Robert Wernick has written more than fifty articles
for* SMITHSONIAN. *His book* The Freebooters *satirizes
World War II.*

Dallas Museum of Art, June 28-September 6, and at
the Brooklyn Museum, October 1-December 1. This
exhibition was made possible by a grant from the IBM
Corporation. The splendid catalog, *Jacob Lawrence,
American Painter*, by Ellen Harkins Wheat provides
the first comprehensive survey of the work of the artist.

These are paintings of scenes of everyday life in Harlem, life in crowded quarters, with flies and rats, frayed
furniture, peeling walls, everything run-down. The
young artist had obviously been looking at the works
of Germans like George Grosz and Käthe Kollwitz
and Mexicans like José Clemente Orozco and Diego
Rivera (SMITHSONIAN, February 1986), whose searing
criticisms of social injustice were widely reproduced at
the time. His work, however, is his own. Where the
Germans and Mexicans deal with the drama of poverty, their brushstrokes and lines come packed with
indignation and invective. Lawrence, on the other
hand, is calm, involved but a little ironic, sympathetic
but unsparing. He was brought up in poverty and

knew it from the inside. He understood how to convey both the sordidness and the kick and vitality of life in the streets. The effect of these early Harlem scenes is very powerful, and the people who saw them the first time—like those seeing them today—found it hard to comprehend how a 19-year-old could have acquired enough mastery over his materials to achieve it. "You just have to believe that what you're doing has value, and that's it," is his own explanation.

Harlem throw rugs become art

The human figures and objects that form the subject matter of his early paintings—and many of his later works for that matter—appear as bright flat patches of color against a background of more subtle color. He likes to attribute his early fascination with color patterns to the bright throw rugs that his mother, like other Harlem mothers, used to scatter around to bring a note of gaiety into their homes. But where did he get the firm sense of design that locks all the figures into such complete and cohesive patterns?

No matter where he got them, these patterns have served the purposes of his vision ever since. One striking feature that recurs frequently is the very shallow space into which the figures and objects are crowded. He often builds his composition on a framework of strong diagonal lines. The perspective tends to be skewed so that everything is thrust forward, almost into the spectator's face, and this helps give the paintings a monumental look, though they are in actuality quite small, usually no more than 20 by 30 inches. They can also evoke the feeling of a compressed, intense, claustrophobic atmosphere, a ghetto atmosphere.

Lawrence's first work was done in poster paints because they were cheapest. He later graduated to egg tempera, casein tempera made with curdled milk, and gouache. All these are water-based paints applied on paper or on gesso-coated hardboard panels. Water is a less flexible medium than oil, but it suits Lawrence's temperament. Drying quickly, with little time for second thoughts, it calls for methodical, thoughtful work.

Lawrence's figures are drawn with great skill, but the skill is directed toward expressing an emotion rather than creating realistic individual portraits. The bodies are distorted, the faces are summary and close to caricature. When he paints pool players, they are just that—pool players—not Joe and Bill and the other guys from next door.

His style of painting lends itself to narrative, and as Lawrence early on worked out for himself, the simplest way of developing a story in art is not by trying to pack everything into a single symbolic scene but by making a series of pictures showing successive or different phases of one overall action.

Among the subjects endlessly discussed and debated at the 306 studio was the place of the Negro in the history of the Western world—a world into which he had been brutally transplanted centuries before. There were heroic figures in the past, but they were barely known; barely, if ever, mentioned in the standard histories and in the schoolbooks that were written by whites. How many people had so much as heard of Toussaint L'Ouverture? Lawrence became intrigued with the man who had led the early successful revolt of slaves against a colonial power, the one that eventually brought independence to Haiti. A few blocks from the studio, in the 135th Street branch of the New York Public Library, which then housed the world's largest collection of printed and pictorial matter on the black past in Africa and America, he devoured everything he could find on Toussaint—his struggles to educate himself, his charismatic leadership, his military campaigns, his eventual betrayal and death in a French dungeon.

It was an epic story, calling for epic treatment. Lawrence decided to portray it with a series of 41 paintings in tempera on paper, each one with an explanatory caption. He conceived the series as a single unit, each panel independent but adding to the cumulative effect of the others. First he penciled in sketches of all the scenes. Then he went over them, filling them all in one color at a time, starting with the darkest, a device that helps give a striking unity of tone to the whole.

Great figures emerge from the past

Other series followed, dealing with more exemplary figures out of the black past. There was one devoted to Frederick Douglass, the escaped slave who became a famous orator and writer for the Abolitionist movement. There was a series portraying Harriet Tubman, another slave who became the most famous and successful organizer (slaveholders put a price of $40,000 on her head) of the Underground Railroad, which guided fugitives to freedom in the North and in Canada. Like Toussaint, they were marginal figures in standard histories. As Lawrence has observed, everyone knows about Molly Pitcher and Betsy Ross, but who had ever heard of Harriet Tubman? Both Douglass and Tubman had been field hands, raised in Maryland, one of the states where it was a statutory crime to teach a slave to read and write, and Lawrence saw both stories as paeans to struggle, to Man's ability to raise himself from any depth.

Works like these, with their controlled energy and their highly personal idiom, made a strong impression on everyone who saw them. But not many people were buying art in the late 1930s. It was, Lawrence says, a turning point in his life when in 1938 he was hired by the Works Progress Administration Federal Art Proj-

Powerful *Square Dance* is from the *Hospital* series, based on personal experience. The patients depicted are participating in a therapeutic session. Lawrence's stay opened up whole new avenues.

In Munich Olympic Games poster, 1972, artist shows black athletes as they strain toward the finish line.

Going to the Apollo Theater in Harlem was a ritual for Lawrence as a boy. Here, a tribute: *Vaudeville*.

ect at $23.86 a week. He was on the Project for 18 months, and when it was over he was able to consider himself a full-fledged professional artist.

In 1941 came more turning points. In that year he married Gwendolyn Knight, an attractive and talented art student who had been a great friend for years. She was a little older and a good deal more sophisticated (she came from Barbados and had been to college).

In that year, too, he produced his first work to attract national attention. It was another major series, this time on a subject closer to home. It was called *The Migration of the Negro*, and it dealt with something that was in his blood and his own youthful experience. His mother came from Virginia, his father from South Carolina; he himself was born in Atlantic City after they settled in the North. They were part of the great movement from Southern farms to Northern cities, which began during World War I and eventually transformed the demographic and political patterns of the

nation (SMITHSONIAN, May 1987). It was a movement on an epic scale, a transplantation of a whole people, on the same scale as the migration from the farms of southern and eastern Europe that had flooded into the industrial cities of the United States a generation or two earlier.

The migration within our own borders was a different sort of affair, a quiet, seething shifting like a rising river that nobody notices till it becomes a flood. It was as if the good burghers of New York had gone to bed one night and awakened to find the sleepy, respectable Dutch-speaking neighborhood called Haarlem turned into the metropolis of America's—some would say the world's—black population.

"I didn't know the term 'migration,'" Lawrence has said, "but I remember people used to tell us when a new family would arrive. The people in the neighborhood would collect clothes for the newcomers and pick out coals that hadn't completely burned in the furnace to get them started." The families all had their tales to

Lawrence's design sense is impeccable. In spare, simple style he paints slave children tumbling on sandy shore, Dorchester County, Maryland, in 1820s, the region where Harriet Tubman was born and raised.

212

tell. Out of such bits of recollection, out of what scattered materials he could find in the library, he constructed scenes for 60 panels, again quite small (12 by 18 inches), painted like early Renaissance works in tempera on gessoed panels. The scenes constitute a panorama of social movement, from the stirrings of restlessness in the rural South, through all the hopes and jeopardies of the journey, the uncertainties of arrival in a strange new world of city streets and tenements, the new racial rivalries and riots in the North, the tensions and adjustments.

Fortune magazine reproduced 26 of the panels in its November 1941 issue. It was the first time a national publication had paid so much attention to the movement of millions of black people, or devoted so much space to the work of a black artist.

An even more important event, from Lawrence's point of view, occurred about the same time, when Edith Gregor Halpert, director of New York's Downtown Gallery, invited him to join her roster of artists, which included Ben Shahn, Charles Sheeler, Stuart Davis and other famous names. It was the first time in America that a black artist had been able to move out of the restricted world of Harlem to be represented by an important New York gallery, the kind of place where major reputations are made. Some black radicals later in the 1960s would denounce him for selling out to the white establishment. He could understand, but went right on in his own way. For Lawrence, the move to the Downtown Gallery was an immense opening up of horizons, a chance for him and for succeeding generations of black artists to enter the mainstream of American art.

The *Migration* series appeared on the gallery walls (and was at once snapped up by the Museum of Modern Art and the Phillips Memorial Gallery) two days after Pearl Harbor had thrust America into World War II. The war caught up with Lawrence in 1943, when he was drafted into the Coast Guard and given the rank of steward's mate—the U.S. Navy in those days could

Travel in Africa furnished new material for the artist. *Street in Mbari* in series on Nigeria shows a bustling and vivid marketplace; yet, with all of its multifarious life, painting is a triumph of design.

Painting the black American experience

not envision black sailors except in menial capacities. But the good luck that has dogged his career brought him a commanding officer who appreciated his talent and eventually arranged to get him a post as a combat artist. He served for a while on a converted yacht that was doing weather patrol in the North Atlantic. It was an integrated ship, the first in the Navy in which whites and blacks were allowed to serve and live together. Later he was on a troop transport that ferried tens of thousands of troops to the battlefields and brought thousands of them back on bunks converted to hospital cots. Most of his Coast Guard paintings somehow got lost in the archives after the war. But a *War* series survives, completed a couple of years later, with some powerful scenes of the cramped, muffled, doom-laden world of the transport.

Out of the service in 1945, Lawrence found himself an established figure, almost a celebrity. His work was selling well and the critics were encouraging. He won prizes and received a Guggenheim fellowship. He was asked to do book illustrations. Black Mountain College, the experimental institution in North Carolina where many of what were to become the big names of the American avant-garde put in an appearance, asked him to teach during the summer session of 1946. It was all very gratifying for a young man from the West 130s, and even Jake Lawrence's level head began to feel askew under the pressure. He checked into a mental institution in 1949 and stayed there eight months. An intelligent doctor, constant support from Gwen, and his own incurable good sense pulled him through. Unlike most patients, he never let himself be overwhelmed by his own problems; the eyes that had looked so keenly at the streets of Harlem and the decks of the USS *General Richardson* did not blink at the Hillside Hospital in Queens. While inside, he produced the 11 paintings of a series called *Hospital*,

which gives as revealing a picture of human beings in one of these institutions as we are ever likely to get. The patients sit slumped in apathy, or they stare at a table loaded with the multicolored capsules that are supposed to cure them, or they dance stiffly in a room where the columns supporting the roof have a disconcerting resemblance to the bars of a cage. They are all submerged in the gray, foreboding universe of the mentally ill.

Since he left the hospital in 1950, Lawrence's life has been a record of steady work, steady success. He has been a popular teacher at Pratt Institute in New York, at Brandeis in Massachusetts and at other schools. In 1962 he made a brief visit to Nigeria and two years later returned for an eight-month stay at the invitation of a society of local artists. The vivid colors, the bustle and animation of the marketplaces and village life of western Africa enthralled him, and for the first time in his life he felt himself out in the open spaces. He had seen the ocean when he was in the Coast Guard, but he'd been shut up in the narrow steel box of a ship. There was plenty of scenery at Black Mountain, but Black Mountain was in a South which at that time did not take kindly to the idea of a black teacher mixing in a white society, and the Lawrences spent all ten weeks there on the campus without even visiting the nearby town of Asheville.

Some changes, but the theme is constant

His style has evolved over the decades. His figures have become more angular, cubistic; "I seem to gravitate to geometric form," he says. His color combinations have become more subtle. But the basics remain the same, and while the winds of fashion have veered and sheered from Action to Hard Edge, from Pop to Minimal, he has kept steadily on his way painting the life around him. As he says, you can never run out of subjects that way.

The subject matter has broadened, though the feeling behind it has not changed. Beginning with his Coast Guard paintings, where white and black sailors together are chipping paint or cleaning bilges, he has recorded the gradual desegregation of American society. He has remained very much a part of the black community and at times has been among its most eloquent spokesmen, as in the group of paintings about the civil rights movement in the 1960s, angry paintings about prejudice and injustice. But, he says, "I never use the term 'protest' in connection with my paintings.

Fascinated by tools and how they are used, Lawrence painted *Cabinetmaker* in homage to craftsmen.

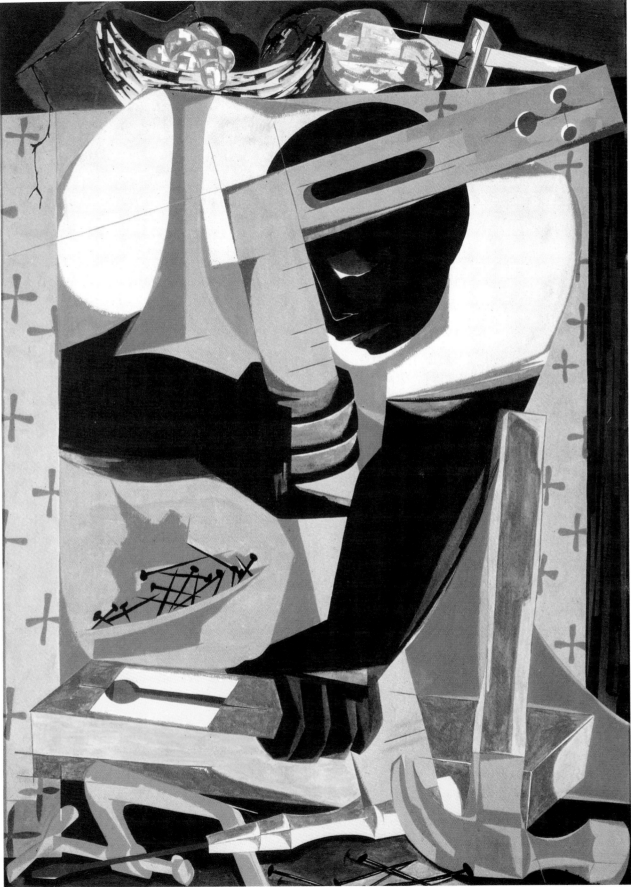

Lawrence painted himself in Seattle studio, but out back window is the everlasting presence of Harlem.

They just deal with the social scene. They're how I feel about things.''

In 1971, about the time that he and Gwen were feeling cramped in their New York quarters, he was invited to take a post as professor of art at the University of Washington in Seattle. Sixteen years later they are still there, though he has retired and is professor emeritus now. He continues to do a little teaching, for students love him—he has a gift, they say, for helping them find their own way without imposing his own personality or style on them. It is impossible to conceive of this man imposing his personal preference on anyone.

The slower, quieter pace of Seattle has had its charms for both Lawrences, though they still speak occasionally of going back to New York. They live in a pleasant house where they both have studio space. Gwen, who for almost half a century has been helping him with advice and criticism, and by sometimes rubbing down the gesso on his panels, has seen her own career bloom. She will be having a show of paintings in what he calls her romantic-realist style at a Seattle gallery next fall.

The soft gray, misty air of the Northwest has had its effect on Lawrence's painting too. The angular forms of his middle years remain, but they have become a little rounded. Far from the harsh lights of New York City, his palette has become, as he says, more tonal, less prismatic.

A recurring theme of these later years is that of builders. Lawrence has always loved a job well done and the way a good craftsman goes about doing it. He has been fascinated by tools since boyhood. He served for six months in the Civilian Conservation Corps, building a dam in upstate New York when he was 17, and he came away with an intimate knowledge of the shovel and "how it feels to throw dirt up above your shoulders." He loves the look and feel of traditional tools—the planes and chisels and awls you can see unchanged from medieval paintings of the workshop of St. Joseph the Carpenter down to our own day—and how they fit the human hand and human movement. He sees the action of builders as not only beautiful in itself but expressive of the creative depths in human nature: "I think of it as Man's aspiration, as a constructive tool—Man building." In the paintings, he blends his workers (black and white together, as you can find in real life now though not much in Lawrence's youth) and their hammers, saws, levels, and the beams and rafters of the buildings they construct in a lively complex of flat, colored shapes.

There have been other projects in Seattle, too: a huge mural, *Games*, for a sports stadium; a mural, *Theater*, for the University of Washington's performance center; a series of paintings on the settlement of the Northwest; projected murals for the state capitol building in Olympia to summarize the past and present of Washington State.

These might seem like unusual subjects for the man who once chronicled Toussaint L'Ouverture. There has been no break with the past, however; he has never forgotten where he came from. The Jacob Lawrence sketching Mount Rainier and the wilds traversed by the early settlers is the same Jacob Lawrence who frequented the poolrooms and churches of Harlem half a century ago. A few years ago, in 1977, he did one of his rare self-portraits (left). He is upstairs in Seattle, in his studio, which, characteristically, takes up more of the picture space than does the artist. It is a clean, spare, methodical studio. He is climbing the stairs into it with an ambiguous expression on his face, baring his teeth, his big capable hands extended, ready for action. In the background is a window, and where you might expect to see Mount Rainier through it, there are instead the familiar brownstones of the West 130s and 140s, squeezing the narrow streets where Jacob Lawrence first learned his trade.

By Jack Fincher

'Meryl is dying to do Scarlett anorexic'

If June 30 marks the 50th birthday of *Gone With the Wind*, the book, can the golden anniversary of *GWTW*, the movie, be far behind? I mention this only to pose a more serious question for today's New Hollywood: Whatever has happened to the sequel?

As usual, creative differences were cited, but that was just Tinsel Town airing its designer linen again. The real reason *GWTW2* sank with hardly a trace is deeply otherwise. I have in my possession the confidential memos (to himself) of one Barry (Bare) B., (UCLA '80), former Production Chief at Razzmatazz Pictures who now manages a Fast Foto franchise in Eugene, Oregon. The memos tell all—and a sordid tale of life in the Santa Monica Freeway fast lane it is, too.

20 June 1983
You've done it, Bare, scored the hottest property of your career. Meryl is dying to do Scarlett anorexic, something about that turnip scene at the popcorn break of *GWTW1*. Dolly lusts to do Scarlett as Belle Watling's illegitimate daughter if she can wear (and keep) wardrobe of cinch-waist, off-the-shoulder ball gowns by Gucci. Pia's husband will put up half the development nut provided a part can be scored for Scarlett's long-lost, half-breed baby sister. Barbra called too, but did not leave a number. Brunching with Burt at Spago.

1 July 1983
Trouble in Culver City. Burt wants Sally in the picture for old time's sake. I go, no way is she Scarlett. Scarlett nothing, goes Burt, she wants Melanie, Melanie's more likable. Wait a minute, Burt, I go, Melanie dies at the end of the first picture. You wait a minute yourself, goes Burt. Does the audience ever actually *see* Melanie die? Besides, if you ask me any broad *that* Goody-Two-Shoes is brain dead from reel one. I go, I'll get back. At least Bob definitely wants to do Rhett. If he doesn't have to dye his hair, learn more than six lines of dialogue or leave Sundance, Wyo-

ming, in ski season. Barbra called again. Said I was out.

15 July 1983
Great news! Steven wants to direct and George wants to produce, or vice versa. They haven't decided which. Doesn't matter, they say, so long as locations shot in Marin County and the story done in flashbacks from the future. Francis thinks he has the answer: for ten mil a computerized new ILM electronic process that will allow everything, a second burning of Atlanta thrown in, to be superimposed on outtakes from *Birth of a Nation*. Told them I'd check public domain and get back.

2 August 1983
Where are you now that we need you, Leslie, baby? Joanne wants *Paul* to do Ashley but Paul thinks Ashley's an aristocratic wimp and won't sign unless he's rewritten as a grass-roots Democrat. But Paul, sweetheart, I go, this is right after the Civil War, Democrats are not even invented yet I don't think. No problem, Bare, goes Paul, we'll have him do a lot of liberal things the audience can identify with, like free the slaves, drink Bud and race fast horses.

3 August 1983
What a joker that Woody is. He wants to script, direct and shoot the picture on 16mm black-and-white in Manhattan, with Mia wigged out as Scarlett. Offers to play Ashley for nothing if he can write his own interior monologues. I see him as a Freudian Hamlet, he goes, possibly Jewish. But Wood, I go, so OK, so you're the resident intellectual, but when this story opens Freud could not be more than a Viennese teenager. Woody very depressed at this.

Now Prissy is problemsville! Whoopi won't sign for the Butterfly McQueen *shtick* unless Quincy does the music, and Quincy won't do the music unless Whoopi gets either the guy or Tara. Priss ain't no jive farmer, Whoop goes, Priss in medical school, and forget Rhett as my main unless it's Eddie. Eddie won't play Rhett unless he gets creative control and billing

above the title. Bob is history. Wanted pitch in the script for conservation of Okefenokee swamp as a national resource.

3 September 1983
Tina says no to Mammy. NAACP says no to Pia, even if she commits not to lip sync spirituals. So lose Pia, lose Mammy. But hold the phone: Dustin wants to do *both* Prissy and Mammy. So help me, right there in Ma Maison, in front of Warren, God and everybody, he goes, give me six big ones up front, Bare, points and a major piece of the cassette action and I'll throw a dozen writers right at it. Dust does love an artistic challenge. Dining tonight with Barbra at Chasen's.

4 September 1983
Not only does Barb concept Scarl as poor white trash with a Brooklyn accent, she wants to produce, script, direct, distribute, write the score, sing the title song, record the cast album, adapt musically for the stage, byline the spin-off novel (ghosted) and establish a four-year college for Southern feminists in Marg Mitchell's name. Suggests Sly as her leading man. All of us lunching at the Polo Lounge Saturday.

6 September 1983
Sly shows. Barb is nowhere. Sly in a volcanic snit. Calms down, agrees to cameo appearance as Rhett for 40 percent of the gross if shooting can be wrapped in a week. Sees Rhett as riverboat renegade revulsed by lawless carpetbaggers in cahoots with corrupt Yankee government, who swims the Mississippi in floodtide with Gatling gun and wastes all the little buggers standing between him and the liberation of New Orleans from the British. Sly's manager and I take turns explaining why Sly's concept, while box-office megabucks it may be, is not exactly viable in today's New Hollywood. Viable, schmiable, Sly goes, he'll get back.

10 October 1983
Woody won't return my calls and Pia is suing for breach of mutuality. We may be in trouble here, Bare.

By Thomas Dozier

The controversy on whereabouts of Columbus' body

After 468 years, the bones of the Admiral seem to have traveled almost as far as they did in life; no one is certain where they all rest

In the Mediterranean world from which he hailed and in the New World to which he sailed, Christopher Columbus probably is honored by more monuments and place names than any other man in history. Yet he remains an enigma. Even after repeated crossings of the Atlantic, he insisted that when he was traveling westward he was sailing uphill. He also concluded from the fact that the weather became progressively warmer from East to West that he was proceeding upwards ever nearer the sun. And, far from proving that the Earth is round, he decided it was pear-shaped.

Columbus died in semidisgrace and poverty in Valladolid, Spain, May 20, 1506. What happened to his mortal remains after that is as much of a puzzle as anything connected with his life.

I first became aware of the mystery of the whereabouts of Columbus' bones a dozen or so years ago. In Spain I had visited the great Gothic pile of the Seville cathedral and stood in awe beneath the elevated tomb (p. 222) of Don Cristóbal Colón, meditating on the greatness of the man whose bones rested in this exalted setting and not bothering over the curious detail in the guidebooks that listed the tomb as being a work of the "late 19th century." My reason subconsciously told me that Columbus must have been buried before the 19th century, but my emotion at standing beneath the actual remains of the Grand Admiral left

The late Thomas Dozier was a veteran foreign correspondent for Time *and* Life, *and author of a number of books on natural history.*

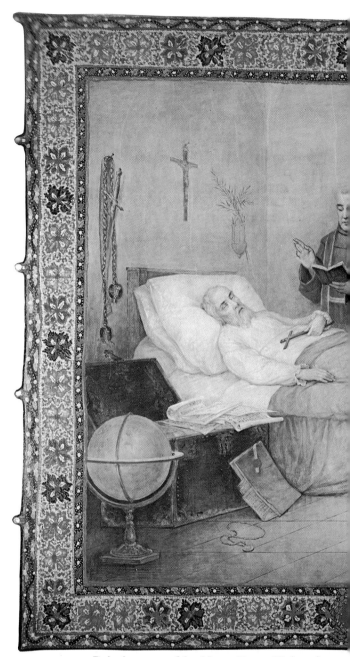

Painting owned by Notre Dame University depicts death scene of Christopher Columbus

no room for questioning. It was only when I visited Cuba in 1959 and was shown the tomb where Columbus *had been* buried that it became clear that his body had been shipped from Havana to Seville.

A few months later in what was then Ciudad Trujillo in the Dominican Republic, I was taken by one of the dictator's aides to the Santo Domingo cathedral and shown the tomb of Columbus. "This," said my military escort, "is where the Grand Admiral is *really* buried." I resolved someday to look into the matter.

on May 20, 1506, in Valladolid, Spain.
The date and place are probably authentic.

Lead coffin found in cathedral in Santo Domingo in 1877 contained bones. Inscription inside lid (top) could mean "Illustrious and Esteemed Baron, Don Cristóbal Colón." Letters on outside (directly above) may stand for *Descubridor* (Discoverer) *de la America, Primer Almirante* (First Admiral).

That opportunity came many years later. On a return trip to Seville, I met Don José de la Peña, who had just retired as Director-General of the Archive of the Indies, the huge library where all available documents relating to the discovery and conquest of America are kept by the Spaniards. It was quite natural that the mystery of Columbus should come up. Where, I asked, was the real tomb of the Admiral? "Ah," said Don José as we sipped dry sherry in an outdoor café, "that is a subject of considerable complication."

This metal chest now holds the fragile lead coffin in the cathedral at Santo Domingo.

Columbus' bones

Bones were believed moved to cathedral in Havana until the Santo Domingo coffin was discovered.

It is reasonably certain that Columbus died on May 20, 1506, in Valladolid. A Requiem Mass was said for him, and he was temporarily buried in the Church of San Francisco in this Spanish city. How long the body lay in Valladolid is not certain. Most historians, including José de la Peña, say that in 1509, three years after the Admiral's death, his eldest son, Diego, moved his father's remains from Valladolid to the Carthusian monastery of Las Cuevas in Triana, a quarter of Seville.

It is about 400 miles from Valladolid to Seville, a wearisome journey for the aged and infirm Columbus when he did it on muleback in 1505, and also a torturous distance for Diego to travel with his father's remains in 1509. But the posthumous wanderings were just beginning. Some 30 years later—the *Encyclopaedia Britannica* says flatly it was in 1542, José de la Peña says the date is uncertain—Columbus' bones were exhumed, along with those of his son Diego, by Diego's widow, Doña Maria de Toledo, and shipped across the Atlantic to Hispaniola (today shared by the Dominican Republic and Haiti), which the Admiral had discovered on his epic first voyage.

Old records show that in 1537 Maria de Toledo obtained royal permission to establish a burial place for the Columbus family in the main chapel of the cathedral of Santo Domingo; in addition to the discoverer and his son Diego, other members of the family buried there in the 16th century were Doña Maria herself, the Admiral's nephews, Christopher and Luis—and, according to de la Peña, a grandson also named Christopher. Some historians also include the Admiral's two brothers, Bartholomé and Diego, but de la Peña insists that brother Diego's remains were exhumed in Triana in 1950.

Don José also discounts one of the wilder theories about the Grand Admiral's bones: that the skeleton exhumed in 1950 was really that of Christopher, his

daughter-in-law having removed the wrong bones.

The amateur bone-tracer must make certain assumptions for himself: first, that Doña Maria took the right bones to Santo Domingo some time between 1537 and 1542. Assuming that, there is then no reason to doubt that the Admiral was reinterred in the main chapel (on the "Gospel" side of the altar) of the Santo Domingo cathedral and that there he remained for almost two-and-a-half centuries, slowly dissolving into dust and fragments alongside the remains of assorted relatives.

In 1795 Spain ceded Hispaniola to France. Local Spanish authorities and one archbishop Portillo, spurred by an officer of the Armada, decided that the remains of their beloved Admiral must not fall into the hands of the French. An exhumation was hurriedly arranged, and a coffin containing "a number of bones, and a quantity of mould" set sail for Cuba, a colony still safely Spanish. There they were ceremoniously reinterred in a vault of the cathedral in Havana. Across the vault was mounted a relief image of the Admiral with an inscription: "O remains and image of the great Columbus, for a thousand ages rest secure in this urn and in the remembrance of our nation."

Assuming the archbishop took the right dust and bones, the inscription writer proved to be too much of an optimist. Just over a century later, the Admiral was again menaced by the fortunes of war and revolution. In 1898, with the help of the United States, Cuba gained its independence from Spain. Determined action was necessary to prevent the Admiral's bones from falling into irreverent hands. This time, Columbus' descendant, the Duke of Veragua, arranged the ex-

Rebuilt cathedral at Santo Domingo,
in Dominican Republic, contains 1877 coffin.

humation from Havana's cathedral and the transfer of
his distinguished ancestor's remains to Seville, a city
unlikely ever to be taken over by non-Spaniards. With
the agreement of the Cubans, the bones that had been
transferred from Santo Domingo in 1795 were placed
aboard a Spanish destroyer bound for Seville, where
they were finally sealed in the monument built to contain them in the great transept of the cathedral.

So far, so good—as long as we assume that in each exhumation and reburial it was indeed the remains of
Christopher Columbus. From all the evidence, it is safe
to say that this was the case up to the point of transfer
from Santo Domingo to Havana in 1795.

By that time, the cathedral in Santo Domingo had
been allowed to fall into a state of near ruin, and the
inscriptions on the tombs of the various members of
the Columbus family were all but obliterated. Re-
building the cathedral in 1877, Dominican workmen
discovered on the Gospel side of the main altar several
coffins of the Columbus family. They were in poor
condition, but on the outside of one were found the
initials "CCA" inscribed in Gothic characters. The
letters, the Dominicans excitedly decided, stood for
Cristóbal Colón, Almirante (p. 219). Other abbreviated
inscriptions were found in the debris. The most important read: *"Illtre. y Esdo. Varon Dn. Criztoval
Colon,"* which could be rendered: "Illustrious and Esteemed Baron, Don Cristóbal Colón." Another legend,
somewhat more mysterious, appeared as *"Ua pte de
los r tos del p mer Al t D Cris toval Colon Des r."* which
might mean in Spanish *"Urna Patente de los Restos
del primer Almirante Cristóbal Colón Descubridor,"*

or in English: "True Urn of the Remains of the First
Admiral Christopher Columbus, Discoverer."

Proudly the Dominicans announced that they had
discovered the true grave of Columbus and that the
bones removed 80 years earlier and temporarily en-
shrined in the cathedral of Havana were those of the
wrong man. The Spanish indignantly declared the discovery a hoax.

The Dominicans proceeded to build a new shrine to
guard the remains of *their* Columbus, placing the cor-
roded lead coffin with its handful of dust and a few
fragments of bones in a heavy metal chest, the sides
of which fold down to reveal its precious contents.
Richard Halliburton, in his book *Seven League Boots*
(1935), recounts being shown the relic:

"I had a profound feeling of awe when these actual
bones of Columbus were revealed," wrote Halliburton.

"The lead box is seventeen inches long by nine inches square, and on the side the initials CCA—Cristo-
bal Colon Almirante—stand out boldly. . . . Of Columbus' remains only a few bones are still intact; the rest
have crumbled to dust which half fills the receptacle.
The skull has distintegrated entirely, or else it was
never there."

Never was there? Why not? And as for the skull's
having disintegrated, this seems unlikely. I have the
skull of a young girl of a pre-Incaic civilization in Peru
that an archaeologist assures me is at least 1,000 years
old; except for a few missing teeth it is perfect.

Adventurer Halliburton's belief in the authenticity
of the Santo Domingo Columbus has been shared by
numerous writers and serious scholars, but the Span-

iards have never budged from their insistence that their Seville Columbus is the right one. Thus for almost a century the world of Columbian studies has been split between the advocates of the 1795 theory (the true bones to Havana and finally to Seville) and those who favor the 1877 theory—the remains were never removed from Santo Domingo.

Now, Don José de la Peña comes up with an explanation of the mystery that is refreshingly simple. After a lifetime of study (the results of which he hopes to publish in book form), Don José has concluded that the mortal dust of the Great Explorer rests in *both* Santo Domingo and in Seville. In the hurried excavation of the ruined tombs in the Santo Domingo cathedral in 1795, Archbishop Portillo and his helpers took only a part of the Admiral's bones and dust, inseparably mixed with the remains of son Diego and probably of other members of the Columbus family, for reburial in the cathedral in Havana. Specifically,

Don José believes that the first words of the acronym found with the caskets in 1877 mean *"Una parte"* ("a part") rather than *"Urna patente"* ("true urn"), thus making the inscription read "A part of the remains of the Admiral Christopher Columbus." This suggests that there was a deliberate sharing of the remains.

As for the inscriptions on and inside the coffin now preserved in Santo Domingo, de la Peña is suspicious that these might well be 19th-century reproductions of what local artisans imagined 16th-century Gothic lettering should look like. He is particularly skeptical about the use of abbreviations, and says "The use of acronyms smacks more of the 20th century."

Says Don José: "The truth is that in the noble struggle between two patriotic factions, Santo Domingo decided to retain part of the bones and let the remainder be shipped away. Columbus belongs to America, but he also belongs to Spain. May he therefore rest in peace both in Santo Domingo and in Seville."

Columbus' remains may yet lie in this splendid tomb in the cathedral at Seville, where they were supposedly reinterred in 1899 . . .

. . . or all or part may rest in the memorial made for them in Santo Domingo's cathedral. Historians still must take their choice.

E asy mis   especialmente encargo que   no fuese

Almirante Colón   Descubridor de America

Article and photographs by Merlin D. Tuttle

Harmless, highly beneficial, bats still get a bum rap

Comprising a fourth of all mammal species, these nocturnal creatures pollinate crops, disperse seeds, and help keep insects down

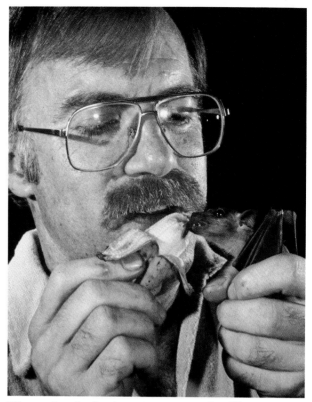

The author feeds a banana to a cave-dwelling nectar-eating bat he has trained to come to his hand.

Barely able to see in the dawn light, I fought my way through yet another tangle of vines and bamboo and shivered in the damp cold. I fervently hoped it was too cold for cobras to be active, and I worried about finding Khao Chong Pran Cave in time to photograph the spectacular morning return of its three million bats.

Suddenly, as I rounded a final pile of boulders, my thoughts were shattered: just in front of me stood a surprised and disgruntled-looking poacher. As we stared apprehensively at each other, I wished I had not left my Thai assistant, Surapon Duangkhae, so far behind. Just beyond the poacher, I could see a 40-foot-wide fishnet sagging with its catch of 30 large fruit bats.

Bats form the largest colonies of any warm-blooded animal, and they are found in all but the most extreme desert and polar regions. Nevertheless, bats are especially susceptible to extinction: they are, for their size, the slowest reproducing mammals; they are highly specialized; their huge colonies, in readily accessible places such as caves, are easily destroyed; and they are relentlessly persecuted.

Sensational media reports portray bats as mostly rabid and dangerous to man, his livestock and crops. In reality, the vast majority of bats are harmless and highly beneficial. Nearly a thousand kinds make up

Cave-dwelling nectar-eating bats, a male and female, are roosting together. They pollinate durian flowers.

almost a fourth of all mammal species and their survival is of great ecological and economic importance.

Worldwide, bat populations are declining rapidly. Some bats already are extinct, and many more may become extinct if human misconceptions are not corrected. The plight of Thai bats is just one of many possible examples.

I went to Thailand to study bats and their conservation needs, hardly dreaming that I would find myself in the middle of a feud between bat poachers and a coalition of school officials, monks and a town mayor. Dr. Boonsong Lekagul, a well-known Thai medical doctor and ardent conservationist, had introduced me to Khao Chong Pran Cave, simply as an excellent site to see a variety of Thai bats. We had barely arrived when I noticed that children were wearing bat T-shirts. I asked why, and quickly became fascinated with the story of guano mining and poaching, and how local people and a school are affected.

Especially in tropical areas, bats are often of considerable economic importance. In this case a monastery, school and many local townspeople were largely dependent upon bats for their survival. The bats of Khao Chong Pran Cave produce tons of droppings (guano), mined for use as fertilizer. Whole families partici-

Poacher cleans bats for market. The boy is wearing a shirt from local school supported by bat guano mining.

A young poacher in Thailand removes bats caught in a net. Small ones are simply killed and thrown away.

pate in the mining, and approximately 9,000 pounds are removed every Saturday. Annual sales total roughly 1.2 million baht ($52,860).

Khao Chong Pran Cave is owned by a monastery, and mining is supervised by the monks and town mayor. In addition to providing a livelihood for local people, profits from guano sales are used to support the monastery and the Wat Chong Pran School, a grade school attended by more than 460 students. In recognition of the importance of the cave's bats, the school sign displays a large stylized bat, and students are taught to respect and protect bats.

The cave has been mined for as long as anyone can remember, but guano production has dropped by some 50 percent over the past five years. Community leaders are concerned. Lost productivity apparently is the result of a decline in the cave's bat population, and they are convinced that the cause is too much poaching.

To stop the poaching, monks have covered one entrance to the cave with a locked door. Two other entrances have been covered with heavy steel grating. At the large entrance that is most used by bats, the monks actually hired an explosives expert who used dynamite to create steep cliff sides. Nevertheless, poaching continues. In Thailand large fishnets are readily available, and poachers have learned to hide them high up on a ridge above the cave. Nets cannot be seen from below by the monks, and the large fruit bats lack sonar and are easily caught.

Restaurant owners buy the big fruit and nectar-eating bats for three baht (15 cents) each and charge 30 baht a plate for their meat. Smaller insectivorous species have little commercial value and are killed simply to facilitate removal from nets.

With Surapon's assistance, I investigated further. Guano miners argued that their activities were traditional and of little consequence to the bats, but the cave seemed so well protected that I doubted that poachers could pose a serious threat. I asked Surapon to arrange for us to meet the poachers, but he quickly reported that such a meeting was impossible, since poachers feared apprehension.

My surprise meeting on the following morning, however, worked out well. At first, the young poacher understandably wanted nothing to do with us. Surapon finally convinced him that I was relatively harmless and offered him an excellent cash tip.

Soon we were following him from net to net and on to meetings with other poachers and even with a restaurant owner who bought bats. I learned that ten poachers were killing more than 10,000 bats per month. On the morning of our encounter he alone caught 90 large fruit and nectar-eating bats. Such a catch, if typical, would have resulted in ten poachers taking more than 300,000 bats annually. The town mayor claims there are actually 20 to 30 poachers, so even this figure could be a considerable underestimate.

Superstition contributes to continued poaching. Many Thais believe that eating bats makes people powerful sexual performers. They mix bat blood with whiskey as an aphrodisiac and for relief of back pain. Such practices, combined with a basic shortage of protein, already have led to the loss of many and probably most of Thailand's largest bat colonies, especially those that live in caves. For example, only three of 12 caves that I visited in the vicinity of Khao Chong Pran Cave still contained more than occasional individual bats, though most had once housed thousands and some perhaps millions of bats. In two of the three caves still occupied, bat populations have declined by more than 80 percent. In the third, Rakang Cave, more than a million bats support an entire village of guano miners, but are about to be destroyed by an expanding limestone quarry. Some species might actually become extinct before they are discovered.

Few Thais realize how much they benefit from bats. Aside from their role as natural insecticides and as producers of prized fertilizer, Thailand's bats also are of considerable economic importance in other, less obvious ways. The second most common bat in Khao Chong Pran Cave, the cave-dwelling nectar-eating bat, is the only known pollinator of durian trees. Throughout Asia the durian fruit has been prized from ancient

Merlin Tuttle is founder and executive director of Bat Conservation International, located in Austin, Texas.

times. Durian crops worth roughly $90 million annually could not be produced without bats.

Tropical rain forests around the world depend heavily upon fruit and nectar-eating bats for seed dispersal and pollination. In such forests up to half of all the species of mammals are bats, and bats are the most important seed dispersing animals. Additionally, more than 130 genera of tropical trees and shrubs are known to depend on bats for pollination.

Even in the United States, we often unknowingly benefit from the activities of tropical bats. Many, if not most, economically important tropical fruits originally were or continue to be dependent upon bats. These include peaches, bananas, mangoes, guavas, breadfruit, avocados, dates, figs and many more. Numerous other products of the world's tropics are equally related to the nocturnal activities of bats. This list includes timber prized for furniture, balsa wood for crafts, kapok filler for surgical bandages and life preservers, hemp fibers for rope, beads for jewelry, carob for candy, latex for chewing gum, and even tequila.

We are only beginning to understand the great value of bats in tropical ecosystems. Quite aside from their critical importance to rain forest survival, bats are essential to maintenance of genetic strains of wild progenitors of modern agricultural plants, such as bananas. Although bananas are vegetatively reproduced on plantations, preservation of their bat-dependent ancestors could prove critical to development of new, more productive or disease-resistant varieties.

Bats everywhere are unusually fascinating animals, and Thailand's bats are no exception. The Kitti's hognosed bat is the world's smallest mammal, the only member of its unique family, and known only from Thailand. It weighs less than a penny and has a bum-

A guano miner works inside Khao Chong Pran Cave in Thailand. Production is dropping as bats dwindle.

This bat is supplementing its normal diet of nectar and pollen with a whole fruit, in this case a crabapple.

The ear (center) and bizarre nose flaps of horseshoe bat are part of sophisticated echo-location system.

The author's tame Leschenault's rousette, one of the flying foxes, licks its chops before a meal.

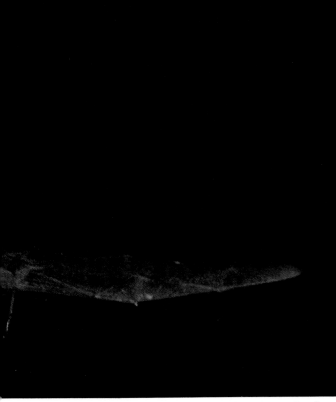

Such bats thus play a role in dispersing the seeds of many plants, as well as pollinating their flowers.

A lesser false vampire bat carries a captured moth. It preys upon large insects and small vertebrates.

A nectar-eating bat pollinates a male banana flower. Many valuable tropical fruits depend on bats.

A male black-bearded tomb bat exhibits the feature for which the species is named. It feeds on flying insects.

blebee-size body. Most of its formerly known cave roosts in Sai Yok National Park are now abandoned. The bats were decimated for tourist souvenirs.

Many kinds of horseshoe and leaf-nosed bats found in Thailand have incredible facial adaptations, apparently useful for sending and receiving sonar signals. Their strange looking nose-leaves, earflaps and other facial appendages may seem ugly at first glance. But, to scientists who understand their function, such faces are beautiful. Using sound alone, bats apparently "see" all but color, and have eyes as well! Even these once relatively common bats are increasingly hard to find.

Teaching a bat to come to the hand

Most people are surprised when given an opportunity to meet bats as they really are. The truth is that bats are among the world's most naturally gentle mammals. One evening at the Ratburi Forestry Station, I invited the foresters to watch my trained bats perform. They were amazed. Within two days of capture at Khao Chong Pran Cave, three cave-dwelling nectar-eating bats already had learned to fly to my hand on call.

Many of Thailand's fruit-eating bats are attractive by anyone's standards. Several species are referred to generally as flying foxes because of their handsome, foxlike faces. The Lyle's flying fox is conspicuous, owing to its three- to four-foot wingspan and its preference for roosting in large tree colonies in monastery courtyards. It survives because of protection by Buddhist monks. One of the world's largest bats, the common flying fox, is now rare on the mainland of Thailand. This giant bat, with its five- to six-foot wingspan, was simply too tempting as a source of food.

Throughout much of the tropics large fruit bats are declining rapidly. They were once abundant with colonies sometimes numbering more than a million. Several species are now extinct. When they are not overly exploited for food, they are killed by farmers who often mistakenly believe that such bats seriously damage their crops. In actuality, fruit bats prefer fruits in native forests and rarely eat any fruit that is not completely ripe. Since commercial crops must be picked green for shipment, they are seldom damaged. Research on bats that visit orchards is badly needed, both to counter misunderstandings and to develop means of avoiding the relatively few legitimate problems.

Most people are either ignorant or misinformed about bats. In Thailand I was unable to find a single person who knew that bats are essential to the durian fruit industry, and no biologists were studying bats. On the contrary, many Thais had heard that bats are dangerous carriers of dread disease.

The truth is, in all Asia, only one person is suspected of having died from bat-transmitted rabies, and only

one more is reported for all of Europe, Asia, Africa, Australia and the Pacific Islands combined. Furthermore, in all that vast area, none is known to have died of any other bat disease. By comparison, some 15,000 people die annually in India alone of rabies from other animals, mostly dogs.

Asians traditionally do not fear bats. In fact bats often are considered to be signs of virtue, good luck and happiness. Why then are these people increasingly concerned about bats being dangerous? The problem apparently stems largely from their blind trust in American knowledge and leadership. Although bats receive legal protection throughout Europe and the USSR, misinformed Americans spend millions annually exterminating bats. Worse yet, we export our grossly exaggerated fears to Third-World countries.

Why are we so uniquely fearful? In part it is because all of our bats are small, secretive and nocturnal, and therefore easily misunderstood and feared. But more important, our bats have been erroneously accused of serving as major carriers and reservoirs of wildlife rabies. In fact, many Americans still mistakenly believe that most bats are rabid and dangerous.

Even local health officials often are unaware that

The greater false vampire bat is a carnivore, feeding on frogs, fish, lizards, birds and sometimes smaller bats.

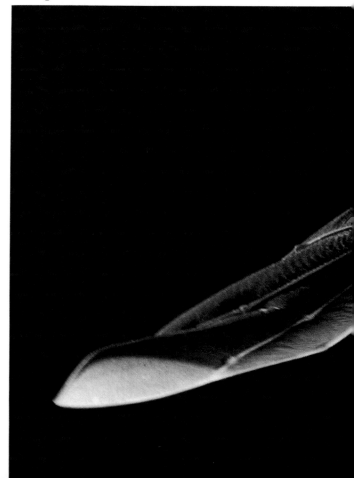

less than half of one percent of bats contract rabies or that even these rarely become aggressive. Bats do not act as symptomless carriers and rarely transmit rabies to wildlife. When people are endangered it is usually because they have foolishly picked up a sick bat that bites in self-defense. I have spent more than 20 years studying some 300 species of bats, often surrounded by millions, and never have seen an aggressive bat or contracted a bat disease.

Mortality statistics show that only ten Americans have died of diseases from bats in nearly four decades of record keeping. More people die annually from dog attacks, falling coconuts or food poisoning contracted at church picnics. Ironically, a federal judge recently concluded that the most serious health hazards involving bats are those created by unscrupulous pest-control companies in the guise of protecting people from bats!

Authorities on bats and public health agree that the only solution to unwanted house bats is to build them out after their nightly or seasonal departures. Beyond that, people simply should be warned not to handle unfamiliar animals, including bats.

Saving bats is important. Tropical rain forests and many economically valuable plants depend on the sur-

vival of huge bat populations, not just a few relict groups. Single cave colonies of insectivorous species can cover thousands of square miles, catching up to a quarter of a million or more pounds of insects nightly, including many economic pests. They are the only major predators of night-flying insects. Bats also are extremely valuable to science. Research on bats, for example, has contributed to development of navigational aids for the blind, to development of artificial insemination and birth-control methods, to production of vaccines, to testing of drugs, and to studies of disease resistance, speech pathology and aging.

Tens of thousands of important bat colonies have been destroyed intentionally by misinformed people and their governments. Many of the world's largest populations are already gone, and more are disappearing rapidly. The million bats in Rakang Cave may be gone by the time you read this article.

Certainly extinction of bats cannot be in mankind's best interest. These fascinating creatures are among our most sophisticated and likeable allies. It's time they received the respect that they have long deserved. Perhaps we, too, can learn from the teachers of Wat Chong Pran School.

But this predator is actually very gentle; the author found they could be quickly tamed and easily handled.

Photographs by Constance Warner

Eyeing animals eyeball to eyeball

*Readers are challenged to identify
the owners of these 22 eyes.
A trip to your local zoo may help.*

Of all the ways of sensing the world around us, seeing it is by far the most awesome. That our fingertips respond to texture, that the fine structure of the nasal passages corresponds so nicely with certain chemicals, that some complicated bones in the ear vibrate meaningfully in the head—all this is somehow less surprising than the idea that the world registers as images and patterns in the mind.

Seeing is all the more awesome when you realize that the eyes of each species are different and therefore, one must presume, transmit different images of the world. Every successful kind of creature sees what it must. Eyes are so designed—with a nearly endless proliferation of form and accouterment. One finds windscreens, goggles, windshield wipers, awnings, turrets, venetian blinds—all determined by such considerations as where the animal lives, or how fast it moves or what and when it eats, or by what it is eaten.

With all this in mind and with thanks to Mrs. Constance Warner, who has photographed eyes of birds and other animals for the Smithsonian Institution's National Zoological Park, we present an animal-watcher's eye test. You will be highly successful if, from the panorama of eyes that appear on these pages, you can identify the owners of more than five eyes. Pay no attention to size; the scale is purely esthetic, not relative.

In an age where the withholding of immediate satisfaction is frowned upon, the answers are obligingly given on page 237. For the more disciplined, clues (of a sort) are provided in the captions.

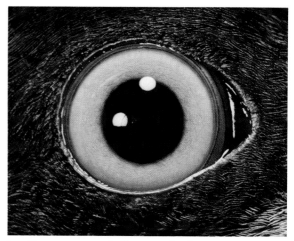

1.   Frogmen, pearl divers and others require glass-clear goggles over the eyes.

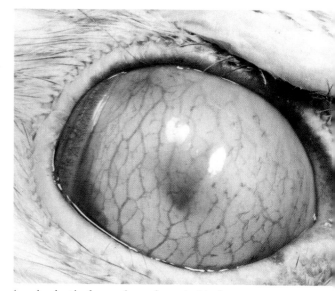

4.   A piratical eye glares from behind a porcelain-like third eyelid.

7.   Binocular vision permits greater depth of field for handling objects.

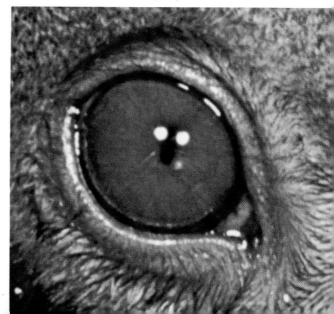

2. One eye watches you; the other can look almost anywhere for insects.

3. An elongated pupil helps some mammals by extending their field of vision.

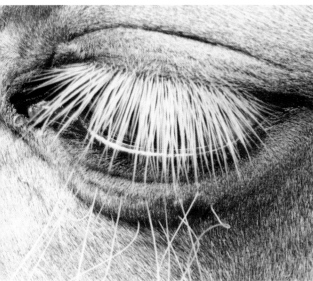

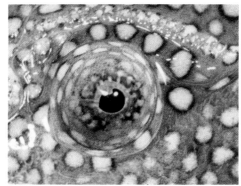

6. An "electric eye" zaps fish passing by overhead with up to 50 volts.

8. Another set of eyelashes, but what are they made of?

Eyelashes provide protection from the dust and glare of the trail.

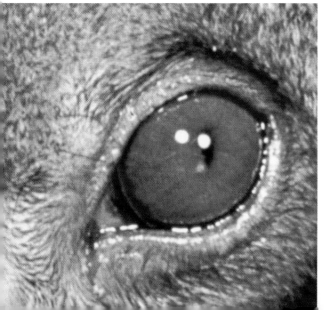

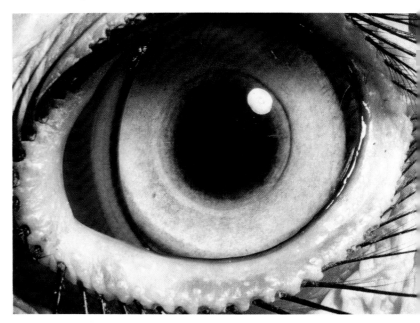

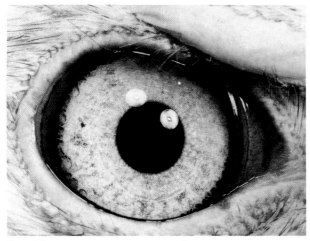

9. A bony canopy protects against glancing blows. See number 4.

10. Coming from the dimness into the icy glare, it is helpful to wink.

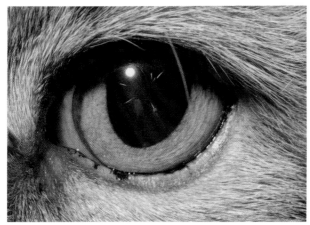

11. A dome-shaped eye with the pupil open is bad for detail, but good for motion.

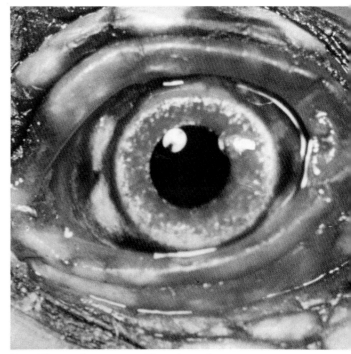

12. The males are usually red-eyed, the females are brown-eyed.

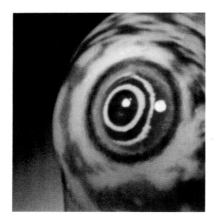

14. No science-fiction nightmare, but a device for regal reconnaissance.

15. When closed, the notched eyelid makes two tiny pinholes for bright light.

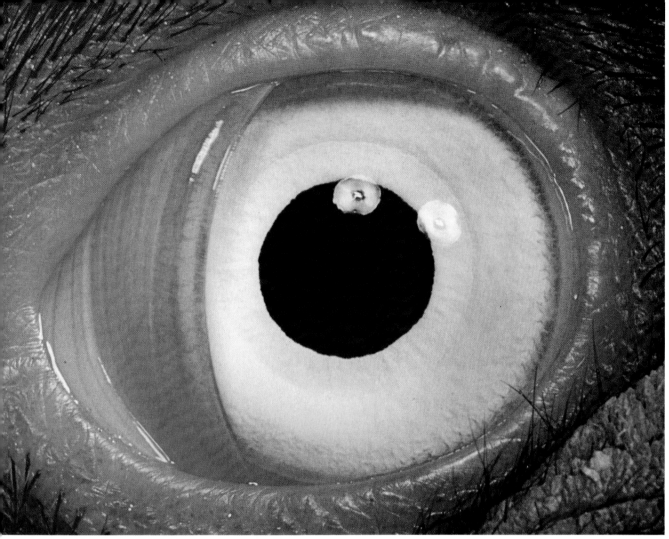

13. Like a windshield wiper, the third eyelid cleans this distant-seeing orb.

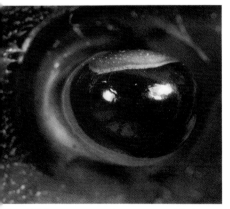

6. This compound eye can withdraw beneath a hard canopy.

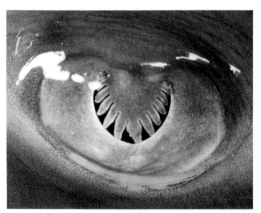

17. For looking up into the glare, it helps to have a venetian blind.

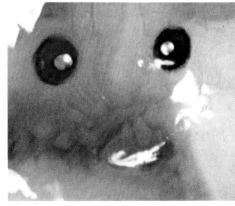

18. With 50 times what shows here, this creature still can't see much.

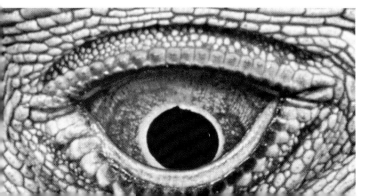

19. More eyelashes, but this time they are made of scales.

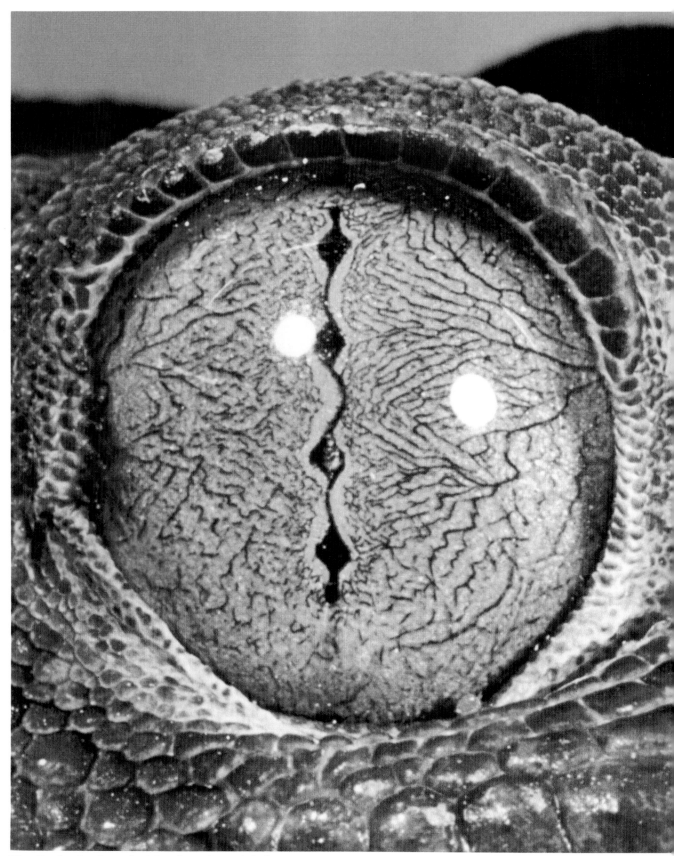

20.   In the daytime, the irises form four pinholes
which in turn form one image on the retina.

Eye-test answers

1. The merganser duck is an accomplished diver.

2. The turreted eyes of the chameleon can revolve in separate directions simultaneously.

3. Goat.

4. This bird of prey is known to hijack the catch of other birds. See answer number 9.

5. Palomino horse.

6. Lurking on the bottom in waters from South Carolina to Brazil, the southern stargazer has eye muscles that are modified to emit electricity. Both eyes are on top, hence the fish's name.

7. Near the low end of the scale of living primates, the African potto sees at night but moves so slowly through the trees that it is known as the "softly-softly."

8. A bird, the hornbill's lashes are feathers.

9. Not even the bony canopy has protected the endangered bald eagle from the direct pressures of man.

10. The king penguin's pupil contracts through a series of star- and square-shapes. Then it winks.

11. House cat. You should have gotten this one.

12. Eastern box turtle.

13. King vulture.

14. One of the stalked eyes of the queen conch— it probably only sees light and dark.

15. Gray potoo, a tropical bird related to whippoorwills.

16. Lobster.

17. When the little skate approaches the surface, an organ called the operculum expands and partly fills the pupil.

18. The 100 or more photoreceptors of the scallop serve only to detect light and dark.

19. Iguana.

20. When the gecko's irises are contracted, this lizard's depth of field and the consequent sharpness of image increases from "F4" to "F22."

The eye behind the camera

There is an aura of preordination in the photographs of Mrs. Constance Warner. A nurse, she worked for and ultimately married a distinguished eye specialist in the District of Columbia. Later, in preparing a paper for a local science group on the natural protection of animal eyes, she went to the National Zoological Park and found that no one there had thought much about the eyes of animals. That did it. With the help of zoo authorities, she set up a studio on the premises and began a long photographic career. She traveled worldwide to photograph animals not available to her at the zoo and, with the exception of poisonous snakes, handled them all herself.

Many thousands of transparencies later, Mrs. Warner is retired from photography. She still makes her home in Washington, D.C.

By Charles Elliott

How to read Proust

". . . it is our *duty*," wrote Cardinal Newman (who knew something about duty), "to live among books. . . ." As an editor in a publishing house, striving without principle to produce still more of them ("Books? . . . I have more than I can use"—David Hume), I should in decency hesitate to press the point. But Newman is right. Reading is duty, and hard reading is hard duty. "Read we must" observed Lord Shaftesbury; "let writers be ever so indifferent."

The question is, how?

I am, happily, in a position to tell you. In half a century of reading, I've learned a few things about it.

● Do not read in bed. It is impossible to stay awake. Of course some people have fallen into the regrettable habit of reading to *put* themselves to sleep, for which purpose they have special "bed books" of a soothing and soporific nature. It should be recognized that reading and sleep are the two great antithetic activities (see below).

● Do not read *on* a bed. Reading in this fashion, I had by the age of 18 developed a callused elbow and a substantial astigmatism. On the other hand both of my daughters seem to prefer the position to any other. They always read that way. They also manage to compose essays, meditate, bite their nails, listen to the radio and talk on the telephone, sometimes all at once, while leaning on an elbow on their beds.

● Read at a desk. A desk forces you to stay upright in a fairly stiff posture. As a rule the light is good. A hard chair, especially one with arms, is preferable to a chair with padding, although certain desk chairs have benefited from unusual elaboration. Li Yü, a Chinese author of the Ch'ing Dynasty, invented a temperature-controlled stool equipped with a special chamber for cooling one's seat in summer and a chair for warming it in winter. He, of course, customarily sat at a desk.

● Do not read in an easy chair. Like a bed it is conducive to sleep, and has the additional drawback of requiring you to cross your legs and wriggle a good deal in order to prop the book at the correct level. Besides giving you a crick in the neck, this plays hob with the crease in your trousers.

● Read on the subway or in any other form of public transportation where the movement does not make you sick. Sitting facing sideways helps. Dozing off under such circumstances is highly unlikely and concentration much eas-

ier than usual. Do not miss your stop. This time is frequently wasted and should not be, as the great English preacher John Wesley knew. "History, poetry, and philosophy I commonly read on horseback, having other employment at other times," he wrote. T. E. Lawrence supposedly read Aristophanes on camelback.

● Set aside specific small chunks of time to be used for reading especially difficult, even repellent, books. For example, do not take *People* magazine into the bathroom with you; take the *Critique of Pure Reason.* I myself read both parts of Goethe's *Faust* (in an excruciatingly bad translation) over the course of several weeks during the time spent removing my tie after dinner each night.

● Read at meals. While this may offend one's spouse and children, and judgment must be exercised, reading at the table has a long and distinguished history. Charles Lamb, as is well known, regarded Milton as suitable supper reading, which he proved by dropping bits of cheese and tobacco ash into the book. It ought to be simple enough to avoid this. A certain delicatessen on Third Avenue is my favorite reading spot above all others, I think. The pea soup (which

Charles Elliott is editor and vice president at Alfred A. Knopf Inc., a subsidiary of Random House Inc.

is served every Monday) is exquisite and the counter provides adequate elbow room.

"Take up Proust after dinner
& put him down"
—Virginia Woolf, June 20, 1928

• Do not attempt to read outdoors. The only exception to this rule is reading when walking, say, to work in the morning. Given a good sense of direction and a bat's ability to evade obstacles without actually looking at them, you should be able to read about three pages a block. I once read six chapters of Balzac's *La Peau de chagrin* before walking into a Madison Avenue bus. It was fortunately stationary at the time. Reading on the beach is not feasible.

• It is better not to read while driving a car or riding a bicycle, though I have known people to do so. I have not checked lately to see whether either of them is still alive.

• Read a variety of books at one time. Some would regard this as less a policy than an apology for mental disorder, but in fact the change of pace is invigorating. Most true readers have six or eight books going simultaneously. This means that it is usually possible to find one of them on the coffee table.

• Do not expect to remember what you read. Few people do, and there is much to be said for slithering through literature like Montaigne, a self-described "man of no retentiveness," who finally took to writing his opin-

ion of a book in the back of it so that he wouldn't make the mistake of trying to read it again as new. With a poor memory one can read *The Thirty-nine Steps* every ten years.

• Wait until you are old enough to read certain books. Only grown-ups should read Dickens, Melville, James and George Eliot. Do not attempt to read Proust before the age of 40.

"I try to read Proust"
—Virginia Woolf, April 27, 1934

• Persist. Especially when reading fiction, the point usually arrives when you will be eager to find out the ending. In certain cases (for example *Finnegans Wake* or *Centennial*) the ending itself may occur first.

• Stay awake. As I have noted, the great enemy of reading is sleeping. I do not know why this should be so; a beekeeper does not worry about falling asleep on the job. Readers, however, must be constantly on their guard. A number of devices, some unsettling, have been employed. Maxine Hong Kingston tells how her father, as a candidate for a civil service examination, first tied his pigtail securely to an overhead hook, then (when drowsiness still overtook him) thrust an awl into his thigh. Petrarch, who must be accounted a failure in this regard, was said to have died with his face in a manuscript.

• Employ special tactics when necessary. For example:

a) *Reading Proust* Select the proper edition, in translation. I recommend the small volumes published in Britain by Chatto & Windus, two of

which make up one of Proust's. They lie flat, the type is pleasantly readable, and they fit into a pocket. Read Proust deliberately and continuously, in regular small doses every day (or every week), preferably under conditions in which no reading matter more attractive than a saltines wrapper is available. Do not give up. Proust gets better in the second volume and by the time you reach Charlus it's whizzo.

b) *Reading diaries and memoirs* Read them at the rate at which they were written. In the case of Pepys, this will take nine years and five months.

c) *Reading philosophy* There is no way to read philosophy. Read *Riddle of the Tsangpo Gorges* instead.

"I followed my new diversion of book binding. I am covering Proust in little shiny squares of gummed paper"
—Virginia Woolf, July 22, 1934

Illustrations by Lane Yerkes

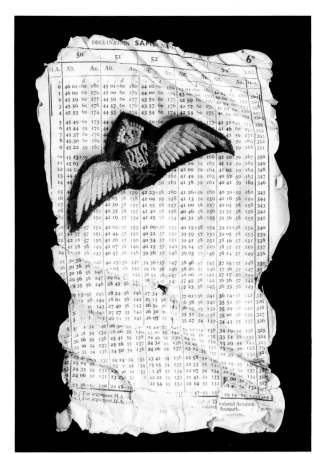

Royal Air Force pilot's wings and navigation tables were among wreckage of British planes in polders.

Kneeling in the soft dirt of a reclaimed polder, Arie van der Graaf examines pipe from B-17 wreck.

By Les Daly

Archaeology with a heart in Holland's drained inland sea

Excavating planes that crashed in its waters during World War II, a Dutch team is helping old wounds to finally heal

"I remember that crash because it was at 3 o'clock on my wife's birthday on Easter Sunday in 1944," a Dutch farmer tells an "archaeologist," actually a Dutch government official. At that moment, he recalls, a flaming fighter plane plunged to Earth and buried itself in his farmland near the southeastern Zuider Zee dike. As unforgettable as that incident was, it was only one of thousands like it that shattered the days and nights of Holland for five years; in staggering fact, Dutch experts estimate that more than 7,000 aircraft crashed in the Netherlands or in Dutch waters during World War II. They were American, British, German, sometimes flown by Australians, Canadians, New Zealanders and others. Too frequently the pilots and crewmen vanished with their planes. They were listed with official certainty as "missing in action and presumed killed."

The Netherlands lies at the corner of the continent of Europe, perhaps the busiest corner in the world during World War II. The location made the Netherlands the direct air route between England and Germany. Much of the corridor passed above the huge inland body of water once called the Zuider Zee, and

He specializes in identifying human remains
from crash sites and records of missing aircrews.

U.S. Air Force hand compass was sifted from mud
during the 1982 excavation of B-24 Liberator.

referred to as the IJsselmeer since it was closed off from the North Sea by a dike built in 1932. It was particularly attractive as a wartime air route because a large body of water was naturally less well defended than a flight path over land would have been.

Thus for more than five years the skies of Holland were filled with planes; early in the war they were Germans attacking and occupying the Netherlands, later streaming westward to devastate Britain, and each time returning again across Holland to their bases in Germany. Later still, as the momentum of war shifted, British, American, Canadian and other Allied fighters and bombers flew day and night above the Netherlands through German fighter squadrons and antiaircraft fire to strategic raids on Germany. Then they passed across Holland again, through more fighters and gunfire, on their way back to England. Thousands of those aircraft, on both sides, never reached home.

The enormity of 7,000 lost aircraft is almost impossible to comprehend. Consider this: the total fighter and bomber combat force of the U.S. Air Force today

amounts to about 3,400 airplanes. To put it another way, the crash of 7,000 aircraft would mean that every square mile of the entire state of New Jersey would have shaken to the impact of a downed plane.

It is well known, of course, that for hundreds of years the Dutch have been draining, drying and developing livable land from their inland seabed. In the past 25 years, however, they have recovered from the mud of the land they "created" the wreckage of 178 World War II aircraft. With these aircraft were the identifiable remains of 72 crewmen; for about 40 years each had been listed only as "missing in action." They were American, British, Canadian; many were German.

The "old lands" of the Netherlands had largely been scoured already, since most aircraft that had crashed on land during the war had been dealt with by the occupying Germans. However, in the 1950s and '60s, as the east and southeast portions of the IJsselmeer were drained to form large "new lands," called polders, more wreckage emerged from the sea bottom. Aircraft and pieces of aircraft lay in the path of development of the new lands—an obstruction and, in fact, a danger.

Color photographs by Bryan and Cherry Alexander

The Dutch recover crashed planes

If there were any doubt that these remains of World War II posed unusual problems, they were dispelled in 1960 when a group of Boy Scouts near the town of Kampen pursued an unprecedented class of merit badge. The industrious Scouts hauled away the tail-turret machine guns and 700 rounds of ammunition from a British Wellington bomber, and restored them to working condition.

"We thought this was a bit too dangerous," relates Col. Arie P. de Jong of the Royal Netherlands Air Force and now an official of the Ministry of Defense. Only a few weeks earlier, an Air Force jet fighter had crashed into the IJsselmeer, and the civilian Ministry of Traffic and Waterways had asked the Air Force to clean up the site. They did, and it was immediately apparent to the government that the Air Force was better trained and equipped than any other agency to cope with the older wrecks as well. By the end of 1960, the Air Force's crash and recovery specialists were given permanent responsibility for safe removal of all old airplane wreckage, with Arie de Jong as their leader.

Since that time, as reclamation has progressed, the Air Force team has been kept busy. The two polders most recently reclaimed from the IJsselmeer together cover about 735 square miles, an area comparable to New York City. They look more like North Dakota, and on Holland's scale they are vast. In a country well sprinkled with farmhouses, villages and little roads that seem to stagger back and forth for the sheer joy of it, the polders are for the most part sparsely inhabited farmland, eerily flat and open, with straight roads running to the sky. Holland is the most densely populated country in Europe and the sudden appearance of emptiness is unsettling. The Dutch call the polders the "land of endless horizons." The phrase is picturesquely accurate. But at the same time the word "endless" seems as artificial and out of place as the "new lands"

themselves in a country that you can drive across in a few hours.

In the midst of the polder farmland, the Dutch have been building sleek, cool concrete towns. They come complete with shopping centers, parking lots, underground utilities and sports complexes; on the flat polder lands they unavoidably bring to mind rows of little houses and hotels on "Boardwalk" and "Park Place." And they frequently stand where aircraft have fallen, bringing in the Air Force specialists. "A grazing cow doesn't have any trouble with an aircraft that is five or six feet below the ground," says Gerrie J. Zwanenburg, who is currently head of the recovery team. "But when you start building houses, that's an entirely different story."

When the Air Force recovery team was formed, the first thing they did, with the cooperation of American, British and German authorities, was to compile a virtual encyclopedia of nearly every aircraft thought to have crashed in Holland. They concede, ruefully, that the German records are the best—"*deutsch greundlich,*" a Dutch expression that refers to something being done "with great thoroughness." British records are also reliable, but often end simply with "nothing heard of this aircraft after takeoff," leaving the Dutch, as they say, "in the blind." Americans, they will tell

Flak-damaged B-24 bomber, burning in a field in 1944, was one of 7,000 planes downed over Holland.

British and American bomber formations often flew over less-defended Zuider Zee to German targets.

On map of partially reclaimed Zuider Zee, dots mark where planes were found by draining or by fishermen.

you amiably, often were unclear about the difference between the Netherlands, Belgium and Germany and "if they say it went down in Holland it might well have been Copenhagen."

These records have become the backbone of the recovery operation, explains Zwanenburg, whose office is at a Dutch air base in the small town of Zeist, not far from Utrecht. His chief objet d'art there is a twin-barrel machine gun he recovered from a downed German Messerschmitt 110 night fighter; he often uses it as an armrest while talking about his work.

"When I hear a report of someone coming upon an aircraft, I go out there with my metal locator," says Zwanenburg with the deliberateness of a plumber being called to fix a pipe. "I check my records to see who was going where and when and what they lost. Then I get my team, maybe eight or ten fellows, perhaps with cranes, bulldozers; maybe with teaspoons. Sometimes we need two or three demolition experts, sometimes medical experts."

The "contemporary archaeologists" also seek additional information in the area where the crash occurred, often finding eyewitnesses with remarkable memories who can provide invaluable details, like the farmer who recalled the crash on his wife's birthday 35 years earlier. Before the recovery operation even begins, they have usually already established which aircraft it is and whether it is likely to be a salvage job alone or one that will involve demolition experts

The author, a frequent contributor to these pages, wrote about cave dwellers in the June 1983 issue and solar dream houses in September 1981.

(there is almost always ammunition and frequently there are unexploded bombs).

"In fact, if the plane is a bomber the first question we must answer is whether it was on the way to a target, or on the way home," says Zwanenburg. "We need to know if it had dropped its bombs or whether it crashed with the bombs aboard. And even then, it might have had a hang-up, a bomb that did not release." He pauses thoughtfully. "If you know you are working on top of four 1,000-pounders," he adds wryly, "then you would rather do it with a small spade instead of two big cranes."

There was, for example, the excavation in 1973 of an American B-17 that had crashed with "a whole load" of 500-pound bombs. Colonel de Jong, who has never quit working with the recovery team although he no longer heads it, wanted to know the ignition time of the fuses and asked for help from the U.S. Air Attaché at the embassy in The Hague. "He got us a very fast answer; the timing was one-fortieth of a second!" de Jong recalls today with still-lingering respect for both the promptness of the answer and the hastiness of the fuses. Further, the mechanisms had been immersed in mud and water for 30 years or so, with uncertain effects. "Knowing those facts in advance determines whether you will have a fast recovery or a very slow and careful one," he points out matter of factly. "We have never had an accident—knock on wood," he adds, tapping the table purposefully.

It is rare that an aircraft hits the water or the ground and remains intact. "Aircraft are designed to fly through the air and are really quite fragile; hitting land or water is like hitting a concrete wall," explains

Col. Arie de Jong, who headed the recovery team when it formed in 1960, still works with the group today.

Gerrie Zwanenburg is now the team leader; when wreck is found, he heads to site with his metal detector.

de Jong. "The engines and the guns are usually the most durable items."

But not always. A half-filled bottle of eau de cologne was found in one aircraft, with a still strong fragrance. The manufacturer managed to acquire it "in the interests of research," an officer recalls, but used it instead in advertising. Functioning fountain pens and legible diaries, cards and letters have been found after more than 30 years. Film from mud-encased cameras was developed and produced recognizable images of raids over Germany. One American aircraft yielded a pair of silk stockings, "obviously a souvenir of better days," de Jong speculates. "At the moment we found them, in the midst of thinking about a wartime operation, it was a surprise."

It is indeed like an archaeological expedition, and the thrill of pursuit is contagious among the team members. For the veterans it is a source of technical and historical interest, and considerable personal satisfaction. For the 19- and 20-year-old enlisted airmen, wearing rubber hip boots to work in the cold wet mud, it becomes a sort of "gold fever" and irresistible. "As soon as they see a piece of an airplane, it turns into a challenge and they want to know more about it and what else is there," says de Jong. Routine coffee breaks are ignored by the men and the digging goes on until darkness despite the regular halt at the end of the working day.

The bed of the IJsselmeer is dark gray clay, the color of lifeless lunar rocks. Beneath the clay is sand. Civilians who visit the site are at first repelled by the gray mud and the cold water. After a few minutes, they ask to put on boots and take part in the excavation. The "fever" infects even the coolest observers who, like the team members themselves, are moved when a hand compass or a good-luck charm is sieved out of mud at the site of a wreck.

Unearthing old planes, reopening old wounds

From the beginning, the Dutch were aware that excavating the long-submerged planes created a poignant dilemma. Unearthing old planes also involved reopening old wounds as crew members once labeled missing in action were identified. At first, the Dutch were not anxious to enter the emotional unknowns among the families of men missing for so many years, hesitant to disturb old scars with new discoveries. "From our side, we were reluctant to give details, saying, 'Well, perhaps that is not decent; that should not be done,' telling how their beloved brother or son or husband spent his last seconds," explains de Jong.

"But much to our amazement, in all cases so far, and there have been hundreds of cases, people *ask*," he says. "I think it is the certainty, the technical certainty that

In the field, van der Graaf (left), Zwanenburg (third from right) and others recover Stirling prop.

Kent Miller (front, third from left) and Charlie Taylor (front, at left) were aboard an ill-fated B-24.

turns out to overrule their sensitivities. Even after this long period, people without exception are eager to know what happened and it satisfies them and is a consolation . . . no one ever says they don't want to know," he says reflectively. "It is something we had to learn."

Gene Miller agrees. Now retired and living in Florida, 11 years ago he was president of the Viking Glass Company in New Martinsville, West Virginia. "I was in my office one day and my secretary came in and told me there was a major who wanted to see me," he remembers. "When the officer came in, he introduced himself and immediately wanted to verify that I was Kent Miller's brother.

"The first thing I said was, 'I think I'd better sit down,'" Miller recalls. "I knew something had turned up about Kent, and I wanted to know." But Miller was shocked when the officer told him that after so many years, Kent's remains had been found. Miller then called his sister, Janet, and said, "If you're standing you'd better sit down, too." Once he had told her the news, he adds, "She started crying. She didn't know whether to be sad or glad."

The last Miller had seen his brother was just before Kent went overseas. Kent had flown low in his bomber and buzzed the glass factory where Gene and his father were working. They had looked up and waved good-bye. The fledgling pilot was 20 years old.

According to official records, Kent Miller had been the pilot of a B-24H Liberator bomber, serial number 427638, that crashed into Holland's inland sea three days before Christmas in 1943. Four crewmen bailed out and later died. One, the copilot, Charlie Taylor, survived the crash-landing and was captured. Five, including Kent Miller, were declared missing in action.

Three decades later, the Dutch built dikes and began draining the polder that would be known as South Flevoland. The water receded about an inch a day and as it subsided to a depth of about two feet, "something that looked like a piece of white wood" emerged. Enlarged photographs revealed it to be an aircraft wing with a U.S. Army Air Forces insignia.

When the water had fully drained, the Dutch built a causeway across the mud and excavated what turned out to be a B-24 bomber, nearly intact. Team leader Zwanenburg worked with identification expert Arie van der Graaf, Dutch colleagues and American authorities to track down the records of the five crew members who had not bailed out. Among them was Kent Miller, missing in action for 32 years.

Gene Miller and his sister were grateful to finally know what had happened to their brother. When a loved one is missing in action, Miller says today, "you may be 99 percent sure, but with no actual proof you think there's a chance they're alive and you always wonder. Knowing the truth at first made us sad; but in the long run it put our minds at ease."

Charlie Taylor, who had been the copilot on that fatal flight with Kent Miller, was luckier than his pilot. When their plane hit the 20-foot-deep water on that cold and cloudy December afternoon, its nose broke off right next to the copilot's seat. Taylor fought his way out of the plane, climbed onto a wing and passed out. The next thing he knew he'd been picked up by the Germans. He never knew what had happened to his crewmates.

Charlie Taylor was astounded when in April 1975 he received a phone call at his home in Scotch Plains, New Jersey, from the Netherlands. They had found the plane in which he went down, the caller said; the remains of five of his fellow crew members had also been found inside the wreck. Soon, Gerrie Zwanenburg and Taylor were in direct contact. "Were there any bombs on the plane?" Zwanenburg asked him. "No," replied Taylor; "we dropped them all over Munster."

That October, Taylor flew over to the Netherlands, where Zwanenburg met him and took him to see the plane. They drove out along a dike, walked a quarter-mile on a sand road and then climbed onto a small pontoon raft that took them to the edge of the giant camouflage-green hulk. "Zwanenburg took me to the top of the fuselage," Taylor relates today. "He showed me where the armor plate had buckled and closed the escape hatch behind the pilot's seat, which is apparently what prevented anyone else from getting out." Taylor had long wondered why he had apparently been the only one to escape, and now he understood.

Taylor realized how lucky he'd been. "As we were walking on the plane I thought—here are the five bodies, still in here; it really shook me up," he says. "They were a great bunch of fellows. I was lucky to get out."

The Dutch still get requests from families in many countries asking for information and in some cases for a special recovery effort for an aircraft in which a man went down. "We need to know the precise location of an aircraft that is still carrying missing aircrew," says de Jong a little apologetically. He is a man who carries his responsibility heavily, who is aware that there are still too many anxious, hoping families somehow counting on him and his colleagues.

"If we thought there was a crewman and knew the precise location we would try to tackle the job, unless it was an impossible location, in the North Sea or in a busy shipping lane," he says. "But the majority of these simply cannot be done because we know too little. Sometimes the family is not even sure it is in the Netherlands."

On the whole, the recovery operation is an endeavor of extraordinary dedication and sometimes mystical coincidence. When aircraft and crew members have been recovered, the Dutch have sometimes found next of kin through advertisements published by the British Ministry of Defence in newspapers in England and in Canada. De Jong remembers receiving a letter from an airman in Dublin asking about his Wellington bomber that had crashed 37 years earlier. The letter was received in his office on the day that the Wellington was uncovered.

On another occasion, a Dutch farmer told a major newspaper that he would like to know the identity of a pilot who had crashed fatally on his farmland, so that he could locate and talk with the pilot's family. At almost the same time, the widow of that pilot was writing to Dutch officials from Brussels, hoping to establish where and how her husband died.

"I telephoned her to tell her the news before she read about it in the newspaper, and she fainted on the telephone," says de Jong. "There is a strange sort of coincidental luck, or possibly even more than that, which I cannot explain. But there is something beyond our own capabilities that plays a role in what we are doing."

Pilot Kent Miller did not survive plane crash into the Zuider Zee; his remains were found 32 years later.

Personal items, navigational equipment excavated from downed American planes form eloquent still life.

Mares and Foals without a Background (1762) was commissioned by the second Marquess of Rockingham.

By Bennett Schiff

Stubbs' horses were all painted from inside out

Equally at home in the dissecting room, the stable, the racetrack and behind an easel, he was a very great English artist

Stubbs usually painted animals and figures first,
added the background only if the patron required it.

This portrait study of Stubbs at the age of 53
was made by his friend Ozias Humphry in 1777.

There are some things in England, even now, that
don't change. When the Queen recently took her first
real vacation abroad in 17 years, giving precedence to
pleasure over duty, she chose to come to the United
States to spend her precious private time mainly looking at horses, the horse in a way being to England what
apple pie is advertised to be to America.

Nothing could exemplify this more vividly than the
grand showing, the largest and most detailed ever put
together, of the work of an 18th-century commoner
named George Stubbs, mounted at London's Tate Gallery and now splendidly installed through April 7 at
the Yale Center for British Art in New Haven (made

possible by United Technologies). The Tate is an elaborate palace on the Thames. The Yale Center is one of
modernist Louis Kahn's purest essays in contemporary
architecture (SMITHSONIAN, July 1979). The two could
not be more different in style, but Stubbs shone in the
one and now shines in the other.

His is work that would glow softly in any surroundings, it being its own source of light through the gentle
incandescence of the color, but it is very much at home
in regal settings, the greatest part of it having been
commissioned by the top levels of the English aristocracy. In fact, next to Paul Mellon's, the British Royal
Collection has more Stubbses today than any other—
18. Mellon still owns 21 after giving the Yale Center no
fewer than 16. The Tate itself possesses 12, two of
which Mellon gave it along with 28 other sporting
paintings. In all, there are now approximately 450
Stubbses of which the whereabouts are known, most of
them spread around in what is left of the inhabited
stately homes of England or in more modest accommo-
dations, part of the family possessions.

In early 18th-century British painting the favorite
subjects were people. English painting then was essen-

Stalwart *Soldiers of the 10th Light Dragoons,* with horse, were painted for the Prince of Wales.

This regiment was the Prince's Own, and his commission to Stubbs was evidence of his pride.

tially English portraiture. The upper-class or aristocratic landed gentleman wanted *pictures* of his wife and children to hang in his manor house. Often enough he also wanted a portrait of himself, if only to hang alongside those of his illustrious ancestors, keeping up the tradition. English painting in that sense was not so much art as it was the acquisition of comforting emblems, medallions of a sort, representing familial intimacy or genealogical pride. Dr. Johnson summed it up, as he usually did with any subject he spoke on (although he was not at his best when it came to music or art), when he said. "I would rather see the portrait of a dog that I know, than all the allegorical paintings they can show me in the world."

For art, the wellborn seeker after knowledge and experience went elsewhere, on what was called the Grand Tour. Men of taste and sensibility—and money—brought back from France and Italy thousands of

outstanding masterpieces which have become the universal artistic heritage and treasure of the country. The elegant literary man Horace Walpole wrote home from his own Grand Tour, saying: "I am far gone in medals, lamps, idols, prints, etc. and all the small commodities, to the purchase of which I can attain. I would buy the Colosseum if I could."

But at home it soon became evident that, if you were going to have portrayed your nearest and dearest, it followed that the next logical step was your horse. The Englishman began to be shown with his horse as well as his wife and children; in many cases, if you were to judge by whom he spent the greater part of his time with, you would have to conclude he preferred his

Bennett Schiff, a member of SMITHSONIAN's *Board of Editors, wrote about Japan's cultural treasures from the daimyo exhibit in November 1988.*

The Countess of Coningsby (c. 1760), here in
Charlton Hunt livery, had her own racing stable.

The stately lady is followed by a little dog,
whose self-importance is almost equal to her own.

horse. Not all was ego, however. More often than not,
he commissioned the growing number of painters who
specialized in such subjects to paint just his horses and
his dogs, preferably in the field. When the British
sporting painter Benjamin Marshall (1768-1835) was
asked why he went to work at Newmarket, then as now
a great center for horse racing, he said: "I have good
reason for going. I discover many a man who will pay
me fifty guineas for painting his horse, who thinks ten
guineas too much for painting his wife."

Of those artists who specialized in painting horses,
George Stubbs is by far the greatest. Stubbs developed
a visual language for displaying the tense suppleness
and power of the animal which, because it is so exact
and so compelling, no one has ever surpassed. And, if
his exteriors are the most beautiful presentations of the
lovely animal, his interiors—the anatomy of the horse—
are works of such extraordinary accomplishment that

they can be compared respectfully with Leonardo's
anatomical studies. Stubbs' horses are literally painted
from the inside out.

The horse was fundamental in the 18th century. You
rode it for pleasure if you could afford to keep one,
and it also got you from one place to another by public
conveyance if you were poor. Before the advent of the
steam engine it was the only means of traveling long
distances on land. The horse also provided the muscle
power needed for growing food. And horse racing,
which reached manic heights in those years, was all of
today's soccer and football and baseball rolled into
one. For work and for pleasure, society depended on
the horse. George Stubbs, you could say, was born to it,
in Liverpool in 1724, his father being a successful
currier and tanner.

Although Stubbs is one of the most straightforward,
even-tempered, direct and clear-cut artists of any time,

Horse Attacked by a Lion was commissioned by Lord Rockingham. "African" background is imaginary.

Unlike the melodramatic lion pictures, *Zebra* is a sober,

there is something enigmatic about him. Now recognized to be one of the major artists of English history—along with Reynolds, Hogarth, Constable, Gainsborough and Turner—he has been given scant attention, often amounting to a mere mention, in the standard art histories. For more than a century he dropped out of the public eye entirely and was brought back to attention only about 25 years ago through the efforts of the English writers Geoffrey Grigson and Basil Taylor. Constance-Anne Parker published a revealing and readable book in 1971. Judy Egerton, formerly associated with Paul Mellon's British collections, now Assistant Keeper of the British Collection of the Tate, who brought together the present exhibition and who wrote the illuminating catalog, has also written elsewhere about his work with meticulous academic distinction and fine analysis. He is now back in the public eye where he belongs.

One great problem in learning more about Stubbs as a man is the paucity of contemporary material on him. There is not a single letter known that Stubbs himself wrote. All writers on Stubbs have had to go to a memoir manuscript of 98 pages written by Ozias Humphry, one of his artist friends, which is in the collection of the Liverpool City Libraries.

Until Stubbs was 15 he worked without any great enthusiasm as a clerk in the family business. There were six families named Stubbs listed in the Liverpool parish registers of the time and five of them were in the

leather business. Horses. And yet it was as an itinerant painter that Stubbs began his professional career.

He was virtually self-taught. At the age of 16 he had attempted, following his late father's advice, to study with a local artist, Hamlet Winstanley, then copying paintings for the Earl of Derby, but disagreed about the subjects he was allowed to paint and left after a matter of weeks. From then on he was on his own. There is very little of his work that can be attributed to any outside influence: a trace here and there of Gainsborough technique in the background of his early horse paintings, perhaps some disposition of space and object gained from Poussin, but that is arguable—and that's about all. Even on a trip to Italy to see what the masters had to show, he was unimpressed. Proclaiming that nature was superior to art, he left Italy after only three months in Rome, a short stay for what was a very expensive and difficult journey in those days.

Before his trip to Italy Stubbs had worked as a portrait painter in York, where he also pursued studies in anatomy, took up French, attended a class in fencing and considered learning to dance, graces which gentlemen of the time were expected to acquire. In an extraordinary venture for an artist of those days, he illustrated *An Essay towards a Complete New System of Midwifery* by the well-known physician John Burton, doing dissections himself and drawing as he went along, at a time when anatomy was considered an

accurate likeness of the first one
ever brought to England.

Against elegant, silvery background, *Hound Coursing
a Stag* is one of Stubbs' liveliest hunting scenes.

extremely suspect thing to do and getting subjects became a challenge to ingenuity. It was, after all, the age
of notorious body snatchers who were suppliers to the
medical profession.

In 1756, on his return from Italy, he found an isolated farmhouse at Horkstow in Lincolnshire and began work on one of the most remarkable publications
of the century, his *Anatomy of the Horse.* You can be
certain that it was more than quiet that Stubbs sought
in that rural setting, far from any neighbors, when you
consider what the dissection of so large an animal
meant in noisome odors and noxious gases in those
small rooms. Here, with only the help of Mary Spencer,
his common-law wife for about 50 years, he carefully
dissected, studied and drew with precise scientific accuracy and consummate draftsmanship the annotated
plates of his great book (pp. 254-55). Then, he wrote
the text. He labored there for 18 months, replacing the
carcasses in turn as they rotted way. It was to be another ten years before the work, the plates masterfully
engraved by himself, was published in London in
1766.

The book brought Stubbs great recognition. One of
the leading anatomists and men of medical science in
Europe, the distinguished Dutch surgeon Pieter
Camper, wrote to Stubbs. "How is it possible," he
exulted, "a single man can execute such a plan with so
much accuracy and industry?" A year later he wrote
again saying he was "amazed to meet in the same

person so great an anatomist, so accurate a painter and
so excellent an engraver. It is a pity you do not like to
pursue the viscera of this useful animal."

The book had a very great effect, as Stubbs had
intended it to, on painters of the time and those to
come. Sir Alfred Munnings, a noted painter of horses
of the following century, head of the Royal Academy
of Arts, described it as "The most unique thing of its
kind ever compiled. This heroic effort, an epic of the
18th century, is as great and unselfish a work as anything could be."

By that time Stubbs was firmly established in London, where he was to live for the rest of his life on a site
now occupied by Selfridges department store, which
faces on Oxford Street. A plaque in the store marks the
approximate location of Stubbs' house.

Soon after he arrived in London to stay, in 1760, he
became acquainted with Domenico Angelo
Tremamondo, who had come from Italy, an exquisite
practitioner of skills much in demand by the young
bloods of the day. Tremamondo opened an establishment to teach *haute école*, the art of classical riding,
and fencing. At this stylish school Stubbs, who probably went to observe the horses in action, met dukes,
marquesses, earls and other nobility, all of whom gave
him commissions. He had sold his first horse picture in
London to Joshua Reynolds himself, a year younger
than Stubbs but already well established as the leading
portrait painter of the nation.

253

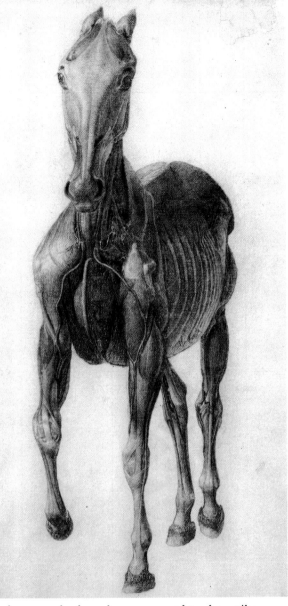

Drawings for *The Anatomy of the Horse,* based on Stubbs' dissections. Here, skin is stripped away.

Surface muscles have been removed to show ribs, blood vessels in neck and forelimbs, some tendons.

It was not only his authoritative knowledge of the structure and movement of the horse that distinguished Stubbs' work, although precisely those characteristics probably made him popular at the time. Scholars today point to his other outstanding qualities as a painter. He was George Stubbs the Horse Painter until he was forgotten, and George Stubbs the Horse Painter when he re-emerged; it is only very recently that he has become, for the experts, George Stubbs the Painter, period. Stubbs' paintings stick together. They are carefully and masterfully composed; the balance, design, arrangement of masses and sight lines are harmoniously unified so that, without knowing quite why—unless you study one—you are rapt with contentment. Look carefully at a large canvas for a bit and

almost invariably a little grouping—hounds, weeds, some wild flowers—becomes a tiny tableau, exquisitely executed, alive in itself. You have evidence, in painting after painting, with never a sign of sloppiness or haste, of the hand of a master.

And, with all that, he was remarkably elegant. Stubbs could paint the sleek, burnished coat of a mare with the same touch that Dutch, French and some English painters used to portray the glint and texture of silks and satins. But here it is living flesh, and pretty soon it is not just horses you are looking at but works of art that reach you with their formal beauty. Still, these are by Stubbs and so they are horses, too. There is in a horse's neck the power, the momentum and the undulating grace of a great wave, in its muscled hindquar-

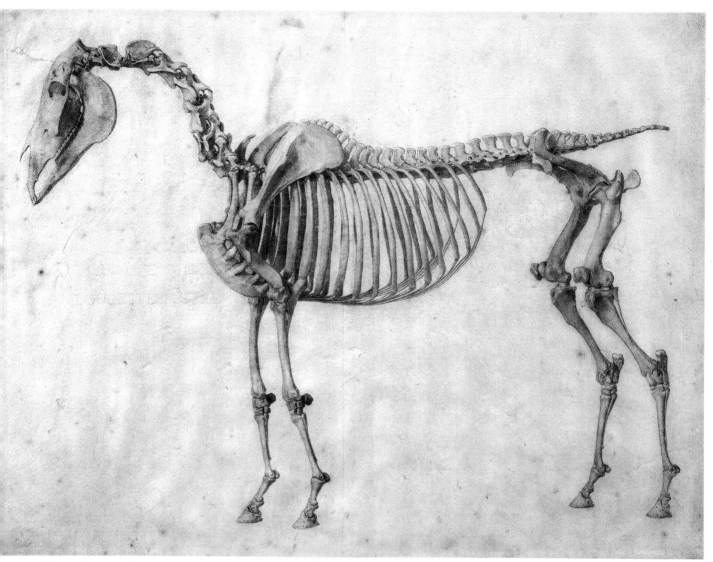

The skeleton. These drawings were later engraved
for the book. They are all graphite on paper.

ters and massive chest, the elemental flow and force of
the land. No false drama, just the horse, Sir.

It is interesting to note that at the Tate at different
times of the day you could see a man or a woman in
riding boots, worn not for fashion's sake but because
the wearer, from the state of the boots, obviously had
come straight from the stable. So universal is the appeal of Stubbs that some people came just for the
horses, while others were remarking on what a superb
formal painter he was, leaving aside the horses.

Like all men of learning in the 18th century, Stubbs
was interested in the wild and the exotic, samples of
which kept pouring into the country, souvenirs sent
back by the intrepid explorers and adventurers of the
age. In addition to the commissioned paintings of

horses in various settings, he painted a number of
pictures of other animals, which are outstanding for
his scientific and dispassionate observation and distinguished for his artistry. Among these were the moose,
the rhinoceros, leopards, lions, a zebra, monkeys, a
cheetah and a tiger which is the very essence of Blake's
"Tyger! Tyger! burning bright. . . ."

Stubbs' paintings of animals were so accurate, held
so much of the spirit of the beast as well, that there is
one case after another where animals were startled by
the paintings—a horse by a life-size painting of a horse,
a dog by a painting of a dog. In the case of the tiger,
Mary Spencer adds a note to the Humphry manuscript:
"For the Duke of Marlborough Mr. Stubbs painted a
large Royal Tiger, when it was nearly finished, it hap-

255

pened to stand on the ground in an out building, where some country [farmerlike] men, followed by a little cur dog came to look at it, soon as the Picture caught the dogs eye, he screamed, ran behind his master, trembled, and was guilty of an indelicacy incident to dogs when terrible alarmed, nor would he by any means, be made to look at it again."

Several major themes occupied Stubbs during his career. He would stay with each for as many as 20 or more years, until he was satisfied. Three themes stand out majestically: a series on mares and foals arranged in balletic friezes as graceful and ethereal as any Botticelli (pp. 248-49), a series of a lion attacking a horse (p. 252), and a series of pastoral paintings of farm laborers which are, simply put, entrancing (below).

He was always busy, always at work, and it is some-

Yale Center for British Art, Paul Mellon Collection

Reapers (1795) is painted in enamels on a clay tablet devised for Stubbs by Josiah Wedgwood.

how difficult to think of him sitting down to read, but he had an extensive library of about 2,000 books; knowing the kind of man he was, you feel he knew what was in them. When he wasn't painting in oils, he was developing a scientific method of painting in enamels on clay tablets in order to preserve, without fading, the original colors of the paint. For this he went to the cultivated potter Josiah Wedgwood for an earthenware plaque larger than any developed to that date, one that would not warp or crack in the kiln. After some years Wedgwood developed one, but Stubbs' work in the medium was never a popular success, beautiful as it is.

Toward the end of his life he suffered a decline in popularity, and there is evidence he had severe financial troubles and had to borrow money from a patron.

In 1795, at the age of 71, he began work on a *Comparative Anatomical Exposition of the Structure of the Human Body with that of a Tiger and a Common Fowl*, which he was still working on when he died 11 years later.

A note by Mary Spencer, in the Humphry memoir, recalls his last hours: "Within an hour of his Death he sayd to his surrounding friends 'perhaps I am going to die,' but continued he 'I fear not death. . . . I had indeed hoped to finish my Comparative Anatomy eer I went, but for other things I have no anxiety'. . . . On the 9th of July 1806, he as usual walked eight or nine miles, came home in very good spirits, went to bed about nine o'clock and at three next morning awoke, as well, he said, as ever he was in his life. On getting up in bed, he was struck with a most excruciating pain in his brest, and by the moaning he made, was heard by his female friend (who slept in the next room) on interrogation, he said the pain would kill him, at four o'clock he got up and dressed himself, went down stairs, and up again, several times, to Arange some papers, his friends, who were assembled, all thought him a great deal better, he left them at breakfast and returned to his bedroom. One of the party immediately followed him, and by her screams soon brought up the rest of the company, who found him sitting in an arm-chair, another chair he had placed so as to rest his legs upon, wrapt himself in his Gown, and the moment she arrived breathed his last."

He was said to have been so strong he could carry the carcass of a horse on his back up to the dissecting rack. More likely, you feel, after a day or two of looking at his work, he would have cradled a live horse in his arms.

The superb *Whistlejacket* (1762), not shown at Yale, was yet another Rockingham commission.

By Lionel Casson

The first Olympics: competing 'for the greater glory of Zeus'

There was bribing, boasting and jeering of losers, and only first place mattered, but judges kept almost no statistics at all

Two pancratiasts battled until one gave up. In regular wrestling, winner got the first three falls.

In Olympia today, morning sunlight floods ancient cŏlonnade in palaestra where wrestling took place.

One midsummer day in the year we calculate to have been 776 B.C., a 200-meter dash was run in a rural backwater in southwestern Greece, and a young local named Coroebus won it. It was an obscure event in an obscure spot but it earned him immortality: he is the first Olympic victor on record.

It came about this way. Not far from his hometown, in the place called Olympia, was a primitive sanctuary to the Greeks' chief god, Zeus. Festivals for the deity had been going on there for centuries. For some reason the people in charge decided to embellish what was traditionally done: they would offer up in addition to the customary sacrificial victims and prayers the honor of an outstanding athletic performance. So they organized a race, the race Coroebus won.

The next embellished festival was scheduled for 772 B.C.—and from then on, every four years, it took place more or less without a break for more than a millennium, right up to A.D. 261. And what began as a simple neighborhood affair soon burgeoned into a celebrated spectacle, boasting a dozen or so different events that pulled in contestants and viewers from all over. They came from the whole ancient world, from as far away as what are now France and Syria. There were other religious festivals, some very important, whose programs included sports, too, but none ever attained the prestige of the Olympics. Then as now, a victory there

Photographs by Alexander Tsiaras

259

Boxers wrapped their fists in leather thongs, fought without a break until one was knocked out or gave up.

Fluted stone segments from fallen columns mark the collapsed Temple of Zeus, built about 470-456 B.C.

was the be-all and end-all for all truly serious athletes.

Despite the growing renown of the Olympics, despite the fact that it attracted tens of thousands of people, the time and place were constant: everybody had to make the long and arduous pilgrimage to the out-of-the-way sanctuary. And when there, everybody, right up to champions of the highest repute and backers who sometimes were heads of state, had to submit to the arrangements, rules and regulations enforced by a local committee—about ten worthy citizens of Elis, the chief town of the area.

That was the way things were at the beginning and that is how the ancient games continued to be: for the greater glory of Zeus, not to improve the political image of any particular state or leader, as is sometimes the case today. And there was little fine talk of promoting international goodwill or anything like that. At the time the festival was launched and for four centuries afterward, the Greeks were organized into a multitude of little independent states, and one or more of these was always at war with another. When the date of the festival drew near, heralds were sent out to announce a sacred truce so that those who wanted to attend could make their way through the battle lines to get to Olympia. After a while, the truce was length-

ened to three months or so because travel time increased as spectators and contestants flocked in from farther and farther away.

For some centuries there were no athletic facilities whatsoever at Olympia, just an open space in which a running track would be paced off, areas for the discus and javelin throw laid out, and so on. Finally, by about 500 B.C., a few amenities had come into existence: a stadium for the runners and a hippodrome for the horse and chariot races (but no stands with seats for the spectators, just a sloping embankment to sprawl on), a bathhouse for the athletes, a headquarters building for the Olympic committee, and, of course, a temple to Zeus. Progress was slow because funding depended upon contributions.

Los Angeles, site of the 1984 summer Olympic Games, is better off than Elis was, for it at least can collect gate receipts; in ancient times, since the games were part of a religious ceremony, no admission could be charged. As it happens, Elis was not poor, but it was in no position all by itself to undertake a building program of the size needed. It was able to start work on Zeus' temple only when a successful war against a neighbor provided enough booty for the labor and materials. Many of the other improvements came, if

Games were invented to honor Zeus, and winning athletes received their olive wreaths at his sanctuary.

at all, from generous wealthy states or individuals.

There was not even a gymnasium until sometime after 200 B.C.; the athletes worked out wherever they could. Though eventually there was the equivalent of a VIP hotel, there were never any facilities at all for ordinary spectators. They arrived hot and tired and stayed that way during the five days the festival lasted. The rich were not too badly off: they slept in tents that their retinue of slaves put up. Most, however, slept in the open and munched on bread, cheese and olives, and drank wine they had brought along or bought from itinerant vendors. Sanitation was rudimentary or nonexistent and water, from springs and cisterns, was always in short supply. It was not until the second century A.D., after the games had been going on for about 900 years, that Herodes Atticus of Athens, at the time probably the richest Greek in the world, finally gave the place an aqueduct and a proper water system. In addition to all this, there was the heat and dust of a Greek summer and the flies—so bad that it is said the citizens of Elis used to offer up a special sacrifice to Zeus to keep them away from Olympia. The story goes that all a master had to do to make a sulky slave turn angelic was to threaten to take him along to the games.

"Aren't you all jammed in together?" asked the Greek philosopher Epictetus of would-be spectators. "Isn't it hard to get a bath? Don't you get drenched when it rains? Don't you get fed up with the din and the shouting and the other annoyances?" The answer in every case was a resounding Yes!—but this did not stop people from coming in droves. After all, the Olympics gave them, as ours do us, the one chance in four years to see many of the world's very best athletes in action. And there were other rewards. They could attend the sacrifices and services—which, now that the festival had gained such fame, were impressive ceremonies. They could get a look at some of Greece's finest works of art: a gigantic statue of Zeus in his temple was one of the Seven Wonders of the Ancient World, and all over the sanctuary grounds were statues of other deities and of winning athletes. Imagine today's Olympics being held, say, in Rome during Easter Week and you get some idea of why so many made the long journey and put up with all the discomforts.

Like a number of key features of Greek life, the games were for males only. With the exception of a special priestess, married women were barred from entrance—and on pain of death, no less. Since the assemblage of spectators was joined by the kinds of people who lived off crowds—pickpockets, beggars, con men, pimps, prostitutes—it was no place for respectable unmarried women. (Other festivals eventually ran events for women athletes, but never the early Olympics.) On one occasion a matron from a great sporting family, who could not bear not seeing her son compete, sneaked in dressed as a trainer; when he was victorious, she enthusiastically vaulted the barrier that marked off

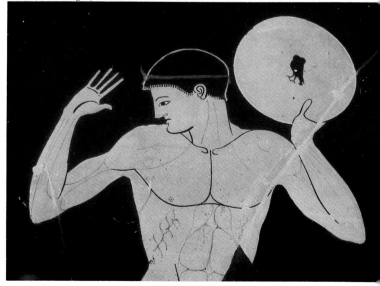

Poised competitor, from fifth century B.C., wields discus with owl, which was symbol of the goddess Athena.

Stone lion heads were originally designed to be drain spouts for water on roof of the Temple of Zeus.

the trainers' section and, in so doing, revealed her sex. Out of respect for the family's long line of winners she was spared execution, but a ruling was passed stating that trainers, like athletes, were to go around naked.

Shortly after 500 B.C. the program of sports reached its more or less final form—three days of major competition given over to about a dozen different events. It most likely started with the most spectacular, the chariot race. The number of entrants varied each year; at a comparable festival, the Pythian Games held in Delphi, there were as many as 41. The competitors lined up, each standing in a two-wheeled chariot that was light, like a modern trotter's gig, but pulled by a team of four horses that would be driven at the fastest gallop they could generate. They made 12 laps around the course—about nine kilometers—with 180-degree turns at each end. As at our Indianapolis 500, viewers enjoyed not only the excitement of a race but the titillation that comes from the constant presence of danger: as the teams thundered around the turns, or one chariot tried to cut over from the outside to the inside, crashes and collisions were common and doubtless often fatal. In one celebrated race at the Pythian Games, competition was so lethal that only one competitor out of several dozen managed to finish!

Next came the horse race, and it, too, offered the spice of danger because jockeys rode bareback on earth just churned up by the chariots. Both of these events were strictly for the very rich; owning a racehorse in ancient times was like owning a Rolls-Royce today, and owning a chariot and team was like owning a fleet of four of them. In the very beginning the owners may have done their own driving and riding, but they soon turned these jobs over to professionals. The prize, however, went only to the owners. Once, for example, a famous mare named Αὔρα (Breeze) threw her rider at the very beginning of the race, but being well trained,

covered the course in perfect style and came in first; the judges awarded her owner the prize. Women owners, who could not even get inside the grounds to watch, could yet win a prize this way, and there are the names of some in the lists of Olympic victors.

The chariot and horse races were the showiest events. But the crowd's favorites tended to be the body-contact sports—wrestling, boxing and the pancratium (a combination of the two)—which the arrangers of the program shrewdly scheduled for the fourth day, the latest possible. Wrestling was the mildest of the three. Unlike today's wrestling, the contestants were on their feet most of the time, since three falls ended a match and even touching the ground with the knees constituted a fall. Ancient wrestlers, like our TV mammoths, ran to size and beef. A certain Milo, who lived around 500 B.C., was so mighty a man that a whole series of fabulous stories grew up about him: that every day he packed away seven and a half kilos each of meat and bread, washing it down with seven and a half liters of wine; that he once carried a full-grown bull around the stadium, then cooked and ate it; that he could tie a band around his head and snap it by swelling his veins.

Classicist Lionel Casson writes often for SMITHSONIAN *on life in the ancient world. Among his subjects: political campaigns in Rome.*

Statues of Zeus were erected with money from athletes fined for dishonoring the games by taking bribes.

A local athlete is honored. Proud hometowns sometimes gave Olympic winners a special purse.

Fight crowds in any age like to see blood, and ancient boxing supplied plenty. The men fought with their hands wrapped in tough leather thongs, they fought continuously with no rounds and they fought till one was knocked out or gave up. It was a rare boxer who, after several years in the sport, still had uncauliflowered ears and all his teeth; boxers' battered physiognomies became a favorite butt of contemporary satirists, whose humor was crueler than ours.

The bloodiest and most popular event was the pancratium, or "all-powerful contest," a modified free-for-all. The contestants punched, slapped, kicked or wrestled, and the bout was over when one was knocked out, gave up or—as happened every now and then—died. No holds were barred, not even the stranglehold, and much of the time, as with today's wrestlers, the contestants were thrashing about on the ground, since a fall did not matter. One pancratiast actually developed a technique in which he would throw himself on his back with his opponent on top and work from there; he was never beaten. There was also biting and gouging, though these were theoretically illegal. The end usually came when one man got such a hold that the other quit to avert a broken bone or dislocated joint.

The first Olympic event to be recorded, Coroebus' race, was a straight run the length of the course, in effect a 200-meter dash. Soon a second race was intro-duced: down the course and back, a 400-meter dash. A long-distance run was added of nearly 4,800 meters, and then even a dash in which contestants ran in armor. These were the only track events; the marathon in today's games is a modern idea. The field events were three: broad jump, discus throw, javelin throw. They were never independent contests but always part of a curious mix called the "pentathlon," the "five-contest": the jump, discus and javelin followed by a 200-meter dash and a wrestling match. If a man took three of the five he was the winner.

It is hard to see how any one athlete could develop high skill in so many different sports. Yet the pentathlon was one of the earliest items in the Olympic program. It was sandwiched in between the spectacular horse events of the second day and popular body-contact bouts of the fourth. The modern Olympics, begun in 1896, made things easier by deleting the wrestling. After 1924, the men's pentathlon was dropped entirely, although the Olympics had already instituted a quite different competition, known as the "modern pentathlon," involving, among other things, horsemanship and pistol shooting. This year's games are going to include, at least for women, a version that goes the ancient pentathlon two better: a heptathlon—a seven-part contest, all track and field.

The fifth and last day was devoted to prize giving. Winners formed a procession and marched to the Temple of Zeus. It was an ancient version of the ticker-tape parade, since bystanders along the route showered them with leaves and flowers. At the temple, each was handed what ancient athletes considered the most precious object in the world, the victor's olive wreath. Its intrinsic value may have been nil, but it was worth a fortune to the man who walked away with it. An Olympic victory, as it happens, was just as great an

Greek charioteer reins in rampaging team; racing was Olympics' most spectacular (and dangerous) event.

Dozens competed, but during the nine-kilometer race, many chariots smashed up taking 180-degree turns.

honor for a winner's fellow townspeople as for himself, and they sometimes showed their gratitude by voting him a cash bonus—sometimes even a pension for life—as well as other perquisites. Moreover, Olympic champions were welcomed as contestants at festivals where bountiful cash prizes were awarded.

All such benefits were for winners only. Vince Lombardi would have been right at home in the ancient Olympics. Winning was everything; there were no seconds or thirds, no Greek equivalents of silver or bronze medals. And modesty in victory was not required. It was expected that a winner would savor his triumph to the full, would publicly exult in it. The Greeks did not go in for our ceremonious "sportsmanship," the generous congratulations of the vanquished. Far from it: losers were jeered and, hiding their heads in shame, slunk away. Even their mothers treated them with scorn. "The wreath or death" was the motto.

Greek record keeping, too, was very different. Almost no records were kept of the actual distance a winner jumped, or threw the discus or javelin, or the exact time it took to win any of the races. In ancient Greek, there isn't even a way to say "set a record" or "break a record." What interested people were "firsts."

In the beginning, Olympic athletes tended to be aristocrats. Only they had enough free time to go in for the extended work needed to train a man up to championship standard, as well as the free time and the money to travel to the festival every four years. Besides, most aristocrats had a good head start since wrestling, running and other sports were the way Greece's gilded youth spent its leisure. As the years passed, though, lesser folk managed to enter the competition, and in increasing numbers. Perhaps this was what prompted a famous crack by Alexander the Great, a very fine runner, when he was urged to enter the dash: "Only if the contestants are kings." One reason that common folk came to compete more was that hometowns took as much pride in a victory as did the victor himself. When a promising lad turned up, they would subsidize him; they did for their athletes what American corporations today do for ours. And once the lad had racked up a win, between bonuses and prize money at other cash-paying festivals, he was set for life. One ancient Olympic victor was offered 30,000 drachmas—the 1984 equivalent of at least half a million dollars in purchasing power—just to take part in some local festival; our barnstorming tennis stars do not do much better. Then as now, the popularity of a man's sport made a difference. Where cash prizes were given, the reward for a win in the pancratium could be six times that for a win in the pentathlon.

There was a price to be paid for getting into the charmed circle of Olympic winners, the same price paid today: endless, grueling training under the iron rule of the best coaches to be found. These had their special techniques, some of which make sense, some of which do not. Runners, for example, were probably paced by men on horseback. Boxers shadowboxed and worked out with the punching bag. Wrestlers worked out with partners called "statues" in the Greek sports jargon. Pancratiasts worked out with a punching bag heavier than the boxer's type, and they not only practiced punching it but kicking it as well. They also let it bash them on the head, presumably to accustom that member to a bash from a fist.

Trainers had their hang-ups about food, then as now. When it came to fish, to eat or not to eat depended on the kind of seaweed the fish fed on. As for meat, pork from pigs pastured along the shore was taboo, since the chances were they had fed on the sea garlic that flourished there. One trainer refused to let his charges go to dinner parties on the grounds that intelligent conversation would cause headaches.

All entrants were eventually compelled by the rules to train continuously for the ten months prior to opening day. The last month of training was conducted at Elis under the gimlet eyes of the judges. This procedure immeasurably impressed the competition since any who saw themselves clearly outclassed would quietly take off to avoid the shame of defeat.

The word "judges," when applied to the ancient Olympic committee, is a misnomer. Although the Greeks called them that, judging was only a small part of their duties. They checked the credentials of the competitors, supervised their training at Elis, served as referees and umpires, heard complaints of fouls and bribery. They were chosen by lot from a list of wealthy locals likely known as generous contributors.

If chosen, a man got the chance to be an absolute autocrat within the area of his competence and to display his importance by strutting about in a special purple robe and carrying a whip, followed by whip-carrying flunkeys. For the judges could punish athletes who had broken training—or committed fouls or accepted bribes—not only by fines or expulsion from

Runners, like these shown c. 530 B.C., contested in only four distances at Olympia: 200- and 400-meter dash and a 4,800-meter Greek "mile," as well as a cumbersome sprint that had to be run in armor.

265

the games but also by scourging, a most unusual procedure since Greek practice was never to lay a whip on a freeman (this was something reserved for slaves). Money from the fines went to erect statues of Zeus inscribed with appropriate sentiments, e.g.: "Show that you win at Olympia with the speed of your feet and the strength in your body, and not with money." The bribes seem not to have come from gamblers or betting combines but from fellow athletes who wanted a victory desperately enough to try buying it. Hometowns were so fervently behind their boys that even bribery did not faze them. When an Athenian pentathlete was fined for trying to bribe his way to a win, the Athenians sent out a top advocate to plead for him; when that failed, they paid the fine themselves.

The original Olympic Games endured for so long because they were part of a religious festival, an offering to the great god Zeus. Ironically, what kept them going was also what brought them to an end. As more and more of the ancient world turned to Christianity, Zeus was gradually forced to abdicate his throne. The Olympics were held, regularly as clockwork, down to

A. D. 261, when a threatened invasion of barbarians, the Herulians, interrupted the long sequence. The games were quickly resumed and continued—whether unbroken or not we do not know—until 393, the year in which the Roman Emperor Theodosius I, a fervent Christian, ordered the closing of all pagan centers. The site was abandoned. Over the centuries it was devastated by invaders, battered by earthquakes and gradually covered by silt from floodwaters of a nearby river. All this, together with endless years of neglect, left it buried until a British traveler found it in 1766. In 1875 the first of a number of German archaeological teams set about a systematic excavation.

Soon afterward, a French aristocrat, Baron Pierre de Coubertin, was passionately promoting the cause of athletics in general and a revival of the Olympic Games in particular. Resurrection of the site spurred him to even greater efforts, and in 1896 he finally achieved his dream: the first modern international Olympic Games. But they were held in urban Athens, not rural Olympia—the modern spectator took a dim view of sleeping alfresco, or even under a tent.

This is the track at Olympia on which athletes ran for fame, fortune and the greater glory of Zeus.

It is 200 meters long and has no stands; spectators sprawled on grassy banks. The judges' box is at center.

By Felicia Lamport

'The bass swam around the bass drum on the ocean floor'

I was having lunch at the faculty club with a recent acquaintance when a young man approached my table, handed me a slip of paper, said "Two more" and walked away. My companion and I were just beginning to discuss the project that we had agreed to lunch about when another man came up, gave me another slip of paper, said "Three, maybe four" with an air of quiet triumph and left. A woman dropped off the next slip. "Only one this time," she said, "not a large number, but after awhile the mind tends to grow number."

"Would it be presumptuous to ask what this is all about?" my vis-à-vis said.

"Not at all," I said. "It's a kind of game—trying to find a word that has two separate pronunciations, two distinct meanings, but only one spelling. Word games used to be used more often, but it's a subject I didn't intend to subject you to since you're an economist." He looked slightly annoyed. "The last economist I tried it on got his wind up before I'd even had a chance to wind up," I explained. "This is more likely to appeal to literary people."

"Economists are not necessarily illiterate," he said. "Can you give me an example or two?"

I handed him the slip the first man had given me. He unfolded it and read aloud: "*The bass swam around the bass drum on the ocean floor.*" He paused to blink, then continued: "*The buck does odd things when the does are in heat. . . .* You sure this isn't some sort of a private code?"

"Something I'd only intimate to my most intimate friends?" I said. "By no means." I handed him the slip the

woman had given me, sure that it would be a good one; her mind moves so supply that she had already added a dozen to the total supply.

"*A crow can scatter wheat seeds, but can a sow sow corn?*" he read, and laughed, but I sighed because the example duplicated one that had already been given me by a physicist obsessed with the game. "Oh, sao-so!" my lunch companion said. "I get it. But what's the problem? There must be dozens of words that meet your three conditions."

"They're rather hard to find. Name one if you can."

His silence lasted quite awhile but his lips kept moving.

"Are you having dessert?" the waitress asked.

"After dessert she deserted . . ." he started off happily, but I interrupted with: "No good; the spelling must be the same."

"Oh." Then after a pause, "But suppose I said: 'She wished she could desert him in the desert'?"

"On the nose—same spelling, two meanings, two pronunciations."

"Give me a few more from your approved list," he said.

"A couple should be enough to present you with at present. First, a rather sweet one: 'After watching the seagull dive for a fish, the dove dove.'"

"Lovely," he said. "Go on."

"OK, a final example," I said. "'The town dump is so full that it may have to start to refuse refuse. And if that makes the mayor blow his fuse, who will refuse him?'"

"That's a double," he said accusingly, and then added on with sudden inspiration: "When my mother-in-law accompanied us on our honeymoon trip to

Niagara, I nearly threw the old dam over the dam."

"Two-thirds OK, but the pronunciation is the same in both."

"Damn," he said. Then, after a pause: "How about: 'In trigonometry, the sine is a *sine qua non*'?"

"Sorry," I said gently, "foreign languages don't count. Although one contribution, 'It's unwise to rub pâté into one's pate,' struck me as so charming that I was tempted to give it a visa."

"Why not?" he said. "Must you be so intransigent?"

I sighed. "You make me feel that my sole object is to object. But I allow one great exception: 'Man's laughter can be crueler than manslaughter.'"

"That's really awe-inspiring. Do these things have a name?"

"Of course: heteronyms, logical relatives of synonyms, homonyms and antonyms."

The next morning's mail brought seven sound ones from my lunch companion—not a bit to my surprise. Heteronyms spread like happy rumors, perhaps because they're so useful in warding off insomnia, migraines or irritation with airplane delays. A two-page list came from a paleoanthropologist on the same day that a novelist swam up to me on Martha's Vineyard and said, "I saw the weirdest thing in town: a hand reaching up from a manhole wielding a threaded needle. It's the first time I ever came upon a sewer in a sewer."

We are, I think, coming close to a close with the contents of the master list, combining the inspirations of several score heteronymophiles for a 49-word total, including 16 you may or may not have spotted on this page.

Musée du Petit Palais, Paris

By Robert Wernick

Camille Claudel's tempestuous life of art and passion

A stunning model and brilliant sculptor, she influenced Auguste Rodin's work, but their stormy affair helped send her to the madhouse

Camille sculpted Rodin's favorite portrait of himself in terra-cotta in 1888—here as it was cast in bronze.

The great Rodin lay, old and infirm, on a sickbed outside Paris. He muttered that he wanted to see his wife. She is right beside you, they said: Rose Beuret, his faithful model, mistress and housekeeper for 50 years, whom he was to marry shortly afterward, two weeks before her death and several months before his own. "No, no," he said fretfully. "Not her. The other one."

The "other one" was at that moment 400 miles away, in a madhouse near Avignon, eating only raw eggs and potatoes she boiled in their skins for fear of being poisoned by Rodin and his henchmen. She was Camille Claudel, who for 15 tumultuous years before the turn of the century had shared Rodin's artistic and emotional life as pupil, model, collaborator, lover. A major sculptor in her own right, her career and her sanity had both passed under a black cloud. She was to live a quarter of a century after Rodin's death in 1917, remembered if at all as a mere footnote to the life of the man who inaugurated modern sculpture.

In the past few years her reputation has enjoyed a vigorous revival. The few and scattered works that have survived have come out of private collections and provincial museums for a couple of major exhibitions. A film is being planned on her life. There have been several books, one of them by Reine-Marie Paris, the

artist's great-niece, who has spent years searching through family and medical records to throw some light on a tragic destiny.

Camille Claudel was born in 1864 in the little town of Fère-en-Tardenois in a grim, windswept corner of the Champagne country. Her brother, Paul, who was to become one of France's leading poets and playwrights, called their home Wuthering Heights, and not only because of the barren moors that surrounded it. It was a house shrill with family discord.

The father, Louis-Prosper, was an upper-level civil servant; the mother, Louise, came from a local landowning family. In little Villeneuve-sur-Fère, where Camille grew up, it was the only family that counted, and it lived by its own rules. The father, said Paul, "had an antisocial and fierce disposition. . . . He made the family into a closed circle inside which we fought from morning to night."

Louis-Prosper adored Camille, his oldest daughter, and encouraged her when she developed an unladylike enthusiasm for modeling clay. Louise, the mother, hated her for not being the boy she wanted to replace her firstborn, who had died in infancy; hated her still more for being unconventional, proud, willful, artistic. Her younger sister, Louise, hated her too. Her

As a young woman, wrote brother Paul, Camille had an "air of courage, of frankness, of superiority."

269

Camille Claudel, a tragic life in art

brother, Paul, adored her, although his early plays are laid in stifling family atmospheres, with warring sisters (a stage direction in *La Jeune Fille Violaine*: "she throws the hot ashes into her sister's eyes").

Both Camille and Paul felt at an early age that they were meant to leave a mark upon their world. Her gift for modeling was extraordinary from the start. She was still a schoolgirl when it was noticed by a well-known sculptor named Alfred Boucher in the town of Nogent-sur-Seine when Louis-Prosper, by some whim of the bureaucracy, was transferred there. Under his encouragement, Camille blossomed. Her earliest works, now lost, were busts of Bismarck and Napoleon.

Louis-Prosper moved his family to Paris when Camille was 17, partly at her insistence because Paris was the center of the art world. "I see her now," wrote Paul in his old age, "in the full glow of her youth and genius, her splendid forehead overhanging magnificent eyes of a deep blue you hardly ever meet with but in novels, her mouth, more proud than sensual, that mighty tuft of chestnut hair, the true chestnut which the English call auburn, falling to her hips. An impressive air of courage, of frankness, of superiority, of gaiety—the air of someone who has received much."

She came not as a student but as a full-grown artist. The earliest of her works that have survived, busts of an old woman and of her brother (opposite), done before she was 20, show an astonishing maturity in the techniques of her craft, in her handling of volumes, in her psychological insight. She showed some of her work to the established academic sculptor Paul Dubois, and he was thunderstruck. "Have you been studying with Monsieur Rodin?" Dubois asked. It was the first time she had heard the name.

Camille meets Rodin

She worked all the time. When she wasn't modeling figures from life, she modeled bones—she made a complete set of human bones, and she carried a rhinoceros' skull around with her like a suitcase. She shared a studio in Montparnasse with her English friend Jessie Lipscomb and two other girls. Boucher used to come by from time to time to comment on their work. One day he won a prize which entitled him to a trip to Rome, and he asked Rodin to visit the Montparnasse studio in his place. Rodin went, he saw Camille, and life would never be the same for either of them.

He was in his early 40s, more than twice her age. He was red-bearded, corpulent, bandy-legged, a snorting sensualist—"a myopic wild boar," as Paul Claudel said. He was also at that time beginning to be recognized as one of the important sculptors of his day.

Soon Camille was working in his studio. They worked together in rare harmony. No one knows when

Seated, sister Louise; mother behind; father, at left with hat; on his left, brother Paul; Camille, in middle.

One of Camille's few surviving early works is of her brother, Paul, at age 13. Original plaster bust is missing.

Rodin's sensitive, poetic *La Pensée*, completed in 1886, is a portrait of Camille when she was 22.

they became lovers, for almost all the documents concerning her have disappeared. When they opened Rodin's desk after his death there was a huge envelope marked with her name, but it was empty.

They had much in common as sculptors. They came to their art with a fresh, clear vision and joy in handling the raw materials. Sometimes their work is so similar that—as in the case of Rodin's *Galatée* and Camille's *Jeune fille à la gerbe* (p.273)—it is impossible to tell which came first. (The comparative tranquillity of the composition might argue that it was Camille who had the original conception.) It is known that she worked on many of the scores of figures that swirl and writhe through Rodin's most ambitious work, *The Gates of Hell* (SMITHSONIAN, July 1981). Since all witnesses agree she was working continuously throughout this period, and since there are very few signed works of hers, the conclusion seems inescapable that part of Rodin's enormous production in the '80s and early '90s was conceived and executed by Camille.

The author, who commutes between Paris and Sea Island, Georgia, writes frequently about the art, history and culture of both continents.

Whatever the actual debt, there is no doubt that these years were the most fertile in Rodin's long career. For a time the "wild boar" was humanized, his capacity for feeling deepened and broadened, as he found himself dealing with a woman who was certainly more to him than a casual conquest. The strength and ferocity of his early work, his savage delight in human muscles, which led him to be called one of the great animal sculptors of all time, had become softened. There were now spiritual horizons beyond the pervasive presence of the flesh. You have only to compare the Brobdingnagian *Le Penseur*, whose thoughts do not appear to go much beyond, say, his next wrestling match, with *La Pensée* (above), with its tender delicacy, its veiled sadness, which he did a few years later and which is a portrait of Camille.

She called him Monsieur Rodin. He called her Mademoiselle Camille. They never lived together in Paris, though he would take her on trips to the country. There were rumors that she bore him one, two or four children, or that she had several abortions.

The few letters of hers to Rodin that have survived are girlish rather than passionate. ("I sleep naked to give me the impression you are with me. But when I

This small but critical view of society was called
The Gossips, The Talkers, The Babblers, The Secret.

Bronze version of original plaster done by Camille
in 1888 shows her fluidity of line and her tenderness.

wake up, it is not the same thing.") She sent him instructions to buy her a medium-size bathing costume at a department store, which, as Reine-Marie Paris points out, would have been a rather bizarre thing for a portly, bearded gentleman to do in the Paris of the 1880s. She made unmerciful caricatures of him, as well as a noble bust (p.269). At times their relationship could lurch into the grotesque: once she took him home to meet her parents, accompanied by Rose Beuret, whom she introduced as Madame Rodin. Her mother's rage when she found out the trick that had been played on her was deep and lasting.

For outsiders, it was the love match of the century. When they were working together or when they appeared at literary salons, where Camille impressed everyone with her grave, quiet beauty, her sudden bursts of laughter and her throaty countrygirl way of talking, they must have struck observers as an ideal combination of artist and muse.

Camille, however, was not content to be a muse. She wanted an independent career. She was never a servile copyist of Rodin—her works all have her own personal stamp. They are less bombastic, more contained, more intimate.

And there were fundamental differences of character. Rodin at bottom remained a man of the people, simple of taste, coarse of grain. He was devoted to Camille, he was generous to her, he worried about her excesses of temperament. But he had strong attachments to Rose, too, who had stood by him in all the hardships and disappointments of his youth, who had spent so many hours wrapping damp cloths around his clay figures to keep them malleable and able to be worked, and who had borne him a son. Besides, he liked her cooking. He would have preferred to go on indefinitely with both women by his side, catering to different sides of his nature, while he tended the fires of his genius; and he was honestly distressed when Camille wouldn't see it that way.

The end of the affair

Rose was a woman of almost preternatural credulity and forbearance, but the time inevitably came when even she knew what was going on, and there were dreadful scenes between her and Camille.

The breakup took years, and it is hard to know exactly what took place and when. Camille may or may not have had an affair with Claude Debussy, who was certainly smitten with her, and it may have roused Rodin to a jealous fury; in addition, he hated Debussy's music. All that is certain is that Monsieur Rodin would not marry Mademoiselle Camille, and that after 1898 she would not let him inside her door—though, according to one account, she used to hide in

Rodin's *Galatée*, about 1890, is at left. On right is Camille's *Jeune fille à la gerbe* of about the same date. It was at this time they worked together and the similarities are clear. What is not certain is the extent to which they influenced each other artistically.

the bushes outside his house in Meudon to watch him surreptitiously as he returned home.

He took it very hard. Camille took it much harder. She disintegrated.

She worked as hard as ever, after she had thrown off Rodin, and some of her most powerful works date from the next few years: the spiral of arrested motion called *La Valse*; the haunting figure of *Clotho*, one of the three Fates, burdened by the tangled threads of human destiny she must weave; the intensely dramatic group called *L'Age mûr* (Maturity), the most pointedly autobiographical of her works (p.275), in which a man slumps into the arms of a withered figure representing old age while a young woman, naked and desperate, on her knees, implores him to return to his youth, to his talent, to Camille; and the terrifying little group of figures bathing insouciantly under a towering wave that will break all too soon.

She was trying to distance herself from Rodin by working out intimate little pieces like *Les Causeuses* (*The Gossips*), which looks monumental enough in reproduction but which you can hold in your hands (opposite). She spent whole days making quick sketches of people in the street, and then making little figurines, "and they are clothed," she boasted, to mark how she was getting away from Rodin's compulsive fascination with nudity. Her drawers and cupboards were full of these little figures, which must have offered

a unique re-creation of Parisian life in all its variety at the turn of the century. But we will never know what they looked like, for she destroyed them all.

She destroyed almost all the works of her last years of liberty, hacking up in summer what she had labored all winter to create. She was losing contact with the world and with herself. She stopped seeing her friends ("I can't afford new clothes," she said, "my shoes are all worn out"), but sometimes, when she received a commission and got her hands on some money, she would round up people off the street and keep them all night in her apartment for a drinking bout. She lived alone in two rooms on the Ile Saint-Louis. The youthful body thickened, her face at 35 was that of an elderly woman. In her brooding solitude, Rodin became a malevolent presence that surrounded her. He was persecuting her, he was sending his agents to assault her or to rob her. He was selling creations he had stolen from her under his own name for hundreds of thousands of francs while she was being dunned for the cost of plaster. Once, she said, a maid put a sleeping powder in her coffee and stole her latest work, for Rodin to sell at a profit.

Her brother, Paul, had been away during almost all of these critical years. He was in the diplomatic service. On one of his leaves, in 1905, he took her on a trip to the Pyrenees. When he came back in 1909 he was appalled. "In Paris," he wrote in his journal, "Camille

Camille Claudel, a tragic life in art

Rodin with Rose Beuret, in 1916, about a year before they married. They both died shortly afterward.

insane, enormous, with a soiled face, speaking incessantly in a monotonous metallic voice."

The reasons for her breakdown have been ardently debated. Perhaps there was a hereditary strain of madness. Paul blamed everything on Rodin. Feminists have blamed the difficulty, the near impossibility, of living an independent creative life as a woman in those years of unabashed male chauvinism.

It was hard, but some women made it, like the painter Berthe Morisot or the writer Colette. Camille, however, was in a special position that helped to doom her. For one thing, she was a sculptor, and sculpture, at least in those days, demanded a considerable capital investment to pay for the fine Italian marble and the founders of the bronze casts. Camille's work was admired by her peers and by the critics, and was bought by a small circle of discriminating collectors, but she never achieved the kind of fame which would have brought her the big public commissions she needed to keep afloat.

And Camille's own nature was not made for half measures. She had told her brother when they were young that he was not to become any old playwright, he must measure himself against Aeschylus and Shakespeare. Her own ambitions were on the same scale. She had gambled all her life and her talent to gain Rodin and to gain glory. Now she saw Rodin ascending the heights, treated as a demigod in his own lifetime, while she sat alone on the Quai de Bourbon with her cats and her broken plaster.

Art imitates life

Across the sea in Norway an interested observer was hearing all the gossip about Rodin and Camille from a Norwegian friend of his, a painter living in Paris. Henrik Ibsen never met either of them, but, Reine-Marie Paris points out, they provided at least part of the theme of his last play, *When We Dead Awaken*. The hero of this curiously prophetic drama is Professor Rubek, a world-famous sculptor who since the creation of his masterpiece many years ago has been dragging on through an increasingly sterile life, turning out busts of society people. At a summer resort he runs into Irene, a deranged woman whom he recognizes as the model for his great statue, the woman who had shared his years of creative ecstasy. In long impassioned dialogues they admit to each other that since they parted, their lives have meant nothing, they are dead souls.

Ibsen, who believed in dramatic logic, kills off Rubek and Irene in a mountain storm at their moment of supreme awareness. Real life was not to be so kind to Rodin and Camille.

Rodin's last 20 years were a constant pageant, a fire-

Bronze cast of Camille's *L'Age Mûr,* or *Le Chemin de la vie,* shows one woman losing a man to another.

Rodin reportedly felt that it was too intimate and revealing a statement, and that it should not be shown.

works display of honors and glory. He was showered with decorations, awards, honorary degrees. Women of all ranks threw themselves into his arms while poets chanted his all-embracing genius. He paraded around Europe, and was photographed in tails and top hat as he went to visit kings and popes and society hostesses.

There was to be neither glory nor medals for Camille. On the 5th of March 1913, three days after the death of their father Louis-Prosper, Paul Claudel asked a doctor for the medical certificate permitting Camille's internment. Five days later two burly hospital orderlies broke into the apartment on the Quai de Bourbon, where she sat cringing among the cats and the accumulated filth of years, and carried her out to an ambulance which took her to the asylum of Ville-Evrard near Paris. When war broke out the next year and the German armies were approaching Paris, the patients at Ville-Evrard were evacuated to the asylum of Montdevergues near Avignon. Camille was to remain there for the next 29 years. There were brief visits from Paul and his family in the intervals of his rise in the foreign service; he became ambassador to Japan and to the United States. Only one friend visited her—Jessie Lipscomb—and she came just once.

A friend said that Paul Claudel never talked of his sister without the word "remorse" coming to his lips. A short while before he died, he noted in his diary, "Always the same taste of ashes in my mouth when I think of her." He was in no position to help her as he would have wished. He was too far away and he never had enough money—he became rich from his plays only after she died. But he must have been tormented by the question: Could he have done more?

There were many to ask questions, both at the time of her internment and afterward. Did they have to take her away at all? And once put away, did they have to keep her in that miserable place all her remaining years? Some of her friends claimed she was never crazy at all. Yes, she was paranoid, she had a persecution mania, but the woods are full of people with persecution manias who go about their daily business more or less satisfactorily without getting into trouble. Camille was never violent. She was unconventional, certainly; the neighbors had been complaining about that filthy ground-floor apartment with its shutters always closed and warned their children not to have anything to do with the shabby old lady who slipped out in the dark to pick up some scraps of food. But as a childhood

French film star Isabelle Adjani, who is producing and starring in a film about Camille, examines a Rodin.

friend of Camille's said plaintively, "Still and all, it isn't a crime to live alone and to love cats. If it was, half the village would be locked up."

The doctors in the asylum never wavered in their diagnoses: Camille went on suffering from persecution mania till the end. But it is characteristic of paranoia that it entails no impairment of the mental processes. Camille's letters from her dungeon run on perfectly lucidly for page after page until her thoughts carry her back to Rodin.

They can make heartbreaking reading. "Mad-houses," she wrote her brother, "are houses made on purpose to cause suffering. . . . I cannot stand any longer the screams of all these creatures."

The doctors tried to get her interested in working again; they offered her modeling clay, but she thrust it away from her angrily. On at least two occasions they recommended that she should be released, and she wrote pleading letters to her mother offering to abandon her share of the inheritance, asking only for a tiny room in the family house that she could creep into. The mother was adamant: she was an old woman, she said, past 75, and she could not bear at any price to take back someone who had caused her so much grief and would only cause her more. "She has every vice," she wrote to the director of the asylum, "I do not want to see her again." When the patients of Montdevergues were brought back to Paris in 1915, she pulled strings to keep Camille where she was, as far from home as possible. She was willing to send her cookies and coffee and pay for her dentist bills, but she also enjoyed getting back at her for the slights and injuries of the past, for that "ignoble comedy that you

acted out for us. Imagine me being naive enough to invite the 'great man' to Villeneuve, with Madame Rodin, the concubine! And you, all sugar, you were living with him, his kept woman. I don't dare even write the words that come to my mind."

Yet Camille clung to her family; it was all she had left. In 1939 when she was 75 years old she wrote to Paul: "At this holiday season I think ever of our dear mamma. I have never seen her since the day when you took the fatal decision of sending me off to an insane asylum! I think of the beautiful portrait I did of her in the shade of our lovely garden. The large eyes in which you could read a secret pain, the spirit of resignation which reigned over her whole face, her hands folded on her knees in complete abnegation; every-thing spoke of modesty, a sense of duty pushed to an excess, that was our poor mother. I have never seen the portrait again (any more than I have seen her)." And then the festering old wounds open again, and the tone turns to shrillness: "I do not think that the odious person of whom I speak to you so often has had the audacity to attribute it to himself, as he has done my other works, it would be just too much, the portrait of my mother!"

To an old friend who popped out of the past to write her in 1935, when she had been locked up for 22 years, she wrote: "I live in a world that is so curious, so strange. Of the dream which was my life, this is the nightmare." The nightmare would not end till she was an old, quite mad woman, quite cut off from communi-cation with the outside world. Her nephews and nieces, Paul's children, remember visits to the asylum to see a little old lady sitting motionless in her hospital gown and staring silently at the floor.

As for Rodin, he had died in the grim November of 1917. There was not enough coal to heat the large rooms of the huge house he lived in, and he contracted pneumonia.

Camille died in the dark days of another war, of an apoplectic stroke, say the hospital records; she had been suffering from undernourishment. When Paul visited her a month before her death, her last words to him were, *"Mon petit Paul."* He asked that her body be taken to the family vault in Villeneuve-sur-Fère, but because of the war, his request was never acted on. In 1955, after Paul's death and in accordance with his will, the family attempted to have her remains trans-ferred to the vault. But her body had long since been moved to a communal grave and no one knew where to find her bones.

A mournful and aging Camille Claudel sat for a photograph at Montdevergues asylum about 1931.

Poling into swampy Sundarbans delta, where tigers are unusually aggressive, village fishermen wear clay masks on the backs of their heads to baffle the enemy (tigers usually leap from behind to attack prey).

By Geoffrey C. Ward

India's intensifying dilemma:
Can tigers and people coexist?

Efforts begun in 1973 to save the animal and its habitat are working, but it is the local villagers who are paying the price

Secure in preserve, tiger takes a plunge; powerful swimmers, they're among the few water-loving big cats.

To the first-time visitor, Kheri District in the north Indian state of Uttar Pradesh seems a lovely, prosperous place. Tall green stands of sugarcane alternate with still-greener fields of wheat and brilliant yellow blankets of mustard. Brightly painted tractors rattle past with well-dressed Sikhs at the wheel. At harvest, the sweet smell of the sugar factories is overpowering and the lines of bullock carts filled with cane waiting to be sold stretch along the roads for miles. The hazy

India's growing dilemma over tigers

blue line of the Himalaya hangs above the horizon; the mountain kingdom of Nepal lies only a few miles to the north.

But the apparent tranquility is misleading: some 20 people are killed each year in encounters with the tigers whose home this region has always been. The Indian tiger has been brought back from the brink of extinction—official figures indicate that its numbers have more than doubled since the Indian government, in cooperation with the World Wildlife Fund and other international conservation organizations, set out to save it just 14 years ago—yet the future of these magnificent animals and of the forests over which they reign remains very much in doubt.

Conservationist Arjan (Billy) Singh has spent his life crusading for survival of the tiger and its habitat.

The conflict between men and animals in Kheri is more clear-cut and dramatic than that found almost anywhere else on the Indian subcontinent, but during the three months I spent traveling through some of India's and Nepal's remaining forests last winter, the problems this region faces seemed symptomatic of what is likely to occur wherever conservationists succeed in rescuing the tiger and even a small sampling of its world.

Until 1947, most of Kheri was considered unfit for human habitation. It is part of the Himalayan terai, a thick belt of deep forest and soggy grassland ideal for tigers and their prey, but hostile to settlement because of its inaccessibility and the malarial mosquitoes that swarmed out of its swamps. Independence changed everything. Eager for additional land on which to grow more food and relocate thousands of refugees fleeing the partition of the Punjab, the new Indian government drained the swamps. The great forests were felled for new farms and commercial profit. Hundreds of thousands of landless people followed in the wake of the first settlers.

Forced into a few pockets of jungle

The surviving tigers withdrew to a few small pockets of surviving jungle. Dudhwa National Park is one of these, a 200-square-mile tract of grassy meadows and groves of lofty *sal* trees that would also have been destroyed had it not been for one of India's best-known and most-controversial conservationists, Arjan Singh. Still vigorous at 70, and known to friends and adversaries alike as Billy because of a boyhood fondness for the adventures of Buffalo Bill, he has farmed in Kheri since 1946 and now lives at the southern fringe of the park on a farm called Tiger Haven.

He is a thorny, blunt man ("Billy talks," says a long-time friend, "the way a tiger would if it could talk"), and to him the great predator's survival is everything. His stubborn efforts to reintroduce three hand-raised leopards and a tigress to the forest have sparked controversy, and there are few conservationists with whom he has not quarreled at one time or another during the past 40 years. But no one faults either his courage or his dedication. He has written four books; has won the *Padma Shri*, one of India's highest civilian awards; and is the sole Asian to receive the World Wildlife Fund's Gold Medal.

Dudhwa is his monument; having persuaded the government to declare it a sanctuary in 1968 in order to save one of India's last remaining herds of swamp deer, he remains its tireless guardian, squinting shirtless in the sun while thumping out angry letters to the newspapers on an ancient typewriter, or speeding through the forest in his open jeep to check out

Pair of tigers are among motifs painted on the walls of village houses on periphery of Ranthambhore Park.

Pugmarks, here unnervingly juxtaposed with human prints, are key tool in estimating tiger populations.

rumors of illicit fishing or look for a lame tiger seen limping along the road.

Billy now fears all his efforts may have been in vain, that the extraordinary animals to which he has devoted most of his life may ultimately be doomed because government has proved unable to keep Man and tiger apart.

The 1973 international effort to save the tiger was begun none too soon. Three of the eight subspecies that once hunted from Iran to Siberia had already vanished; two more seemed about to share their fate. And even in India, where there are said to have been 40,000 tigers at the century's turn, fewer than 2,000 were believed to survive in the wild, many of them in scattered groups too small to maintain their numbers, let alone multiply.

In setting out to save the magnificent predator that has become its national animal, India had twin objectives: "to ensure the maintenance of a viable population of tigers" and "to preserve for all time, areas of biological importance as a national heritage for the benefit, education and enjoyment of the people." The core areas of the tiger reserves, off limits to humans, were meant to be "breeding nuclei, from which surplus animals would emigrate to adjacent forests." Broad buffer zones, where human incursions were to be restricted, would shield the breeding grounds from disturbance.

A visitor can only marvel at the seriousness with which India, faced with so many challenges, has worked at wildlife preservation in recent years: in 1975 there were just 5 national parks and 126 sanctuaries in the whole country; those numbers have grown steadily since, and now encompass 54 national parks and

Survivor of two attacks by the same tiger, old farmer who lives near Dudhwa Park displays frightening scar.

In Sundarbans, clay dummies are electrically wired to shock attacking tigers; dummy at right was mauled.

Running at full tilt, a male tiger closes in on his prey, a fleeing sambar, in Ranthambhore Park.

248 sanctuaries. Fully 12 percent of India's national forests are set aside for wildlife, more than 38,610 square miles. To create these havens the local populace has often been called upon to make great sacrifices. Villagers had to be moved from their forest homes, and the grazing of livestock and gathering of wood, grass and wild honey that had gone on for centuries was abruptly ended.

"It is an enormous investment for a poor country to have made," says R. L. Singh, the director of Project Tiger, a patchwork of 15 prime tiger reserves. "Our task now is to manage it wisely."

That investment has already paid off, at least in the short term. Even Billy concedes that there are many more tigers now than there were 14 years ago.

Just how many more, however, is a matter of controversy. Tigers are secretive, mostly solitary creatures and precise facts about them are hard to get. The most recent official figure is 4,005 animals, the grand total of the national tiger census in 1984, which includes all national parks and state sanctuaries, plus an estimate of all the animals said to live in the forests outside their precincts.

This census is a considerable undertaking: hundreds of thousands of square miles of forest are divided into individual blocks; then, in a given week, each square is systematically crisscrossed by forest department employees who search for tiger pugmarks while noting all the wildlife they see along the way. Some 10,000 men take part, equipped with glass plates on which they trace any prints found and record their location. Forest officers then compile the results and are supposed to be able to identify the size and distinguishing features of each individual animal.

The bureaucratic completeness of these tallies is sometimes breathtaking. One park director told me last winter that he not only knew exactly how many tigers prowled his forest but the precise number of male and female mongooses and pythons living there, too. The census has recently come under a good deal of critical fire. R. L. Singh admits that roughly half the men taking part have had little or no training and, although one former field director went so far as to claim that each tiger's footprints are as unique as are human fingerprints, many researchers question the whole notion of identification by pugmarks. "It's all nonsense," Billy says. "I've been tracking tigers almost every day now for 40 years and even I am unable to differentiate from pugmarks alone between tigers of the same size

The author, a biographer and historian, writes often about India and its wildlife; his article on Benares appeared in SMITHSONIAN, *September 1985.*

One out of every five chases, which last for about two minutes, will result in a successful kill. No man eating has taken place here; the open terrain minimizes incidents of surprise or mistaken identity.

and sex, unless there's some abnormality—and even that doesn't always show up." During one count at Dudhwa, he told me, some field-workers solemnly turned in pugmark tracings that had five toes—one more than tigers actually possess. And an Indian researcher named Ullas Karanth has shown that there are simply not enough prey species in the parks he studied to support anything like the numbers of tigers some of their directors claim.

Seeing a tiger has become something of a national craze among middle-class Indians, and tourists are permitted inside the parks provided they do not go on foot. For some reason, tigers don't seem threatened by people mounted on elephants or riding in vehicles.

The real problem is not with casual visitors. It is the village poor living around the parks who run the real risks from tigers. According to R. L. Singh, about 600 people have been killed in the past dozen years. Between 50 and 60 people annually die from tiger attacks: 15 to 25 of them are killed in the Sundarbans, a vast, thick mangrove forest on the border between India and Bangladesh; the same number die in Kheri; and the rest are scattered across the subcontinent.

Most killings are still simply cases of mistaken identity—accidents. Since long before the advent of firearms, tigers seem to have been innately wary of humans on foot. And even when a tiger is surprised on a kill, it follows a fairly standardized routine to scare off anyone who ventures too close. First it gives a warning roar (I have heard this sound twice, and found it awesomely persuasive both times). Then it roars even louder. Then, if the intruder somehow *still* fails to back off, it may make a mock charge. Finally, as like as not, it will turn and run rather than launch an all-out attack.

Human beings walking upright and sticking to forest roads are relatively safe, then; it is when they wander off into the undergrowth and lean over, cutting grass or collecting firewood, so that they lose their distinctively human look, that the likelihood of tragic error seems to intensify.

One afternoon Billy invited me along on his daily

walk through the dense forest behind his house. I struggled to keep up with him as he paced ahead on his thick legs, a short, carved "tiger stick"—the only weapon he carries—cradled in his arm. We ducked beneath branches, picked our way through mud, stepped over fallen logs and twisted roots.

"There you are," he said, stopping suddenly and pointing straight ahead. Only a few yards away, I could just make out the bent backs of three men cutting grass. Even to me, their silhouettes looked like those of browsing deer. "That's just one reason why mixed use won't work," Billy said. "Tigers and Man cannot share space. It really is as simple as that."

Surviving two attacks by the same tiger

Encounters between people and tigers are usually but not always fatal. I met two survivors: a young Nepalese woman, mauled last winter while cutting grass in Royal Chitawan Reserve, who was still ambulatory despite the two neat round holes left behind her ears when her attacker's canines pierced first her skull and then her brain; and Shiv Shankar, a grizzled, 63-year-old farmer who lives near Dudhwa. He managed to survive two attacks by the same tiger, thereby surely qualifying for the *Guinness Book of World Records.* Flames from an overturned kerosene lamp scared off his attacker the first time; several days later, the shouts of his horrified companions drove the animal away again. I asked him to what he attributed his extraordinary good luck. He thought for a long moment. "I have always drunk a great deal of milk," he said.

The tiger's champions like to point out that one hundred times more people die in India annually of snakebites than die from tiger attacks; that the risk of a mauling is seven times less to a villager living on the edge of a national park than is, say, a traffic accident to an American commuter.

But to the family and friends of a tiger victim, statistics don't mean much and, increasingly, grief is being transformed into anger. This past March, a tiger killed a teenage girl just inside the boundary of Corbett Park, northwest of Dudhwa; and when her friends and relatives banded together to recover her body, the tiger charged into the angry crowd and killed one of her protectors. The grief-stricken villagers eventually recovered both corpses and bore them to the home of the park director, breaking his windows, smashing up forest department vehicles and demanding action.

"Why is man eating such a problem at Dudhwa?" I asked Billy, hoping to slow his headlong pace through the jungle.

"This was the most ecologically vulnerable area," he answered, continuing to push through the undergrowth. Dudhwa has a special problem, he explained:

At Ranthambhore Park, a tiger plunges into lake in pursuit of sambar after watching them wade in from

there is no adequate buffer zone. Cultivators have been allowed to plant sugar right up to the forest edge, and sugarcane, so tall and so thickly grown that two men cutting it ten feet apart cannot see each other, strikes tigresses as ideal cover in which to bear and hide their cubs. The cane field becomes their home, and when, at harvest time, the cutters move into it, the tigresses defend it fiercely.

"The sugarcane problem is unique to Dudhwa," Billy says, "but the clash will come everywhere. When this place became a park ten years ago, there were 21 villages and small settlements on the outskirts; now there are 80. Population is out of control everywhere in India, and the problem will spread as more and more tigers grow familiar with humans and come to see them as prey. Familiarity breeds contempt."

Anything that moves is a target of opportunity for a tiger, Billy explained as we headed back to his house. Their primary prey is deer, but when hungry enough they have been known to feed eagerly on anything from baby elephants to frogs and locusts—and instinct teaches them to sample whatever they kill. A herds-

a hidden spot on shore. The large, heavy deer, which often feed in water, are the tiger's main prey here.

man killed trying to stop an attack on his buffalo at the park's edge may become a substitute for that buffalo. The next time, another herdsman may become the primary target.

Man eating is not new and it was once a good deal worse. Tigers accounted for the deaths of about 500 human beings and 20,000 cattle in a single district of the Bombay Presidency in 1822. Between 1902 and 1910, an average of 851 people were killed and eaten every year in India. The notorious Champawat tigress alone killed 436 people before Col. Jim Corbett, the most intrepid dispatcher of Indian man-eaters, managed to hunt her down.

A man-eating tiger, Corbett wrote after a lifetime of hunting them, "is a tiger that has been compelled through stress of circumstances beyond its control to adopt a diet alien to it. . . . The stress is, in nine cases out of ten, wounds, and in the tenth case, old age." Another circumstance helping to produce that fatal stress has traditionally been the degradation of the tiger's habitat and the disappearance of prey species on which it normally depends. In order to survive in a

steadily shrinking forest, old or ailing tigers turned first to livestock and then to humans.

Now a third, still more troubling variety of man-eater seems to be emerging, and the irony is that the brand-new "stress of circumstance" that seems to produce it is the success of the parks themselves as breeding grounds. Tigers are territorial. Although they often cover 15 miles in a night in search of food, the jungles through which they move so quietly are divided by them into distinct territories connected by a complex network of trails, their limits marked in a variety of ways—warning roars, scratch marks on the trees, the meticulous spraying of trees and other natural boundary markers.

The barriers between animals are not impenetrable: a tigress will sometimes share her territory with her grown daughters, and a resident male allows several breeding females to occupy segments of his range. But he rarely shows similar generosity toward other males, including his own sons, and so, as tigers continue to breed within the undisturbed core areas of the parks, young animals—or weakened old ones— are driven out toward the periphery. The forest corridors between parks that the planners of Project Tiger had hoped to maintain for just such immigrants have largely failed to materialize under the competing pressures of population and agriculture, and these hungry displaced animals are forced to cling to the forest edge. Increased confrontations seem inevitable.

They have already begun at Chitawan where, until 1980, there had been no documented cases of man eating at all. Since then, Charles McDougal, the American tiger expert who has been conducting research there for many years, told me 13 people have been killed and eaten around that park, most of them by battered animals that had lost out in the struggle for territory.

Openness of terrain minimizes danger

It is not the growing numbers of tigers alone, but the ever-increasing isolation of the forests in which they are forced to fight to survive that is making things worse. This seems to be demonstrated in reverse at Ranthambhore, in the desert state of Rajasthan. It is one of the most populous tiger reserves (I saw seven tigers there in just two days last year), yet Ranthambhore has never experienced man eating. Unauthorized intrusions have until recently been kept to a minimum by the dedicated project director, Fateh Singh Rathore, and his foresters, and the unusual openness of the Ranthambhore jungle minimizes the danger of accidents. A stalking tiger can recognize his potential prey over much longer distances here than he can almost anywhere else in India. But most important, its director believes, is that his young tigers, unlike those elsewhere, still have an escape route to follow when they reach maturity, a sizable patch of tattered forest just a few miles away across the fields; he has recently found pugmarks and other signs of tigers there, and has lobbied hard to have that area declared inviolate too.

There is one region where generalizations about Indian man-eaters have never applied—the Sundarbans. There seems to be no shortage of natural prey in this huge, forested delta, and the swampy terrain precludes permanent human habitation. Yet, since at least the 17th century, tigers have systematically preyed upon the villagers who slip up its canals and inlets in small boats to fish, cut wood and collect honey. In 1666, Francois Bernier, a French visitor, wrote, "Among these islands, it is in many places dangerous to land, and great care must be had that the boat, which during the night is fastened to a tree, be kept at some distance from the shore, for it constantly happens that some person or another falls prey to tigers. These ferocious animals are very apt . . . to enter into the boat itself, while the people are asleep, and to carry away some victim."

There are now officially said to be some 260 tigers in the Indian Sundarbans alone, the largest concentration on Earth, and they continue to be mysteriously aggressive. In fact, one out of every three is thought to be an "opportunistic" man-eater, one that will kill and eat any vulnerable human it happens to encounter. No one is certain why. Some believe the daily tides that wash away the tigers' scent markings force the animals to be unusually combative in order to hold on to their territories. Another possible explanation is that too much salt water might affect their livers, rendering them especially irritable; freshwater ponds have been dug here and there in hopes of restoring their equanimity. Authorities have also urged villagers to wear clay masks on the backs of their heads to confuse tigers on shore (tigers are reluctant to attack their prey from the front) and they have erected clay mannequins throughout the forest's buffer zone, each dressed in unwashed, villagers' clothing and wired to a souped-up car battery. The hope is that any tiger that attacks one of them and receives a 230-volt shock will learn a valuable lesson and may pass that lesson along to its offspring. Eleven dummies had been mauled by last March and the annual number of Sundarbans killings (which used to run between 55 and 60) has been roughly halved. It is too early to tell whether one or more of these programs or other, un-

Tourists are permitted inside the tiger reserves but they may not go on foot; instead, they are brought in by elephant or by wheeled vehicle. Seeking big tips, guides sometimes try to get a rise out of tigers.

Sunrise over Corbett National Park, first to be established (in 1936); its 201 square miles support perhaps 100 tigers.

Surprised tiger growls at an intruder; usually, it will threaten rather than attack.

known factors have been responsible for the change.

Despite the continuing difficulties around the periphery of the Sundarbans, however, the great forest's inhospitableness to Man and the large number of tigers that live undisturbed within it make it one of the most likely places for a permanent tiger population to persist.

"The tiger will survive in India," R. L. Singh says, "only so long as it behaves. The moment we try to be sentimental about any aberrant, defaulting tiger, the tiger will be doomed. Such tigers must be eliminated immediately. We are serving people first." He claims personally to have shot three man-eaters during his six years as field director at Dudhwa, and a total of ten animals was officially done away with. "The fault is Man's, of course," Billy says, "but the tigers are always made to pay."

Old-time professional hunters, forced to find other work since tiger shooting was banned in 1970, have eagerly volunteered to oversee the culling of undesirable animals. "Despicable," Billy adds. "They used to get $10,000 a tiger from their clients before hunting was stopped. They just want to get back into the act." Their unselfishness does seem suspect since they also want the right to contract rich overseas hunters and fly them in to do the shooting, a process that could take weeks while more innocent villagers die.

Some have suggested that "troublesome" tigers be transported to a forest where they are less likely to encounter humans. But other tigers often already oc-

cupy such places. Some years ago, a young Sundarbans tiger that had wandered out of the core area and killed first livestock and then a herdswoman, was tranquilized, taken to a spot deep in the jungle and released. The resident male killed it before the week was out.

Compensation for livestock killed by a tiger ranges up to 2,000 rupees (about $154) for a prime animal, provided the killing took place outside a park. (If a cow or buffalo strays inside the forest and is killed, its owner gets nothing.) The family of a human victim receives 5,000 rupees (roughly $384). Bureaucratic confusion often delays payment and sometimes causes it to be overlooked entirely. A man convicted of killing a tiger, on the other hand, must pay a fine of 5,000 rupees *and* serve six months in jail.

Despite the risk, villagers often take matters into their own hands. Last year, in and around Dudhwa, at least 13 tigers died in mysterious circumstances. One had its head blown off by a bomb planted in its kill; a forest guard was found burning the corpse of another tiger rather than have his superiors find out that one of his charges had been slaughtered. And Billy himself came upon the skeleton of a third surrounded by the reeking corpses of close to 150 vultures; someone had poisoned the tiger's kill, the tiger had eaten from it and died, and the poison remaining in its body, in turn, had done in the overeager scavengers that had fallen upon it.

Billy has not mellowed, but he has matured. In the old days, battling single-handed to defend his park's borders, he pummeled with his big fists the woodcutters and graziers and poachers he captured, sometimes even hauling them behind his tractor to park headquarters. He is as vigilant as ever but now sees that the poor are not the real enemy.

"How can you blame the cultivator?" he asks. "He has one acre of land and one bullock to plow it. If a tiger takes that bullock, what is he to do? No wonder he wants tigers done away with. It is government's fault. They have set up these parks and now they walk away from the problem."

"The local people hate the park," Billy told me as I drove off to talk to villagers in the surrounding countryside. "And they hate me. You'll see."

I left Tiger Haven along a twisting forest track, pulled onto the tarmac road and almost immediately passed a wealthy landowner's concrete house surrounded by the thatched huts of his tenants. A gaudy tent was set up in the landlord's garden with loudspeakers lashed to poles, so that his daughter's wedding ceremony that evening could be shared with his neighbors. A little farther along, I pulled over to let the groom's party pass, perhaps 75 laughing men in beards and turbans, dancing to the crash and blare of a brass band on their way to the home of the bride.

I stopped beside a field, where an old man was plowing behind a haggard bullock. His name was Kanthulal and he had lived there all his life. Things had been much better before the park was established, he said; he had been able to collect his firewood without fear of arrest, could buy timber and thatch to shore up his house after the monsoon. Hunters had kept the tigers down. Now he lived in fear. The wife of a boyhood friend had been killed cutting cane; he had himself twice seen tigers padding along the road and often saw their fresh pugmarks on his way to the fields in the early morning.

Two young cyclists stopped and walked their bicycles across the ruts to join us. They agreed. "Government cares *only* about tigers," one said. "They do not care about us."

"We might as well be dogs," the third man added. "In my village no one stirs from his hut once the sun has gone down."

I thanked them and continued on, past teams of cutters half-hidden in the cane, and stopped beside the prosperous-looking young Sikh who was supervising their work. A tiger had recently slipped into his compound at night and taken a fine buffalo. He had been helpless because he was not permitted a rifle. Forest officers had visited him but had done nothing.

Billy was right: no one who lived around the park seemed to have a good word to say about it. Nor did most of the villagers who clustered in and around the other reserves I visited seem anything but resentful of the parks' existence, and their smoldering hostility sometimes flares into open warfare. At the Keoladeo Ghana bird sanctuary in the desert state of Rajasthan a few years ago, for example, eight men were shot dead by police when they refused to pull their animals out of the park in which their fathers had grazed them for a century. Shortly before that, herdsmen at nearby Ranthambhore beat Fateh Singh Rathore, the field director, almost to death for trying to bar their herds from his forest.

Hard times make things still worse. The Ranthambhore region has been hit by drought three years in a row now, withering what little fodder the seared, chewed-over landscape outside the park normally provides. This past summer, thousands of cattle swarmed through Ranthambhore's ravines, and political pressure forced the field director from his post. Ranthambhore survives and so do its tigers—but the future remains uncertain.

Forest resources are rapidly vanishing

The villagers' view is ecologically shortsighted, of course. Most know only what their fathers knew—and the forest resources upon which their fathers relied have all but vanished. According to satellite data, every year India loses more than three million acres of forest, an area a little larger than Connecticut. There are more than 730 million people in India, and perhaps a billion head of domestic livestock, almost all of it undernourished and forced to forage to survive. "We face ecological disaster," Prime Minister Rajiv Gandhi has said of the disappearing vegetation, and with aid from abroad the central and state governments have undertaken massive reforestation projects. But trees continue to fall, precious grasslands are steadily devoured, whole hillsides tumble into riv-

A group of tiger cubs surprisingly pops up in India's Kanha Reserve, one of nine which has been set aside for the failing king of the jungle as part of internationally supported conservation program.

ers. You can see what is happening almost anywhere along the Indian roads. Brightly painted trucks overloaded with newly cut logs careen around the curves. In the purple evening light, bands of barefoot women hurry home with heaps of branches balanced on their heads. Long lines of lean buffalo, gaunt cattle, scrawny goats drift out of the forest, leaving more acres stripped, and plod toward villages already shrouded in blue woodsmoke. Increasingly, the parks are becoming green islands in a human sea.

Indian conservationists have always hoped that in ensuring survival for the tiger, human survival would be enhanced as well. "We are here to preserve the habitat, not the individual tiger," R. L. Singh says.

"But how can local villagers be expected to understand that?" Billy asks. "No provision is made for supplying them with alternative fuels, for teaching them other ways to build their houses or thatch their roofs or feed their animals. We must face the fact that the park does not benefit them. Why should they want to preserve it?"

Valmik Thapar, a shaggy young naturalist and filmmaker who has been studying and writing about Ranthambhore's tigers for a decade, agrees: "Villagers must be involved in these parks, must be made to feel a part of the necessary changes, not their helpless victims. The future of Indian wildlife ultimately rests with the villages that surround them." He and Fateh Singh Rathore have proposed that local banks provide villagers who pledge to stay out of the forest with low-interest loans for buying improved livestock, for example, and that those new animals be stall-fed on grass planted and maintained outside the reserve by the forest department itself. "The ideal," Thapar says, "is that the parks will eventually provide so many benefits to the villagers that they demand that more degraded forests be made into parks."

Billy concurs, but such programs take time to implement. "Meanwhile," Billy argues, "the only real answer that is fair to both sides is to keep people and tigers apart." He wants a high electrified fence put up around Dudhwa to keep tigers in and people out, and a permanent ban on the growing of sugarcane within five miles of it.

But thousands of people would be thrown off the land. Something else would have to be provided for them to do. Isn't this sort of undertaking too large to assume for a country with limited resources and so many pressing problems?

"Saving the tiger—and the forests it lives in—is itself

a large undertaking," Billy answers. "If we are serious about it, we have no choice."

"Why do you go on?" I asked Billy. "The odds must sometimes seem hopeless." "A quirk of personality," he says, eyes flashing with their old fire. "I could not live with myself if I gave up."

Conservation is always a question of priorities and Billy's are clear: "Tigers need unmolested forest in which to multiply. People can breed anywhere." But government inevitably has a more crowded agenda.

His body a finely tuned hunting machine, a tiger moves stealthily through the grasses of Ranthambhore.

The question remains whether in a democracy like India—where, as Billy says, "Tigers don't vote; people do" and where many of those voters are understandably preoccupied with their own day-to-day survival—government can make ordinary citizens see in time that their own future well-being and that of the Indian forests and the superb animals that still rule some of them really are inextricably linked.

On my last evening at Dudhwa, I sat with Billy across a stream from a tiger's kill. The moon cast just enough light for us to make out the tiger's silhouette, but we could clearly hear him muttering as he tore at his kill, alarming but natural sounds that have been heard here since the beginning of time.

Then, a new and ultimately more ominous noise drifted toward us from across the cane fields at our back: the amplified drone of the wedding priest in the nearby village. A new family was beginning; still more people would soon edge toward the tiger's last retreat.

It was already hard to hear the cracking of the bones.

Trenches near Beaumont-Hamel, once churned up
by shellfire, have been softened by time and weather.

By James D. Atwater

Echoes and voices summoned from a half-hour in hell

*At the Somme in July 1916, brave men of
the Newfoundland regiment were senselessly
ordered forward to all but certain death*

Astonishingly, there is no one there. The billows of
land roll on to the horizon, gentle shades of green
blending into far-off blue. There must be some mistake. You are alone in a part of the world that you had
always imagined as being filled with masses of men
waiting for their moment in history—7:30 A.M. on Saturday, July 1, 1916—and the order to begin the Battle
of the Somme.

And something else is wrong. There is no noise.
Somehow you had assumed there would always be
noise, a lingering rumble, at least, of the tornado of
sound that swept across these fields more than 70 years
ago, shaking the soul of everyone who heard it,
clamping down like a magnet until it became part of
everyone and everything, the men and the landscape.

To get to Beaumont-Hamel, where the Newfoundlanders fought, you leave the main road and veer off to
the left, studying the map carefully. Only then do you
begin to notice what at first seem to be tiny, enclosed
parks set down beside the main road or incongruously
placed in the middle of a farmer's field, a single-track
dirt road leading up to a wooden gate.

The small patch of earth Newfoundlanders fought for is marked by a bronze caribou, the island's emblem.

They are the cemeteries for the British Army dead, men from England and Scotland and Wales and Australia and the other parts of the empire who died here during the Great War. The effect is not as overwhelming as it sometimes is in the far larger cemeteries of Normandy that commemorate the Americans who were killed a quarter-century later, and at places near Château-Thierry and Verdun, but if the impact is less dramatic it is perhaps more insistent. Men died here, lots of them, and here, and here, and here.

On the Newfoundlanders' field of battle the old trenches can still be seen. Smoothed and softened by time, they lie like a gentle range of miniature mountains and valleys. They are grassed over, but narrow; sandy paths wind along the bottoms of the trenches. In the intervening years, enough people have felt compelled to stand where the men had been to wear away the turf. A crag of rocks and bushes rises steeply ahead, topped by a great, dark, metal statue of a caribou (above), the symbol of the Royal Newfoundland Regiment. His magnificent antlers are lifted high. He is looking out toward the German lines.

What drew me to the Newfoundlanders was a kind of terrible fascination with what had happened to their regiment on the Somme. Even in a war of senseless bloodletting, few units, if any, lost so many men in such a short period of time for so little gain. What happened to the Newfoundlanders summed up what happened to the British Army on July 1, 1916, the bloodiest day in its long history, the bloodiest of any army in World War I. Some 57,000 men, about half of those who attacked, were killed, wounded or captured—30,000 of them in the first hour alone. Fighting defensively, firing their Maxim machine guns with deadly accuracy, the Germans suffered only 8,000 casualties. On that disastrous day 790 men of the Newfoundland regiment climbed out of their trenches and, laden with equipment, began to walk toward the German lines. In just over a half-hour, 272 men were dead or mortally wounded. More than 400 of them were hit but survived. The Newfoundland regiment had virtually vanished. Not a yard of territory was taken. Later, talking to survivors, I could find no one who had even got off a single shot.

Minutes before zero hour on July 1, 1916, British troops near Beaumont-Hamel (left) wait to go into battle. Then, just before they had to go over the top, tons of explosives blew up (above), hurling earth high into the air—and alerting the Germans.

The day and the tactics, the loss of so much life for so little, the stubborn sending out of men, unit after unit, to die uselessly, was the responsibility of Sir Douglas Haig, commander of the British Expeditionary Force in France. He felt predestined to win a victory so glorious that it could finish the war. Before the battle, Haig wrote to his wife: "You must know that I feel that every step in my plan has been taken with the Divine help."

Haig's plan, which offered some hope of ending the bloody stalemate of trench warfare, was intended to relieve pressure on Verdun (see map, p. 296), where the Germans were inflicting heavy casualties on the French. First the Germans would be shelled with the heaviest bombardment ever —the rumble was clearly heard on the

English coast 135 miles to the west. Then infantry were to punch a hole through the German lines. Next, Haig intended to deploy three cavalry regiments to exploit the opening, very much in the way that German tanks would exploit the breakthrough at Sedan in 1940 (SMITHSONIAN, February 1986).

But the Germans survived the seven-day bombardment and, on the bright, hot morning of July 1, saw, disbelievingly, one of the most astonishing sights of the war. Because most of their troops were inexperienced, the British commanders had sent them out in lines, at a steady pace, bayonets held high, so that they would not get disorganized. After watching the scene, poet Siegfried Sassoon wrote in his diary: "The sun-

light flashes on bayonets as the tiny figures move quietly forward. . . . I am staring at a sunlit picture of Hell."

The tragedy of the day changed the idea of war forever, not only for the British, but for the rest of the world. "Idealism," wrote historian A. J. P. Taylor, "perished on the Somme." A cadre of young British poets serving in the line began to write verses about the damnation of Man by war that described the true horror of the trenches. "What passing-bells for these who die as cattle?" Wilfred Owen would ask in *Anthem for Doomed Youth*, answering, "Only

The author is former senior editor of Time *and former Dean of the University of Missouri School of Journalism, where he now teaches.*

the monstrous anger of the guns."

Haig kept up the pressure on the Germans for four months until, in November, the Allies finally "won," gaining an area about 25 miles long and 7 miles wide. The British lost 419,654 men, either killed, wounded or captured; the French, 204,253; the Germans, about half a million.

In 1918, when Germany launched a last, desperate offensive and part of the British Army nearly broke, German soldiers took the Somme, only to lose it again in a weekend when the British rallied, beginning the counter-attack that would end the war.

The Somme—and Verdun—turned the battlefields of World War I into a charnel house that the British did not forget. During World War II when Gen. George C. Marshall (and the Russians) pressed for an invasion of Europe sooner than England wanted, Lord Cherwell, a onetime aide to

Winston Churchill, explained his country's hesitation, "It's no use," he remarked, "You are arguing against . . . the Somme."

I went to Saint John's, Newfoundland, to talk to some of the survivors of July 1, 1916, to hear what they remembered, to learn what I could about the road they had traveled to the Somme and why they did not break and run. The blood had flowed in such gouts, one man recalled, the field smelled "like a slaughterhouse."

When the war began in August 1914, there was no military unit in Newfoundland, not even a band of overage reservists to use as a cadre. There were no uniforms, nothing, and there was little chance of getting any help from across the Atlantic. To mobilize for war, the city of Saint John's created the Patriotic Association of Newfoundland. The leadership of the association was carefully

selected to represent the three-way split in religion in the colony: Church of England, Methodist and Catholic. Newfoundland promised Britain it would recruit, train and equip a volunteer fighting force of 500 men and would raise all the money itself.

Newfoundland's population was about 250,000 in 1914. It is only 580,700 today. The island had no soldiers, but it had boys and young men who had some quasi-military training in special units organized by the city's large and active churches. Groups like the Anglican "Church Lads' Brigade," besides fostering leadership and developing character, taught parade-ground drill and marksmanship.

On the first night of enlistments, Sid Frost, a young accountant, was part of the crowd jammed into the C.L.B. Armory. When I talked to him, he still vividly remembered the surge of excitement, the shouts back

Sixty seconds after the attack began, a ragged line of soldiers advances across open ground toward barbed wire and enemy machine-gun nests. In the trench behind them, a second wave of men waits to join the battle.

and forth between friends, and the fact that Leonard Stick, one of his buddies, managed to duck around some of the screening procedures to capture the honor of being the first man to join the Newfoundland Regiment. (Stick was to win a battlefield commission during the first day of the Somme.) Within a week, 275 were on the rolls and every person who enlisted seems to have remembered his number. It was a badge of honor. Every man I talked to in Saint John's proudly and promptly recited his for me. Sid Frost's was 58.

He was 22 when he enlisted, but many were younger than the minimum of 19 set by the Patriotic Association. John Ryan was 17. No matter; he lied about his age and began earning $1 a day as a private, far less, however, than he could have expected to get around the docks of Saint John's. To appear older than his 15 years, Walter Day went down to the brigade hall wearing a black shirt and Australian-type slouch hat, and got in with no trouble at all.

The recruiters and doctors examining the recruits surely must have known most of the boys in town and could have told who was underage and who was not. There must have been a kind of quiet conspiracy, one joined in by the parents of the underage boys to allow them to get in on the great adventure. And some par-

Before Newfoundlanders had been issued uniforms they were hastily introduced to the mysteries of this Colt-Browning machine gun.

ents with initial misgivings were brought around. George Chalker was just 15 and weighed only 112 pounds, and they took him, or at least they did until his father came down and dragged him home. A few months later, his father relented and young Chalker went off to war, afraid, like all the others, that the whole show would be over before he got a chance to kill some Germans.

With the whole populace apparently pitching in, the Patriotic Association rapidly created a training camp at nearby Pleasantville, so close to town that relatives and friends could walk over after supper to see their soldiers in the making.

The boys' brigades contributed 47 tents to the encampment and Governor Sir Walter E. Davidson sent over three marquees used on ceremonial occasions at Government House, his official residence. Three local firms— Reid Newfoundland, Bowring Bros. Ltd. and Newfoundland Produce Co. —offered to give free transportation to anyone who volunteered from the seaports up the coast, who had to

travel by sea to get to Saint John's. Mr. J. Clouston offered to donate four cooking ranges. Mr. K. R. Prowse said that the new battalion could use the old golf links "for any purpose for which it may be required."

Since no suitable khaki material was available in Saint John's for the first 500 men recruited, the association authorized the making of puttees from fabric that was navy blue. The resulting wrappings, used to bind a man's pants between knee and ankle, became a symbol of great prestige. To have been a member of the "First Five Hundred," as Col. Gerald W. L. Nicholson noted in the Fighting *New-foundlander*, the official history of the regiment, was to be known forevermore as a "Blue Puttee."

Initially, Newfoundland's bankers and merchants and civic leaders calculated it would cost $520,000 to raise, equip and keep the original 500 in the field for a year. All through the first year, the association raised money as best it could. One event that occurred on October 1, 1914, especially conveys the spirit of what it was

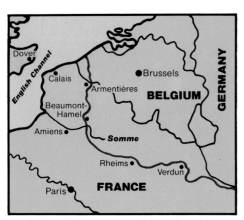

Map of Somme area shows situation on Western Front (red) at time of battle.

like to live in Saint John's at the time. It was a show put on at the Casino Theater by the Women's Patriotic Association and, as described by the *Daily News*, it caused "a spontaneous outburst of patriotic ardour and enthuiasm. Even the staidest, caught up by the inspiration of the moment, let themselves loose and joined heartily in the national songs."

Part of the show was composed of a series of tableaux, the curtain opening to reveal local residents posed motionless, more or less, as they tried to depict such motifs and sentiments as "The Hero of the Hour," "The Triple Entente" and "The British Empire." The most popular scene, entitled "The Widow's Mite," showed a widow offering her two sons to Britannia. Mr. Goodridge sang "Tommy Atkins" and "Soldiers of the King" and Miss Mare sang "All the Nice Girls love a Sailor." Then Miss Louise Anderson sang "It's a Long Way to Tipperary," changing the last lines to "Good-bye, dear old Narrows,/Farewell Pleasantville,/It's a long long way to Terra Nova,/But my heart's right there." Terra Nova of course,

was Newfoundland, and the narrows was the opening of the harbor that led to the North Atlantic and the fields of France.

Thousands went out to Pleasantville to watch the departure of the men, or to march along with them down to the harbor. Thousands more, many thousands—the biggest crowd in the history of Saint John's until that time—lined the streets and climbed poles and roofs along the route. More than 400 of the 526 men and officers had been born and raised in Saint John's; they not only were hometown boys, they represented the very best in the community. The war had a face and it was a familiar one. Sid Frost was one of the few who did not have a retinue of friends and relatives. As he strode along, a boy of about 8 came up to him and asked, "You don't have anyone?" Frost said no. The boy asked if he could carry Frost's bag, and the two marched along together down Water Street by the harbor.

The buildings were bright with flags and decorations, and so were the ships in the harbor. The church brigades' bands played as each company was lined up and marched onto the S.S. *Florizel*, a passenger-freighter used in the spring to haul seals slaughtered on the ice to the north.

The men would later recall that the holds still smelled faintly of seals. On board they began to sing "Tipperary." Their voices were joined by those of the thousands on shore, and the sad, homesick song of the British Army filled the harbor. Standing on deck, Frost caught sight of the boy who had carried his kit. He was waving from the dock. After the war, Frost was to meet the boy again and learn that the youngster had known no one else that day to say good-bye to. Their needs had matched perfectly.

The next evening, the *Florizel* steamed off through the narrows to join a convoy. She was accompanied past the headlands by boats and launches, and cheers followed faintly

in her wake as she finally pulled away.

The route to the Somme was long and wandering. After serving guard duty in Scotland, the Newfoundlanders were blooded in the ill-fated landings at Gallipoli and later posted to Egypt. In Gallipoli they got a new commanding officer, Lt. Col. A. L. Hadow, an Englishman who before the war had served with small units in the distant reaches of the southern Sudan.

None of the men I spoke to remembered Hadow with affection, but they all recalled him with respect. He was a demanding man. One evening he sent the battalion on a 14-mile march into the desert. A total of 76 men fell out and the ordeal so enraged some of them that they shouted at him in derision. Somehow they got away with it. Under his stern command, the regiment began to regain its strength, after the hardship endured at Gallipoli, and to develop a new sense of confidence. Frost remembered that the men began to sing a song that seems insulting when the words are isolated on paper, but were admiring when bellowed out on a march:

I'm Hadow, some lad-o
Just off the staff,
I command the Newfoundlanders
And they know it—not half.
I'll make them or break them,
I'll make the blighters sweat,
For I'm Hadow, some lad-o
I'll be general yet.

Sixty-two years later, Frost—who had been a banker in Saint John's—raised a voice that was husky but still strong and boomed out the refrain for me, remembering every word. He was smiling as he sang.

Finally France, the troopship pulling into Marseilles, then a jolting ride up the Rhône Valley through Lyons, a detour around Paris and, at last, a small town in the northeast, out of earshot of the rumble of guns, called Pont-Remy. General Nicholson records that the men who climbed down from the railroad cars to fall in and march across a bridge paid little

Daddy, what did YOU do in the Great War?

This recruiting poster from 1914 employed guilt to ensure patriotism.

Bound for war at last, troops of Newfoundland regiment
are ferried to steamer for crossing the North Atlantic.

attention to the river moving slowly below. It was the Somme.

At 9 P.M. on June 30, the regiment assembled on its parade ground: 25 officers, 776 privates and noncommissioned officers. The Newfoundlanders were not to take part in the initial attack, but to have the honor of participating in the coup de grace that would carry the day—taking the third line of German fortifications. Captain Frost was assigned a man with a can of white paint and a brush. They were to go out onto the battlefield after the Germans had been routed and paint the name of their unit on the captured guns so no one else would get credit for taking them.

As villagers watched, the troops swung into place and the familiar parade ground sounds—so haunting at every staging area in the world—echoed across the evening fields: the cry of voices raised in command, the slap of hands on rifle stocks, the crisp thump of rifle butts slammed to the ground. When all was ready, Colonel Hadow rode up on his charger, waved

his hand and the Newfoundlanders set out for Beaumont-Hamel.

It was cold that night, John Ryan remembered, cold and still as the men marched toward the lines for five hours. Ryan recalled swearing in front of a chaplain and being royally chewed out. The men hunkered down in groups in the bays of the trenches. Even then the platoons were breaking up into clusters of individuals as the isolation of battle started.

At dawn, the trenches slowly came alive. Curiously, no one I talked to could remember whether or not the battalion was served the customary tot of rum before the battle, a clout of a drink that in other regiments made a few inexperienced young soldiers so drunk they passed out. The Newfoundlanders followed the soldiers' ritual of checking their equipment. In addition to his rifle, each man carried 170 rounds of ammunition, rations, two empty sandbags, two Mills grenades, a helmet, a water bottle, a field dressing kit and a water-proof sheet. Everyone also had to carry a share of

the regiment's heavy gear needed to take and hold ground: wirecutters, stakes, picks, shovels and sledgehammers. Some men hauled parts of 32 bridges specially built to help the unit cross over the German trenches. Each man in the attacking infantry wore on his back a triangular piece of metal designed to reflect the sun and show observers watching with binoculars from the rear how well the advance was going.

In all, like the 60,000 other soldiers up and down 18 miles of front, each Newfoundlander would tote upward of 66 pounds of equipment into the battle that the brigade commander assured would be a "great victory" and probably the "beginning of the end of the war."

At 6:25 A.M., the final artillery bombardment began—the shells roaring over the Newfoundlanders' trench raising morale even higher. Everyone imagined the havoc being wrought in the German lines. The men had nothing to do but wait until their moment of attack, set for 8:40. The first wave was to go at 7:30.

At 7:20 there was a tremendous explosion off to the left (pp. 294-295). Walter Day remembers peering over the top of his trench and seeing a mountain of earth rising into the sky and holding there for an instant before beginning to tumble to the ground. At first he thought that the blast had magically lifted the entire village of Beaumont-Hamel into the air. The explosion was caused by 40,000 pounds of ammonal that had been packed into a tunnel under the German fortification that commanded the terrain the Newfoundlanders were supposed to cross. The blast was intended to destroy the fortification, but because the British chose to blow the mine before zero hour what it also did was alert the Germans that an attack was imminent.

When the mine exploded, Ryan could not believe the Germans had been given such a clear warning. "That's it," he thought as he watched the earth fall. "We're licked."

"Within five minutes," the official British history notes, "it seemed that every enemy machine gun along the front was firing incessantly. The divisions were caught forming up." A German regimental historian later wrote: "Ahead of us, wave after wave of British troops were crawling out of their trenches and coming towards us at a walk, their bayonets glistening in the sun."

Sometime that morning, John Ryan learned just how badly the assault was going. With no warning, a British officer rolled into the Newfoundlanders' trench. Ryan never did learn what regiment he came from, but it made no difference. He clearly recalled the man gasping, "They've wiped out all of us."

As the Newfoundlanders waited, other units of the 29th Division struggled out of the trenches, adjusted their heavy loads and started their walk to destruction. Machine guns in the valley around Beaumont-Hamel swept the field. German artillery, 66 batteries in all, including 11 hidden until the attack rained shells on the advancing British. The German barbed wire turned out to be uncut by the seven-day bombardment. Whole battalions were swept away. The Second South Wales Borderers went into action at 7:30 in the first wave. "Within five minutes," the official history notes, "nothing remained of [the Borderers] but a few scattered individuals lying within 100 yards of the German trench."

By about 8:15 A.M., any man who stole a glimpse of the battlefield knew that the attack was a horrendous blunder, but the generals were not so sure. There were, to be fair, confusing signals coming from a distant corner behind the front lines along a lane known as Station Road. Trying to make what they could out of the confusion that morning, observers spotted flares rising into the sky from the area, the agreed-upon signal to indicate that the position had been captured.

Young Newfoundlanders cheerfully lounge for informal portrait on troopship. Trip took 16 days from Saint John's to Plymouth.

The message went against all logic and all the evidence before the generals. The 29th Division clearly was being slashed to pieces. As it turned out, the flares actually were German signals to their own artillery. But, records the official history of the division, "when the military machine gets in motion, it is hard to divert or stop. Those in command had imperfect and rather encouraging reports. If our men were really fighting in the Station Road on the right . . . they must be supported and a determined effort made to prevent them from being cut off and undone by the very brilliance of their success." Accordingly, Brig. Gen. D. E. Cayley sent out the order to attack with his two leading battalions, the First Essex and the Newfoundlanders.

Cayley's call came at 8:45 A.M. The Essex could not get under way. Their trenches were too clogged with the dead and dying from other units for

their companies to get organized. In the Newfoundlanders' lines, Colonel Hadow took the call directly from Cayley and was ordered to advance "as soon as possible."

Hadow asked Cayley if he meant the battalion should attack without the aid of the Essex.

The reply was yes.

Hadow asked: "Has the enemy frontline been captured?"

Cayley hedged: "The situation is not cleared up."

Decades later, thinking back about what happened next, Sid Frost would still turn red with anger. What Hadow should have done, said Frost, was to ask for a delay until the situation became clearer, or to point out that the communications trenches in front of him were so filled with bodies that his troops could not use them to get to the front lines. They would have to advance in the open, in full view of German machine gunners,

Once in Britain, reinforced Saint John's contingent took advanced training and, on June 10, 1915, received its regimental colors.

Pvt. Ron Dunn, now 90, was Lewis gunner and one of 438 wounded at the Somme.

before even reaching their own barbed wire.

Instead, Hadow passed the word to attack. There was no time to change formations or tactics to conform to the new situation. The men would have to advance just as they had practiced—platoons in columns, heading for the gaps in the British wire that opened into no-man's-land, the maneuver predicated on the assumption that there would be little opposition, since by then the attack was supposed to have swept far ahead of them.

Hadow was the first man out of the trench. He moved about 20 yards ahead and gestured with his ash walking stick toward the German lines. But, like other battalion commanders, he had been ordered not to advance with his men. The chance that he would be killed was too high. So Hadow had to endure the worst moment in the life of a commander. When the bugles blew, he was forced to drop into a trench and watch his men die.

The battlefield had become an inferno. Zeroed in, the German artillery was firing for effect and the chatter-ing Maxim machine guns swept the ground, concentrating on the diagonal gaps in the British line of wire, well marked by limestone, that served as gateways to no-man's-land.

Still, there was, as far as I can determine, absolutely no hesitation in the ranks of the Newfoundlanders. Bill Newbury, John Ryan, Walter Day, Robert Tetford, Fred Coxworthy and all the rest climbed the trench ladders and quickly tried to line up in formation.

Then they began to fall. Newbury recalls Capt. Eric Ayre, commander of D Company, standing up and waving his hand and dying on the spot. Captain Ayre was not the only member of his family to die on the Somme that day. Two cousins, both lieutenants, were killed with the Newfoundlanders, and his only brother, Capt. Bernard Ayre, died with a Norfolk Regiment (p. 303). The survivors remember obliterating noise and horror that crushed the senses. When Captain Ayre was killed before his eyes. Newbury fully expected he would be the next to go. He and another man had been assigned the job of carrying a wooden ladder that was to be used to cross the second line of German trenches.

They were just starting out when Newbury heard a sound like the quick roll of a drum. He glanced up and saw a swath of German machine gun bullets splintering the steps of the ladder. At that instant, the other man carrying it was killed. Another man helped Newbury pick up the ladder and they started again. Then the second helper was killed. Newbury abandoned the ladder and went on alone. Ahead of him he could see the men of the leading companies—A and B—falling in windrows.

Expecting to be hit any second, he kept on and, somewhat to his surprise, found himself at the line of British barbed wire. On his own, with only a few men around him, Newbury got about 200 feet into no-man's-land when a Maxim hit him in both knees. He spun, fell and floundered on the ground, unable to crawl to the shelter of a shell hole.

By then, the world of the surviving Newfoundlanders had been reduced to a few yards of shell-torn earth and their lives; those who had not yet fallen expected to in a few moments.

Ryan would always remember the towers of black and white smoke thrown up by the exploding German shells and the stink they made. "I can smell them yet," he told me, wincing. Ryan was near Capt. James Ledingham, the commander of Company A, when the captain was hit in three places. Ledingham later was able to crawl back to safety. He recovered, went back to duty and was killed in battle in October 1917.

When the attack began, the job of Robert Tetford (No. 277) was to help carry a wooden bridge 25 feet long that was to be used to span the German trenches. As he and Edward Brown (No. 545) started forward, Brown was killed instantly. "He was hit just here," Tetford told me, gently placing a finger on the middle of his forehead. "Just here" was a phrase I was to hear often as I talked to the Newfoundlanders, and always in the same context—to signify a bullet hitting a man in the exact center of his forehead. The Newfoundlanders would say the phrase quietly but very precisely, looking at me closely to see if the import registered. Annihilation had come so swiftly, so precisely, so completely that the phenomenon deserved to be regarded with some awe.

When Brown dropped, the bridge fell and Tetford dived into a shell hole. Billy McNiven (No. 279) fell dead across his legs. Three or four other dead men were with them, Tetford recalled. As he lay there, a shell fragment ripped a flesh wound in his stomach.

All that day in the warm sun, Bill Newbury lay on the battlefield trying not to move in his agony so that the light reflecting off the triangle of metal on his back would not draw more German fire. That night the British came out to get him. Someone tried to lift him, but the pain was too sharp. He asked to be put back on the ground. Later they came after him with a stretcher, but again the pain was too great to bear as they tried to move him. He asked to be left alone.

The next morning, Newbury's knees were so caked with mud that the bleeding had stopped. Determined not to be taken prisoner, he began to crawl back toward the British lines. A machine gunner would spot him occasionally and stitch the ground nearby with bullets. Newbury would lie still until the shooting stopped, then creep on again. When he got to a British trench, he saw that the lip of the parapet was covered with bodies.

For a while he did not see how he could make it; he had planned on simply rolling in. Finally, with one last desperate effort, he forced his shattered knees to lift him for an instant and toppled over the corpses and down into the trench. When the pain eased, he looked around and discovered that all of his companions were dead.

According to one witness, Colonel Hadow was a "shaken man" after watching his troops go into battle, as well he might have been. But, in the fashion of the day for British commanders, he seems to have exhibited no feeling of remorse or anguish for his role in ordering his battalion to what he must have known would be its death. In his diary, Hadow simply noted: "The regiment was nearly wiped out." I wrote to his son to ask if his father had ever talked much about what had happened on July 1, 1916. The reply was polite but unilluminating. No, his father had never spent much time talking about what had happened during the war.

The most appropriate praise was delivered by the commander of the 29th Division. He wrote: "It was a magnificent display of trained and disciplined valour, and its assault only failed of success because dead men can advance no farther."

But back in Saint John's it seemed at first to have been a famous victory. "British Launch Great Offensive," headlined the *Evening Telegram* on July 1, 1916. "German Trenches and Prisoners Captured over a 20-mile Front." On July 13, twelve days after the assault, the city still did not know

what actually had occurred. Then the casualty lists began filling column after column of the *Telegram*. Nearly everyone in Saint John's must have known one of the casualties or at least known who one was—by recognizing his name from a Sunday school class long ago, or remembering him playing center forward on a soccer field.

And yet the news accounts, editorials and letters in the papers reveal none of the anguish that must have swept over the city. The suffering is all described in the heroic style of the time. Nor is there a flicker of honest feeling in the official report of Colonel Hadow, which finally arrived on July 29. "I deeply deplore the losses, but it will be some consolation to the people of Newfoundland to know that nothing could have been finer

Regimental commander Lt. Col. A.L. Hadow was an ambitious disciplinarian.

than the conduct of the regiment and it has established a reputation in this our first battle, which will ever be remembered."

The event demanded a scream, and yet none was recorded publicly, as far as I could tell. What must it have been like to walk that city at night in early July 1916? Did the sound of keening pursue you down the street?

Then I talked with Walter Day, the man who had enlisted at 15, climbed the trench ladder at 17 and somehow lived through the next 40 minutes. He was in a veterans' hospital in Saint John's, and although he was 78 years old and had just suffered a mild heart attack, he was still a vigorous man with a thick, strong hand and an eagerness to help a stranger from the United States understand what it had been like on the Somme. He nodded toward a fan in one corner of the ward. "The bullets hummed just like that," he said.

Day remembered hearing from friends and family back home how the news of the attack had devastated Saint John's, and I pushed him for an example. Then he recalled being told about the men in black: the priests and ministers who went up and down the rows of streets, paying condolence calls on the bereaved. "You could tell who had lost someone by watching where they went," said Day, and suddenly some human element of the tragedy came home—friends and neighbors watching with a mixture of sympathy and dread from behind their curtains while the clergymen went to call on families just up the street, watching with the cold realization that next time someone might ring their own bell.

Day and the other old men could not quite understand what it was they had done that would cause an American to come so far to seek them out. They talked to me in living rooms that often had pictures of themselves, young and strong and half-smiling into the camera, taken during World War I. They were too polite not to talk to the man who had suddenly showed up on their doorstep, although they often were not in good health, and one or two such as Bill Newbury, rubbed old wounds as they spoke.

Some of the men were deaf and leaned close to catch my questions that wives or daughters, sitting nearby, proudly erect, had to rephrase and ask in louder, sharper voices. The cheeks of the men turned red as they concentrated, trying to remember how it had been—it was all so long ago.

They spoke with little bitterness. Some seemed to feel that the whole experience had been some kind of cosmic, practical joke. They had joined the service with such innocence and marched into battle with such confidence, only to find the odds so stacked against them.

When I asked why they had pulled themselves out of the trenches and walked into the deathtrap, even after it had been sprung, they could not understand the point of the question. The Newfoundlanders had done what they were trained to do, what everyone expected them to do, what they had known they should do. It was as simple as that.

I was in Saint John's on June 30, the night the Royal Newfoundland Regiment has its annual dinner, and was invited to attend the affair. A sprinkling of my new friends were there, along with veterans of World War II,

British field commander, Sir Douglas Haig, devised the Somme plan of battle.

Close-rank gravestones in the Beaumont-Hamel cemetery mark the resting place of the British, Scottish and Newfoundland dead.

The body of Cpl. Robert Pitman, like those of many others, was never found.

when Newfoundland had sent over an artillery unit (they had tried sending infantry once).

Suddenly, there was a burst of applause. Men were starting to laugh and to crane their necks to look at the head table. I turned to see a former naval officer drinking out of what looked like a small, shallow bowl. When he was done, he turned it upside down over his head to show that it was empty, and then kissed the bottom before handing it back to a steward who was standing by with a tray full of bottles. One of my companions explained that this was a tradition that the battalion had learned from the Scots while occupying Edinburgh Castle before shipping out for Gallipoli and the Turks. The bowl was really a quaffing cup. On ceremonial occasions it was filled with brandy or a mixture of liquors, and each officer was supposed to follow the ritual I had just observed while his friends cheered him on.

The cup gradually worked its way around the room and then the steward was handing it to me. Standing, I performed the ritual and drew the cheers, holding the cup empty above my head and kissing the bottom. I sat down, more aglow from the moment than the brandy, and only then realized the full symbolism of the event and the evening.

I had just drunk from the same cup that the young officers—half my age, most of them—had undoubtedly passed back and forth on the nights before the battle. It was about 10 P.M. in Newfoundland—1:30 A.M. in France. The battalion would have just about completed its long march up to the lines.

A few hours later, Colonel Hadow would make his decision and climb out of the trench and wave his stick toward the German lines. Within a half-hour, almost all of the men who most likely had drunk from the same cup I had just held would be dead or wounded.

On the old battlefield near the village of Beaumont-Hamel, the compulsion to play soldier is too great to resist. You walk along the twisting trenches and peer toward where the Germans had been trying to sense what it had been like that day. But the sloping sides of the trenches are carpeted with grass that is brightly flecked with wildflowers.

The playacting does not work. You feel like a trespasser. Still, there is nothing to be done but to climb out of the trench and start for the German lines. All around you, the Newfoundlanders had surged up out of the earth, struggled to hoist ladders and other gear to their shoulders and walked into a hurricane.

The remains of the German trenches are only a short walk farther on. Near one or two of them are scattered pieces of rusted rubble, indefinable pieces of battlefield equipment that have been slowly disintegrating over the years.

Looking back, through German eyes, the perspective suddenly changes. You automatically start looking for targets, imagining how they would have been arrayed—groups of men, struggling to get through the gaps in their own barbed wire. Somewhere, an easy shot away, Fred Coxworthy had climbed over six dead men to reach no-man's-land.

Just inside the cemetery gateway, in a niche behind a brass grille, is a book in which visitors have left their names and addresses, and sometimes their thoughts. "In memory of Willie Scott, my brother." "We remember." "So ended the golden age." Every thought I have seems presumptuous or falsely solemn, and so, in the end, I write nothing at all. Leaving the battlefield, I reach down and pick up a piece of gray, stony chalk and take part of the battlefield of the Newfoundlanders home with me.

Memento mori for Saint John's businessman C.R. Ayre honors his four officer grandsons, all killed on July 1, 1916.

Picture Credits